World
Development
Report
1983

Published for The World Bank
Oxford University Press

Oxford University Press

NEW YORK OXFORD LONDON GLASGOW
TORONTO MELBOURNE WELLINGTON HONG KONG
TOKYO KUALA LUMPUR SINGAPORE JAKARTA
DELHI BOMBAY CALCUTTA MADRAS KARACHI
NAIROBI DAR ES SALAAM CAPE TOWN

ISBN 0-19-520431-X cloth
ISBN 0-19-520432-8 paperback
ISSN 0163-5085

The Library of Congress has cataloged this serial publication as follows:

World development report. 1978–

[New York] Oxford University Press.
v. 27 cm. annual.
Published for The World Bank.

1. Underdeveloped areas-Periodicals. 2. Economic development
Periodicals. I. International Bank for Reconstruction and Development.

HC59.7.W659   330.9'172'4   78-67086

Foreword

This Report is the sixth in an annual series assessing development issues. Part I reviews recent trends in the international economy and their implications for the developing countries. As in previous years, Part II is devoted to a special topic; this year the focus is on the management and institutional aspects of development.

The early recovery in the world economy foreseen in last year's *World Development Report* did not materialize. The recession has lasted longer than expected and has set back global development more decisively than at any time since the Great Depression. The indications of an upturn are now firmer, but the international financial system remains severely strained and protectionism continues to be an ominous threat.

Part I examines how alternative policies may affect the future prospects for recovery. The Report concludes that the present financial crisis is manageable, provided concerted efforts are made both nationally and internationally. It is essential for the industrial countries to maintain the momentum of their recovery, to promote freer trade, and to ensure growth in capital flows. Equally important, developing countries must for their part continue their efforts to adjust their economies to the new external circumstances and thereby regain the confidence of their creditors.

The interdependence of the global economy has become strikingly evident over the past three years. Not only does recession in the industrialized countries lead to stagnant export markets and lower capital flows for the Third World; retrenchment in the developing countries also means less employment in the developed countries. The recession has badly hurt all countries, though self-evidently the poor are less able to withstand the shock. But the ability of different countries to cope with the current difficulties has varied greatly. This Report seeks to learn from those significant differences in country performance.

Even with optimistic assumptions about sustained growth in the industrialized countries over the next decade, limited capital flows and trade growth are likely to be serious constraints to developing-country growth. Raising living standards and combatting poverty in the developing countries will depend more than ever on achieving greater efficiency in the use of human and material resources. The stress on efficiency in Part II of this Report should not be seen as signaling any change in the Bank's focus on poverty issues.

Governments everywhere must wrestle with difficult management problems as they seek to fulfill their heavy and varied responsibilities. To ease this burden, many countries have found it advantageous to give managers within the public sector greater autonomy over operational decisions, to involve local communities in the design and implementation of service delivery programs, and to use prices and market mechanisms more in place of administrative interventions. At the same time, successful measures to overcome skill shortages and strengthen public services have included making training more job related, building more effective career development systems, and linking incentives more closely to performance.

Good economic management depends, first and foremost, on the adoption of policies that stimulate enterprise and efficiency, but it depends also on the quality of the public sector institutions responsible for executing these policies and for providing public services. Developing countries' governments typically have had to work in very difficult conditions, beset by shortages. It is all the more remarkable that so much should have been accomplished over the past thirty years in building up systems of government. The Report draws on this experience to identify common problems and possible ways of addressing them.

This Report tackles a difficult and important subject not previously broached so directly by the Bank. It is a staff report and the judgments expressed in it do not necessarily reflect the views of our Board of Directors or the governments they represent. As in previous years, the Report includes updated World Development Indicators, which set out selected social and economic data for more than a hundred countries.

A. W. Clausen

This Report was prepared by a team led by Pierre Landell-Mills and comprising Ramgopal Agarwala, Richard Heaver, Dominique Lallement, Geoffrey Lamb, Selcuk Ozgediz, and Mary Shirley, assisted in particular by Engin Civan, Rahul Khullar, Leonie Menezes, Manon Muller, Hossein Partoazam, Joost Polak, and Paramjit Sachdeva. The Economic Analysis and Projections Department, under the direction of Helen Hughes, prepared the material on which Part I is based and supplied data for the whole Report. The work was carried out under the general direction of Anne O. Krueger, with Peter Wright as senior adviser and Rupert Pennant-Rea as principal editor.

With respect to Part II, the team would like to acknowledge the considerable assistance provided by the staff of the Development Administration Division of the United Nations, International Center for Public Enterprises, International Labour Organisation, International Monetary Fund, and Secretariat of the Development Assistance Committee of the OECD. In addition to Bank staff and those who prepared background papers (listed in the Bibliography), many others made helpful comments or contributions. Among these were Jose Abueva, Pierre Amouyel, John Armstrong, Michael Bentil, Rodrigo Botero, Peter Bowden, Robert Chambers, Kenneth Davey, Reginald Green, Metin Heper, Leroy Jones, Christopher Joubert, Mahn Jae Kim, David Korten, Melody Mason, Gabriel Mignot, Jon Morris, David Murray, Bernard Schaffer, Amartya Sen, Frank Sherwood, Arthur Turner, and Peter Wilenski. However, none of the above is responsible for the views expressed in the Report.

The authors would also like to thank the many other contributors and reviewers and the production and support staff—especially Rhoda Blade-Charest, Banjonglak Duangrat, Jaunianne Fawkes, Christine Houle, Carlina Jones, and Gerry Quinn.

Contents

Text tables

Text figures

Boxes

Definitions

The principal country groups used in the text of this Report and in the World Development Indicators are defined as follows:

- *Developing countries* are divided into: *low-income economies*, with 1981 gross national product (GNP) per person of less than $410; and *middle-income economies*, with 1981 GNP per person of $410 or more. Middle-income countries are also divided into *oil exporters* and *oil importers*, identified below.

- *Middle-income oil exporters* comprise Algeria, Angola, Congo, Ecuador, Egypt, Gabon, Indonesia, Islamic Republic of Iran, Iraq, Malaysia, Mexico, Nigeria, Peru, Syria, Trinidad and Tobago, Tunisia, and Venezuela.

- *Middle-income oil importers* comprise all other middle-income developing countries not classified as oil exporters.

- *High-income oil exporters* (not included in *developing countries*) comprise Bahrain, Brunei, Kuwait, Libya, Oman, Qatar, Saudi Arabia, and the United Arab Emirates.

- *Least developed countries* include Afghanistan, Bangladesh, Benin, Bhutan, Botswana, Burundi, Cape Verde, Central African Republic, Chad, Comoros, Djibouti, Equatorial Guinea, Ethiopia, the Gambia, Guinea, Guinea Bissau, Laos, Lesotho, Malawi, Maldives, Mali, Nepal, Niger, Rwanda, Samoa, Sao Tome and Principe, Sierra Leone, Somalia, Sudan, Tanzania, Togo, Uganda, Upper Volta, Yemen Arab Republic, and the People's Democratic Republic of Yemen.

- *Industrial market economies* are the members of the Organisation for Economic Co-operation and Development (OECD, identified in the Glossary) apart from Greece, Portugal, and Turkey, which are included among the middle-income developing economies. This group is commonly referred to in the text as *industrial economies* or *industrial countries*.

- *East European nonmarket economies* include the following countries: Albania, Bulgaria, Czechoslovakia, German Democratic Republic, Hungary, Poland, Romania, and USSR. This group is sometimes referred to as *nonmarket economies*.

Economic and demographic terms are defined in the technical notes to the World Development Indicators.

Official Development Assistance. The data on Official Development Assistance in Table 18 of the World Development Indicators, in Table 2.11, and in Box 10.2 are not comparable with the ODA data in Table 2.12 and in Chapter 3. The former are based on the OECD Development Assistance Committee (DAC) definitions which show disbursements of all types by donor countries. The latter show grants and concessional loans received by the developing countries as reflected in their balance of payments. The principal differences are that the DAC definitions cover technical assistance and contributions to multilateral institutions, including paid-in capital. The data on ODA receipts generally exclude these two, and in the case of the multilateral institutions include only the disbursement of concessional loans.

Billion is 1,000 million.

Tons are metric tons (t), equal to 1,000 kilograms (kg) or 2,204.6 pounds.

Growth rates are in real terms unless otherwise stated.

Dollars are US dollars unless otherwise specified.

All tables and figures are based on World Bank data unless otherwise specified. Growth rates for spans of years in tables cover the period from the end of the base year to the end of the last year given.

Glossary of Acronyms and Initials

CMEA Council for Mutual Economic Assistance.

DAC The Development Assistance Committee of the OECD (see below) comprises Australia, Austria, Belgium, Canada, Denmark, Finland, France, Federal Republic of Germany, Italy, Japan, Netherlands, New Zealand, Norway, Sweden, Switzerland, United Kingdom, United States, and Commission of the European Communities.

EEC The European Economic Community comprises Belgium, Denmark, France, Federal Republic of Germany, Greece, Ireland, Italy, Luxembourg, Netherlands, and United Kingdom.

GATT General Agreement on Tariffs and Trade.

IDA International Development Association.

ILO International Labour Organisation.

IMF International Monetary Fund.

NGO Nongovernment organization.

ODA Official development assistance.

OECD The Organisation for Economic Co-operation and Development members are Australia, Austria, Belgium, Canada, Denmark, Finland, France, Federal Republic of Germany, Greece, Iceland, Ireland, Italy, Japan, Luxembourg, Netherlands, New Zealand, Norway, Portugal, Spain, Sweden, Switzerland, Turkey, United Kingdom, and United States.

OPEC The Organization of Petroleum Exporting Countries comprises Algeria, Ecuador, Gabon, Indonesia, Iran, Iraq, Kuwait, Libya, Nigeria, Qatar, Saudi Arabia, United Arab Emirates, and Venezuela.

SOE State-owned enterprise.

UNCTAD United Nations Conference on Trade and Development.

UNDP United Nations Development Programme.

USAID Agency for International Development, US Department of State.

1 Overview

The recession that has afflicted the world economy since 1980 seems at last to be easing. But the economic conditions of many developing countries have worsened since the last *World Development Report* was published. Many middle-income countries have faced a greater liquidity crisis than was expected, brought on by high interest rates and reduced demand for exports. Low-income countries dependent on the export of raw materials have suffered from historically low commodity prices in real terms.

The developing countries' present difficulties are the culmination of events dating back a decade or more. They are a consequence partly of conditions in the industrial market economies and partly of their own policies. Part I of this Report underlines the increased interdependence of all countries brought about by the increase in trade and capital flows, and looks ahead to how the world economy might evolve during the next decade. Part II discusses how developing countries have managed

their development efforts, and how these might be improved. Chapter 12 sets out concluding themes which should be read in conjunction with this overview.

The 1980–82 recession

The recession of the past three years was no simple repetition of the mid-1970s (see Table 1.1). Following the jump in oil prices in 1973, GDP growth rates in the industrial economies fell sharply for two years and then recovered rapidly in 1976, although in the three subsequent years growth was still well below the average for the 1960s. In contrast, growth rates were initially less depressed by the 1979 rise in oil prices, but subsequently failed to match the recovery seen after 1975. The second recession was shallower than the first, but it has lasted longer since industrialized countries tightened monetary controls to bring down inflation. As a result, unemployment in the industrial

TABLE 1.1
Key indicators, 1973–82
(percent)

Indicator	1973	1974	1975	1976	1977	1978	1979	1980	1981	1982[a]
World trade growth (volume)[b]	12.5	4.0	−4.0	11.5	4.5	5.0	6.5	1.5	0.0	−2.0
Industrial countries										
GDP growth	6.3	0.6	−0.7	5.1	3.6	3.9	3.2	1.3	1.0	−0.2
Unemployment	3.4	3.7	5.5	5.5	5.4	5.1	5.0	5.6	6.5	8.0
Inflation rate	7.7	11.6	10.2	7.3	7.4	7.3	7.3	8.8	8.6	7.5
Developing countries										
Oil importers										
GDP growth	6.5	5.3	4.0	5.3	5.6	6.6	4.2	5.0	2.2	2.0
Debt service ratio[c]	12.6	11.4	13.3	12.6	12.7	15.7	14.7	13.9	16.6	21.5
Oil exporters[d]										
GDP growth	9.1	7.2	3.7	8.2	4.8	2.4	1.2	−1.3	1.5	1.9
Debt service ratio	12.2	6.7	7.8	8.4	11.1	14.9	15.5	13.0	15.7	19.1

a. Estimated.
b. IMF data for 1973 to 1981; GATT data for 1982.
c. Service on medium- and long-term debt as a percentage of exports of goods and services.
d. Excludes China.

countries, which stayed high at about 5 percent after the first recession, has since climbed to more than 8 percent.

Developing countries are directly affected by fluctuations in the industrial world (see Figure 1.1). Overall their growth rates have been higher, but even those that have grown fastest have not been able to avoid the cyclical influence of industrial countries. They have also been affected by high interest rates. Both effects were powerful in the

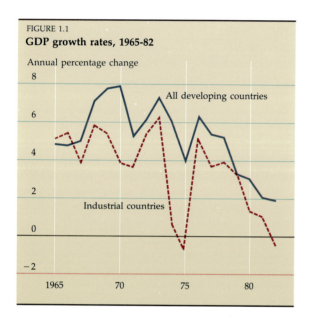

FIGURE 1.1
GDP growth rates, 1965-82

Annual percentage change

early 1980s—many developing countries have been squeezed between stagnating foreign exchange earnings and soaring interest payments on their debt.

Developing countries have reacted to these pressures in different ways. Those middle-income countries that had adopted outward-oriented trade policies—mainly in East Asia—have managed to maintain the momentum of export expansion and avoid serious new debt problems. But some countries, including several in Latin America that had borrowed heavily and adjusted less (or inappropriately) during the 1970s, have been hit by the high interest rates and have had to deflate in response to a liquidity crisis. In Latin America as a whole, according to preliminary estimates, GDP fell by 3.6 percent between 1980 and 1982.

The two largest low-income countries—China and India—have come through the current recession with encouraging resilience. They were not so heavily dependent on foreign trade, had little commercial debt, and so were not much affected by high interest rates. They have also made impressive progress in agriculture; India's low GDP growth in 1982 was largely due to the failure of the monsoon.

Low-income countries in Africa, being more dependent on primary commodity exports, have suffered badly from the world recession. Their per capita income has continued to fall, and there is now a real possibility that it will be lower by the end of the 1980s than it was in 1960. To prevent this happening will require policy reforms by many African governments, a recovery of commodity prices, and a large expansion of international aid to the region.

All developing countries will find the difficulties of the past few years greatly eased by a recovery in the world economy. Since January 1983 there have been encouraging signs that recovery is under way. In addition:

• Nominal interest rates have fallen well below their peak, reached in 1981. Taking account of the foreign exchange holdings of developing countries, each percentage point off Eurodollar interest rates saves them over $2 billion net in interest payments in a full year. The ratio of debt service to export earnings is expected to fall from a peak of 20.7 percent in 1982 to below 17 in 1984.

• Oil prices have come down, partly in response to the recession, but also because of conservation measures. For net oil-importing developing countries every dollar off the price of a barrel of oil reduces their import bill by approximately $2 billion in a full year. Some oil exporters have overborrowed and are now seriously strapped for foreign exchange. However, they should benefit if, as seems likely, oil prices harden again in the medium term. (This subject is discussed in Chapter 3.)

It would be premature to assume that the industrial countries will achieve sustained and steady growth such as they experienced in the 1950s and 1960s. Continued rapid growth in the early 1970s was checked by the recession of 1974–75, and the subsequent recovery in 1976–79 was not sustained. For the present, inflation has been curbed, but interest rates and exchange rates continue to fluctuate widely, reflecting (and often contributing to) a pervading sense of uncertainty. Industry and agriculture have been slow to adjust to new patterns of comparative advantage. The objective of the industrial countries must be continued recovery with restructuring, but as yet there are too few signs that underlying structural problems are being adequately tackled.

International collaboration

Development is a long-term proposition; its impetus is maintained by policies that must be both directed at fundamental change and viable in the short term. In the 1960s developing countries as a group made considerable progress in raising productivity and real incomes, and in improving social indicators such as literacy and life expectancy. Progress continued into the 1970s, but more slowly as countries encountered short-term economic difficulties. Since 1980 short-term problems have been on a larger scale and now threaten the development strategies of numerous countries.

The requirements of a far-sighted recovery strategy come, in part only, from policy reforms introduced by the developing countries themselves. Others are the responsibility of the international community, and particularly of the industrialized countries.

The crisis of the past few years has highlighted the bonds that join the economies of the developed and developing countries. The most publicized bonds—the financial links between banks in the industrialized countries and borrowers in developing countries—were once the least visible. Yet they in turn are intertwined with international trade: borrowing countries can service their debts only if they earn enough foreign exchange from exporting. These truisms would hardly be worth repeating were it not that government policies often seem to defy them.

Trade and protectionism

Protectionist sentiments have been growing in the industrial countries. The main reasons have been an implacable rise in unemployment and the financial difficulties of companies that are no longer internationally competitive. The temptation to seek relief by import controls has been considerable, at times irresistible. Among many measures to protect ailing industries, governments have erected a formidable set of controls against the textile exports of developing countries. The Multifibre Arrangement, covering as much as 15 percent of developing-country manufactured exports, is the most extreme example of trade restriction since governments started to undo the protectionism that contributed to the depression of the 1930s. In other industries, too, the exports of developing countries have faced new (particularly nontariff) trade barriers.

Nevertheless, as Chapter 2 illustrates, protectionism has not prevented a substantial growth in trade. Developing countries increased the volume of their exports by an average 5.1 percent a year in 1970–80 (for manufactures alone, the growth rate was 15.9 percent a year). Also, their market share of manufactured goods consumed in industrial economies has increased from 1.7 percent in 1970 to 3.4 percent in 1980. But the danger lies in the future. Although gains in price and efficiency from freer international trade are still widely appreciated, developing countries are often victims of short-sighted government action. The political challenge is first to halt and then to reverse the drift toward protectionism. The ministerial meeting of GATT held in November 1982 set the stage for liberalization. Greater participation by developing countries in GATT would help strengthen its role as the most appropriate forum for continued negotiations to reduce trade barriers.

Debt and capital flows

Capital markets have become highly integrated over the quarter century since currency convertibility was established. While this integration has many merits, a sharp rise in international interest rates can turn an acceptable debt service burden for a developing country into a debt crisis.

Viewed globally, the world debt situation is manageable, though recent difficulties require close international cooperation to achieve a sustained recovery in international trade and to assist those borrowers facing acute debt servicing problems. Such problems can have one of two causes—shortage of liquidity or genuine insolvency. The first arises when a borrower is temporarily unable to earn or borrow enough foreign exchange to meet its debt service payments, often because interest rates are themselves unexpectedly high. Insolvency has far more serious and permanent connotations: a borrower simply does not have the resources to service its debt, even though it makes maximum use of available resources.

The debt problems of most major developing countries are caused by illiquidity, not by insolvency. Sustained high interest rates alone may convert a liquidity problem into a solvency problem. A recovery in world demand, lower interest rates, and determined restructuring of their own economies will restore the ability of developing countries to service their debts. In the meantime, they need continued inflows of capital to ease their liquidity shortage.

3

That need has been recognized by several initiatives taken over the past year. Central banks have cooperated to provide emergency loans to some countries, notably through the Bank for International Settlements. The International Monetary Fund's resources have been substantially expanded. During 1982 the debts of twelve developing countries were rescheduled and thirteen others were under negotiation in the first quarter of 1983.

But the ad hoc debt rescheduling characteristic of the past is no solution for countries with deep-seated problems. Close collaboration by creditor governments, commercial banks, and the international financial institutions is needed to facilitate long-term adjustments to restore financial viability.

While steps are being taken to ease the debt difficulties of the main middle-income borrowers, too little has been done to assist the low-income countries seriously affected by the 1980–82 recession. They depend on official aid for 84 percent of their foreign capital inflows, so their capacity to import and to invest is directly affected by the aid programs of the industrialized countries. Aid as a proportion of the GNP of DAC members was no higher in 1981–82 (0.37 percent) than in the late 1960s. In real terms official development assistance from all sources, including members of OPEC and the CMEA, rose by 5.7 percent a year in the 1970s. Concessional aid for Africa would need to rise at about double this rate over the next ten years if the per capita income of the low-income African countries is to rise by 2 percent a year—a very modest target.

National development efforts

The benefits of international cooperation can do no more than supplement the efforts of the developing countries themselves. Earlier *World Development Reports* have reviewed cross-country experience in selected sectors to identify policies that promote development. This year Part II of the Report takes a wider perspective, exploring management issues that cut across all sectors. The underlying concern is the search for greater efficiency in the pursuit of governments' social and economic objectives. The current economic slowdown makes the task more urgent, as well as more difficult.

Too often development is discussed only in terms of policies, without regard to the institutions and people who decide and execute them. This Report seeks to redress the imbalance. It examines the role of the state, stresses the importance of appropriate incentives (especially prices) to foster development, and discusses the institutional arrangements needed to formulate a consistent development strategy and carry it out. The Report draws on country experience to identify ways of making state-owned enterprises and project management more efficient, and, more generally, improving the performance of the bureaucracy.

This stress on efficiency is compatible with efforts to assist the poor, although in times of financial stringency governments often cut programs for the poor. Well-designed programs to improve management of public projects, reduce inflationary budget deficits, make bureaucracies more responsive, limit nonessential activities, and share the management burden with the private sector so that vital public services are performed well—all these complement efforts to assist the poor. Today's difficult economic situation requires more than ever a critical appraisal of those well-intentioned initiatives that have gone awry—the costly subsidy that mainly benefits the better off, or the state enterprise that employs a bloated labor force at relatively high wages. To raise the standard of living of the very poor, scarce resources must be carefully targeted as well as efficiently managed.

Role of the state

The boundary between the state and the private sector is never clear-cut and varies widely from country to country. For this reason, it is misleading to discuss efficiency in terms of ownership. What matters more is creating the conditions that encourage efficiency in both private and public sector activities. Such an environment is largely determined by governments, not simply in the way they affect the private sector through legislative and fiscal measures but also by the way they manage their own affairs.

State-owned enterprises are an obvious example of how a government's approach to management can influence the whole economy. Both developed and developing countries are keen to find ways to make state enterprises more efficient. The more successful initiatives have been those which defined unambiguous and attainable objectives, gave a wide measure of freedom to managers to meet those objectives, and developed performance indicators that enabled government to monitor progress.

The state's role as employer—in many developing countries, the largest employer in the modern sector—also influences the whole economy. Most developing countries have abundant unskilled labor combined with a shortage of skilled workers. The results are political pressure to overstaff the public sector at the lower grades, which is inefficient and expensive, and fierce competition between the public and private sectors at the top. Experience has shown that the public sector can keep competent staff only by offering pay and other benefits that do not lag much behind the private sector and by offering a premium to key specialists.

A third area in which governments can improve their own administrative arrangements is in the making of economic policy. Current structural adjustment problems underline the need for greater attention to policy analysis. Planning has been excessively concerned with producing detailed, long-term blueprints for development, to the neglect of both policy analysis and the preparation of public investment programs. The process of planning—formulating a development strategy, analyzing policy, and assessing investment options—matters more than the plans themselves.

Many countries still lack the close links among policy analysis, investment analysis, and budgeting needed to define and carry out a development strategy. They also need more timely and reliable feedback, which can be obtained by better monitoring of the economy. Selective tracking of government activities is the key, whether through data collection, auditing, or project evaluation. In particular, more of the resources of central statistical offices should be devoted to assembling essential data on national accounts and other information relevant for policy analysis.

Even when governments have effective methods for managing state-owned enterprises, their own employees, and the formulation of economic policy, they can still find themselves overstretched by the range of responsibilities they have assumed. Administrative capacity is limited in every country; in some developing countries it is the scarcest resource of all. Reducing the burden on senior administrators is therefore a precondition for greater efficiency, and much can be achieved by decentralizing—both within the public sector and to groups outside it.

Burden-sharing

Day-to-day decisions can be devolved to those who are responsible for carrying them out, and who

have the advantage of detailed knowledge not possessed by those at the center. Decentralizing is a way to increase the responsiveness of government to those it serves and can involve those outside government—community organizations, for example—whose active support is often necessary in promoting development. It can also take the form of subcontracting, with some public services provided by private operators.

Decentralizing is not solely a matter of involving a wider range of people in discharging the responsibilities of the public sector. Governments, including socialist governments, can also make greater use of markets and prices, since they avoid the heavy administrative requirements of centralized planning controls. While greater reliance on markets may appear to carry risks, many governments have learned that their own interventions can easily misfire. The costs of market failure need to be balanced against those of bureaucratic failure. The practical advantage of relying more on markets is that the public sector can then concentrate on improvements in those activities for which market solutions are inappropriate.

However, the willingness to use prices to allocate resources is on its own not enough. Governments also need to ensure that prices really do reflect relative scarcities. Relative prices changed rapidly during the 1970s, partly because of floating currencies and two sharp increases in the cost of oil. Many countries failed to adjust their domestic prices to these international changes, so price distortions assumed serious proportions. Cross-country analysis for 1970–80 reveals that the best economic performances tend to be closely associated with the lowest price distortions (the details are given in Chapter 6). However, countries that have tried to correct price distortions have seldom found it easy. To obtain good results, adjustment programs must be tailored to the circumstances of individual countries and managed with close attention to timing, pace, and scope.

Political commitment

The underlying assumption of this Report is that all governments of developing countries, whatever their political complexion and their concern for equity, do attach priority to economic and social development. Governments nevertheless vary greatly in the commitment of their political leadership to improving the condition of the people and encouraging their active participation in the development process. When political leaders are recognized for their integrity, vision, and concern for the public welfare, these qualities can be reflected in the ethos and performance of the public service and will have a profound effect on all sections of society. But if corruption is rife, public bureaucracy is likely to become demoralized and self-serving.

Perhaps the most important task of national economic management is to enlist the skills and energies of the population at large in raising the productivity of capital and labor. The routes followed in pursuit of these objectives must depend on the nature of the political system, but the morale of the labor force will always be a critical factor.

The economic fluctuations of the 1970s, and their culmination in the recession of 1980–82, have underscored the uncertainty of the economic environment in which farmers, businesses, and governments have to operate. Readiness to take risks and show flexibility in responding to unforeseen events are therefore essential ingredients of successful management.

Part I World Economic Recession and Prospects for Recovery

2 The prolonged recession

The world economy had another difficult year in 1982. Few countries managed to improve on their previous year's growth, and more than twenty experienced declines in output. The recession that had started in 1980 thus continued for a third year, making it the longest since the depression of the 1930s. Even those developing countries with excellent growth records had to struggle for modest gains in the face of depressed export markets and high debt servicing costs.

Some countries were less badly affected than others (see Table 2.1). As a group, Asian countries—which account for two-thirds of the population of the developing world—increased their per capita incomes in each of the three years of the 1980–82 recession. By contrast, Latin American and low-income African countries suffered declines in per capita incomes, although some among them were exceptions. These variations in performance can mostly be explained by the different policies pursued in the 1970s by individual countries.

The growth of developing countries depends on steadily expanding trade and capital inflows, both of which are closely related to the level of world economic activity. This chapter first highlights the dominant influence of the industrialized countries on the length of the recession. It then examines how successful developing countries have been in expanding their market share in developed economies and in increasing trade among themselves. It also analyzes how movements in commodity prices have changed the developing countries' terms of trade, and summarizes trends in workers' remittances. The chapter then describes how developing countries have financed their deficits—without serious strains until 1980, but with considerable difficulty since then. It looks in detail at the state of international indebtedness, and concludes by reviewing variations in economic performance

TABLE 2.1
Growth of GDP, 1960–82

Country group	1980 GDP (billions of dollars)	Average annual percentage growth				
		1960–73	1973–79	1980	1981	1982[a]
All developing countries	2,231	6.0	5.1	3.0	2.0	1.9
Low-income	544	4.5	5.1	6.1	3.7	3.7
Asia	492	4.6	5.6	6.6	4.1	3.9
China	283	5.5	6.3	6.8	3.0	4.0
India	159	3.6	4.4	6.6	5.6	2.8
Africa	52	3.5	1.5	1.2	0.1	0.8
Middle-income oil importers[b]	920	6.3	5.5	4.2	1.1	1.1
East Asia and Pacific	204	8.2	8.5	3.6	6.9	4.2
Middle East and North Africa	28	5.2	2.9	4.7	0.1	2.7
Sub-Saharan Africa[b]	43	5.5	3.7	4.0	3.7	4.0
Southern Europe	201	6.7	5.0	1.5	2.4	2.2
Latin America and Caribbean	444	5.6	4.9	5.7	− 2.4	− 1.2
Middle-income oil exporters	687	7.0	4.8	−1.3	1.5	1.9
High-income oil exporters	221	10.7	7.5	7.5	−1.8	−11.7
Industrial countries	7,395	5.0	2.8	1.3	1.0	−0.2

a. Estimated.
b. Does not include South Africa.

among the developing countries. A discussion of the various sources of the historical data is to be found in the Technical appendix.

The delayed recovery

Over the past ten years, the industrial market economies have experienced two recessions separated by a four-year period of modest growth. The first recession, in 1974–75, was sharper than the opening years of the second (1980–81), but was followed by a swift recovery in 1976. In 1982 the rebound never came; in fact, GDP fell by 0.2 percent (see Figure 2.1).

The contrast between the recovery of the mid-1970s and the continuing recession of the early 1980s has its roots in the policies adopted by the governments of the largest industrial countries. In the 1970s these governments reflated their economies out of recession by a conventional combination of fiscal and monetary expansion. By the end of the decade they were dissatisfied with the results. Inflation, though below its 1974 peak, remained stubbornly high. Interest rates had shown a secular tendency to rise, weakening financial confidence and discouraging investment. Many structural flaws had become apparent, having developed almost unnoticed during decades of rapid growth. Some industries had failed to adopt new technology and to keep their cost structures competitive with producers in the more advanced developing countries. Labor markets had grown increasingly rigid, so that real wages had resisted the fall implied by the productivity slowdown and terms of trade losses in the 1970s. Partly in consequence, unemployment rates fell only slightly

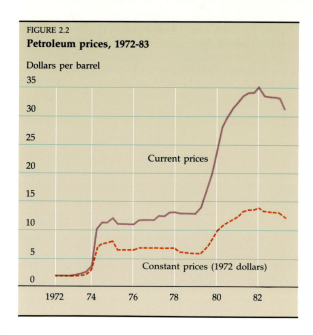

FIGURE 2.2

Petroleum prices, 1972-83

Dollars per barrel

during the four years of growth after 1975.

All these factors, combined with a second surge in oil prices in 1979–80 (see Figure 2.2), prompted most governments to change their policies. As a priority they put greater emphasis on reducing dependence on imported oil. Energy intensity—the amount of energy required to produce a dollar of real GDP—has fallen by 2.5 percent a year since the 1979–80 rise in oil prices, compared with a decline of only 1.7 percent a year after the 1973–74 surge. Oil production in non-OPEC countries also increased substantially, by almost 50 percent between 1973 and 1982. As a result, OPEC's share of internationally traded crude oil fell from 87 percent to about 65 percent.

These changes were the consequence of policies initiated in the mid-1970s and then pursued with increased vigor after 1979. In other areas, however, government policies in the industrial countries marked a definite break with the past. In particular, their monetary stance became more restrictive, which has helped bring inflation down sharply. Having risen by 10.6 percent in 1980, consumer prices (measured by the deflator for private consumption) in the major OECD countries rose by 8.9 percent in 1981, by 6.8 percent in 1982, and at an annual rate of 6.0 percent in the first quarter of 1983.

Since increasing monetary restraint was accompanied by continuing large fiscal deficits, short-term interest rates remained high. In real terms, adjusting for the rate of inflation in the United States, they have risen steadily since the middle

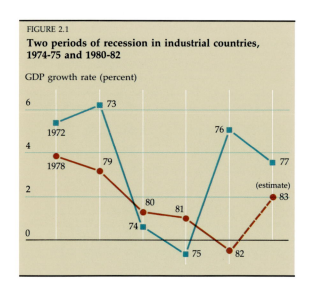

FIGURE 2.1

Two periods of recession in industrial countries, 1974-75 and 1980-82

GDP growth rate (percent)

of 1977. If the export prices of developing countries are used as a deflator, the fluctuations are even more marked and the recent increase has been dramatic (see Figure 2.3). The high level of real interest rates was a major reason the recession of 1980–82 lasted longer than that of 1974–75. Corporate finances in the industrialized countries came under considerable pressure, leading to heavy destocking and investment plans being delayed or even canceled. Companies also reduced their work forces, so that unemployment rose steeply: from 5.0 percent of the labor force in 1979, it increased to 5.6 percent in 1980, 6.5 percent in 1981, and 8.0 percent in 1982.

By the end of 1982 the pace of destocking was starting to slow. Helped by the marked fall in inflation rates, monetary growth in most industrialized countries turned positive in real terms. Oil prices were falling, encouraging expectations that inflation would fall even further. All these factors have helped improve business confidence, and there are signs that 1983 will show an upturn in output. Whether the current positive trends will be sustained in the medium term is hard to predict; possible scenarios and their implications for the world economy are discussed in Chapter 3.

As stressed in Chapter 1, the links between the industrialized world and the developing countries are close and pervasive. Growth has been faster in the developing countries during most of the past ten years, yet they have not been able to escape the cyclical pull of the industrialized economies. This pull is exerted principally through international trade and capital flows.

International trade

The rapid economic growth of 1950–73 was accompanied by even faster growth in international trade. In the peak period from 1965 to 1973, when world GNP grew at about 6 percent a year, trade in goods and services grew at more than 8.5 percent a year. Reductions in barriers to trade and capital movements stimulated productivity and income growth, making it easier for governments to reduce restrictions still further.

After 1973 slower growth in the industrial economies was accompanied by slower growth in international trade. The average annual growth in the volume of world exports of fuels fell from 9.0 percent in 1965–73 to 0.5 percent in 1973–80, and of manufactures from 10.7 percent to 6.1 percent. Overall, growth in exports slowed to about 5 percent a year in 1973–80. But at the same time the

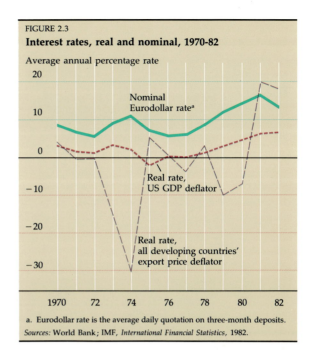

FIGURE 2.3
Interest rates, real and nominal, 1970-82

Average annual percentage rate

a. Eurodollar rate is the average daily quotation on three-month deposits.
Sources: World Bank; IMF, *International Financial Statistics*, 1982.

developing countries became an increasingly important market for the developed countries.

During the 1970s the export growth of the developing countries slowed down even more than that of the industrial countries, largely as a result of declining oil exports. The volume of total exports of the oil producers fell by half a percent a year from 1973 to 1980. But both low-income countries and middle-income oil importers expanded their exports by 8 percent a year. From 1977 on China was particularly successful in boosting its non-oil exports, accounting for the fast export growth of the low-income Asian countries. Low-income African countries, however, barely managed to increase the volume of their exports during this period.

After 1979, the recession hit world trade: exports grew by only 1.5 percent in 1980, stagnated in 1981, and declined by an estimated 2.0 percent in 1982. Trade in fuels was largely responsible, falling by more than 16 percent between 1979 and 1982. Other categories also slowed down markedly, with exports of manufactures growing just under 2 percent a year. Among developing countries, only a handful managed to increase their exports, mainly in manufactures. By improving productivity and quality, they were able to increase their price competitiveness and diversify into new products.

Developing-country exports

For developing countries as a group, exports of both fuel and manufactures have increased in im-

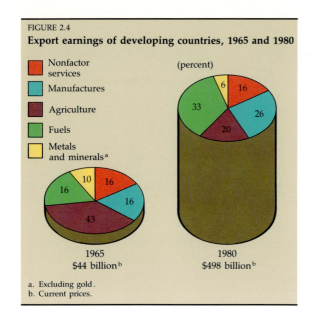

FIGURE 2.4
Export earnings of developing countries, 1965 and 1980

- Nonfactor services
- Manufactures
- Agriculture
- Fuels
- Metals and minerals[a]

(percent)

1980
$498 billion[b]

6 / 16 / 26 / 20 / 33

1965
$44 billion[b]

10 / 16 / 16 / 16 / 43

a. Excluding gold.
b. Current prices.

income oil importers, the share declined from 60 percent in 1965 to 36 percent in 1980. Developing countries can no longer be caricatured as exporters of primary products and importers of manufactures. Some have even become significant exporters of capital goods, accounting in all for about 6 percent of the world's total.

These changes should not obscure the fact that for many developing countries—particularly the poorest—primary products still dominate their exports. Many countries are highly dependent on one export commodity: coffee still represents almost 90 percent of Burundi's recorded exports and more than 50 percent of Colombia's. Other examples include cocoa in Ghana (70 percent), sugar in Mauritius (more than 65 percent), and copper in Zambia (more than 70 percent).

Commodity prices

The decline in nonfuel commodity prices of importance to developing countries, which began at the end of 1980, continued into 1982 (see Table 2.3). This trend was finally reversed in December 1982. At their lowest point, nominal prices of these commodities had fallen to their 1978 level. But in

portance over many years (see Table 2.2). The share of agricultural commodities in their total merchandise exports declined from 50 percent in 1965 to 23 percent in 1980 (Figure 2.4). Even for the low-

TABLE 2.2
Exports of developing countries, 1965–82

	Value 1980 (billions of dollars)	Average annual percentage change at constant 1980 prices		
		1965–73	1973–80	1980–82[a]
Total merchandise[b]	434	7.9	3.4	−0.5
Nonfuel primary products	126	4.6	5.9	0.6
Fuels	163	8.0	−1.8	−5.1
Manufactures	130	15.6	12.4	4.1
Nonfactor services	78	11.3	9.4	2.6
Goods and nonfactor services	512	8.2	4.2	0.0

a. Estimated.
b. Includes gold.

TABLE 2.3
Trade prices in current dollars, 1965–82
(average annual percentage change)

	1965–73	1973–80	1981	1982[a]
World export prices[b]	5.7	13.7	−2.2	−4.0
Nonfuel primary products	7.0	6.6	−7.0	−12.0
Fuels	7.5	32.8	12.5	−3.8
Manufactures	5.1	11.0	−4.8	−2.1
Industrial countries' GDP deflator	6.1	9.9	−0.7	0.9

a. Estimated.
b. Goods and nonfactor services.
Sources: World Bank; IMF, *International Financial Statistics,* 1982.

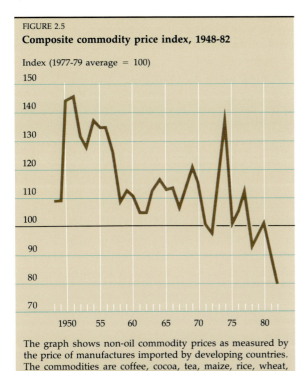

FIGURE 2.5

Composite commodity price index, 1948-82

Index (1977-79 average = 100)

The graph shows non-oil commodity prices as measured by the price of manufactures imported by developing countries. The commodities are coffee, cocoa, tea, maize, rice, wheat, sorghum, soybeans, groundnuts, palm oil, coconut oil, copra, groundnut oil, soybean meal, sugar, beef, bananas, oranges, cotton, jute, rubber, tobacco, logs, copper, tin, nickel, bauxite, aluminum, iron ore, manganese ore, lead, zinc, and phosphate rock.

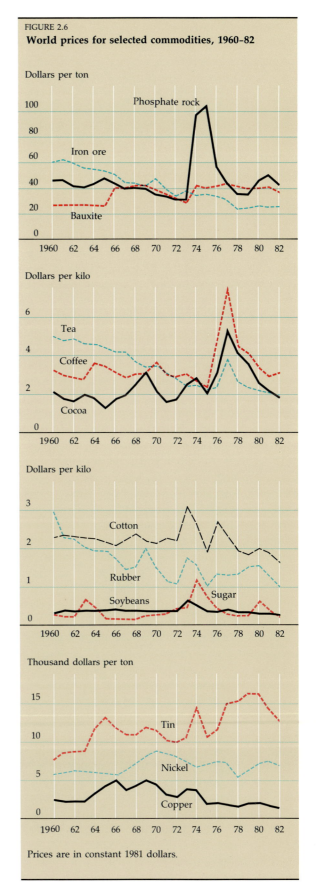

FIGURE 2.6

World prices for selected commodities, 1960-82

Prices are in constant 1981 dollars.

real terms—after adjusting for the rise in prices of manufactures imported by developing countries—commodity prices in US dollars were lower in 1982 than at any time since World War II (see Figure 2.5).

Food prices fell most—by 30 percent (in nominal terms) between 1980 and 1982—and nonfood agricultural commodities by 24 percent, while metal and mineral prices declined by 17 percent. The worst affected commodities were sugar (down 71 percent), rice (down 39 percent), cocoa (down 33 percent), and the fats and oils group, which declined by about 23 percent on average (see Figure 2.6).

The adverse impact of this fall in prices on countries exporting primary commodities was mitigated in two ways. First, part of the trade in primary commodities is governed by long-term bilateral agreements at prices unaffected by short-term price movements in the free market. Second, for developing countries heavily reliant on imports of food products (accounting for about 13 percent of total nonfuel merchandise imports of developing countries), the low prices of grains and fats and oils have partly offset their loss of purchasing power. For Africa this effect was small.

Notwithstanding these mitigating factors, the fall

in commodity prices in 1980–82 was devastating. It had several causes. The prolonged recession in the industrial countries greatly reduced demand, while high interest rates made the holding of stocks costly. On the supply side, the past three harvests have generally been excellent. Record or near-record crops have been harvested in North America (wheat, coarse grains, soybeans, and cotton), South America (grains and soybeans), and Western Europe (particularly sugar). Grain supplies have been so plentiful that the Soviet Union's four consecutive poor grain harvests have had little impact on prices. Supplies of tropical beverages, especially coffee and cocoa, have also been abundant. The 1976–77 price peaks for beverages led to considerable replanting and new planting, and these investments have started to increase output. A severe frost in Brazil in 1981 stemmed the fall in coffee prices, but its effect will be only temporary.

Since the price elasticities of tropical food products are low, the fall in prices has not led to much growth in demand; hence, with bountiful harvests, stocks have accumulated. Even with an improvement in economic activity, it will take several years of good income growth or, alternatively, a succession of poor harvests, for the historically large stocks of sugar, cocoa, and coffee to clear.

The acreage-reduction programs adopted by the US government for the 1983–84 crop year will lower the world supplies of wheat, rice, coarse grains, soybeans, and cotton. The payment-in-kind program for wheat and coarse grains is designed to transfer US government-held stocks of grain to farmers in exchange for leaving their cropland idle. If the implementation of such schemes coincides with both a recovery in economic activity and a poor harvest, stocks may be quickly run down and prices could rise sharply.

For industrial raw materials—such as natural fibers, rubber, and metals and minerals—income elasticities are larger than for foodstuffs. Consequently, reductions in consumption and trade during this recession have been more severe. Some mines have closed down. With reflation, the recovery in prices and consumption of these raw materials is likely to be greater than for foodstuffs.

During the past two to three years international stabilization agreements have been in operation for five commodities—coffee, cocoa, rubber, sugar, and tin. Of these, only the price of coffee has been significantly affected, mainly because the export quota scheme of the International Coffee Agreement is the most restrictive. However, support of the coffee price has resulted in a large buildup in

stocks in producing countries which, given future production and consumption prospects, will not be easily reduced.

The recession, in conjunction with the high level of energy prices and environmental issues, has forced industrial countries to limit their processing of minerals. For example, high electricity prices have forced the Japanese government to rationalize its aluminum industry, while economic and environmental factors may result in plant closures in the lead and zinc industries. The European community is considering reducing its zinc-smelting capacity. Pollution problems have caused the closure of significant copper-smelting capacity in the United States. These changes may mean opportunities for investment in processing minerals in the developing countries when demand picks up.

Terms of trade

The nonfuel primary producers among the developing countries suffered a decline in their terms of trade during the past decade. Except in the case of Africa, the deterioration after the 1979–80 oil price rise was greater than it had been after the 1973–74 rise. Nonetheless, although some low-income African countries benefited from the falling prices of grain, as a group they suffered by far the sharpest decline in terms of trade after 1979; this was also the case in the mid-1970s. And all oil-importing countries benefited from the fall in real oil prices in 1982.

When export prices fall in relation to import prices, exporters obtain partial compensation if demand for their products expands significantly. This effect is summarized in the purchasing power of their exports (see Table 2.4). After both oil shocks, foreign exchange earnings from trade continued to improve for all but the low-income African countries. For the low-income Asian countries considered as a group, the terms of trade gains from higher oil prices accruing to China more than offset the declines experienced by India.

Protectionism

Moves to liberalize trade continued during the 1970s, with the implementation first of the Kennedy and then of the Tokyo Round of the GATT negotiations. The Tokyo Round agreement on codes of conduct to govern many nontariff barriers was an important new approach to reducing protectionism. The Generalized System of Preferences also lowered barriers to trade in developing countries' products.

TABLE 2.4
Terms of trade of developing countries, 1973–82
(1978 = 100)

Developing countries	Change in terms of trade (percent)[a]		Change in purchasing power of exports (percent)[b]	
	1973–76	1979–82	1973–76	1979–82
Low-income				
Asia	12.1	−3.2	58.5	15.7
Africa	−15.3	−13.8	−18.7	−3.5
Middle-income				
Oil importers	−9.5	−10.7	4.5	2.5
Oil exporters	59.9	31.8	71.0	11.5

a. Ratio of export unit value index over import unit value index.
b. Product of terms of trade and export quantum index.

Not all trade barriers were reduced, however. The desire to maintain farm incomes in the industrial countries continued to provide a reason for protecting agriculture. Tariff and nontariff barriers against clothing and textile imports from developing countries also grew. Although some tariffs on processed primary products were reduced in the Tokyo Round, others remained. And subsidies continued to be used to promote exports of capital goods.

Recession and sharply rising unemployment after 1979 prompted an upsurge of protectionist pressure. Restrictions on trade among the industrial countries—notably in automobiles, steel, and agricultural products—began to increase. While these measures affected relatively few developing countries, they made protectionism in general more respectable. The industrial countries stepped up their restrictions against exports from developing countries, sometimes by increasing tariffs, more often by import quotas or "voluntary" agreements to restrain exports. They also used other means such as restrictive "quality" requirements and health regulations to achieve protectionist ends. Governments increased subsidies on capital goods exports, which benefited those developing countries buying the goods, but harmed those who were competing with industrial countries in the capital goods market. Other kinds of subsidies were also increased—to foster industries (such as shipbuilding), to aid regions, and to encourage ill-defined activities such as research and development.

The overall impact of the increase in protectionism is hard to gauge. Barriers imposed by the industrial countries were most effective in agriculture, where the developing countries' share of the industrial countries' market for basic foodstuffs declined during the 1970s (see Table 2.5).

As for processed agricultural commodities, developing countries raised their market share from 3.5 percent in 1970 to 3.7 percent in 1980—an average annual growth of only 0.6 percent. This slow growth was due in part to disincentives to production in the developing countries. Developing countries were also squeezed in third markets, as a result of industrial countries' increasing the volume of their subsidized agricultural exports such as sugar and beef.

In manufactures trade, the developing countries have made more progress. The rapid expansion of exports of manufactured products from the mid-1960s would not have been possible without the increase in their share of industrial-country markets. Table 2.6 shows that they doubled their share between 1970 and 1980, though at 3.4 percent in 1980, it was still only a trivial part of the total. Market penetration increased by more than 8 percent a year between 1970 and 1977, and still managed to grow at 7.6 percent a year in 1977–80 despite the marked increase in barriers against

TABLE 2.5
Share of developing-country exports in the consumption of selected agricultural products in industrial countries, 1970–80

Product	Share in estimated consumption (percent)		Import penetration (average annual percentage change)
	1970	1980	1970–80
Sugar	7.8	3.9	−6.7
Tobacco	21.1	30.2	3.6
Beef and veal	2.3	0.9	−9.0
Wheat	0.9	0.1	−19.3
Rice	1.4	1.9	3.1
Maize	5.1	1.4	−12.1
Tomatoes	5.3	4.7	−1.2

TABLE 2.6
**Share of developing-country exports
in the consumption of manufactured goods
in industrial countries, 1970–80**

Country or trading group	Share in estimated consumption (percent)		Average annual percentage change	
	1970	1980	1970–77	1977–80
Australia	2.1	5.5	14.9	2.9
Canada	1.3	2.1	5.5	4.2
EEC[a]	2.5	4.6	6.6	7.5
Japan	1.3	2.4	7.8	12.9
Sweden	2.8	3.8	4.0	4.2
United States	1.3	2.9	10.6	5.1
Total	1.7	3.4	8.4	7.6

a. European Economic Community.

clothing, textiles, and footwear. The growth of market penetration continued to rise in a variety of other products (see Table 2.7), reflecting rapid diversification in some developing countries' exports.

The number of developing countries exporting manufactures continued to increase throughout the 1970s. While northeast Asian countries remained the most rapidly growing exporters of manufactures, several southeast Asian and Latin American countries also expanded their manufactured exports considerably in the late 1970s. China's export expansion was mainly in manufactures (at about 18 percent a year in 1977–81). A wide range of

relative newcomers, such as Malta and Mauritius, also made good progress.

The growth of market penetration does not mean that protection was ineffective. Without trade restrictions, exports would undoubtedly have grown faster, even in manufactures. Moreover, the protectionist threat must have reduced investment in export-oriented activities in many developing countries, increasing supply constraints.

Protection is also very costly to the protectionist countries themselves. They have to pay more for goods than they need to, so losing an opportunity to buttress their anti-inflationary efforts. Their poorest consumers are worst affected, since developing countries generally specialize in the low-cost goods that take a large part of the spending of the poor. Even minor protectionist measures can hamper the restructuring of industrial economies, postponing the investment in new industries and companies that is needed to revive growth.

Finally, the more developing countries can increase their exports and growth, the bigger the market they provide for exporters in the industrial countries. Between 1973 and 1980 the share of industrial-country exports of merchandise to developing countries increased from 23 percent to 28 percent (see Table 2.8). The United States, for example, now sells two-fifths of its exports to developing countries. Buoyant world trade is essential for, as well as reflects, the well-being of the global economy.

TABLE 2.7
**Share of developing-country exports in the consumption of selected
manufactured goods in industrial countries, 1970–80**

Manufactured goods	Share in estimated consumption (percent)		Import penetration (average annual percentage change)	
	1970	1980	1970–77	1977–80
Food	3.5	3.7	3.4	−5.4
Clothing, textiles, and footwear	3.1	10.5	15.5	9.5
Clothing	4.0	16.3	18.6	9.0
Textiles	2.3	5.4	9.1	9.3
Footwear	2.6	16.3	24.3	8.6
Leather products	6.2	17.3	12.6	8.3
Wood products	1.9	3.6	6.6	8.3
Paper	0.2	0.5	11.2	20.6
Chemicals	2.0	3.8	7.8	11.0
Nonmetallic minerals	0.3	1.1	13.7	15.7
Base metals	3.5	4.1	−0.6	14.0
Machinery	0.4	2.1	20.6	15.9
Cutlery and handtools	0.8	3.3	16.2	13.4
Metal furniture	0.6	1.6	12.2	5.3
Radios, televisions, and the like	1.1	6.7	23.5	13.6
Other	4.0	8.0	7.2	10.9
Total	1.7	3.4	8.4	7.6

TABLE 2.8
Share of industrial-country exports to developing countries, 1973 and 1980

Exports	Total exports (billions of dollars)		Share to developing countries[a] (billions of dollars)		Percentage share	
	1973	1980	1973	1980	1973	1980
Machinery	141	434	38	149	27	34
Total merchandise	398	1,228	90	339	23	28

a. Includes high-income oil exporters.

Trade among developing countries

Developing-country exports were increasingly drawn to industrial countries in the 1950s and 1960s because the latter were growing rapidly and were liberalizing trade when others were not. But trade among developing countries ("south-south" trade) accelerated in the 1970s, increasing its share of their exports from 20 percent in 1973 to 24 percent in 1980; the rapid growth of markets in oil-exporting countries provided part of the south-south impetus, as did expansion in the newly industrializing countries.

South-south trade has built up in different forms. In Latin America regional trading arrangements encouraged trade diversion: relatively capital-intensive and high-cost goods were traded, rather than those exports that reflected the comparative advantage of Latin American countries. In East Asia, by contrast, regional trade helped to promote a more efficient division of production. The newly industrializing countries were expanding their demand for raw materials, while starting to export more sophisticated goods and services, some to countries within the region. This created opportunities for the region's primary producers—and for those countries that produced cheap, low-quality manufactures, since they could fill the gap

left as the newly industrializing countries moved up market. Regional trade expanded because trade policies stimulated responses to new market opportunities rather than as a result of formal trade agreements. Trade with the rest of the world also continued to grow fast. Thus, while regional trade grew as rapidly in East Asia as it did in Latin America, its share of total trade stayed constant in the former but rose in the latter.

Workers' remittances

Workers' remittances continue to be a significant source of foreign exchange for labor-exporting countries. The remittances received by some countries have been more than half the value of their exports; for a few countries, remittances have been larger than their exports. Even when remittances have been small in relation to exports, they have provided a higher standard of living for some families. Although the working conditions of migrant workers are sometimes poor, continuing emigration suggests that the private returns far outweigh the physical and psychological costs of being away from home (see Box 10.3).

The middle-income oil importers have been the largest recipients of remittances (see Table 2.9). This group includes the traditional labor exporters

TABLE 2.9
Flows of workers' remittances to developing countries, 1970–82

Country group	Billions of current dollars					Average annual percentage growth	
	1970	1973	1980	1981	1982[a]	1970–80	1980–82[a]
All developing countries	2.3	6.7	24.0	25.5	27.6	26.4	7.2
Low-income							
Asia	0.1	0.3	3.0	2.8	3.2	40.5	3.3
Africa	0.1	0.1	0.3	0.4	0.5	n.a.	29.1
Middle-income							
Oil importers	1.7	5.5	16.9	18.4	20.0	25.8	8.8
Oil exporters	0.4	0.7	3.8	3.9	3.9	25.3	1.3

n.a. Not applicable.
a. Estimated.

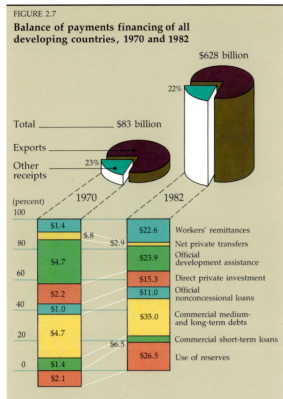

FIGURE 2.7

Balance of payments financing of all developing countries, 1970 and 1982

$628 billion

22%

Total _____ $83 billion

Exports _____

Other receipts

23%

1970   1982

(percent)
100

$1.4	$22.6
$.8	Workers' remittances
$2.9	Net private transfers
$4.7	$23.9
	Official development assistance
$2.2	$15.3
	Direct private investment
$1.0	$11.0
	Official nonconcessional loans
$4.7	$35.0
	Commercial medium- and long-term debts
$6.5	Commercial short-term loans
$1.4	$26.5
$2.1	Use of reserves

The height of the pie charts indicates total receipts of foreign exchange of all developing countries in current dollars. The financing of the resource gap is shown in the bar charts; the height of the blocks indicates the share of each component, and the numbers show the absolute amount in billions of current dollars.

in southern Europe (such as Turkey, Yugoslavia, and Portugal) whose workers go to northern Europe, as well as some of the countries which benefited from sending labor to the oil-surplus states: Jordan, Republic of Korea, Morocco, Philippines, Sudan, and the Yemens. Remittances to the low-income labor exporters of Asia also increased; although the total was small in comparison with the receipts of the middle-income group, it was an important source of their foreign exchange earnings. Some oil exporters (for example, Algeria, Egypt, Mexico, and Tunisia) also exported labor and their remittance receipts increased by 25 percent a year in 1970–80. The traditional labor importers in northern Europe hardly increased their immigrant work forces in the 1970s, but the boom in the Middle East boosted remittances considerably between 1973 and 1980. In 1980 remittances emanating from the industrialized countries amounted to about $19 billion, while the high-income oil exporters are estimated to have paid out about $5 billion. Since then remittances have

grown much more slowly, largely reflecting a slowdown in activity in labor-importing countries.

Capital flows

The growth of developing countries' exports during the 1970s was slightly exceeded by the growth in their inflows of medium- and long-term capital. Most significant was the increase in private lending, which rose at an average rate of 22 percent a year in 1970–80 and provided about half of total medium- and long-term capital flows during the period. Private direct investment contributed 14 percent of the total, and grew by 19 percent a year. Official development assistance (ODA) provided 28 percent of the total and expanded by 18 percent a year. The relative importance of these various sources of foreign exchange financing is shown in Figures 2.7 and 2.8.

Private sources

The share of medium- and long-term debt owed by the developing countries to private lenders has doubled since the early 1970s to an estimated 60 percent in 1982. The share is even higher (more than 70 percent) when banks' short-term credit is included; at the end of 1982, short-term credit totaled more than $150 billion. The dramatic increase in medium- and long-term borrowing reflects the developing countries' progress in building up creditworthiness, as well as market developments that favored a rapid expansion of lending. Private loans

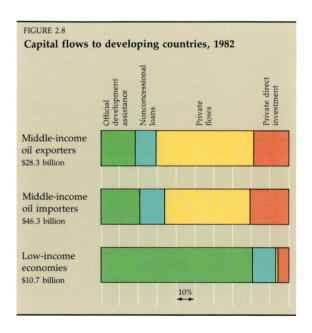

FIGURE 2.8

Capital flows to developing countries, 1982

Official development assistance · Nonconcessional loans · Private flows · Private direct investment

Middle-income oil exporters
$28.3 billion

Middle-income oil importers
$46.3 billion

Low-income economies
$10.7 billion

10%

went almost exclusively to the middle-income countries. At the end of 1982, more than 70 percent of their medium- and long-term debt was owed to private sources, while more than 80 percent of the debt of low-income countries was still owed to official sources, mostly at concessional terms. Some of these countries, either because of their strong reserve position or because they had progressed so little toward full creditworthiness, held deposits with the international banking system that were greater than their outstanding borrowings from it (see Table 2.10).

Some of the expansion of bank lending over the past decade has substituted for direct investment.

The relatively low interest rates during most of the 1970s encouraged this trend, as did restrictions placed by a number of host countries on direct investment. Multinational firms could often substitute debt for equity flows. In an effort to encourage direct investment, some countries have set up insurance schemes for foreign investors (see Box 2.1).

Official sources

Aid is provided for a variety of reasons—political, economic, and humanitarian—which are reflected in its geographical distribution. About two-thirds

---

Box 2.1 Insuring international investment

Twenty-two capital-exporting countries, including almost all OECD countries, as well as India and the Republic of Korea, have set up national investment insurance schemes. They offer insurance of new investments against noncommercial risks abroad to nationals or residents of the insuring country. Eligible investments have generally included equity and quasi-equity; the definition of investments extends increasingly to nonequity forms of international business transactions such as service and management contracts and profit or production-sharing arrangements. In general, coverage is available for three types of political risk: expropriation, currency incovertibility, and war. Periods of insurance tend to range between fifteen and twenty years. While a few schemes offer separate coverage for individual types of political risks, most of them provide only for blanket coverage of all risks at a flat premium. Premium rates vary among the schemes, but flat premiums tend to range between 0.5 percent and 1.5 percent a year of the insured amount.

As a rule, only investments flowing into developing countries are eligible. Whereas only one scheme explicitly requires the existence of a bilateral agreement with the host country as a precondition for insuring a project, many schemes strive to safeguard their exposure through general bilateral investment protection agreements between home and host countries.

Assistance to the development of the host country by promoting investments, promotion of the home country's exports or its access to raw materials, as well as promotion of mutually advantageous economic relations, are basic objectives of the national schemes. While some schemes concentrate on one or more of these targets, others strive, with varying priorities, to integrate all of them. All schemes operate under the auspices of their respective governments. Most are required, or at least expected, to operate on a self-sustaining financial basis.

According to OECD estimates, as of December 1981 the share of total OECD investment in developing countries covered by national investment insurance averaged about 10 percent—but varied between less than 1 percent and 87 percent. Many of the schemes appear inactive, with total coverage remaining under $100 million, and sometimes even under $10 million.

National investment insurance may be subject to a number of constraints such as:

• Inability to achieve a viable spread of risk, especially by small home countries

• Country or project ceiling, or both

• Failure of developmentally valuable investments to obtain insurance as a result of home-country-related policy considerations

• Inability to accord coverage to all members of international consortia on

equal terms and conditions

• Unavailability of national insurance to (potential) investors from some capital-exporting countries, in particular, capital surplus OPEC countries, which do not operate national schemes.

Since the early 1970s some private insurance underwriters have started to issue policies to cover noncommercial risks for firms operating in developing countries. In the past ten years the capacity of private insurers increased significantly.

The private insurers were successful mainly by making their programs complementary to national insurance schemes. Despite some disadvantages of private insurance—higher premiums (up to 5 percent) and shorter period of coverage (one to three years)—it provided coverage that could not be obtained under the national schemes because of their restrictions (for example, host-country ceiling and limitation to new investments by nationals).

To overcome the weaknesses of national and private insurance programs for noncommercial risk, international or multilateral investment insurance systems have been considered repeatedly since the early 1960s. Thus far only one regional scheme has been established: the Inter-Arab Investment Guarantee Corporation headquartered in Kuwait, which insures investment from Arab member states in other Arab member states.

TABLE 2.10
Net liabilities of selected developing countries, end-December 1982
(billions of dollars)

Country	Amount	Country	Amount
Brazil	51.77	Cameroon	0.60
Mexico	48.49	Sudan	0.20
Argentina	16.43	Tanzania	0.06
Korea, Rep. of	15.12	Sri Lanka	0.05
Chile	7.99	Bangladesh	−0.10
Portugal	7.48	Ghana	−0.14
Yugoslavia	7.28	Uruguay	−0.15
Nigeria	5.48	Kenya	−0.23
Philippines	5.37	Ethiopia	−0.23
Algeria	4.05	Pakistan	−0.46
Turkey	1.36	India	−0.56
Thailand	1.30	Egypt	−1.80
Indonesia	0.97	China	−6.64

Note: A negative sign denotes a net asset position as reported to the Bank for International Settlements (BIS).
Source: BIS.

of bilateral ODA goes to middle-income countries, while virtually all multilateral ODA goes to low-income countries. Because middle-income countries have borrowed heavily from private markets, ODA constitutes only a small fraction of their total capital inflows—20 percent in 1980. By contrast, even though low-income countries receive only 35 to 40 percent of total ODA, it has provided more than 75 percent of their external capital during the 1970s. Even among low-income countries, ODA's financial contribution varies widely. In the populous countries of South Asia, it was equivalent to only 5 percent of gross domestic investment in 1980, and 15 percent of imports. By contrast, ODA was equivalent to more than 40 percent of investment in low-income Africa and 20 percent of imports.

Although most DAC countries have accepted a target for ODA of 0.7 percent of their GNP, their

TABLE 2.11
ODA flows from major donor groups, 1970–81

	1970	1975	1981
	Billions of dollars		
Total ODA	20.0	31.6	37.6
Source	*Percent*		
DAC	88.5	68.4	68.0
OPEC	4.8	27.9	25.9
Nonmarket economies	6.7	3.7	6.1

Note: The figures reflect disbursements reported by donors and therefore differ from net ODA flows given in Table 2.12. (See also under Official Development Assistance in the Definitions.)
Sources: DAC and UNCTAD.

overall average has remained at about half that level since the early 1970s. Some DAC countries, notably the Netherlands, Norway, Sweden, and Denmark, have met and even exceeded the 0.7 percent target. Others—particularly the United States—have slipped further below it. ODA flows from OPEC countries increased rapidly in the first half of the 1970s but have since stabilized. Nonetheless, the share of ODA in their GNP remains far higher than in the case of the industrialized countries. ODA in real terms from DAC countries declined by 5 percent in 1981, and recovered by 10 percent in 1982, due in part to deferred disbursements from the previous year. The 1982 figure reflects the appreciation in the dollar which raised both the purchasing power of dollar aid receipts and the burden of debt denominated in dollars. ODA disbursements by source are set out in Table 2.11.

Not all official lending to developing countries qualifies as ODA. Official loans on terms close to market rates—mostly export credits and loans from multilateral development banks—have been growing more rapidly than ODA, rising from 19 to 29 percent of official flows between 1970 and 1980. While export credits are available to almost all countries, loans at near market terms from multilateral development banks often provide a bridge for countries not sufficiently creditworthy for purely private finance, but able to handle some debt on commercial terms.

Financing deficits in the recession

In the early 1980s many countries ran into serious balance of payments problems. Recession in the industrial countries reduced the export earnings of developing countries, while high real interest rates increased their debt service obligations. Some lenders, concerned about the ability of individual borrowers to surmount these difficulties and uncertain about world economic prospects, became less willing than they had been to increase their lending.

The outcome (partly estimated) for all developing countries in 1982 indicates the extent of the deterioration (see Table 2.12).

● The current account deficit was $118 billion, the same as in 1981 and more than twice that in 1980. It was equivalent to 5 percent of GNP and 25 percent of exports of goods and nonfactor services. By contrast, in 1975—the previous peak deficit year—deficits were 3.3 percent of GNP and 17.5 percent of exports.

TABLE 2.12
Developing countries' balance of payments, 1970–82
(billions of current dollars)

	1970	1978	1979	1980	1981	1982[a]
Current account						
Resource balance	−7.2	−28.8	−22.2	−42.3	−91.6	−85.7
Workers' remittances[b]	1.4	14.2	18.1	19.7	20.8	22.6
Interest payments[c]	−2.7	−16.8	−24.3	−32.9	−41.8	−49.5
Other current transactions	−3.5	−4.4	−2.9	−3.4	−6.0	−5.6
Current account balance	−12.0	−35.9	−31.3	−58.9	−118.6	−118.2
Financed by net capital flows	12.7	65.1	81.1	81.6	96.6	85.2
Official development assistance[d]	4.7	16.1	19.6	24.4	23.2	23.9
Official nonconcessional loans	1.1	5.3	7.3	9.8	10.1	11.0
Private loans	4.7	35.1	42.6	35.3	47.7	35.0
Private direct investment	2.2	8.4	11.6	12.1	15.6	15.3
Use of reserves and other capital[e]	−0.7	−29.3	−49.7	−22.8	22.0	33.0
Memorandum items						
Debt outstanding	69.4	311.7	370.3	424.2	491.6	548.0
Official	34.0	120.4	136.1	157.2	177.6	199.0
Private	35.3	191.3	234.2	267.0	314.0	349.0
Resource gap as percentage of GNP	1.4	1.8	1.2	1.9	4.3	3.7
Current account deficit as percentage of GNP	2.3	2.2	1.6	2.7	5.5	5.0
Net capital flows as percentage of GNP	2.5	4.0	4.3	3.7	4.5	3.6
Debt service as percentage of GNP	1.8	3.2	3.5	3.4	4.1	4.7
Debt service as percentage of exports	13.5	15.4	15.0	13.6	16.3	20.7
Interest payments as percentage of GNP	0.5	5.0	5.5	5.9	2.0	2.1
Deflator[f]	38.4	83.0	91.7	100.0	99.3	98.4

a. Estimated.
b. Net of remittance payments.
c. Interest payments on medium- and long-term loans.
d. Net official development assistance, defined as net disbursements of concessional official loans plus net official transfers.
e. Other capital includes net short-term borrowing, capital not elsewhere indicated, and errors and omissions.
f. US dollar GDP deflator for industrial countries.

TABLE 2.13
Developing countries' current account balance, excluding official transfers, 1970–82
(billions of current dollars)

Country group	1970	1978	1979	1980	1981	1982[a]
All developing countries	−12.0	−35.9	−31.3	−58.9	−118.5	−118.3
Low-income						
Asia	−0.7	−1.9	−5.4	−11.6	−6.6	−4.2
Africa	−0.6	−2.6	−3.0	−3.7	−5.5	−5.5
Middle-income						
Oil importers	−7.5	−21.8	−36.2	−56.2	−67.7	−58.8
Oil exporters	−3.2	−9.6	13.3	12.6	−38.7	−49.8

a. Estimated.

● Export earnings fell for the second consecutive year, to a level 7 percent below that of 1980—the result of declining dollar prices of exports and stagnant volumes.

● Interest payments on medium- and long-term debt rose to nearly $50 billion, 50 percent above their 1980 level. The London Interbank Offer Rate (LIBOR) for six-month dollar deposits, which determines interest payments on the bulk of private bank loans, averaged 16.6 percent in 1981 and 13.5 percent in 1982.

The external deterioration affected different groups of developing countries in different ways (see Table 2.13). For oil importers the high interest rates and depressed export markets of 1980–82 came on top of the 1979–80 rise in oil prices, to which most countries had barely started to adjust. Between 1978 and 1980 their current account deficit rose from $26 billion to $72 billion, even though they reduced the rate of growth in the volume of their imports from an average 7 percent a year in 1975–79 to only 4 percent in 1980. In 1981 they held the volume of their imports constant, but this did not stop the deficit from rising to a new peak of almost $80 billion. Exports were falling rapidly while interest payments still rose. In 1982 export earnings fell again; since capital-importing countries were unable to increase their borrowing, they had to cut back their merchandise imports.

The oil-exporting developing countries initially benefited from the 1979–80 rise in oil prices. However, as the momentum of expanding imports ran into progressively weakening demand for oil, their current account swung from a surplus of $13 billion in 1980 to large deficits in both 1981 and 1982. Their imports rose $45 billion in current prices between 1980 and 1982, while exports fell $13 billion. That $60 billion swing accounted for the entire widening of the current account deficit of all developing countries during the period. Although the oil exporters slowed down the growth in their import volume in 1982, their external deficit, at 7 percent of GNP and 28 percent of exports, was clearly in need of correction.

In the 1970s medium- and long-term borrowing exceeded current payments needs and resulted in a substantial buildup of foreign exchange reserves. The $80 billion expansion of the combined current account deficits of developing countries between 1978 and 1982 was accompanied by notable shifts in financing patterns. Medium- and long-term finance rose 30 percent over this period, but this increase met only a quarter of the rise in the current account deficit (see Figure 2.9).

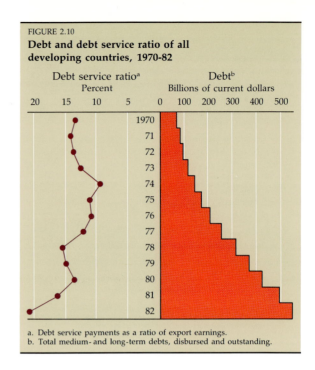

FIGURE 2.10
Debt and debt service ratio of all developing countries, 1970-82

a. Debt service payments as a ratio of export earnings.
b. Total medium- and long-term debts, disbursed and outstanding.

Within this total, long-term private lending, which had expanded to $48 billion in 1981, fell back in 1982 to close to the level in 1978. Net receipts of ODA expanded by 50 percent between 1978 and 1980 but have subsequently stagnated, placing severe strains on low-income countries that cannot borrow privately. Net private direct investment, which began to accelerate in the late 1970s, also stalled as growth in developing and industrial countries declined. Most of the extra financing needs since 1980 have therefore been met by both reserve movements and short-term borrowing.

International debt

While the developing countries' medium- and long-term debt increased by 20 percent a year in the 1970s, the resources needed to service the debt were also growing rapidly. The ratio of privately owned debt to exports, as well as total debt service to exports, was no higher in 1980 than it had been in 1970 (see Figure 2.10). Although the average effective interest rate on total developing-country debt increased from 6.3 percent in 1970 to 8.9 percent in 1980, this rise was less than the annual increase in the prices of their imports or exports, and less than the inflation rate in the industrialized countries. The real interest rate on debt was therefore very low.

After 1980 the position changed. Although the

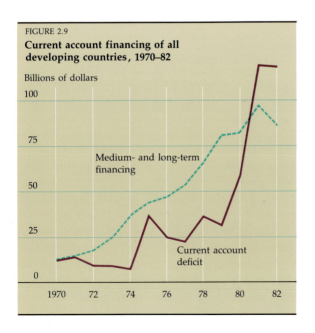

FIGURE 2.9
Current account financing of all developing countries, 1970–82

Billions of dollars

Medium- and long-term financing

Current account deficit

rate of growth of debt halved to an estimated 11 percent in 1982, the slowdown in export earnings was sharper. As a result, the ratio of debt to exports rose from 76 percent to 104 percent between 1980 and 1982; if short-term debt is included, this ratio exceeded 150 percent. For oil-importing developing countries, the ratio was far higher than at any time since 1970; for oil exporters, it was no lower than it had been before the 1973–74 oil price rise (see Figure 2.11). Since a large part of developing-country debt is denominated in dollars, the appreciation of the dollar in foreign exchange markets has added to their debt burden.

Boosted by higher interest rates, the ratio of debt service obligations to exports rose sharply from 13.6 percent in 1980 to 20.7 percent in 1982 (see Table 2.14). Although the incidence of lower export earnings, more debt, and higher interest rates varied widely among countries, the importance of lower export earnings is indicated by a hypothetical calculation: had export earnings risen at 10 percent a year in 1980–82 (about half the average increase in the 1970s), the debt service ratio would

TABLE 2.14
Debt service ratios for all developing countries, 1970–82

Country group	1970	1980	1981	1982[a]
All developing countries	13.5	13.6	16.3	20.7
Low-income				
Asia	13.3	7.9	8.4	10.1
Africa	6.5	8.8	11.6	28.3[b]
Middle-income				
Oil importers	14.0	14.9	18.0	23.0
East Asia	6.7	7.0	7.6	8.6
Latin America	13.0	33.3	39.6	53.2
Oil exporters	13.9	13.0	15.7	19.1

a. Estimated.
b. The sharp rise in 1982 reflects the accumulation of arrears and does not allow for any reschedulings in 1982.

have risen by less than three percentage points instead of the seven points it actually did. Of that three-point increase, about half would have been due to higher debt levels and half to higher interest rates.

The way developing-country debt evolved during the 1970s left most borrowers particularly vulnerable to the pressures of the early 1980s.

• Debt was increasingly composed of loans at variable rates, their share rising from less than 10 percent in 1970 to more than 40 percent by 1980. Variable rates were initially welcomed by many bankers and borrowers. By eliminating the interest rate risk for lenders, variable rates made banks more willing to lend long-term during a period of rising inflation. Variable rates also promised to stabilize real interest rates on long-term debt, if interest rates changed in line with inflation. However, the tightening of monetary policy in major countries in recent years raised real as well as nominal rates. Being more reliant on variable rate loans, developing countries found that market interest rates affected their total interest obligations more quickly than before. (By the same token, they benefited promptly from the interest rate declines in 1982 and early 1983.)

• The practice of syndicating loans also helped to boost private financial flows to developing countries, by spreading the risks of such lending among many banks. With heightened uncertainty about economic prospects, however, banks have had to devote more resources to risk assessment, increasing their costs and discouraging some smaller banks from further lending. Although the quantity and quality of information available to lenders have improved, many are still dissatisfied with it.

• Facing difficulty in obtaining long-term loans

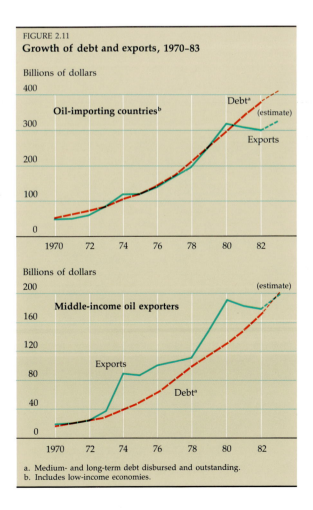

FIGURE 2.11
Growth of debt and exports, 1970–83

Billions of dollars

Oil-importing countries[b]

Debt[a] (estimate)
Exports

Billions of dollars

Middle-income oil exporters

(estimate)
Exports
Debt[a]

a. Medium- and long-term debt disbursed and outstanding.
b. Includes low-income economies.

(official as well as private), countries looked increasingly to short-term borrowing or to running down their reserves. These expedients are customarily adopted to smooth out short-term fluctuations in earnings. Their use through the prolonged downturn of 1980–82 may have permitted a higher level of imports than would otherwise have been possible, but it has left many countries vulnerable to further shocks. By increasing their net short-term debt, countries also became more exposed to rising interest rates and to sudden withdrawal of support by commercial banks.

While these three factors help explain how debt difficulties worsened in the 1980s, those difficulties have affected individual countries rather than whole regions or groups. The deteriorating aggregate ratios of the past few years understate the predicament of a number of countries (including some of the largest debtors), while exaggerating the problems of others. Genuine difficulty can be measured by the number of countries that have sought formal rescheduling or major refinancing of their debts. Since 1980 more than twenty countries have negotiated to reschedule their debt—a far higher number than in any comparable period (see Box 2.2). Most have rescheduled through the Paris Club, the traditional forum for renegotiating official debt. They have typically been small, primary-producing countries that rely heavily on official sources of finance and that have been hard

Box 2.2 Restructuring developing countries' debts

Two kinds of institutional arrangements exist to restructure the two major types of debt, official and commercial. Debts to governments and commercial credits covered by official guarantees are renegotiated in the Paris Club or in aid consortia; debts to commercial banks are renegotiated with committees of bankers. Debt restructuring generally takes two forms—either a repayment of existing debt through refinancing arrangements or a rescheduling of existing loans. There have been substantial refinancings of debt to commercial banks in the past: for example, Argentina (1976) and Jamaica (1979). But the bulk of the more recent official and commercial bank debt renegotiations have involved formal reschedulings.

The terms of reschedulings are usually relatively short. In Paris Club agreements, rescheduled debts, which cover one to two years of original obligations, are normally repaid in seven to ten years with three to four years' grace. But exceptions have been made. Between 80 and 90 percent of eligible maturities are consolidated. Sometimes the nonconsol-

idated portion of the debt may be paid during the grace period rather than on the original due dates. Moratorium interest charges on rescheduled commercial credits are normally set at the rate at which new credits are offered.

Rescheduled commercial bank debt is repaid over five to ten years. Debt relief agreements with commercial banks normally reschedule principal amounts due. Occasionally some interest arrears are consolidated but they are normally paid in about half the time allowed for consolidated principal. Currently both the Paris Club and commercial banks require the debtor country to have agreed on a stabilization program with the IMF.

A number of countries have recently sought and obtained debt relief without any formal agreement with their banks. This somewhat confirms the view that mechanisms for debt renegotiations have become adequately institutionalized. Furthermore, the most complicated debt renegotiations—such as those with Poland and Romania—have been put in place. In recent negotiations, however, the IMF has played an increasingly im-

portant role putting together viable debt restructuring packages with commercial banks.

A number of problems, however, continue to mar the smooth working of debt-relief procedures. Debt renegotiations essentially address liquidity problems. Countries with deep-seated economic difficulties often require debt relief for several years in a row: without it, their solvency can be impaired. Delays in implementing bilateral agreements under the Paris Club are not unusual. This in turn delays the return of export credit insurance and the renewed flow of commercial credits. Most important, debt renegotiations have not succeeded in maintaining the creditworthiness of many countries. In some measure this has been due to the overwhelming concern with liquidity problems to the exclusion of long-run development issues. Both government and commercial bank creditors need to recognize that, without additional capital to support real adjustment, debt restructuring may not serve the ultimate purpose of debt renegotiations, that is, the restoration of creditworthiness.

hit by declines in commodity prices.

Several of the largest debtor countries, which have relied chiefly on private sources of finance, have also sought to reschedule their debt. These arrangements have generally been made through ad hoc committees of creditors, in conjunction with programs agreed with the International Monetary Fund (IMF). The IMF has made a particular effort to ensure that these arrangements do not result in debt merely being transferred from private to official creditors, but that additional new private loans are also committed.

In several major countries with debt servicing difficulties, such as Brazil and Mexico, the problem is basically that of liquidity; in these cases, al-though the productivity of investment has been relatively high, difficulties arose because of the sharp increase in interest rates and sudden decline in short-term capital inflows. In others (such as Argentina, Bolivia, Jamaica, Madagascar, Nicaragua, Senegal, and Zaire), the low return on investment has also contributed to debt servicing problems.

The impact of the recession on developing countries

There is considerable variation in the impact of the international recession on individual countries, but there are also broad similarities. Most countries

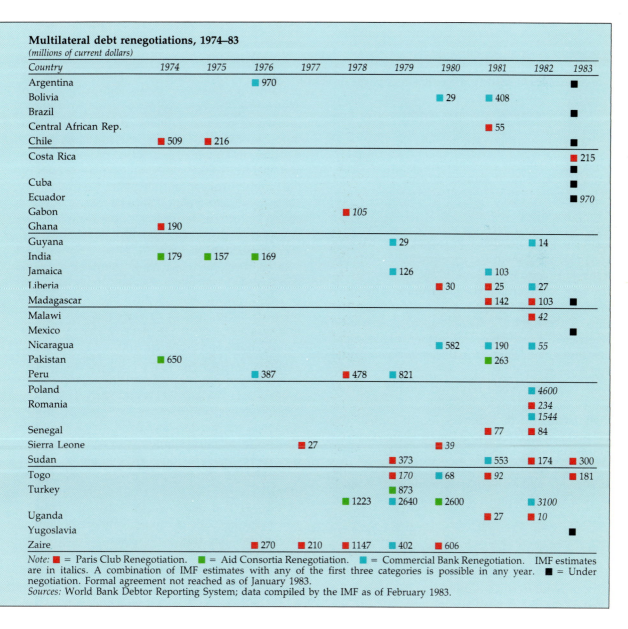

Multilateral debt renegotiations, 1974–83
(millions of current dollars)

Country	1974	1975	1976	1977	1978	1979	1980	1981	1982	1983
Argentina			970							■
Bolivia							29	408		
Brazil										■
Central African Rep.								55		
Chile	509	216								■
Costa Rica										215 ■
Cuba										■
Ecuador										*970*
Gabon					*105*					
Ghana	190									
Guyana						29			14	
India	179	157	169							
Jamaica						126		103		
Liberia							30	25	27	
Madagascar								142	103	■
Malawi								42		
Mexico										■
Nicaragua							582	190	*55*	
Pakistan	650							263		
Peru			387		478	821				
Poland								4600		
Romania								234		
									1544	
Senegal								77	84	
Sierra Leone				27			*39*			
Sudan						373		553	174	300
Togo						170	68	92		181
Turkey						873				
					1223	2640	2600		*3100*	
Uganda								27	*10*	
Yugoslavia										■
Zaire			270	210	1147	402	606			

Note: ■ = Paris Club Renegotiation. ■ = Aid Consortia Renegotiation. ■ = Commercial Bank Renegotiation. IMF estimates are in italics. A combination of IMF estimates with any of the first three categories is possible in any year. ■ = Under negotiation. Formal agreement not reached as of January 1983.
Sources: World Bank Debtor Reporting System; data compiled by the IMF as of February 1983.

have experienced, in varying degrees:

- Import reductions because of stagnant or declining foreign exchange earnings, reduced inflows of external capital, and rising debt service requirements
- Falling government revenues due to declining economic activity, the stagnation in trade, and the difficulty of imposing new taxes during a recession
- Cutbacks in investment plans and the slowdown of ongoing projects because of shortages of domestic and external funds
- Shortages of funds to finance the operation and maintenance of existing facilities.

The severity of such problems depended not only on economic structure but also on the choices countries made among the various ways of adjusting to external shocks: some adjustment paths are efficient, others less so. Current account deficits can be reduced by slower growth, which cuts the demand for imports, or by switching production to additional exports and efficient import substitutes. Countries with access to external capital could use this capital to help make these structural adjustments or to help postpone making adjustments. Countries that choose to maintain consumption levels by reducing investment eventually pay the price of a more difficult adjustment in later years, or must be willing to accept a longer period of slower growth. Others, which restructure investment programs, increase domestic saving, and give incentives to export may have to accept slower growth and consumption during the transition period, but are likely to emerge as stronger economies in the long run. For the low-income or least developed countries, however, the choices were more difficult, since consumption levels were already low and further cuts to maintain investment implied particularly severe social and human costs.

Although the world recession sharply curtailed growth in most developing countries—in 1980–82 their GDP growth rate was less than half the 1973–80 average—the low-income economies of Asia did much better than those of Africa. Among the middle-income oil-importing countries, East Asia as a group markedly outperformed Latin America in 1981 and 1982 (see Table 2.1).

Low-income countries

The position of the low-income sub-Saharan African countries continued to deteriorate in 1980–82. Most had fared significantly worse in the 1970s than in the 1960s, and GDP per capita declined in many countries from 1973 to 1980. As the World Bank's report *Accelerated Development in Sub-Saharan Africa* noted, inappropriate policies—chronic fiscal deficits, farm prices and marketing arrangements that deterred production, and overvalued exchange rates—contributed to slow growth in the 1970s. These long-standing problems have been greatly exacerbated by the 1980–82 recession, with falling demand for primary product exports. To make matters worse, a severe drought is afflicting not only the Sahel region, but also southern Africa. Drought conditions in 1982 contributed to a decline in agricultural production. This was not offset by any growth in official development assistance, which was virtually stagnant in 1981 and 1982. To cope with their worsening balance of payments, countries sharply curtailed economic activity to reduce imports.

Many African governments (for example, in Malawi, Mali, and Sudan) have recognized the importance of adjusting policies, and particularly of eliminating the bias against agriculture. Despite the world recession, policy changes have produced encouraging results. For example, Sudan devalued its exchange rate, raised producer prices, and altered its tax regime—all geared to restoring the incentive for cotton cultivation. Concessionary aid helped finance critical imports for the irrigated cotton sector. The result was a 51 percent increase in cotton production in 1981–82 followed by a further 27 percent last year.

In contrast, the low-income countries of South and East Asia, notably India and China, were able to face the difficulties of the 1970s, and even of the early 1980s, from a stronger position. In part this was because of the policies they pursued. China, India, and Sri Lanka initiated liberalization programs in the second half of the 1970s. Pakistan and Bangladesh adopted structural adjustment programs in the late 1970s and early 1980s. The low-income Asian countries have mostly shown discipline in monetary and fiscal policy and have also made significant progress in correcting price distortions and providing appropriate incentives to encourage efficiency and growth. India, for example, grew by an average of 6.5 percent a year in 1980–81 and, although growth slowed to 2.8 percent in 1982 due to drought and the prolonged world recession, this increase was still high compared with earlier drought years. By adjusting prices to reflect economic costs more closely, the government helped to promote a rise in public savings in 1981–82, while private savings also grew. Improved efficiency in power and railways allowed higher capacity utilization in industry. And despite the world recession, exports continued to grow rapidly in response to export incentives and the greater availability of essential imports.

Middle-income oil importers

The recession also affected middle-income oil importers in diverse ways. The middle-income countries of Asia saw a deterioration in their terms of trade, yet they still performed remarkably well. The Republic of Korea and the Philippines managed to grow by an average of 2 and 4 percent a year respectively during 1980–82, and Thailand by 6 percent a year. Although the reliance of the newly industrialized countries of Asia on manufactured exports makes them vulnerable to downturns in trade and to protectionism, their manufactured exports did not decline. By emphasizing efficiency and competitiveness, and by being relatively cautious in their foreign debt and fiscal policies, they have created an economic resilience that can weather difficult conditions. Their relatively low level of price distortions was conducive to better resource allocation and use, which permitted respectable growth of exports and GDP during the latest recession. It also meant that the returns on foreign borrowing were higher.

In contrast, from 1980 to 1982 the GDP of middle-income oil importers in Latin America fell by almost 2 percent a year. The recent decline in oil prices has alleviated their import burden, but falling world demand and prices of primary commodities reduced export earnings. Even more important, sharply rising interest payments exacerbated their worsening balance of payments. Their heavy indebtedness made the Latin American economies especially vulnerable to rising interest rates and any slowdown in their exports. The size of the external debt of the oil importers in Latin America is not high in relation to the level of economic activity, but it is exceedingly high compared with their export earnings. In 1981 their ratio of debt to GDP was identical to that of other developing countries (24 percent), but the ratio of debt to exports was 158 percent compared with 95 percent for other developing countries. Furthermore, more than 50 percent of this debt was at variable interest rates compared with 21 percent for all other developing countries. By 1982 their debt service burden had risen to 53 percent of exports compared with 8.6 percent for East Asian oil importers. To service their debt, they therefore had to reduce their imports, and thus their growth, considerably.

Long-standing domestic problems added to the vulnerability of these economies to recession. Negative real interest rates and other financial policies dampened savings and contributed to capital flight. High protection led to inefficient manufacturing industries and limited exports, and fiscal and monetary policies led to high rates of inflation. The immediate result of such policies was the overvaluation of exchange rates and a tendency to import too much, export too little, ship capital abroad, and borrow heavily. During this period many countries embarked on programs to adjust their policies by reducing protectionism, encouraging exports, eliminating price controls, and adjusting exchange rates. While important progress was made in some cases, in others the sequence of policies was unfortunate. For example, when the liberalization of foreign capital inflows preceded trade liberalization, borrowed capital flowed into inefficient activities with low social returns. At the same time these policy reforms often had little impact on fiscal deficits and inflation.

Where policies have been changed, middle-income oil importers, like the low-income countries, have shown that they can reap substantial benefits, notwithstanding the world recession. For example, Turkey, which initiated a major economic reform program in 1980, has made notable progress. Its GDP grew by more than 4 percent a year in 1981 and 1982, inflation dropped from 107 percent in 1980 to 25 percent in 1982, and an upsurge in exports, together with modest import demand, brought the current account deficit down from 4 percent of GDP in 1981 to 2 percent in 1982.

Middle-income oil-exporting countries

Paradoxically, some of the countries now facing the greatest problems are oil exporters, despite the marked improvement in their terms of trade over the past decade. Their problems have well established antecedents in the history of other resource-rich economies. A country that is well endowed with natural resources reaps a rental income from their exploitation. Usually the government appropriates the bulk of the rents in the form of royalties, direct profits, or production-sharing fees, and such revenues can be used for heavy public spending.

The oil exporters used their revenues to expand development expenditures, putting more funds into social and physical infrastructure than they could otherwise have done. Sometimes, however, they overinvested in capital-intensive sectors that contributed little to employment, drawing resources out of agriculture and small-scale enterprises.

The erosion of the tax base has been a further problem for resource-rich countries. With windfall gains from oil, it is difficult to persuade taxpayers that their contributions are necessary for growth. But if the tax base erodes, governments find themselves short of revenues when income from oil or other resources declines.

For all these reasons many middle-income oil exporters have found themselves in difficulty in the 1980s. For example, in Egypt, the fall in revenues from petroleum exports, as well as diminished earnings from the Suez Canal, workers' remittances, and tourism, caused the current account deficit to widen to nearly 14 percent of GDP in 1982. The fiscal deficit rose to 22 percent of GDP that same year.

Sometimes capital-intensive investments were further expanded by external borrowing on the assumption that revenues would continue to grow. At the beginning of the recession, as the demand for oil was falling, it was tempting to maintain public spending by borrowing even more. The Latin American oil exporters, for example, increased their debt by 23.3 percent a year between 1972 and 1981 (compared with 19.4 percent for the region's oil importers), and by 1981, 70 percent of the debt was at variable interest rates (compared with 56 percent for the rest of the region). As interest rates rose and oil revenues fell, these heavily borrowed countries found themselves in difficulty.

Here, too, there were variations. Some oil exporters, such as Mexico and Nigeria, had difficulty servicing their debts when oil revenues fell. Others, Malaysia and Indonesia, for instance, have maintained creditor confidence and access to financial markets. In both countries the accumulated foreign exchange reserves from past oil revenues also provided a cushion against the decline in export earnings.

Summing up the experience of all developing countries, the past three years underline the importance of incentive-promoting policies. The most successful countries have been outward oriented, and have also emphasized the role of prices and markets for improving efficiency, as well as better management of the public sector. The ability of some Latin American countries to withstand external strains after 1979—particularly higher interest rates and lower commodity prices—was seriously compromised by their earlier domestic policies. For sub-Saharan Africa, the main new factor has been the sharp decline in commodity prices—again, coming on top of continued weaknesses in economic policy and management.

What is needed for sustained world economic growth is concerted action by both the industrial and the developing countries. The former to help provide a more stable and favorable external economic environment through steady but noninflationary expansion, a more open trading system, and continued steady growth in both commercial and concessionary capital flows. The latter, by adopting policies that increase efficiency. These policies are discussed at length in Part II.

3 The outlook for developing countries

The previous chapter has placed the difficulties of the past few years in their historical perspective. This chapter looks ahead to the middle of the next decade. It concludes that most developing countries should be able to regain their growth momentum, but to do so will require a more favorable world environment, coupled with significant efforts by the developing countries themselves to make better use of their resources. Even in those circumstances, the outlook for some of the poorest countries is somber.

In common with previous *World Development Reports*, no attempt has been made to predict the future. This chapter instead provides a consistent framework for exploring the links between countries and between economic variables, so as to illustrate the effects of different policies and events on the developing countries. To assist this analysis, three sets of projections—Low, Central, and High growth scenarios—have been prepared through 1995; the results are summarized in Table 3.1. The Central case does not represent the most probable outcome; it is merely the middle set of the three scenarios that serve to illustrate the likely impact of different policies. All three have required judgmental adjustments, particularly with respect to policy changes. A more detailed explanation of the methodology used in elaborating these scenarios is given in the Technical appendix.

The purpose of assessing the outlook as far ahead as 1995 is to abstract from cyclical fluctuations and concentrate on underlying trends. However, the recession of 1980–82 was so severe that it is bound to affect statistical averages for several years. In order to avoid distorting the picture, the years to 1995 have been divided into two periods—1980–85 and 1985–95.

Before examining the domestic determinants of growth in developing countries, this chapter discusses the external factors that affect economic performance. These include growth in industrial countries, energy, trade, workers' remittances, and capital flows. The analysis focuses mainly on the Central case, but indicates policies that would make the High and Low scenarios more likely.

Growth in industrial countries

The Central case assumes that GDP in industrial countries will grow at about 3.8 percent a year during the recovery period and up to 1990, and thereafter at about 3.5 percent a year. Though governments are likely to proceed cautiously for fear of reigniting inflationary pressures, a rate of growth

TABLE 3.1
Past and projected growth of GDP, 1960–95
(average annual percentage change)

Country group	1960–73	1973–80	1980–82	1982–85	1985–95 Low	Central	High
All developing countries	6.0	4.7	1.9	4.4	4.7	5.5	6.2
Low-income							
Asia	4.6	5.4	4.1	4.5	4.5	4.9	5.3
Africa	3.5	1.4	0.5	2.9	2.7	3.3	3.9
Middle-income							
Oil importers	6.3	5.2	1.2	4.5	4.4	5.7	6.9
Oil exporters	7.0	3.7	1.7	4.0	5.3	5.7	5.8
Industrial countries	5.1	2.5	0.4	3.0	2.5	3.7	5.0

approaching 4 percent following a recession would be modest compared with past industrial-country recoveries. Nonetheless it would enable the waste and social costs represented by 30 million now unemployed to be substantially reduced.

As unemployment declines, in time labor shortages will appear and restrain industrial countries' growth. If present immigration policies remain unchanged, declining population growth rates and other demographic changes will reduce the growth of the labor force in industrial countries from about 1.25 percent a year between 1960 and 1980 to about 0.7 percent a year in 1985–95. Over the projection period technical progress is assumed to produce an annual growth in per capita output of about 2.8 percent, a level comparable to that of the past two decades. The GDP deflator (in dollars) for the industrialized countries is assumed to average 6.4 percent in 1982–95; real short-term interest rates are assumed to average 3 percent over the same period.

Energy

The links between energy prices, energy demand, and economic growth have become complex. Progress made so far in conservation has only scratched the surface of what is technologically possible and likely to be economic at higher energy prices. Conservation is more than the adjustment of thermostats, retrofitting, switching to smaller cars, and similar measures, which represent the main efforts undertaken to date. It also implies innovation in design and hence new investment. Significant gains can still be made.

Those gains depend on policies that reduce the energy used per unit of output and induce a shift from dependence on imported oil at high prices to greater use of cheaper alternatives, domestic or imported. Such policies include raising energy prices; taxation and other fiscal incentives; investment in domestic supplies of energy; training; and promotional and educational efforts. These measures encourage more energy-efficient processes in industry, transport (fuel savings, railway electrification), households (improved woodstoves), and electric power (loss reduction, use of waste heat, and improved load management). Some developing countries—notably Brazil, China, and the Republic of Korea—have reduced their commercial energy intensity in recent years and shifted to cheaper substitutes. Other countries have yet to correct their policy stance and develop well-defined programs for managing energy demand.

The slowdown in economic activity is another major cause of the slower rise in energy demand since 1973. Nevertheless, the global demand for energy can be expected to rise again rapidly toward the end of the 1980s. If GDP in the industrial countries grows at nearly 4 percent a year and in the developing countries at about 5.5 percent a year between 1985 and 1995, world commercial energy consumption is likely to rise by about 2.3 percent a year in 1985–95, compared with 3 percent from 1970 to 1980. For developing countries alone, the growth rate is likely to reach about 4.5 percent a year. This projection assumes not only Central case GDP growth, but also further progress in conservation and the production of new energy supplies.

Rising demand for energy would influence the course of energy prices. In the short run, energy prices could soften considerably in response to low demand and the urgent needs of energy exporters for revenue; the 1983 price is now forecast to be some 20 percent lower than in 1982. A sustained period of depressed oil prices (and hence energy prices) would almost certainly slow the pace of energy conservation and affect the production of other forms of energy. As GDP growth recovers, however, real oil prices will rise, and energy demand may be expected to grow more quickly than the availability of cheap, incremental supplies. By the mid-1990s the real price of oil is expected to be about 20 percent above its 1981 peak. The Central scenario assumes that the oil-price rise in real terms averages 1.6 percent a year between 1982 and 1995.

Despite their conservation efforts, which led to a decline in their consumption of oil, the long-term dependence of industrial countries on imported oil will not diminish substantially, since their own production—particularly in the United States and the North Sea—is also expected to decline gradually. The OPEC countries will therefore remain the main exporters of petroleum, with OPEC prices exerting a strong influence on international energy prices.

With the price of oil rising over the medium term, the future pattern of energy consumption is likely to differ markedly from that of the 1970s. Oil consumption is expected to grow by less than 1 percent a year in 1985–95, contributing only 11 percent of the increase in global energy consumption between 1980 and 1995, compared with 43 percent during the 1970s. Coal, primary electricity (nuclear and hydroelectric power), and natural gas are expected to compensate for the declining share

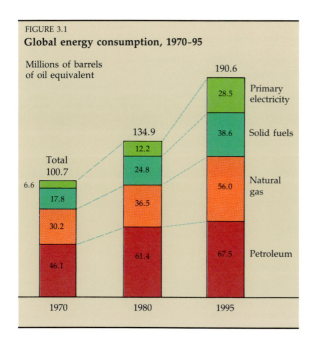

FIGURE 3.1
Global energy consumption, 1970-95

Millions of barrels of oil equivalent

Total 100.7

Primary electricity
Solid fuels
Natural gas
Petroleum

of oil in total energy consumption (see Figure 3.1). The industrial countries, as well as some developing countries, will turn increasingly to coal to meet their energy needs (see Table 3.2). Although its use tends to be constrained by environmental concerns and high transport costs, the expected slower rise in the production costs of coal will give it a competitive edge over other fuels. Of the projected increase in global energy demand between 1980 and 1995, coal is expected to supply 35 percent, primary electricity 29 percent, and natural gas 25 percent. Rising project costs have resulted in a sharp reduction of synthetic fuel projects. Hence nonconventional fuels will play only a minor role during the 1980s and early 1990s.

The prospect of rising real oil prices underlines the urgency of adopting appropriate national energy policies. At their heart lie domestic energy prices. They have to signal the real long-run cost of energy to all energy suppliers and users so that the desired structural changes in supply and demand, for particular fuels and for energy as a whole, will take place. Further, since the risks and costs of interruptions in supplies and sudden price increases are high for oil-importing developing countries, it is important for them to accelerate the development of their own energy resources. Fortunately, many developing countries, including some oil exporters, have moved or are moving domestic energy prices toward world prices. Despite the anticipated short-term weakness in the oil markets, energy development in the develop-

ing countries at prevailing (or even somewhat lower) oil prices remains profitable, particularly if the high cost of interruptions in supply is taken into account. Short-term fluctuations in the price of oil should neither lead to complacency nor deter countries from pursuing conservation and production goals.

Trade

Foreign trade enables developing countries to specialize in production, exploit economies of scale, and increase foreign exchange earnings needed to pay for imports. A good export record also strengthens creditworthiness and permits greater access to private loans. As Figure 3.2 shows, the developing countries' exports are directly affected by growth in the industrial countries. They are also influenced by the level of protectionism in the industrial world. The Central case assumes that industrial countries will institute no new protectionist measures between now and 1995.

The sensitivity of developing-country exports to activity in the industrial countries can be illustrated by a calculation based on some simplifying assumptions. If GDP in the industrial countries were to rise by just 5 percent a year between 1982 and 1984, the oil-importing developing countries would increase the value of their exports by 20 to 30 percent and the volume by about 10 percent.

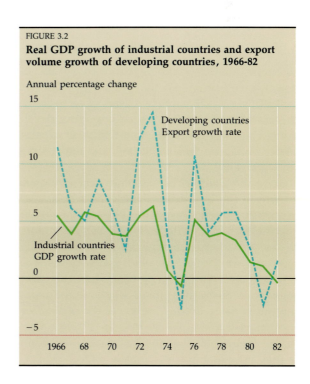

FIGURE 3.2
Real GDP growth of industrial countries and export volume growth of developing countries, 1966-82

Annual percentage change

Developing countries Export growth rate

Industrial countries GDP growth rate

TABLE 3.2
Commercial primary energy production and consumption by country group, 1970–95
(million barrels per day of oil equivalent)

Country group	1970 Production	1970 Consumption	1980 Production	1980 Consumption	1995 Production	1995 Consumption
Low-income	5.5	6.0	10.8	11.0	19.1	18.8
Petroleum	0.7	1.3	2.4	2.7	3.8	3.8
Natural gas	0.1	0.1	0.4	0.4	1.3	1.3
Solid fuels	4.4	4.3	7.3	7.2	12.1	11.8
Primary electricity	0.3	0.3	0.7	0.7	1.9	1.9
Middle-income						
Oil importers	3.4	6.1	5.6	10.8	13.5	22.0
Petroleum	1.1	3.7	1.0	6.2	1.8	9.0
Natural gas	0.2	0.2	0.4	0.4	1.5	1.6
Solid fuels	1.5	1.6	2.6	2.6	5.2	6.4
Primary electricity	0.6	0.6	1.6	1.6	5.0	5.0
Oil exporters	14.6	2.9	16.9	5.1	29.0	11.1
Petroleum	13.6	2.0	15.0	3.6	21.9	5.9
Natural gas	0.7	0.6	1.5	1.1	5.7	3.6
Solid fuels	0.1	0.1	0.1	0.1	0.4	0.6
Primary electricity	0.2	0.2	0.3	0.3	1.0	1.0
High-income oil exporters	11.8	0.7	17.4	1.6	15.7	3.0
Petroleum	11.7	0.6	16.5	0.9	14.2	1.8
Natural gas	0.1	0.1	0.9	0.7	1.5	1.2
Solid fuels	0.0	0.0	0.0	0.0	0.0	0.0
Primary electricity	0.0	0.0	0.0	0.0	0.0	0.0
East European nonmarket economies	22.5	21.2	34.2	32.2	44.1	43.7
Petroleum	7.4	6.5	12.4	11.2	11.9	12.5
Natural gas	3.8	3.8	8.0	7.6	14.6	13.5
Solid fuels	10.6	10.2	12.4	12.0	13.8	13.9
Primary electricity	0.7	0.7	1.4	1.4	3.8	3.8
Industrial countries	43.2	63.1	49.9	74.2	69.1	92.0
Petroleum	12.6	32.1	14.1	36.8	13.5	34.1
Natural gas	13.1	13.0	13.6	14.6	14.0	17.5
Solid fuels	12.8	13.3	14.0	14.6	24.9	23.7
Primary electricity	4.7	4.7	8.2	8.2	16.7	16.7

Welcome though such an improvement would be, it would still be muted by comparison with the mid-1970s. In 1977, after two years of recovery in the industrial countries, the oil-importing developing countries raised the value of their exports 42 percent above their 1975 level, and the volume by 24 percent.

Since the Central case assumes that economic growth in the industrial countries will be slower in 1985–95 than it was in the 1950s and 1960s, it is postulated that world trade will also grow more slowly. The 5 percent annual growth of world trade projected for 1985–95 is about the same as was achieved in 1973–80, but greater than that projected for 1980–85 (see Table 3.3). Within this total, the industrial countries are expected to increase their exports more slowly than in 1973-80. One reason for this slowdown is that a large proportion of their output of goods is already traded—30 per-

cent of their production of machinery, for example. Increases in the trade of industrial countries are therefore likely to be slower in relation to GDP growth than they have been in the past.

Slower growth of industrial countries' trade will undoubtedly restrain the growth of developing countries' exports. Nonetheless, the developing countries are expected to increase their share of world trade. The low-income countries are projected to maintain the same growth in their exports as they managed in 1973–80, although China's initial export drive is assumed to slow down. The middle-income oil importers would have the fastest growth of all, also about the same as that achieved between 1973 and 1980. By contrast, exports by oil-exporting developing countries would rise the slowest, consistent with the slow growth in energy demand.

Although the Central case assumes no new pro-

TABLE 3.3
Past and projected growth of export volumes, 1965–95
(average annual percentage change)

Country group	1965–73	1973–80	Value 1980 (billions of dollars)	Central case projections	
				1980–85	1985–95
All developing countries	8.2	4.2	512	4.3	6.8
Low-income					
Asia	7.3	9.9	36	4.9	7.2
Africa	6.7	0.3	12	3.0	4.2
Middle-income					
Oil importers	9.6	8.1	272	4.7	8.8
Oil exporters	7.4	−0.6	192	3.7	3.2
High-income oil exporters	9.9	0.8	192	−6.5	1.2
Industrial market economies	8.8	5.5	1,513	2.6	4.8
World[a]	8.7	4.9	2,394	2.3	5.1

Note: Export volumes include goods and nonfactor services.
a. Including East European nonmarket economies.

tectionist measures, some of the existing ones, if not removed, will become a stronger brake on exports. The Multifibre Arrangement, for example, hampers newcomers to the textile and clothing trade, while allowing little growth for established exporters. In some other sensitive products, the pace of market penetration may slow as exporters face stiffer competition when they attempt to export manufactured goods that compete more directly with those produced in the industrial countries. Thus exports are expected to grow somewhat more slowly toward the end of the projection period. Table 3.4 shows the projected exports by category.

The projected increases in trade prices associated with the Central case are shown in Table 3.5. Economic recovery is expected to benefit exporters of nonfuel primary products. The prices of metals,

TABLE 3.5
Past and projected increases in trade prices, 1970–95
(average annual percentage change)

	1970–80	1980–95
World export prices[a]	13.3	5.6
Nonfuel primary products	9.1	5.8
Fuels	29.1	7.6
Manufactures	10.6	5.2
Industrial countries' GDP deflator[b]	10.1	5.5

Note: Projections are based on the Central growth scenario.
a. Including nonfactor services and gold.
b. In US dollars.

wheat, sugar, and nonfood agricultural raw materials are assumed to move up quickest, given their responsiveness to cyclical fluctuations and earlier reductions in capacity. For many foodstuffs (particularly tropical beverages and fats and oils), abundant supplies are likely to persist. Over the long term—up to 1995—prospects vary considerably for different commodities. In real terms prices are projected to grow for metals (especially copper, nickel, and aluminum) beef and most agricultural raw materials (especially natural rubber, timbers, and cotton), while those for some foodstuffs (especially bananas) are expected to be less buoyant (see Figure 3.3).

TABLE 3.4
Exports of developing countries, 1980–95

Exports	1980 value (billions of dollars)	Average annual percentage growth at 1980 prices	
		1980–85	1985–95
Total merchandise[a]	434	4.2	6.6
Nonfuel primary			
products	126	2.6	2.6
Fuels	163	3.7	2.8
Manufactures	130	6.6	12.0
Nonfactor services	78	5.0	7.6
Goods and nonfactor			
services	512	4.3	6.8

Note: Projections are based on the Central case.
a. Includes gold.

Workers' remittances

Projections up to 1995 reflect a constrained outlook for workers' remittances. In northern Europe, record unemployment means that the demand for migrant labor is unlikely to grow in the next few

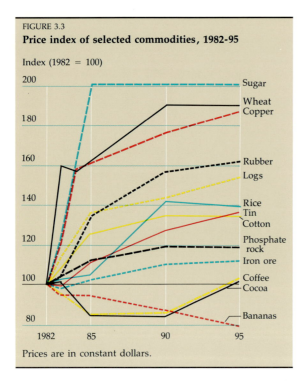

FIGURE 3.3
Price index of selected commodities, 1982-95

Index (1982 = 100)

Sugar
Wheat
Copper
Rubber
Logs
Rice
Tin
Cotton
Phosphate rock
Iron ore
Coffee
Cocoa
Bananas

1982   85   90   95

Prices are in constant dollars.

years and restrictive immigration policies might continue. Even in the long term, these countries will probably require fewer foreign workers than in the 1960s and early 1970s. In the high-income oil-exporting countries, real oil revenues are projected to increase at a much slower rate than during 1970–80, and the demand for foreign labor is unlikely to grow substantially.

The projections in Table 3.6 reflect broad trends only, being subject to several imponderables. The factors determining the pattern of migration during the next decade and beyond will include the changing structure of skills demanded in the labor-importing countries and the ability of labor-exporting developing countries to provide those skills.

TABLE 3.6
Workers' remittances to developing countries, 1980–95

Country group	Billions of current dollars		Annual percentage growth (1980–95)
	1980	1995	
All developing countries	24.0	91.3	9.3
Low-income			
Asia	3.0	7.5	6.3
Africa	0.3	1.8	12.7
Middle-income			
Oil importers	16.9	68.9	9.8
Oil exporters	3.8	13.1	8.6

Note: Projections are based on the Central growth scenario.

The resource gap

Capital inflows contribute to development by supplementing domestic savings and by financing imports. Foreign borrowing also permits flexibility in managing the balance of payments, thereby fostering a relatively stable environment and an efficient use of resources. Some forms of capital can also promote transfers of technology, which may have large payoffs. Such inflows have been important to development throughout history—including, notably, that of North America and Australia in the 19th century. The demand for foreign capital by today's low-income developing countries, whose average per capita income is only 2.4 percent that of the industrial countries, is likely to be substantial in future.

The amount of foreign capital going to developing countries reflects many factors: savings and investment patterns in the countries providing capital; the willingness of their governments to lend to the developing world, and of their businesses to invest there; the willingness of developing countries to spur growth through borrowing; and their capacity to absorb and service foreign capital on the terms offered. None of these factors can be predicted with certainty, depending as they do on the prospects for interest rates, GDP, and export growth, and on economic policy and management in the developing countries. Overall, the projections in the Central scenario envisage an annual real increase in net capital flows of just 3.6 percent in 1982–95, compared with an average of over 10 percent in 1970–80. The outlook varies for different types of capital (see Table 3.7). These are discussed below.

Commercial borrowing

By 1982 current account deficits and debt burdens had become major constraints for a large number of developing countries. Measures have since been taken to ease the liquidity problems of major borrowers. However, the recent fall in oil prices has placed some oil-exporting countries in jeopardy, where previously the prospect of stable export revenues had given confidence to commercial bankers.

A period of transition to more viable external financing is unavoidable; for some countries, it has been under way for some time. Following a period of adjustment, during which foreign borrowing is expected to be sharply curtailed, capital flows are projected to resume their growth, but at a far slower

TABLE 3.7
The financing of current deficits for all developing countries, 1982–95

	Billions of current dollars		Annual percentage growth		
	1982[a]	1995	1970–80	1980–82	1982–95
Current account balance[b]	−118.2	−276.2	17.2	41.7	6.7
Net capital flows	85.2	294.2	20.4	2.2	10.0
Official development assistance	23.9	81.2	17.9	−1.0	9.9
Official nonconcessional loans	11.0	42.0	24.5	5.6	10.9
Private loans	35.0	109.6	22.3	−0.4	9.2
Private direct investment	15.3	61.4	18.6	12.5	11.3
Use of reserves and other capital[c]	33.0	−18.0	. .	. .	. .
Memorandum items					
Debt outstanding	548.0	1,996.8	19.9	13.7	10.5
Official	199.0	809.8	16.5	12.5	11.4
Private	349.0	1,187.0	22.3	14.3	9.9
Resource gap as percentage of GNP	3.7	1.6	n.a.	n.a.	n.a.
Current account deficit as percentage of GNP	5.0	2.7	. .	. .	. .
Net capital flows as percentage of GNP	3.6	2.9	. .	. .	. .
Debt service as percentage of GNP	4.7	3.5	. .	. .	. .
Debt service as percentage of exports	20.7	12.0	. .	. .	. .
Interest payments as percentage of GNP	2.1	1.5	. .	. .	. .
Deflator[d]	95.7	213.8	10.3	−1.6	6.4

n.a. Not applicable.
. . Not available.
a. Estimated.
b. Excludes official transfers. These figures are different from the current account given in Table 2.11, which includes official transfers.
c. Short-term borrowing.
d. US dollar GDP deflator for industrial countries.

rate than in the 1970s. Even when the projected adjustment is achieved, the developing countries will have repaired only some of the recent damage to their external financial positions. Moreover, if uncertainty leads lenders and borrowers to discount more heavily their expectations of future export earnings, they may seek to reduce debt and debt service in relation to exports to levels even below those previously considered acceptable.

Only about one-third of the total debt owed to private sources is guaranteed or insured by creditor governments. Commercial banks have become increasingly concerned about their debtors' liquidity being sufficient to cover repayments on all their loans. That can be achieved only if an adequate volume of new loans continues to be made by the banking system as a whole. The risk is that individual banks will lose confidence in a particular borrower and precipitate a general withdrawal. Unilateral reschedulings or moratoria are sometimes suggested as a response, but these do great harm to the functioning of the international financial system. Short-term loans from the Bank for International Settlements, allowing time for agreements to be reached under the aegis of the International Monetary Fund, are a far better way to

deal with payment crises, providing at the same time an opportunity for the more orderly renegotiation of debt. Thereafter, cofinancing with international development agencies of projects with well-assured returns, can give lenders confidence in the willingness of other banks to lend. Such financing facilitates adjustment; a vigorous adjustment program by developing countries to reduce their need for new loans is essential to retain or reestablish creditworthiness.

That the international banking system will weather the present crisis is not in doubt, considering the small fraction (about 6 percent) of banks' assets represented by their claims on developing countries. For a few banks in a few countries it is nonetheless possible that losses may be sustained, which could pose problems for the international banking system. Consequently, the margins demanded in future are likely to be higher than in the past, and the growth of lending much slower.

Concern about the concentration of debt in the larger developing countries may limit or halt the growth of lending to these countries in relation to total loans. Similarly, concern about the adequacy of banks' capital may limit the growth of their total loans in relation to their capital. In the 1970s, by contrast, both these ratios increased. Even if commercial banks are willing to expand their lending more rapidly, they may be unable to do so if regulatory action to limit international lending, as now contemplated, is introduced. Deregulation of banking in the United States and revived domestic borrowing may also increase the relative attractiveness of the home market.

Reflecting these considerations, the Central scenario assumes that medium- and long-term lending to developing countries increases in real terms by an average of 3.5 percent a year in 1982–95—or about in line with the GDP growth of industrial countries and one-third the real rate in the 1970s. Having grown faster than the developing countries' production and trade over the past decade, the relative importance of private loans may well diminish in future.

Private direct investment

Some of the expansion in bank lending over the past decade substituted for private direct investment. This trend was encouraged by the relatively low interest rates through most of the 1970s and by the restrictions host countries placed on direct investments. The restrictions were often a reaction to past experiences of investments that were unnecessarily subsidized or were seen as having been inconsistent with development objectives. For multinational firms, it was often easy to substitute debt for equity.

The outlook for direct investment has become more attractive recently, since the cost of borrowing has risen and an understanding has been reached between investors and some host governments. Moreover, the outflows related to direct investment—in the form of profit remittances—are directly dependent on the success of the enterprise, and there is more flexibility as to timing. With the prospects for bank lending more constrained, direct investment may contribute a greater share of the capital flows to developing countries. However, the scope for substitution is limited to the private sector; direct investment cannot be used to finance most development infrastructure.

Flows from official sources

Table 3.7 shows that developing countries will depend on ODA for a large part of their net resource inflows. Yet the outlook for ODA is not encouraging. Only a few countries seem determined to raise the share of their GDP to ODA; and the GDPs themselves are not expected to rise fast. Some countries—notably the United States and members of OPEC—may even reduce their ODA ratios. The Central case projection assumes that ODA increases only in line with industrial-country growth, and that there is no further reallocation of aid from middle- to low-income countries. In that case, ODA would be about 60 percent higher in real terms by 1995 than it was in 1980. As a share of total gross capital flows, however, ODA would continue to fall—to 28 percent, compared with 30 percent in 1980 and 37 percent in 1970—even with the projected slowdown in commercial lending.

The strong implication of this analysis is that ODA as currently planned falls far short of the needs of the developing countries, especially of the low-income countries, if world poverty is to be seriously tackled. This is not a simple issue of charity, but rather a complex one of world economic interdependence. Over the past five years, low-income countries received only 37 percent of total ODA; there has been no clear long-term trend toward increasing this share, which was no higher in 1981 than in 1971. Given the special problems of the least developed nations, which even with sound policies lack creditworthiness, there is a strong argument for channeling a larger share of bilateral aid to them.

Overall, the projections summarized in Table 3.7 imply that by 1995 total capital inflows would decline to 2.9 percent of developing-country GDP, about half the 1981 ratio and close to that of the early 1970s. Netting out factor income and the need for reserve accumulation, the net transfer of foreign resources would be 1.6 percent of GDP by 1995. Debt is projected to decline significantly in relation to exports (see Figure 3.4). While this would ease debt servicing burdens, the slower growth of financial flows would give countries less flexibility than in the 1970s.

Implications of the Low case

The assumption underlying the Central case is that industrial countries will resume an average growth rate higher than in the 1970s, though well short of their record in the 1950s and 1960s. It is, of course, possible that the industrial countries will fail to tackle their structural problems. The Low case illustrates the consequences of their managing to grow by only 2.5 percent a year between 1985 and 1995 (see Table 3.1).

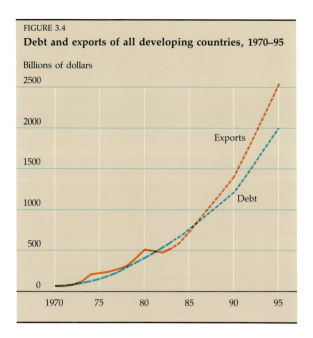

FIGURE 3.4

Debt and exports of all developing countries, 1970–95

Billions of dollars

Exports

Debt

Such slow growth would have several severe implications. Some of them bear on the industrial countries themselves. The Low case growth rate would barely match the industrial countries' performance in 1973–79—years of inflation and mounting unemployment in the industrial countries. With slow growth in the 1980s and 1990s, unemployment would mount, reinforcing protectionist pressures. Restrictions would be directed particularly at developing countries because their relatively labor-intensive exports compete with vulnerable manufacturers in the industrial countries. The negative impact of low growth in the industrialized countries on trade in general, and on the exports of developing countries in particular, would therefore be disproportionately high. With lower export prospects lowering their creditworthiness, commercial capital flows to developing countries would also be negatively affected.

The growth of aid would be curtailed, even if it were to remain a fixed ratio of the industrial countries' GDP, as assumed in the Central scenario. In the difficult international environment associated with the Low case, more bilateral aid would tend to be distributed following nondevelopmental criteria; this could be particularly harmful to the low-income countries. At the same time, lower demand for oil exports would also reduce the revenues of the high-income oil exporters, and probably their aid. Labor remittances are likely to be affected more than proportionately; not only would the growth in migrants' wages be necessarily less under the Low case, but pressures to reduce their

numbers, already quite strong in host countries, would grow.

It is easy to envisage a downward global economic spiral emerging from the Low case, with catastrophic consequences for the developing countries. Indeed, it would be difficult to forestall such a global crisis if the industrial countries' recovery were to taper off into a decade of very slow growth. If anything, the assumptions about the trends associated with the Low case are optimistic. The aid effort of industrial countries and high-income oil exporters is not projected to decrease as a ratio of their total GDP. No allowance is made for migrants being expelled. No new curbs are assumed to be imposed on international capital movements, and commercial capital flows have been reduced merely in line with the lower performance of developing countries. The inroads of protectionism have been limited to the equivalent of a 15 percentage point increase in the average tariff of industrial countries (see Box 3.1).

Despite these moderate assumptions, the impact of the Low case on the developing countries is alarming. The ten-year decline in the per capita incomes of low-income African countries would continue. In the case of the large and relatively closed economies of India and China which dominate low-income Asia, their high saving rates and lower reliance on foreign capital would afford them some protection against the adverse impact of the global economic deterioration. Yet their per capita incomes would still probably not grow by much more than 2.5 to 3.0 percent, substantially slower than in the Central case. However, the outlook presented by the Low case for Bangladesh and some of the smaller Asian countries would be not much better than for the low-income African countries.

The middle-income oil-importing countries, mostly highly dependent on trade and on commercial capital, would also be badly affected. Their per capita income growth rate would fall by about one-third, to about the same rate as in the industrial countries. With such a growth rate, unemployment, already a serious problem in most middle-income developing countries, would become intractable. It might in turn endanger social stability and governments' ability to devise and implement rational economic policies, and hence even to maintain the Low case growth rates.

With the projected slowdown in growth, pressures would mount to increase the share of consumption in income, and thus reduce domestic savings. The Low case assumes that these pres-

Box 3.1 The implications of a 15 percent across-the-board increase in protection in industrial countries

If governments give ground before protectionist pressures generated by higher unemployment, thus eliminating most of the gains achieved in the GATT rounds of tariff negotiations, a serious deterioration in the world trading system would result. To illustrate, the implications of an increase in protection (import licences, quotas, voluntary import restraints) by an amount equivalent to a rise in tariffs of 15 percentage points can be estimated. This assumption is not extreme: protection was much higher in the 1930s. Quantifying the costs of protection is difficult. However, using the Brussels world model (see Technical appendix) it is estimated that even if such protection were introduced gradually, the GDP of both developing and developed countries would be significantly reduced by 1995 as follows:

	Reduction in GDP	
		Billions of
	Percent	1980 dollars
Low-income countries	−0.8	9
Middle-income oil importers	−3.4	70
Industrial countries	−3.3	390

Middle-income oil-importing countries would be hit harder than low-income countries by such a development because they are more open and thus more vulnerable to protectionist measures taken by their trading partners. In the large low-income countries, traditional agriculture, which is less sensitive to external disturbances, still accounts for a large share of total output.

It is striking that developed countries would suffer a loss in GDP growth equal to that of the middle-income countries—a loss of their own making, demonstrating that measures to protect declining industries backfire by harming other sectors, reducing efficiency, and probably worsening income distribution.

sures would be resisted. Most important, however, it has been assumed that the developing countries would be able to continue to benefit from a relatively open trading system. Otherwise, falling efficiency would become increasingly likely for many developing countries.

The possibilities for faster growth

Emerging from the second worst recession of this century, with concerted policies to sustain economic recovery, limit wage increases to productivity growth, liberalize trade, and adjust to changing comparative advantage, economic growth in the industrial countries could once again reach 5 percent a year. Developing countries would share the benefits. They could expand their GDP by between 6 and 7 percent a year; over the ten-year period to 1995, their GDP would nearly double.

With rapid growth, labor shortages would in time emerge in the industrial countries, making them more open to labor-intensive manufactures imported from the developing countries. The growth rate of exports of developing countries could then match, and even exceed, the achievements of the 1965–73 period. Given such fast growth, particularly in the manufactured exports of newly industrializing countries, trade among developing countries would also be stimulated. With higher export growth, developing countries would become creditworthy for larger amounts of commercial borrowing. Aid flows could more easily be increased, disproportionately benefiting the low-

income countries. And, under these much more favorable circumstances, more countries could rely exclusively on commercial borrowing, allowing a greater concentration of aid on the poorest.

This scenario is simulated in the High case summarized in Table 3.1, which assumes that the industrialized countries would return to a growth rate matching the achievements of the 1950s and 1960s. Aid and workers' remittances would rise in line with faster growing incomes. Trade would expand, not only in line with income growth, but even more rapidly. Under this High case, low-income Asian countries would double their per capita incomes in twenty years. The middle-income countries could grow even more quickly than in the 1960s. In relative terms, the improvement for low-income Africa could be greatest—from stagnation under the Central case to marked growth, which by 1995 would reverse the decline of the 1970s.

With regard to energy, the High case assumes worldwide progress in energy conservation such that real oil prices would not rise any faster than in the Central case. Also, there is sufficient production capacity in the oil-exporting countries to meet some increase in demand without accelerating the rise in oil prices. Oil-importing developing countries could therefore expect to obtain considerable benefits from higher export earnings without having to pay higher oil prices.

If prosperity in the developing countries is linked to growth in the industrial countries, the reverse is also true. The severity of the 1980–82 recession was in part due to the absence from the developing countries of the kind of buoyant demand provided during the 1974–75 recession. Without such demand, the recovery now getting under way will also be slower and more arduous. It is therefore greatly to the advantage of industrial countries to stimulate growth in the developing countries.

The greatest immediate dangers are renascent protectionism, unduly restrictive policies toward commercial bank lending, and parsimonious aid—the consequences of slow growth in the industrial countries. All three are symptoms of introspection in difficult times. All three would contribute to increasing those difficulties, and not only for the developing countries. A determined effort to resume the liberalization of trade, prudent but dynamic international lending policies, and more generous aid need not await the resumption of fast global economic growth; on the contrary, they are necessary to help bring it about.

Domestic determinants of developing-country growth

This chapter has so far focused on the impact of trends in the industrial countries on the developing countries. These external factors are indeed important in an increasingly interdependent world. However, within the constraints imposed by the global environment, it is domestic policies that hold the key to developing-country performance.

For developing countries, GDP growth of only 2.5 percent a year in the industrial world would greatly complicate economic management. Many of the policy changes needed would be much harder to introduce under conditions of slow growth. To redirect investment and production to those activities in which countries have a comparative advantage needs growth. Just as the Central scenario assumes a considerable improvement in the domestic performance of developing countries, so also the Low case depends partly on their performance. The three growth scenarios in Table 3.1 assume the same policy improvements in developing countries. Without those improvements, their growth would be even lower.

Growth depends partly on a country's ability to generate savings and then on how efficiently it invests and manages the new capital. In addition, growth is influenced by a country's ability to promote exports and save imports. These four determinants of growth—savings, returns on investment, export promotion, and import restraint—are summarized by country group in Table 3.8.

Domestic savings

During the past two decades developing countries have had remarkable success in increasing their savings. Markedly lower than in industrial countries in 1960, savings rates in most developing countries are now generally higher. Although the shocks of the 1970s partly reversed earlier trends in the industrial countries, they only slowed them down in the developing countries. The exception to this generally satisfactory performance has been sub-Saharan Africa, where the savings rates of the low-income countries have fallen well below those of twenty years ago. This decline is in part related to the region's extreme vulnerability to terms of trade shocks, which have raised the amount of domestic production needed to pay for a given quantity of imports, thus leaving less for domestic savings. It is also related to the slow economic growth and high population growth of the region; with falling per capita incomes, it would have been extremely difficult to maintain earlier savings rates. In addition, the policies pursued by many African countries were in part to blame, not only for the slowdown in GDP growth but also for the fall in savings. In particular, subsidies on consumer goods and the losses of state enterprises were a significant drain on public savings.

In the Central case, an increase in savings rates over the present low level has been projected for the low-income countries of sub-Saharan Africa, though still not attaining the rate achieved in the 1960s. But for the oil-exporting countries, savings rates are unlikely to be sustained now that the rate of increase in oil prices has tapered off.

Returns on investment

Better use of capital offers the greatest scope for raising the growth rates of developing countries. Return on investment—the additional output per unit of investment—measures the result of the combined influence of many forces, some external, some purely related to domestic policies and actions. Intercountry comparisons show that some countries regularly obtained higher returns on investment than did others. The Central case postulates that the rate of return on investment, after improving markedly from current levels, will stabilize around the 20 percent level experienced during the 1970s. Policies to improve the return on investment are discussed in Part II of this Report. While raising efficiency is by no means easy, there are clearly many areas for potential improvement.

TABLE 3.8
Past and projected indicators of domestic performance, 1960–95

Country group	Indicator	1960–70	1970–80	1985–95
All developing countries	Saving as percentage of GDP	19.6	24.2	24.0
	Return on investment (percent)[a]	26.8	20.5	20.0
	Import elasticity[b]	1.4[c]	1.7	1.3
	Manufactures export ratio[d]	2.0[c]	4.4	3.0
	GDP growth (annual percentage change)	5.7	5.3	5.5
	Population growth (annual percentage change)	2.4	2.1	2.0
Low-income Asia	Saving as percentage of GDP	20.2	24.6	23.1
	Return on investment (percent)[a]	20.6	18.7	19.8
	Import elasticity[b]	−0.2[c]	1.7	1.4
	Manufactures export ratio[d]	0.9[c]	2.9	1.6
	GDP growth (annual percentage change)	4.7	4.9	4.9
	Population growth (annual percentage change)	2.3	1.9	1.7
Low-income Africa	Saving as percentage of GDP	10.9	8.8	8.6
	Return on investment (percent)[a]	24.6	10.0	21.2
	Import elasticity[b]	2.1[c]	1.6	1.8
	Manufactures export ratio[d]	1.0[c]	4.1	2.8
	GDP growth (annual percentage change)	3.4	1.6	3.3
	Population growth (annual percentage change)	2.4	2.8	3.1
Middle-income oil importers	Saving as percentage of GDP	19.6	21.8	24.6
	Return on investment (percent)[a]	26.9	22.8	22.3
	Import elasticity[b]	1.9[c]	1.1	1.4
	Manufactures export ratio[d]	2.6[c]	4.9	3.1
	GDP growth (annual percentage change)	5.8	5.8	5.7
	Population growth (annual percentage change)	2.5	2.3	2.2
Middle-income oil exporters	Saving as percentage of GDP	20.4	29.3	24.6
	Return on investment (percent)[a]	34.4	19.5	17.9
	Import elasticity[b]	0.8[c]	2.2	1.0
	Manufactures export ratio[d]	0.5[c]	2.0	3.1
	GDP growth (annual percentage change)	6.6	5.3	5.6
	Population growth (annual percentage change)	2.6	2.7	2.5

a. Real increase in GDP valued at current prices divided by investment at current prices.
b. Rate of growth of import volume divided by rate of growth of GDP.
c. Refers to 1965–70.
d. Rate of growth of volume of exports of manufactures divided by the rate of growth of world GDP (excluding centrally planned economies).

Foreign trade

Historically, countries with above-average export growth have enjoyed above-average GDP growth. This applies to countries grouped by region and income level, as well as to the developing world as a whole. With slow industrial-country growth and protectionist barriers, it will be harder for developing countries as a group to raise the rate of growth of their exports. In textiles, with continuing strong protectionist measures imposed by the industrial countries, the success of one country in expanding its exports could well be achieved at the expense of another. Nonetheless, it is still worthwhile for developing countries to strive to expand their exports, because that in itself stimulates a more efficient use of resources and strengthens creditworthiness.

In spite of growing protectionism, developing countries have achieved significant export growth (particularly of manufactures) during the 1970s. In fact, the elasticity of exports of manufactures of developing countries with respect to world income (excluding centrally planned economies) increased steadily from the 1950s to the end of the 1970s. The Central scenario assumes that this export elasticity will increase by about 30 percent over the level reached in the early 1980s, but will remain significantly lower than that in the 1970s. With firm policies to promote exports, the elasticity could be raised further; the High case assumes that such policies will be pursued.

In the past most developing countries' imports increased somewhat faster than their GDPs. Until recently they have managed to finance this growth with fast-expanding exports and capital inflows.

But the current recession has greatly reduced the availability of foreign exchange and has limited the inflow of imports. When world growth resumes, the recent compression of imports will have to be reversed, and it may therefore be expected that initially the volume of imports of developing countries will expand faster. However, the Central scenario assumes that over the long run developing-country imports will grow only a little faster than GDP and more slowly than in the past. Such an improvement is compatible with the pursuit of open trading policies that foster productive efficiency in line with comparative advantage.

Population growth

Continued progress in reducing fertility and mortality is a prerequisite for population growth rates to remain broadly stable up to 1995. Despite the considerable gains achieved in most Asian and many other middle-income countries in lowering fertility, the battle is far from won. If low-income Africa could match the birth rate of low-income Asia (which reflects the remarkable performance of China and, to a lesser extent, India), its population growth rate would decrease by 40 percent. In addition to the direct impact on per capita income (an eightfold acceleration if total income growth is not affected), there would be an indirect impact: reduced population growth allows resources to be invested in improving productivity and welfare, instead of being stretched out to cover more people. Conversely, failure to match lower mortality with lower fertility would reduce the projected gains in per capita incomes. These issues will be explored in depth in *World Development Report 1984.*

Conclusions

Steady growth in the industrial world is vital for developing countries. At the same time, domestic policies are critical for their performance. And these are within their control. The scenarios discussed in this chapter convey one clear policy message: while there is some scope for improving resource mobilization, the principal area for improvement is in the efficiency of resource use. One major source of greater efficiency is trade—by better exploiting comparative advantage. To improve economic performance requires both policy reforms and strengthened institutions for management— the subject of Part II of this Report.

Even with policy improvements, the outlook for many developing countries is somber. The Central scenario—which assumes some improvement in policies—has per capita GDP in developing countries rising less rapidly during 1980–95 than during the 1970s. And low-income countries in sub-Saharan Africa manage hardly any increase. Even in the High case, per capita income growth matches only what was achieved in the 1970s; by 1995 low-income sub-Saharan Africa still fails to regain its 1970 per capita income.

Earlier *World Development Reports* explored the link between growth and poverty alleviation. It has been estimated that even with an annual GDP growth rate of 5 to 6 percent between 1975 and 2000, more than 600 million people will remain below the poverty line in developing countries in the year 2000, unless the pattern of growth is modified to put more emphasis on poverty alleviation. The current projections clearly suggest more moderate growth prospects and thus reinforce the need for policies not only for stimulating growth but also for curbing population growth and meeting basic needs. They also underline the importance of bolstering improved domestic policies with adequate inflows of capital—especially concessionary aid directed to the low-income countries.

Part II   Management in Development

4   The search for efficiency

Part I of this Report has highlighted the economic difficulties facing most developing countries, lending urgency to efforts to improve their performance. Part II concentrates on the measures needed to produce such an improvement.

Over the past two decades, governments in most developing countries have played an activist role in development, building infrastructure and often engaging directly in productive activities. Their policies have also been critical in determining the environment in which the private sector operates. Much of this activism has produced encouraging progress: over twenty years, developing countries have on average achieved growth rates that had not been managed before, either by the developing countries or by today's developed market economies at a similar stage of their development. In relation to expectations and potential, however, progress in many countries has been unsatisfactory.

To bring performance into line with potential, governments must play a central role in ensuring:
- A stable macroeconomic environment, by adopting sustainable monetary, fiscal, and foreign exchange policies
- A system of incentives that encourages resources to be allocated efficiently and used optimally
- A pattern of growth whereby benefits are widely shared.

Since the world is beset with uncertainty, governments need the flexibility to respond to unforeseen events and to resolve the inevitable conflicts between competing interest groups.

After the experience of the past ten years, the importance of macroeconomic management needs no underlining. In a hostile world environment of modest growth, high interest rates, and fluctuating exchange rates, the macroeconomic policies of developing countries will continue to be critical in ensuring price stability, balance of payments equilibrium, and conditions conducive to growth. While recognizing the importance of shorter-term macro-

economic policies, Part II of this Report is chiefly concerned with management for long-term development.

Faced with widespread poverty and slow economic growth, governments are naturally keener than ever to promote development. But their progress is constrained by weak institutions and management. These constraints vary greatly among countries, and their capacity to deal with them reflects differences in population, incomes, natural resources, and political systems. In many countries, however, managerial weaknesses are explained in part by the shortage of experienced and well-trained people. While this bottleneck will ease as education spending yields dividends, the immediate need is to use existing resources, including managerial skills, more effectively and economically.

Although managerial capacity places an overall limit on a country's development, it is far from homogeneous. The skills needed to frame macroeconomic policy differ from those needed to run a productive enterprise; and large organizations place greater demands on management than do small ones. Governments tend to be involved in the management of big organizations, such as running state farms and marketing boards, rather than relying on peasant farmers, small traders, and individual truckers. And the mistakes that big organizations make have more serious consequences.

The main criterion for judging economic management is "efficiency"—a concept that has meaning only in the context of an agreed set of objectives. This chapter first clarifies the concept, then illustrates the potential long-term gains from increasing efficiency, and provides an analytical framework for Part II of this Report.

The analysis of efficiency

The search for efficiency is not merely a matter of finding technically optimal solutions; it is also a political process. Governments seeking change have to start with existing institutions that have their own historical inertia and underlying political interests. The process of reform therefore involves negotiation and compromise, accepting "second-best solutions" that are politically feasible. This Report recognizes that individual countries attach different weights to particular political and economic objectives, and so draws from the experience of countries with a wide range of political and economic systems.

In every country efficiency has two distinct but related aspects that are critical to economic performance: efficient resource allocation—through prices, markets, and administrative interventions (discussed in Chapters 6 and 7); and operational efficiency—to maximize the use of labor and capital through the sound management of enterprises, projects, and programs in both the public and private sectors (discussed in Chapters 8, 9, and 10).

These in turn contain both static and dynamic dimensions. In static terms, efficiency may be defined as maximizing the present value of output from a given level of inputs. Alternatively, when the goal is to achieve a particular social objective (such as malaria eradication) or to provide a specific service (for example, a telephone link), efficiency may be defined as cost minimization. Either way, a key factor determining efficiency is the

Box 4.1   The concept of efficient pricing

An economy is considered *production efficient* if the supply of any good (or service) cannot be increased without reducing the supply of some other good. One important way in which economies can make goods available is by exporting some goods in exchange for others; thus production efficiency also implies that a country has made best use of its foreign trade possibilities. If a country cannot affect prices in the rest of the world (a reasonable assumption for most developing countries), its foreign trade possibilities are defined by the relative *border prices* of exports and imports.

This definition in turn helps determine *opportunity costs*. The opportunity cost of any good or service is the value of forgone alternatives. If the alternative to using a good were to export it, for example, the opportunity cost would be measured by the border price of the good and the resulting foreign exchange that could have been used to purchase some other import or to replace some other export. The *scarcity value* measures what the good is worth to the economy—calculated, for example, by the value of the extra exports the good enables to be produced. If the economy is producing efficiently, scarcity values must be equal to opportunity costs, and their common value is the *efficiency price*—which, for imports and exports, will then be identical to the border price. For nontraded goods, efficiency prices can be measured by the

opportunity cost of their production when the alternative would be to produce traded goods, or by their scarcity value in displacing traded goods.

An economy is *efficient*, as opposed to just production efficient, if it is impossible to make anyone better off without making someone else worse off. In addition to producing efficiently, the final consumers must have exhausted all possibilities of mutually beneficial exchange. This in turn requires that they all face the same market prices, and that these are equal to efficiency prices. However, an economy may be efficient and yet produce a distribution of income and wealth that is deemed unacceptable. The government may then impose taxes and subsidies or intervene in other ways to improve the distribution of income and wealth. Such intervention may make consumer prices deviate significantly from efficiency prices. But by preserving production efficiency, the largest possible quantity of goods and services will be made available for distribution among consumers. Hence the concepts of production efficiency and efficiency prices remain important for producer prices (for example, before indirect taxes are added) even when market prices (consumer prices) are distorted.

Shadow prices, also known as *accounting prices*, are the same as efficiency prices if society is concerned exclusively with efficiency in the sense here defined. Typ-

ically, however, societies are interested in other objectives—a more equitable distribution of income, for example—as well as efficiency. In this event, shadow prices are measures of social costs and benefits that reflect concern with these other objectives.

The case for removing distortions and moving market prices closer to efficiency prices rests on the argument that prices influence production decisions, and the reform will increase production efficiency. Since choices between alternatives depend on *relative* prices, it may not be enough to eliminate a few distortions, since this could move relative market prices even further from relative efficiency prices. In some cases, however, it may not be desirable to eliminate distortions (such as carefully targeted food subsidies or indirect taxes), since this will prejudice other social objectives; but in many cases these social objectives are best served by other instruments or by more carefully chosen taxes and subsidies. Thus, it is often possible to confront producers with efficiency prices while keeping indirect taxes and subsidies for distributive purposes. From a policymaker's viewpoint, the appropriate prices are those that best achieve these broader social objectives. Choosing appropriate prices is therefore equivalent to choosing the best set of taxes and subsidies, a choice central to the design of public policy.

pricing of inputs and outputs to reflect relative scarcities. Prices of goods that deviate significantly from their scarcity value (or "opportunity cost") may be regarded as "distorted" (see Box 4.1).

Efficiency must also be viewed in a dynamic context. The process of capital accumulation allows new technology to be incorporated into the economy, which implies both discarding obsolete plant and retraining staff. Efficiency therefore requires capital and labor to be priced according to their marginal productivities at international prices. In other words, labor costs per unit of output must be kept internationally competitive and interest rates should reflect the cost of foreign borrowing. If this is done, countries will invest and expand in ways that reflect the relative scarcity of capital and labor—avoiding, for example, capital-intensive production methods if they have abundant manpower.

It is precisely this dynamic element that lends so much importance to sound macroeconomic management. Efficient financial institutions are vital for mobilizing savings for investment, while smoothly operating financial markets ensure that money goes to investments yielding the highest returns. Yet both these tasks will be undermined if macroeconomic policy attempts to keep interest rates negative in real terms.

This view of efficiency is consistent with government goals for alleviating poverty and meeting basic needs. The ability of a government to tackle poverty is much enhanced when economic growth is rapid, while many initiatives to boost efficient production—such as reducing capital subsidies or keeping producer prices up to international levels—also directly affect the welfare of the poor by creating jobs and raising farm incomes. There will, of course, be occasions when the goals of efficiency and distribution conflict and will have to be traded off. There is, however, usually more than one way to achieve distributional objectives. The effect of different options on both efficiency and distribution should be carefully evaluated so that the desired objectives can be achieved at the lowest possible cost.

The potential for greater efficiency

During the past two decades, developing countries have invested heavily to expand their agriculture and industry, build their infrastructure, and provide essential services. Their investment rate rose from about 20 percent of GDP in 1960 to about 26 percent in 1980, compared with the 23

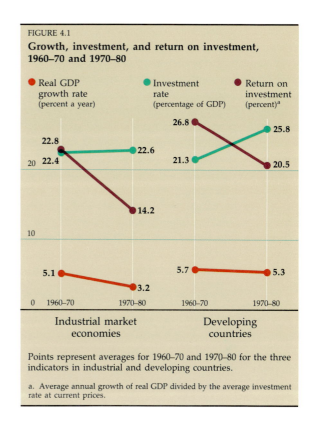

FIGURE 4.1

Growth, investment, and return on investment, 1960–70 and 1970–80

- Real GDP growth rate (percent a year)
- Investment rate (percentage of GDP)
- Return on investment (percent)[a]

Points represent averages for 1960–70 and 1970–80 for the three indicators in industrial and developing countries.

a. Average annual growth of real GDP divided by the average investment rate at current prices.

percent average for industrial market economies in 1980. Although this rise in investment was partly financed by foreign capital, it was chiefly made possible by higher domestic savings rates. Despite increased investment, however, the annual growth rate of GDP in developing countries has remained at about 5 percent, indicating that GDP growth per unit of investment has declined by nearly a quarter between the 1960s and the 1970s (see Figure 4.1). This decline in the aggregate return on investment in the 1970s—a rough index of the trend in the total productivity of the economy—had many causes: the recession in world trade, oil price shocks, strains in the financial system, lower returns on capital locked in aging industry, ineffective macroeconomic policies that postponed rather than promoted adjustments, and more capital-intensive investment—all have played a part.

The declining returns to investment, combined with rising real interest rates, were an important factor behind increasing debt servicing difficulties in 1980–83. In sixteen countries of twenty-two requiring debt rescheduling during 1982–83 (see Box 2.2), the rate of return on investment had declined below 20 percent in the late 1970s and early 1980s. The decline in the return on investment has been even more marked in the industrialized countries, and many of the efficiency issues discussed in this

Report are relevant in developed as well as developing countries.

The implications of this lower productivity are profound, given the conclusion reached in Chapter 3 that foreign lending to developing countries is likely to slow down in the 1980s. For developing countries even to maintain the growth rates of the 1970s, they will either have to boost their own saving—at great sacrifice to consumption—or they will have to maintain the present investment rate but make better use of resources. Certainly, a recovery in the world economy alone will improve productivity; but with good management the gains can be much greater, particularly in the following areas.

Macroeconomic policies

In many developing countries, ineffective exchange rate and monetary and fiscal policies and excessive borrowing during the 1970s resulted in inflation and unsustainable balance of payments positions. This led unavoidably to significant retrenchment, with adverse effects on both the rate of investment and its productivity. Abrupt policy changes introduce uncertainty, which dampens overall investment rates, while controls on interest rates have resulted in savings being channeled to less productive uses.

Distorted incentives

Several studies have shown that output losses due to inappropriate trade policies alone could have reduced GDP in some developing countries by up to 10 percent. As reported in Chapter 6, Bank cross-country analysis for the 1970s confirms the findings of the 1960s that price distortions slowed GDP growth in developing countries. During the 1970s the growth rate of countries with highly distorted prices was as much as 2 percent less than the average for developing countries.

Low-yielding investments

Losses from the misallocation of resources as a consequence of poor investment analysis can also be enormous. In the mid-1970s a series of unviable investments by Indonesia's national oil company, Pertamina, costing over $10 billion, cast a shadow over the country's creditworthiness later in the decade. In the Ivory Coast the rate of return on $8 billion of public investment undertaken in 1976–

80 was approximately 40 percent lower than in 1970–75. This deterioration—which was partly due to heavy investment in six large sugar complexes, with production costs that were three times the world market price—led the government to greatly strengthen its project appraisal procedures. Industrial economies have also made costly mistakes—witness the Anglo-French Concorde, where the only two airlines that bought the aircraft have difficulty covering even their operating costs, and none of the development costs (several billion dollars) will be recouped.

Investment delays

Since governments are under constant pressure to start new projects, they frequently adopt an investment program that exceeds their financial and managerial capacity. They then stretch projects out over longer periods than initially intended, with a consequent loss of output. For a sample of countries, the World Bank has estimated that, assuming an opportunity cost of capital of 10 percent, the cost of a two-year delay in the implementation of a project—a common occurrence—would amount to 20 percent of the cost of investment. In practice, some delays are due to overoptimistic scheduling and unforeseeable contingencies and some to justified postponement owing to changed circumstances. But there is undoubtedly considerable scope for shortening the costly gestation period for investments through better project planning and execution. Embarking on fewer projects would also help.

Low capacity utilization

In industrial market economies, fluctuating demand and technical obsolescence are the main causes of excess capacity. In developing countries, unreliable infrastructure and market distortions—especially underpricing of capital and shortages of materials and skilled staff—often figure more prominently. Underused capacity is costly, in terms of forgone output and the ripple effect on the rest of the economy. For example, if in 1981 the Indian fertilizer industry had operated at 85 percent of rated capacity instead of 67 percent, India would have saved some $400 million of foreign exchange spent on importing fertilizers. Irrigation also provides a good illustration of the potential for efficiency gains (see Box 4.2), as does transport. The Republic of Korea, for example, increased the efficiency of its rail freight (as measured by the ton-

Box 4.2 Irrigation design and management

Public and private investments in irrigation in developing countries have increased dramatically over the past twenty years, reaching about $15 billion in 1980. But the returns are much below their potential: one recent estimate for South and Southeast Asia suggested that an additional 20 million tons of rice, enough to provide the minimum food requirements of 90 million people, could be produced every year with inexpensive improvements in water distribution.

A simple measure of the efficiency of an irrigation system is how much water is lost in distribution. Although losses of 25 percent are regarded as acceptable, they are often much higher due to management weaknesses in the operation of the system. For instance in Pakistan 50 percent of the water distributed over 13 million hectares is lost. If this ratio could be cut to 30 percent, the volume of water saved would equal the capacity of three Tarbela dams (equal to a $9 billion investment).

Losses can often be reduced by relatively cheap improvements in irrigation design. In Maharashtra, India, the public distribution system traditionally consisted of unlined canals serving forty-hectare blocks. Where these have been replaced by lined tertiary canals serving eight-hectare blocks, water available at the field has increased by 40 percent, and net returns on the investment by some 160 percent. In Madhya Pradesh, combining underground water supplies with dams and canals has raised the rate of return on investment from 10 to 29 percent.

Box 4.3 The costs of poor road maintenance

The worldwide road-building boom of the 1960s and 1970s threatens to become the road-maintenance crisis of the 1980s and 1990s. Over the past ten years, roads in many developing countries have been allowed to deteriorate beyond the point where normal maintenance could be effective. Traffic loading has been much heavier than intended, and maintenance has been widely neglected. Funds budgeted for highways have been mostly absorbed in expanding rather than maintaining the network.

In several West African countries roads have had to be rebuilt at costs 20 to 40 percent higher than necessary had they been properly maintained earlier. For tarred roads, rehabilitation or reconstruction costs $125,000 to $200,000 per kilometer, four to eight times what it would have cost had roads been maintained and strengthened as weaknesses arose. In a recent survey of twelve developing countries, more than 25 percent of the tarred road network in eight of them required rehabilitation, strength-

ening, or resealing.

To prevent further deterioration, maintenance budgets need to be increased by at least 25 percent in three-quarters of the countries for which recent studies are available; in more than half, the required increase exceeds 75 percent. But more money is not the only answer. Maintenance costs could be significantly reduced by improved efficiency. For example, use of plant and equipment is often extremely low, sometimes only a quarter or a third of the rates achieved by the best maintenance organizations. Of a sample of seventeen countries, ten had utilization rates of 35 percent or less. Only three countries—the Dominican Republic, Malawi, and Niger—had rates of 50 percent or more. In 1981 Malawi was the only country to reach a 75 percent utilization rate, a reasonable target for all countries.

The lack of spare parts and fuel is often to blame for poor plant utilization. In addition, maintenance costs are frequently inflated by serious overstaffing.

And foreign aid donors have sometimes undermined efficiency by:

- Making finance for new equipment readily available, but leaving it to the country to buy spare parts
- Promoting an uneconomic proliferation of different makes and models of equipment through tied aid or other procurement regulations
- Supporting capital projects that divert the country's own resources from more urgent maintenance work.

When road authorities are not able to afford maintenance work, the costs passed on to road users are larger than the "savings" in public expenditure. Over the life of a road, the total operating costs of vehicles are typically four to ten times the costs of road construction and maintenance. Since operating costs may easily double on poorly maintained roads, the economic loss is considerable. Moreover, in most countries the extra costs chiefly involve spending foreign exchange on spare parts, fuel, and replacing vehicles.

---

nage carried per wagon per kilometer per day) by almost 60 percent between 1970 and 1980, and Mexico managed a 47 percent improvement. Savings affect capital as well as running costs: a 2,000-kilometer railway in Africa with an operational fleet of 90 locomotives would need to invest $35 million less if it could manage a 90 percent availability rate of locomotives instead of 60 percent. Actual availability rates vary widely—between 75

and 90 percent in Asia, but only 30 to 70 percent in Latin America and Africa.

Poor maintenance

Because of inadequate maintenance budgets, public sector assets are often run down much faster than they would be if routine maintenance were correctly carried out (see Box 4.3). For example, in Brazil it is estimated that a significant proportion of the federal highway network built in the past ten years already needs major rehabilitation, while in Nigeria most of the roads built in the 1970s had to be rebuilt three to five years later. The poor state of the US interstate highway system is partly attributable to underfunding of maintenance work.

The framework for improving efficiency

Although both policy and institutional aspects of efficiency are interwoven, for the purposes of analysis it is useful to distinguish between them. In both, however, the state plays a pivotal role: it is government that determines the policy environment in which enterprises and farmers must operate; government that provides the social and physical infrastructure that underpins productive activities; and government that frequently contributes to production through state-owned enterprises.

In many countries the expansion of the public sector has stretched its managerial capacity to the point where serious inefficiencies result. Chapter 5 examines the role of the state, indicating a need to reassess priorities, prune what has become unmanageable, and strengthen the effectiveness of the state's core responsibilities. Less reliance on controls and more on incentives to achieve social and economic objectives would also reduce the

administrative burden on the public sector. When governments have tried to control too much economic activity, efficiency has been impaired—usually because key prices (such as exchange rates, interest rates, and energy prices) have been distorted. Chapter 6 details the potential gains to be derived from reducing price distortions.

The virtues of microeconomic efficiency can be magnified or undermined by the choice of macroeconomic policies. Successful macromanagement requires a strong capacity for policy analysis, backed by mechanisms to translate policies into actions and a reliable monitoring and evaluation system. These important linkages are frequently lacking in developing countries—issues which are taken up in Chapter 7.

The state's role as a producer is considered in Chapters 8 and 9, the former focusing on state-owned enterprises and the latter on the design and execution of government projects and programs. These chapters pinpoint the important causes of inefficiency that project and enterprise managers cannot themselves resolve, even within a framework of sound economic and budgetary policies. Country-wide skill shortages, poor personnel management, and weak administrative structures and procedures all constrain the initiatives that can be taken by the individual agency or enterprise. Chapters 10 and 11 consider these systemic issues associated with managing public bureaucracies.

5 The role of the state

Some economic activities are universally recognized as the sole responsibility of the state; others, it is widely agreed, are best left to private initiative. Between these extremes, governments have tended to expand their sphere of activity for a variety of reasons. They face demands from many competing constituencies. They often come under strong popular pressure to intervene more, not only to protect the public but also to regulate economic activities and actively to promote economic growth and social welfare. In response, the government may engage in production directly or may act indirectly through controls. This chapter describes how the public sector has grown worldwide, then discusses the division of labor between public and private sectors, and concludes with a review of how state intervention may be designed to promote efficiency.

Public spending

For as long as records have been kept, the ratio of public revenue and expenditure to GDP has tended to grow in most countries (see Figure 5.1). In industrial countries, public spending has risen from less than 10 percent of GDP in 1900 to about 40 percent in 1980; in Sweden, the ratio has reached 65 percent. However, public administration alone is generally less than one-tenth of total public expenditure.

Growth

The expansion of public spending has not been a smooth process. In many instances, its ratio to GDP has remained stable for long periods, only to jump during a war or when some main source of new revenue was found. Thereafter it has seldom declined significantly. The dangers of this ratchet effect can be seen in countries that set their spending on the basis of revenue from export taxes at times of exceptionally high prices; when prices collapsed, expenditure could not easily be reduced and fiscal difficulties arose. Many coffee- and copper-exporting countries were caught in this way during the 1970s; more recently, some oil exporters have also been affected. A few, such as Papua New Guinea, have prudently set aside windfall gains in a special development or revenue equalization fund.

Components

Since the public sector is such a hybrid of central departments, state and local authorities, semi-autonomous agencies, and state-owned enterprises (SOEs), it is hard to compare the composition of its spending. Some activities performed by central government in one country may, in another, be the responsibility of SOEs or local governments. Comparisons are further complicated by the variety of intrastate transactions (subsidies, transfers, and loans). Moreover, consolidated data are rarely available for the government as a whole. Although the level of public activity can be measured by its contribution to value added or by its current spending plus investment, neither measure captures the state's other roles—as a redis-

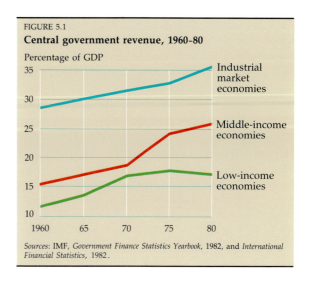

FIGURE 5.1

Central government revenue, 1960-80

Percentage of GDP

Sources: IMF, *Government Finance Statistics Yearbook*, 1982, and *International Financial Statistics*, 1982.

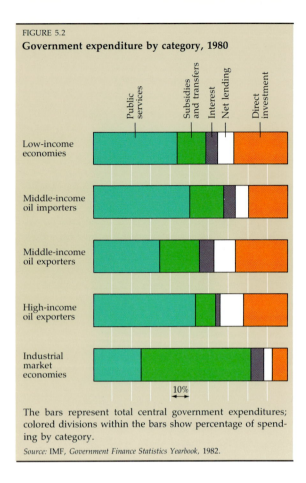

FIGURE 5.2
Government expenditure by category, 1980

Public services

Subsidies and transfers

Interest

Net lending

Direct investment

Low-income economies

Middle-income oil importers

Middle-income oil exporters

High-income oil exporters

Industrial market economies

10%

The bars represent total central government expenditures; colored divisions within the bars show percentage of spending by category.

Source: IMF, *Government Finance Statistics Yearbook,* 1982.

tributor of income through subsidies and transfer payments and as a borrower and lender.

Bearing these difficulties in mind, several different categories of public spending need to be distinguished: services, subsidies and transfers, investment, interest payments, and net lending. Figure 5.2 shows how these vary in importance in different country groups. Data for selected countries are set out in Figure 5.3, which shows that no simple correlation exists between the composition of government expenditure and per capita income.

Public services. Also known as "public consumption," public services comprise all current government spending on wages and salaries and goods and services (including military outlays). Expenditure on wages and salaries to provide public services is defined as central and local governments' contribution to GDP. For industrial market economies, the share of public services in GDP has grown only slowly in recent years. The comparable shares for low- and middle-income countries are lower, but have grown faster (see Table 5.1). Among industrial countries, spending on public services in

1980 ranged from 10 percent of GDP for Japan to 29 percent for Sweden. For some developing countries, substantial mineral revenues have enabled the share to rise even higher: 39 percent in Mauritania, for example. Growth in the share of public services in GDP, too, has varied widely over the past two decades—hardly any increase in the United States, but a doubling in some countries (Denmark, Mexico, and Togo).

Subsidies and transfers. These items include welfare payments to individuals and subsidies to parastatals. In developed countries a large and growing part of this spending has gone for social security, medical care, and unemployment compensation. In developing countries welfare payments are much smaller, and the main items are subsidies.

Investment. Investment takes two forms: (a) capital spending by the government itself (on roads, schools, and hospitals, for example), which averages about a quarter of total capital formation in developing countries, but in 1977 went as high as 69 percent in the Sudan and 77 percent in Ghana; and (b) investment by SOEs. The latter also contribute to GDP through their current spending; their role is discussed in more detail below.

Interest payments. In many developing countries interest payments are growing rapidly, reflecting higher interest rates and increasing indebtedness.

Net lending. A relatively minor item, net lending is normally associated with the financing of investment by SOEs.

By summing these components, one finds that the public sector in most developing countries accounts for 15 to 25 percent of value added in GDP and some 50 to 60 percent of total investment. For industrial countries as a group, the public sector's contribution to value added is a little higher but its share in investment is lower.

The state as producer

In most developing countries the bulk of production is in private hands. Agriculture, commerce, personal services, and small-scale manufacturing

TABLE 5.1
Cost of public services as a share of GDP

Country group	1960	1980
Low-income economies	8	11
Middle-income economies	11	14
Industrial market economies	15	17

Note: Shares are GDP weighted.

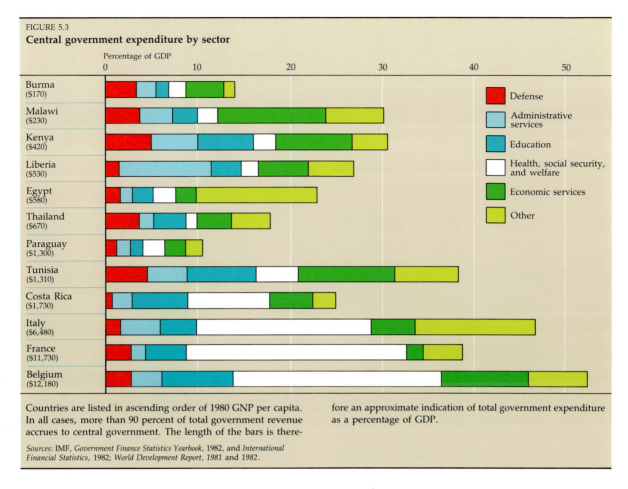

FIGURE 5.3
Central government expenditure by sector

Percentage of GDP

Legend:
- Defense
- Administrative services
- Education
- Health, social security, and welfare
- Economic services
- Other

Countries (with 1980 GNP per capita):
- Burma ($170)
- Malawi ($230)
- Kenya ($420)
- Liberia ($530)
- Egypt ($580)
- Thailand ($670)
- Paraguay ($1,300)
- Tunisia ($1,310)
- Costa Rica ($1,730)
- Italy ($6,480)
- France ($11,730)
- Belgium ($12,180)

Countries are listed in ascending order of 1980 GNP per capita. In all cases, more than 90 percent of total government revenue accrues to central government. The length of the bars is therefore an approximate indication of total government expenditure as a percentage of GDP.

Sources: IMF, *Government Finance Statistics Yearbook*, 1982, and *International Financial Statistics*, 1982; *World Development Report*, 1981 and 1982.

are typically dominated by the informal private sector, while large-scale manufacturing, mining, and finance are usually the preserve of SOEs, transnationals, and a few large, domestically owned enterprises. Electricity, gas, and water are provided mainly by state-owned utilities, and SOEs also play a significant role in transport and communications. In contrast, the pattern of ownership varies considerably in mining and manufacturing (see Figures 5.4 and 5.5).

In industrial market economies the contribution of SOEs to GDP averaged about 10 percent in 1980, up from 9 percent in 1970. For developing countries for which data are available, the average has risen from 7 percent at the beginning of the 1970s to about 10 percent by the end of the decade. Most countries are grouped in the 7-15 percent range, but there are variations from as low as 2 to 3 percent in the Philippines and Nepal to as high as 38 percent in Ghana and Zambia and 64 percent in Hungary, excluding cooperatives which produce another 17 percent (see Figure 5.6). SOEs also contribute substantially to investment; in most of the developing countries for which data are

available, SOEs account for at least a quarter of total capital formation, and in a few cases significantly more (see Table 5.2). Even these figures understate the weight of SOEs in modern sectors of the economy. SOEs may be responsible for producing and marketing major exports of foodstuffs.

TABLE 5.2
Investment by SOEs as a percentage of gross fixed capital formation in selected countries

Country	Years	Percent
Algeria	1978–81	68
Burma	1978–80	61
Zambia	1979–80	61
Pakistan	1978–81	45
Ivory Coast	1979	40
Ethiopia	1978–80	37
Venezuela	1978–80	36
India	1978	33
Bangladesh	1974	31
Brazil	1980	23
Korea, Rep. of	1978–80	23
Peru	1978–79	15

Source: Peter Short (1983).

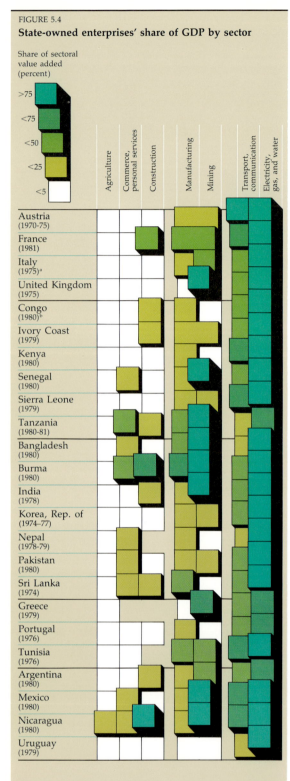

FIGURE 5.4

State-owned enterprises' share of GDP by sector

Share of sectoral value added (percent)

>75
<75
<50
<25
<5

Sectors: Agriculture; Commerce, personal services; Construction; Manufacturing; Mining; Transport, communication; Electricity, gas, and water

Austria (1970-75)
France (1981)
Italy (1975)[a]
United Kingdom (1975)
Congo (1980)[b]
Ivory Coast (1979)
Kenya (1980)
Senegal (1980)
Sierra Leone (1979)
Tanzania (1980-81)
Bangladesh (1980)
Burma (1980)
India (1978)
Korea, Rep. of (1974-77)
Nepal (1978-79)
Pakistan (1980)
Sri Lanka (1974)
Greece (1979)
Portugal (1976)
Tunisia (1976)
Argentina (1980)
Mexico (1980)
Nicaragua (1980)
Uruguay (1979)

The blocks indicate the range of sectoral value added attributed to SOEs. The color and height of the blocks indicate percentage shares. Developed countries are shown first, followed by developing countries grouped by region.

a. Enterprises with more than twenty employees.
b. Gross output.

Sources: UNIDO; World Bank; Peter Short (1983).

They may dominate domestic credit markets, particularly in small economies, because of their borrowing privileges; in the late 1970s, SOEs were responsible for 40 percent or more of domestic credit outstanding in Benin, Guinea, Mali, Senegal, and Bangladesh.

The size of the SOE sector needs to be considered alongside the state's role in providing basic services. Many developing countries are plagued by frequent power cuts, overcrowded ports, deteriorating roads, water shortages, unreliable telephone service, and poor schools and health facilities. The task of improving such services is hampered if the state is also involved in less essential activities. This argues for tailoring a government's responsibilities to match its financial and managerial capacity.

Governments cite a wide variety of reasons for creating SOEs. Whereas some have an ideological preference for public control, others have traveled the same route for more pragmatic reasons. They may have wanted to wrest control of key enterprises from foreign owners (Egypt in 1956 and Madagascar in 1974) or from minority ethnic groups (Uganda in the 1970s); in other instances, enterprises were inherited by the state after independence (Bangladesh in 1972) or a revolution (Portugal in 1974), or as a result of private sector bankruptcies. Governments have used nationalization to capture the rents from the exploitation of minerals and, where national security is involved (as in arms manufacture), to exercise direct military control. In other instances, governments have decided to take the lead in starting a major new industry in the absence of private investors, or have rescued a bankrupt private firm.

The key factor determining the efficiency of an enterprise is not whether it is publicly or privately owned, but how it is managed. In theory it is possible to create the kind of incentives that will maximize efficiency under any type of ownership. But there is a great difference between what is theoretically feasible and what typically happens. As a commercial entity, an SOE must sell in the marketplace. As a public organization, it is given other objectives and is exposed to pressure from politically powerful sectional interests. SOEs are often operated as public bureaucracies, with more attention to procedures than to results; and ready access to subsidies can erode the incentive for managers to minimize costs.

In some cases, SOEs are not necessarily the only or the best vehicle for achieving the goals of government. Other alternatives have sometimes proved more efficient. On occasion, public monopolies have been replaced by competing private firms (see Box 5.1), and in other instances governments have exercised control indirectly by taxing and subsidizing private companies or by controlling their prices. Public stabilization funds may be an alternative to state marketing boards; measures to stimulate the capital market can promote industrialization without the state being directly involved. And governments have used management contracts to tap private managerial and technical skills to provide better services (see Box 5.2).

Though private management has much to contribute, it would be misleading to portray it as universally efficient. In poor countries, managerial capacity is weak in both the public and private sectors. However, the greater potential for competition and the ever-present possibility of bankruptcy exercises a discipline over private businesses that is lacking in the public sector. When services can be provided efficiently by small businesses, such as individual truckers, reliance on the private sector economizes on management. Recognizing that, some governments have decided to reduce the size of the public sector, while others are actively considering doing so. This choice has nothing to do with political ideology: Hungary legislated in 1982 to allow the formation of private companies employing up to 150 people. In Belgrade street cleaning is contracted to a private company, while in New York the same task is undertaken directly by the city government.

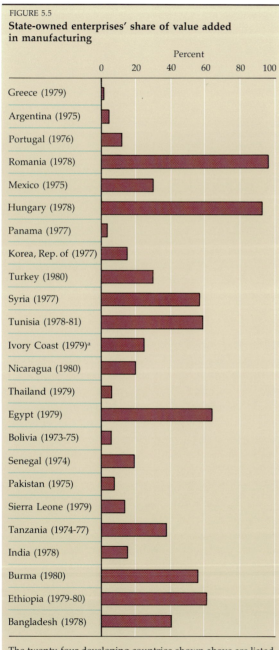

FIGURE 5.5

State-owned enterprises' share of value added in manufacturing

The twenty-four developing countries shown above are listed in descending order of 1980 GNP per capita. The length of the bars indicates the percentage of the countries' manufacturing value added attributed to nonfinancial SOEs.

a. Includes mining.

Sources: UNIDO; World Bank; Peter Short (1983).

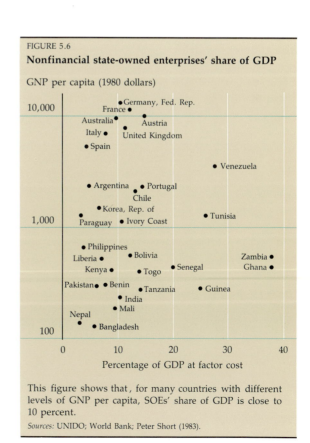

FIGURE 5.6

Nonfinancial state-owned enterprises' share of GDP

This figure shows that, for many countries with different levels of GNP per capita, SOEs' share of GDP is close to 10 percent.

Sources: UNIDO; World Bank; Peter Short (1983).

Box 5.1 Bus services: the comparative advantage of private operators

In many cities bus services are dominated by large, publicly owned or highly regulated companies operating full-size buses (forty to sixty seats). Most require government subsidies to cover their deficits. The experience of cities that have allowed competition shows that smaller, private companies running smaller buses (twenty-five seats or fewer) offer more frequent and convenient service and are profitable.

Public transport in Buenos Aires, for example, is provided by about fifty private companies operating 23–25 seaters. The government sets their routes, but most have to compete on each route. As a result, the buses are well maintained and run frequently; 94 percent of the routes enjoy service for eighteen hours or more a day. An earlier experiment with full-size buses run by a large (initially private, later public) company failed: the company's service deteriorated rapidly and by 1959 its annual losses totaled about $44 million; in 1962 it was dissolved.

In Calcutta the State Transport Corporation (CSTC) was given a monopoly in the early 1960s. In response to public demand, private buses were permitted in 1966. The private buses charged the same fares and earned a profit, while CSTC lost money. Today, private buses operating without subsidies account for two-thirds of all bus trips. On similar routes at the same fares, CSTC still requires subsidies of $1 million a month. The success of the private companies has been attributed to quicker repairs (only half of CSTC's buses are running at any one time), better fare collection (CSTC loses an estimated 25 percent of its fares through evasion), and higher labor productivity (CSTC employed thirty staff per bus in 1980, one of the highest staffing levels in the world).

Chiengmai, a city of about 100,000 people in northern Thailand, allows virtually free competition between large buses following fixed routes and minibuses which adapt their routes according to the demands of the passengers. Minibuses normally charge twice as much as regular buses, yet account for more than 90 percent of all trips. The passengers clearly prefer the convenience of the minibuses. The main bus company loses money; the minibuses make modest profits.

Some of the doubts about private bus operators are not borne out in practice. For example, city authorities may fear that bus companies pursuing profits would not serve poorer communities or work off-peak hours. Yet in such cities as Istanbul, Calcutta, Bangkok, Hong Kong, and Nairobi, minibuses are the only transport serving many low-income communities, especially illegal squatter areas or centers with narrow streets. Private bus companies are also criticized for keeping down the incomes of their drivers. But the limited empirical evidence shows that drivers in Istanbul and Calcutta earn more than the average household income.

The state as regulator

Economic output will be maximized only when resources are allocated by a mechanism that takes full account of their relative scarcity and costs. At one theoretical extreme lies centralized planning, where allocations are all determined administratively; at the other, an unregulated market system. In reality, all countries use a combination of markets and government intervention. This reflects the experience that no planning organization is capable of calculating relative scarcities for all goods and services, while entirely free markets can have major failings.

Markets may not perform perfectly because of insufficient information or because they do not take adequate account of indirect losses and benefits (the so-called externalities such as pollution or worker training). Nor can free markets handle public goods (such as national defense), where the cost of supply is independent of the number of beneficiaries, or natural monopolies. Finally, markets do not act to correct inequalities in income and wealth. Some market failures are so evident that they cannot be ignored; in addition, govern-ments will always have legitimate noneconomic objectives that can be pursued only by intervention. The challenge for every government, whatever its political complexion, is to intervene in ways that minimize economic costs to achieve desired goals. Designing mechanisms that alleviate market failures without creating "bureaucratic failures" has been a difficult task. All too often the attempted cure has been worse than the disease:

- Import restrictions have led to high-cost domestic industry that penalizes consumers. They enable those lucky enough to obtain an import license to reap windfall gains from the scarcities that are created. One estimate for Turkey in 1968 suggests that rents associated with import restrictions alone amounted to about 15 percent of GNP; for India in 1964, the estimated loss of welfare was put at 7 percent of GNP.
- Credit allocation and subsidized interest rates have resulted in a bias toward capital-intensive industry.
- Minimum wage laws have reduced the demand for labor.
- Regulations have created large black markets. Some are associated with the vast traffic in drugs,

but in other cases clandestine activities are linked to crops that governments have overtaxed or underpriced. Coffee and cocoa in West Africa are examples of how black markets can undermine controls, at great cost in lost revenues and often in output as well.

• Prices set low to benefit consumers—especially for food—have frequently discouraged producers, creating scarcities and greater dependence on imports.

To overcome these weaknesses, almost all the economic reforms attempted by market and centrally planned economies have placed greater reliance on prices to decentralize decisionmaking. Where administrative skills are generally at a premium, the theoretically optimal solution to a public management problem—such as a value added tax to fund government operations without introducing fiscal distortions—may prove impractical, and a second-best solution must be sought. The option of using price incentives in place of administrative solutions always merits serious consideration. Not only do price incentives lighten the administrative burden but they also reduce costly distortions. The use of market mechanisms does not require or assume private ownership. Both in socialist countries and within the public sector in "mixed" economies, reforms based on

market mechanisms have been effective without changes in ownership. China, for example, has reformed its commune system to allocate land to individual farmers (see Box 5.3). It has also introduced a pricing system for medical services that allows patients to choose.

The difficulty lies in ensuring that prices reflect costs. In any economy a vast amount of rapidly changing information on the supply and demand for goods and services must be handled promptly and accurately. Competitive markets permit the necessary flexibility and responsiveness and, because they decentralize the task of handling information, also economize on scarce administrative resources.

Changes in government policy can lead to dramatic improvements in enterprise efficiency (see Box 5.4). In addition to ensuring that firms operate within a pricing framework that reflects scarcities, governments can help to improve the efficiency of enterprises in several ways.

Fostering competition

Japan has demonstrated the importance of competition to promote efficiency. The Japanese market was large enough to provide healthy competition even in industries producing for the domestic

---

Box 5.2   Management contracts for water supply in the Ivory Coast

The water and sewerage service in the Ivory Coast is provided on a management contract by a private company, Societe de Distribution d'Eau de la Cote d'Ivoire (SODECI). It was started by a French water supply company; today 52 percent of its shareholders are Ivorians. Although the company still depends partly on expatriates, the general manager and most of the other managers are Ivorians.

A unit in the Ministry of Public Works is responsible for planning and building all large new investments in water. This unit is also responsible for supervising SODECI. Under its contracts, SODECI is paid a fee related to the volume of water sold. The fee is calculated on the basis of agreed standards for staff, equipment, energy, and other inputs, plus a margin based on agreed overheads and profits, indexed against inflation. SODECI therefore makes a reasonable profit, whereas other (usually public) water supply companies in West Africa mostly operate at a loss. SODECI's fee is only part of the water tariff, which is set to cover not only operation and maintenance costs but also debt service.

Despite rapid expansion, water supply in the Ivory Coast offers one of the highest standards in West Africa. The systems are well designed, equipped, maintained, and operated. Water quality and pressure are uniformally good. Consumption is metered and water losses are low. Several factors contribute to these good results:

• The institutional separation of investments from operations makes it easier to evaluate SODECI's performance and assures government control over the expansion of the system.

• By setting water tariffs to reflect costs

fully, the Ivory Coast can finance its high standard of service. Water rates are among the highest in Africa, which means that consumers, rather than taxpayers, pay for the service they receive. Rates for smaller users are low, so the poor can afford the service.

• During periodic traffic reviews, the government can carefully scrutinize SODECI's costs; between reviews, SODECI has a strong incentive to keep down its costs.

• As a private company, SODECI is free (within the contracted limits) to hire, fire, and compensate its staff. This freedom, plus a strong emphasis on training (SODECI is the only water supply company in West Africa with its own training center), enables the company to attract, train, and keep qualified people.

Box 5.3 The search for efficiency in China: the rural production responsibility system

Since 1979 China has embarked on a far-reaching program of economic reform to increase efficiency within a system of public and collective ownership and central planning. The basic components of this program are:

- Greater decentralization of production and investment decisions to enterprises and farms
- Stronger incentives, with more direct links between material rewards and the work of households and individuals
- Greater use of market mechanisms in allocating resources.

Although the reforms extend to all aspects of China's economy, the most striking changes so far have been in the rural areas. Until recently, farmers had little autonomy: they were told what to grow—how much, where, and with what inputs. The bulk of their output had to be delivered to the government or their collective, and their incomes were only partly determined by the amount and quality of their crops.

While still retaining collective ownership of land and most agricultural equipment, the government has introduced significant changes in the organization of production and marketing and in the distribution of income. Under the new "production responsibility system," farmland and sometimes draft animals

and implements are assigned to individual households for several years (usually five). Households may farm the land as they wish, but must undertake to provide an agreed amount of their output at fixed prices to the government and to their village production team. Beyond these obligations, which account on average for one-third of a household's total production, farmers can keep whatever they produce.

The method of allocating land varies in different parts of the country. In most areas allocation depends on household size or the number of laborers in a household. In some places, however, those households that agree to deliver most to the village get the largest farms. Where the main activities are growing vegetables or raising livestock, instead of assigning land to households, production contracts are negotiated between village leaders and groups of households or workers to deliver a fixed amount of output. The groups receive an agreed payment when they deliver, with bonuses for surpluses and penalties for shortfalls.

Crops subject to compulsory delivery have been reduced in number and limited mainly to staples such as grains and cotton. For these crops, a multi-tier price system has been introduced. Within fixed quotas, the government buys crops at

lower prices, thereby levying a form of taxation. Beyond these quotas, however, farmers can sell in markets governed purely by supply and demand. As an incentive, the government has recently reduced the size of the fixed quota. The government is also encouraging the establishment of collective and private commercial ventures to market consumer goods and agricultural inputs in rural areas. And it is providing credit for private and collective activities in raising livestock and for handicrafts, for example.

Since these reforms are at an early stage, many questions remain. In particular, it is unclear whether the new system can retain the advantages of the old system in financing social services for the poor and in organizing large-scale investment. Nonetheless, the reforms have already produced impressive results. During 1978–82, gross agricultural output rose at 7 percent a year, more than double the average rate in the preceding twenty years. Because of higher procurement prices, farmers' real incomes (which barely increased in 1957–77) have risen even faster—at about 10 percent a year during 1978–82. The quantity, quality, and variety of agricultural produce available in urban areas have also improved substantially.

---

market and protected from international competition. The gradual liberalization of imports according to a fixed timetable was an added pressure for efficiency (discussed in Box 6.3 in the next chapter). Brazil is another example of a country where, despite import protection, domestic competition has helped increase efficiency.

In smaller countries, however, attempts to promote internal competition by restricting the size of companies have usually resulted in uneconomically small producers. A better approach is to reduce tariffs and achieve the right mix of incentives between exporting and import-competing industries. The partial liberalization of imports in the Republic of Korea and Brazil during the 1960s increased the competitive pressure on industry. The experience of several East Asian countries shows

that exporting also stimulates productivity gains, as manufacturers strive to penetrate competitive markets. A case study of a successful public company in India, Hindustan Machine Tools, suggests that even modest export sales can have this effect.

Reducing uncertainty

The level of business uncertainty in developing countries is often much higher than in developed economies. Uncertainty encourages companies to build up inventories and cash balances, while discouraging innovation and investment. For example, a policy of short leases (no more than five years) in the Turkish marble industry fostered mining methods that accelerated the destruction of the ore body and discouraged investments that would have added value to the rock.

While a certain amount of uncertainty is unavoidable, governments can reduce it by providing information on their own intentions and the economy in general, by making regulations less arbitrary, and by providing guarantees and insurance. Consultation between business and government can be encouraged by creating a forum for public and private participants to meet and air their views. A good example comes from Japan, which established several liaison agencies in the Ministry of International Trade and Industry (the Commerce and Industry Deliberation Council in 1927, the Industrial Rationalization Council in 1949, and the Industrial Structure Council in 1961). These bodies allowed industrial leaders, academic specialists, and officials to discuss and modify government policy. The Republic of Korea also brings government and business together through monthly meetings, chaired by the country's president, which focus on the export targets set by firms. Participation in this open forum provides an incentive for both sides to do well. Mauritius has a national economic council to bring together government, labor, and business representatives.

Government controls can also breed uncertainty. This is particularly the case when licenses for investment and imports are issued on an ad hoc basis, and when there is a danger of delays or changes in procedures. Some countries (such as India and Turkey) have frequently changed the quantities of imports permitted and have shifted items back and forth between quota and liberalized lists. In Tanzania, applications for import licenses must be submitted three months in advance for six months' worth of imports; then applicants are typically granted only a fraction of their requests. In 1980 an Indonesian cement manufacturer and its distributors were found to need twenty-four different licenses (health, environmental, transport, and so on) to operate, while an importer had to produce between 25 and 100 pages of documentation to obtain one piece of equipment. A study of industrial licensing in India in 1973 found the process took two to three years—and sometimes only the first phase of a project would be approved; subsequent reforms have helped to alleviate this bottleneck.

Simplifying procedures

Several countries are trying to speed up government procedures. Brazil, for example, created a Ministry of Debureaucratization to cut down on regulations and licensing. Since 1979 Brazil has eliminated some of the millions of documents previously required from private firms—saving them, to date, an estimated $1 billion. In the Philippines, the approval time for export incentives was shortened from ninety to sixty days in 1979; exporters were granted advance tax credits or duty rebates on imported inputs only seven days after exporting the finished product. In the Republic of Korea export and import procedures are being computerized.

"One-stop" agencies help to centralize and simplify industry's contacts with government. Indo-

---

Box 5.4 Reform of the Turkish fertilizer industry

In 1980 the Turkish government initiated a program to improve the performance of state-owned and private fertilizer plants in Turkey, after a detailed analysis of the industry had indicated serious shortcomings in eight out of seventeen plants. The industry lacked foreign exchange to import raw materials and local credit to finance working capital. Most older plants were profligate consumers of energy, while others used expensive feedstocks. Most plants suffered from a pricing policy that caused even the most efficient to lose money heavily. Public sector plants lacked skilled workers and competent managers because of wage controls. The state-owned firms also suffered from inadequate organization and lack of management autonomy.

The government's reforms have addressed these failings. As a result of raising fertilizer producer prices close to international prices, the financial viability of most companies has been restored and they have started to expand output and invest in improvements. This has been supported by giving the firms better access to working capital and foreign exchange for imports of raw materials. Moreover, the organizational and man-agerial systems in key state enterprises are being revamped and staff training has been expanded. A major investment program has begun to rationalize eight plants by removing technical bottlenecks and improving their energy efficiency. While it will take several years to correct all the industry's deficiencies, progress has already been dramatic. Capacity utilization increased from a low of 41 percent in 1979 to 67 percent in 1981 and is expected to climb further by 1986 at the end of the rationalization program.

nesia converted its industrial coordination board into a one-stop agency in 1979. Businessmen can now get licenses that previously involved several different ministries, although bureaucratic delays are still a problem. Turkey has centralized export promotion incentives in the Office of Incentives and Implementation. The Singapore Economic Development Board acts as the official liaison with foreign investors and assigns people specially to help cut through red tape.

Encouraging technological development

Promoting technology in developing countries generally requires removing barriers to innovation and increasing access to information. A study of sub-Saharan Africa found that low crop prices discouraged the transfer of agricultural innovation. High taxes, licensing procedures, and measures that reduce competition can have the same effect.

The most important source of new technology for developing countries is foreign firms. Since their presence can raise delicate political issues, some countries have tried to emulate the Japanese in separating foreign investment from the import of technology. With increasing competition to attract foreign investment, however, few countries can close their doors to the companies and import only their technology. Other attempts to restrict transnationals—by requiring them to purchase local inputs or work with domestic partners, for example—can discourage them completely from locating in the market.

One way to increase access to foreign technology is through exporting. A study of industry in the Republic of Korea found that it enjoyed virtually free access to technological and managerial information through foreign buyers, who were the most important single source of ideas on product innovation. Buyers' suggestions also improved the organization of production and upgraded management techniques.

Governments can help spread information to small and medium-size companies by encouraging subcontracting. Large firms typically provide de-signs, quality control, and technical services to their contractors. In some countries, such as Sri Lanka and Bangladesh, governments have promoted special agencies to inform large firms of the capabilities of smaller companies and to assist subcontractors in meeting quality control and delivery standards. Removing cascading sales taxes—which tax transactions between firms but not within a single firm—can also encourage subcontracting.

Conclusions

The role of the state changes as the economy does. In least developed countries, the indigenous private sector consists largely of subsistence farmers and small family traders, while the modern sector is dominated by expatriate or minority-owned firms concentrated in a few export crops or mining. Under such circumstances, governments generally feel that only they have the resources and the purpose to promote development. In more advanced economies, with the potential for greater private sector activity, the state may play more of a regulatory role, concentrating on rectifying market failures.

This chapter has suggested that government interventions can result in large losses of efficiency and should therefore be selective. In the face of compelling political and social pressures, governments will always be tempted to do more than can be accomplished efficiently. Yet today's widespread reexamination of the role of the state is evidence of a new realism. In the search for greater cost-effectiveness in the provision of services, governments are exploring ways of tapping private initiative and simulating competitive conditions. The most common approach is to use private contractors in a variety of fields, from road maintenance to garbage collection. This serves to mobilize new managerial resources and, if well supervised, can greatly improve the quality and reduce the cost of services. Where reliance is placed on markets, however, governments are finding that price distortions can exact a heavy toll. This is the subject of the next chapter.

6 Pricing for efficiency

In the industrial market economies prices play a pivotal role in the allocation of resources. The centrally planned economies have also started to move in that direction, and in developing countries there is a growing body of evidence on the benefits of using prices to reflect scarcities and encourage growth. Remunerative prices helped foster South Asia's agricultural development in the 1960s, and competitive exchange rates contributed to the export successes of several East Asian countries in the 1970s.

Yet government development programs often still concentrate more on the quantity of saving, investment, and output than on prices. Where governments have intervened directly in prices, they have often produced unintended results. Price controls to improve income distribution, for example, have sometimes ended up hurting the poorest—as when low food prices, intended to benefit the urban poor, reduce the incomes of the (more numerous) rural poor. Similarly, import controls designed to save imports and improve the balance of trade have often harmed exports and home production and ended up worsening the trade balance. Controlled low interest rates intended to help investors and farmers often ended up reducing the pool of savings available and forcing small investors and farmers to rely on high interest rates in black or informal markets. Pricing policy became increasingly critical in the 1970s because of the international upheavals in energy prices, interest rates, and exchange rates.

This chapter reviews the extent of price distortions in developing countries in the 1970s and assesses their impact on growth. The main conclusion is that during the 1970s price distortions were serious in many developing countries. Those countries with the worst distortions experienced significantly lower domestic saving and lower output per unit of investment, thus leading to slower growth.

Price distortions

The issue of price distortions has been widely researched and debated in recent years and has been reviewed in several earlier *World Development Reports* . Distortions exist when the prices of goods and services, as well as of capital and labor, do not correctly reflect their scarcity. For goods that are internationally traded, scarcity is generally indicated by international prices (a fuller discussion is given in Box 4.1).

Price distortions may be caused by monopolistic tendencies in the private sector or by government intervention. It is possible for government interventions, if properly designed, to correct distortions. In most instances, however, price distortions are introduced by government directly or indirectly in pursuit of some social or economic objective, sometimes deliberately, sometimes incidentally.

In most cases, these price-distorting policies have their origin in a complex set of political and economic factors. In the 1950s the dominant theories of economic development played down the power of prices and the degree of flexibility in resource allocation. Instead, inward-looking trade policies were favored by governments in many newly independent countries, partly in reaction to the colonial power's keenness to export their agricultural products and to import industrial products from the metropolitan country. In other countries, particularly in Latin America, governments wanted to be less dependent economically on the dominant industrial powers. Many of the controls leading to distortions were imposed in response to scarcities of foreign exchange, or capital, or certain goods (particularly during and after World War II); but the controls were often continued even after their rationale had vanished. Often distortions have arisen as the unintended by-product of inflation under a regime of fixed exchange rates.

As background research for this Report, the available facts on price distortions have been collated for thirty-one developing countries, representing more than 75 percent of the population of the developing world excluding China. The analysis concentrates on distortions in the prices of foreign exchange, capital, labor, and infrastructure services (particularly power). Distortions are not measured against some theoretical ideal, but are practical approximations commonly used in policy analysis. For example, to measure distortions in the pricing of foreign exchange, one should ideally measure the effective exchange rates for imports and exports as they deviate from the "equilibrium" rate. In practice, it is difficult to calculate equilibrium exchange rates; policy discussions generally focus on changes in real effective exchange rates from a base period, together with the effective protection or taxation of traded goods. Similarly, distortions in interest rates are judged by how far interest rates were negative in real terms; in wages, by movements in real wages relative to productivity adjusted for changes in the terms of trade; in the value of money, by high and accelerating inflation; and in infrastructure prices, by the rates of return in utilities. The estimated price distortions are found to be inversely related to growth and efficiency, but there is no strong evidence of such distortions leading to any gain in equity.

Exchange rates

Changing the real exchange rate can be a powerful tool for balancing trade without burdening the administrative system and without distorting domestic incentives. Yet in the 1970s in many countries with a large balance of payments deficit, the exchange rate was allowed to become overvalued in relation to the purchasing power of the currency. This lack of competitiveness became particularly serious in sub-Saharan Africa, where the average real effective exchange rate appreciated by 44 percent between 1973 and 1981. (The real effective exchange rate is here defined as the import-weighted exchange rate adjusted by the ratio of the domestic consumer price index to the import-weighted combination of consumer price indices in the trading partners.) Several African countries now find that producers of traditional export crops cannot be paid enough to cover their costs of production, even though these are the crops for which they have a strong comparative advantage. (Cocoa in Ghana is an obvious example and is discussed

in Chapter 8, Box 8.1.) While the problem was generally less severe for other regions, in several countries an overvalued exchange rate harmed not only the balance of payments but also their growth. Even in such countries as Argentina, Chile, Sri Lanka, and Uruguay, which initiated programs of economic reform during the 1970s, the real exchange rate was subsequently allowed to appreciate and thus weakened their reform programs.

Trade restrictions

Trade restrictions have often led to high and variable rates of protection between different manufacturing industries. By contributing to an overvalued exchange rate, such restrictions have inadvertently discriminated against both exports and agriculture. In several countries (such as Cameroon, Ghana, Senegal, Tanzania, and Turkey), this bias against exports has been supplemented by export taxes or even outright restrictions, sometimes leading to increased agricultural imports at the expense of domestic production.

When import controls are intended to protect infant industries, they are rarely geared to promote an industry's long-run growth potential; nor are they reduced even after the industry has reached adolescence. The loss of efficiency resulting from such policies can be considerable. In extreme cases—steel in Bangladesh, tin cans in Kenya, and cars in Thailand—the foreign exchange cost of importing raw materials and capital significantly exceeds the foreign exchange cost of importing the finished products. Apart from these losses, the system of protection in many developing countries has become a serious administrative burden and, by giving windfall gains to those who obtain import licenses, often makes the distribution of income more unequal as well.

Interest rates

Overvalued exchange rates and low tariffs on imported capital goods encourage capital-intensive techniques at the expense of creating jobs. These tendencies are strengthened when interest rates charged to borrowers (and paid to savers) fall short of the inflation rate. At various times in the 1970s, negative real interest rates were almost a worldwide phenomenon. But they were particularly severe and persistent in countries such as Argentina, Brazil, Ghana, Jamaica, Nigeria, Peru, and Turkey, frequently reaching double figures. Such negative real interest rates not only penalize savers and stimulate capital outflows but also encourage excess demand for credit—which is then suppressed by rationing loans, causing more administrative burdens.

Costs of labor

Capital-intensive investment has also been encouraged where the price of labor has been increased by unrealistic minimum wage laws and social security taxes. In many mineral-based economies, especially in Africa and Latin America, the drive for higher mining wages has spread to other sectors. This has pushed labor costs far above those of competitors, and encouraged rural people to leave the land in pursuit of the high wages paid to those lucky enough to find jobs in the urban sector. In some Latin American countries in the 1970s, social security contributions have added up to 20 percent to the cost of labor. In the 1970s wage negotiations in several countries (such as Ivory Coast and Sri Lanka) failed to allow for deterioration in the country's terms of trade. As a result, real wages grew significantly faster than productivity adjusted for changes in terms of trade.

Infrastructural services

The rapid increases in international costs of energy and capital in the 1970s required correspondingly higher prices for infrastructural services, which are generally both energy and capital intensive. With the exception of some oil-exporting countries and some energy products, most developing countries have adjusted domestic energy prices to international levels. However, infrastructure prices have been raised too slowly to judge by the low rate of return on capital achieved by power utilities. A review of sixty countries conducted by the World Bank in 1980 showed that about half had low (less than 4 percent) rates of return, while several incurred losses. In transport and water supply, rates of return are not available for any sizable sample of countries, but the indications are that most countries fail to recover the full costs of these services. Such underpricing not only increases demand for these capital- and energy-intensive services but also undermines the financial viability of the agencies supplying them.

Inflation

The 1970s was a decade of rising inflation the world over, with most developing countries experiencing double-digit rates. Nearly all the countries that had high—15 percent a year or more—inflation in the 1960s (such as Brazil, Chile, Republic of Korea, and Uruguay) continued in that category in the 1970s, and many others joined their ranks. In several countries (such as Argentina, Bolivia, Chile, Ghana, Mexico, Nigeria, and Turkey), the rate of inflation in the 1970s was high, and several times that in the 1960s. Rapid and accelerating inflation undermines allocative efficiency because it increases uncertainty and induces savers to invest in unproductive "inflation hedges" such as real estate, consumer durables, gems, and foreign currency deposits. Some countries have developed complex systems for indexing wages and prices to compensate for inflation, though this is administratively costly and tends to penalize those (mostly poor) people outside the indexation system. Where indexation does not exist, the "inflation tax" contributes to a growing sense of social and economic injustice.

Linkages among distortions

Most price distortions are connected: some counteract each other, others are reinforcing. For example, an overvalued exchange rate tends to offset the degree of protection given by tariffs, but it increases the bias against exports caused by export taxes. Consumer subsidies may moderate the pressures for raising wages but exacerbate inflationary pressures through increasing budgetary deficits. Low interest rates and transport prices for farmers, along with subsidized inputs, may counterbalance the losses they suffer from an overvalued exchange rate. Similarly, agricultural protection works not only through its effects on agriculture but also through its effects on wages and industrial efficiency.

It is therefore not enough to judge the efficiency of allocation on the basis of individual distortions—as is done, for example, when growth is related just to inflation or just to interest rates. Some composite measure of price distortions is needed. Nor is it enough to analyze only static efficiency. Price distortions that produce a loss of static efficiency might nevertheless increase dynamic efficiency, or they might produce cumulative dynamic losses. Finally, it is hard to know at what point investment encouraged by protection or subsidized interest rates becomes profligate. The answers to these questions must be sought from empirical evidence.

That evidence is set out in Figure 6.1. For each

TABLE 6.1
Indices of price distortions and various components of growth in the 1970s

Country	Distortion index	Simple group average	Annual GDP growth rate (percent)	Simple group average	Domestic savings income ratio (percent)	Simple group average
Malawi	1.14		6.3		14	
Thailand	1.43		7.2		21	
Cameroon	1.57		5.6		18	
Korea, Rep. of	1.57		9.5		22	
Malaysia	1.57	1.56	7.8	6.8	20	21.4
Philippines	1.57		6.3		24	
Tunisia	1.57		7.5		27	
Kenya	1.71		6.5		19	
Yugoslavia	1.71		5.8		27	
Colombia	1.71		5.9		22	
Ethiopia	1.86		2.0		8	
Indonesia	1.86		7.6		22	
India	1.86		3.6		20	
Sri Lanka	1.86		4.1		13	
Brazil	1.86	1.95	8.4	5.7	22	17.8
Mexico	1.86		5.2		22	
Ivory Coast	2.14		6.7		24	
Egypt	2.14		7.4		12	
Turkey	2.14		5.9		17	
Senegal	2.29		2.5		8	
Pakistan	2.29		4.7		7	
Jamaica	2.29		−1.1		16	
Uruguay	2.29		3.5		14	
Bolivia	2.29		4.8		20	
Peru	2.29	2.44	3.0	3.1	21	13.8
Argentina	2.43		2.2		22	
Chile	2.43		2.4		14	
Tanzania	2.57		4.9		12	
Bangladesh	2.57		3.9		2	
Nigeria	2.71		6.5		21	
Ghana	2.86		−0.1		9	
Overall average	2.01		5.0		17.4	

. . Not available.
a. Increase in real GDP valued at current prices divided by investment at current prices. This is the reciprocal of the incremental-capital-output ratio, adjusted for differential rates of inflation in investment goods and GDP. It is thus equivalent to income rate of return on revalued capital.
b. GDP growth rates were negative.
Source: World Development Report 1982.

of the major prices, distortions are classified as high, medium, or low on the basis of available figures and the qualitative judgments of Bank staff. For a particular country the degree of distortion may be widely different for different prices. A composite index was therefore obtained by calculating an average of price distortions (see Box 6.1). Figure 6.1 ranks countries in order of increasing distortion in the 1970s: Malawi, Thailand, Cameroon, the Republic of Korea, and Malaysia have the lowest distortion, while Argentina, Chile, Tanzania, Bangladesh, Nigeria, and Ghana are in

the "high" category. It is interesting to note that these groups contain a mixture of countries, unconnected by geography, natural resources, or degree of government activism.

Price distortions and growth

A large body of theoretical literature has demonstrated how price distortions result in a loss of efficiency. At an empirical level, studies of Brazil, Chile, Pakistan, Philippines, and Turkey relating to the 1960s estimated that the costs of distorted

Additional output per unit of investment[a] (percent)	Simple group average	Annual growth rate of agriculture (percent)	Simple group average	Annual growth rate of industry (percent)	Simple group average	Annual growth rate of export volume (percent)	Simple group average
25.3		4.1		7.0		5.7	
27.6		4.7		10.0		11.8	
26.3		3.8		8.6		2.5	
31.1		3.2		15.4		23.0	
32.6	27.6	5.1	4.4	9.7	9.1	7.4	6.7
23.1		4.9		8.7		7.0	
31.4		4.9		9.0		4.8	
32.7		5.4		10.2		−1.0	
18.4		2.8		7.1		3.9	
27.4		4.9		4.9		1.9	
30.7		0.7		1.4		−1.7	
40.1		3.8		11.1		8.7	
15.6		1.9		4.5		3.7	
22.2		2.8		4.0		−2.4	
35.5	26.9	4.9	2.9	9.3	6.8	7.5	3.9
23.4		2.3		6.6		13.4	
25.5		3.4		10.5		4.6	
24.2		2.7		6.8		−0.7	
24.5		3.4		6.6		1.7	
12.8		3.7		3.7		1.2	
28.1		2.3		5.2		1.2	
. .[b]		0.7		−3.5		−6.8	
20.9		0.2		5.2		4.8	
22.7		3.1		4.3		−1.6	
21.5	16.8	0.0	1.8	3.7	3.2	3.9	0.7
10.7		2.6		1.8		9.3	
15.1		2.3		0.2		10.9	
23.9		4.9		1.9		−7.3	
22.3		2.2		9.5		−1.9	
23.8		0.8		8.1		2.6	
. .[b]		−1.2		−1.2		−8.4	
23.2		3.0		6.1		3.5	

prices due to trade restrictions alone could have amounted to 4 to 10 percent of their GNP. Those countries that embarked on programs of correcting prices in the 1960s (for example, Brazil, Colombia, and the Republic of Korea) also showed significant gains in output (and employment) resulting from these liberalization efforts. More recently, as recounted in the 1981 *World Development Report*, it has been found that countries which avoided distorting trade policies were typically more successful in adjusting to external shocks in the 1970s than those with distorted prices.

Statistical analysis of the relationship between the price distortion index and growth in the 1970s confirms these earlier findings. The average growth rate of those developing countries with low distortions in the 1970s was about 7 percent a year—2 percentage points higher than the overall average. Countries with high distortions averaged growth of about 3 percent a year, 2 percentage points lower than the overall average.

The relation between price distortions and the various components of growth is presented in Table 6.1. High distortions are associated with low do-

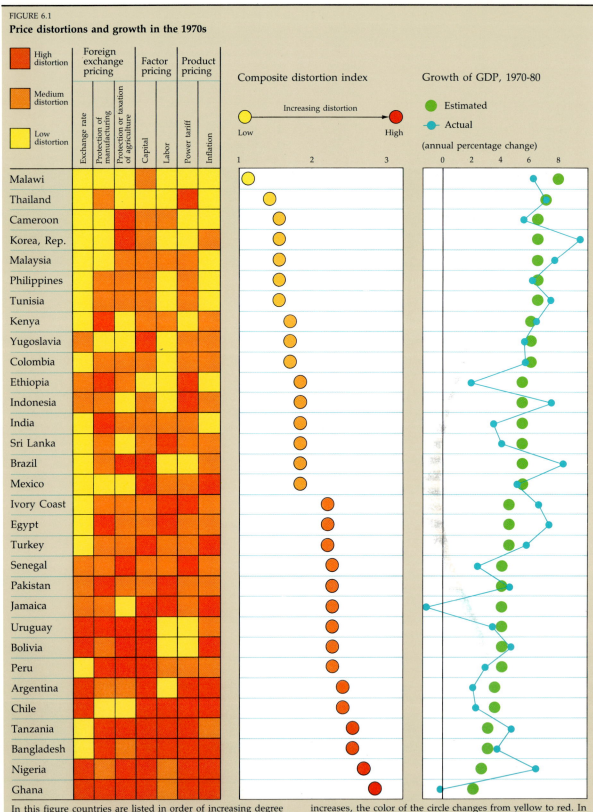

FIGURE 6.1

Price distortions and growth in the 1970s

In this figure countries are listed in order of increasing degree of distortion in prices. In the first section, the color of the squares indicates the degree of distortion in the principal categories of prices. The middle section is a composite index of price distortion for each country: as a country's distortion index increases, the color of the circle changes from yellow to red. In the right hand section, the blue circles show the actual annual rate of growth of GDP; the green circles are estimates of GDP growth obtained by a regression relating growth to the distortion index.

Box 6.1 Price distortions and growth: a statistical analysis

In Figure 6.1 the distortion indices in major prices are classified as low, medium, and high. For statistical analysis, these categories were replaced by numbers 1, 2, and 3 respectively. For the panel of thirty-one countries, the degree of distortion in each price, thus defined, was found to be negatively correlated with the GDP growth rates during the 1970s, with the exchange rate distortion being the most significant.

These distortions are interrelated among themselves and each distortion affects growth through a complicated set of interactions on various elements of the economy. There are therefore major conceptual and statistical problems in any attempt to identify simultaneously the effects of individual distortions on overall growths or the relative importance of different distortions in the total mix. In these circumstances the composite distortion index in Figure 6.1 is obtained as a simple unweighted average of the individual distortions.

The figures on growth rates and distortion indices show that the relatively high (top one-third) distortion countries had growth rates about 2 percentage points lower than the average (which is about 5 percent a year) and the low (bottom one-third) distortion countries, were about 2 percentage points higher than average.

The regression equation relating growth to the composite distortion index shows that price distortions can explain about one-third of the variation in growth performance. Many other elements, not least natural resource endowment as well as other economic, social, political, and institutional factors, would need to be considered in a more complete explanation to account fully for the variation in growth rates. Thus as shown in Figure 6.1, Brazil, Egypt, Indonesia, Nigeria, Republic of Korea, and Ivory Coast did much better than would have been predicted by the regression equation, and Ethiopia, Ghana, and Jamaica considerably worse.

While the degree of distortions in prices has a significant association with growth, the analysis indicated virtually no correlation with the distribution of income. For twenty-seven countries for which figures are available on income distribution, the analysis shows that the distortion index explains hardly 3 percent of the variation in equity, when the latter is measured by the proportion of income going to the bottom 40 percent of the population.

mestic savings in relation to GDP and with low value added per unit of investment (this latter association being statistically stronger). Distortions also affect growth rates in agriculture and industry, with a marked influence on exports. In short, the statistical analysis clearly suggests that prices do matter for growth.

However, price distortions alone can explain less than half the variation in growth among countries;

the rest is the result of other economic, social, political, and institutional factors. So a country well endowed with natural resources (such as Nigeria) or with an active and mobilized labor force (such as China) could still grow relatively fast even if its price structure is distorted. With fewer price distortions, however, its growth would be significantly faster.

7 National economic management

Every government has a fundamental responsibility to establish a sound macroeconomic policy framework within which economic agents can function efficiently. It is important that this framework be flexible enough to permit the economy to adjust to external disburbances, that it provide adequate incentives for longer-term growth, and that it permit the attainment of the objectives of equity and social advance.

The macroeconomic policy framework is composed of a series of interlocking policies that affect all aspects of economic behavior. The key elements are fiscal, monetary, exchange rate, wage, and trade policies. They combine in determining the rate of domestic inflation, the rate and pattern of capital accumulation and resource utilization, and the amount of foreign exchange earnings, the maintenance of balance of payments equilibrium and foreign borrowing, and ultimately, the pace of economic activity and growth. There are no simple generalizations about a single set of appropriate policies that will apply to all countries in all circumstances. Similarly, there are no institutional arrangements for managing economic policy that are uniformly suitable. The appropriateness of policies and institutions varies with a country's level of development, size, and natural endowment.

The establishment of planning agencies for formulating comprehensive development strategy represented an important institutional departure in many developing countries. In some countries finance ministries continued to oversee economic policy, primarily through their control of the budget and supervision of the central bank. Both arrangements have their weaknesses. Finance ministries tend to be preoccupied with short-run questions of financial management and pay inadequate attention to long-term development issues. Planning agencies have generally failed to fulfill the high hopes placed in them in the 1950s and 1960s, and have often been limited to assembling public investment programs with only weak links to budgets and policymaking. In most countries, the institutional arrangements do not exist to coordinate short-term financial management with longer-term policy analysis and investment planning, or to respond quickly to changing circumstances.

This chapter reviews the experience of macroeconomic management and draws lessons for the future. It underlines the importance of:

- Policy flexibility to permit adjustment to changing circumstances
- Stabilization efforts that also permit price adjustments that increase efficiency
- Managing the system of incentives rather than formulating comprehensive long-term targets for investment, production, and consumption
- Improving the capacity of public sector entities to formulate sound investment programs, with particular emphasis on appraising major public sector projects
- Consulting and coordinating both within government and with the public
- Concentrating on a few selected policy issues and programs in place of elaborate blueprints
- Improving the provision of information to keep better track of the key economic developments.

Macroeconomic policies and adjustment

The challenge of macroeconomic management is to adjust established policies in light of changing domestic and international economic circumstances. This often requires overcoming vested interests the given policies have created.

In the past few decades developing countries have accumulated considerable experience in macroeconomic policy adjustment. Brazil, Colombia, and the Republic of Korea are among the best-documented examples of countries that undertook sustained programs of stabilization and price adjustment in the 1960s. In all three, realistic and flexible exchange rates were adopted, trade regimes liberalized, exports modified, and interest rates allowed to increase in response to market conditions. In all three, there were significant improvements in export performance, industrial growth, and domestic savings, leading to faster growth in GDP and jobs.

These long-term benefits were not obtained without some short-term costs in a temporary reduction of output and incomes. Experience suggests that the best policy is to avoid as much as possible internal imbalances that require subsequent adjustment. Economies with consistently good growth records in recent years, such as Cameroon and Colombia, have maintained this balance by avoiding large fiscal deficits and rapid monetary expansion. But when imbalances do arise, the sooner they are corrected, the smaller the ultimate costs of adjustment tend to be.

The existence of short-term costs suggests that reforms may need to be gradual, as long as gradualism does not imply timidity or policy reversal on the part of the government. Experience suggests that the costs of stabilization are reduced and the benefits of import liberalization enhanced if external assistance is provided in a timely manner in support of stabilization and liberalization packages.

In the 1970s the developing countries' capacity to manage their economy was tested to the limit. Energy prices surged twice, inflation rose to new peaks and then came down sharply, exchange rates fluctuated widely, and international interest rates were higher for longer than at any time in history. Growth rates in the industrial countries slumped as they faced the most protracted recession in fifty years. The problems of managing in a hostile environment were thus superimposed on the "normal" problems of macroeconomic management.

Policy reform has not proved easy to manage. In the 1970s major changes were initiated in the Southern Cone of Latin America, starting in 1974 in Uruguay, 1975–76 in Chile, and 1976 in Argentina. In the second half of the 1970s, Sri Lanka embarked on a program of adjustment. More recently, Ivory Coast, Jamaica, Kenya, Peru, Philippines, and Turkey have also attempted varying degrees of adjustment. The elements in these programs usually include a lower exchange rate, more export incentives, less industrial protection, tighter monetary policy, higher real interest rates, less direction of credit, higher energy prices, and smaller consumer subsidies. In addition, programs usually try to restrain public sector spending and increase the scope for the private sector and market forces. Similar reform programs in socialist economies are described in Boxes 5.3 and 11.6.

Some of these adjustment programs are of relatively recent origin and it is too early to judge their overall effectiveness. In others the reforms have had an uneasy course. Chile started with widespread distortions and made major changes over a remarkably short period; adjustment was followed by rapid growth in GNP and considerable success in controlling inflation. However, distortions have subsequently reemerged in certain key areas and there has been a rise in unemployment and a weakening in the financial position of many enterprises. In Sri Lanka, GNP, investment, and employment have grown faster since 1977, although the balance of payments and inflation have worsened (see Box 7.1). Turkey's case is particularly interesting; it has achieved rapid growth in exports and has brought inflation down sharply, but has managed only modest growth in private investment and employment. On average, those countries where adjustment led to low price distortions have managed a significantly better growth performance in 1979–82 than have those with high distortions.

Many other countries are now showing interest in adjusting their price structure. For them, the question is not whether to adjust but how. Experience suggests that the process of adjustment has to be managed carefully with regard to timing, pace, and scope. For example, countries have found difficulty in liberalizing trade and financial markets while simultaneously trying to moderate inflation through restrictive monetary and fiscal policies. The benefits of liberalization operate through changes in relative prices, which require new investment and are easier to bring about when economic growth is rapid. The pace of adjustment has also to be tailored to the circumstances of each country—its political resilience, the degree of distortions in its pricing system, and the resources (especially foreign exchange) it has available during adjustment. The Republic of Korea's successful reforms in the early 1960s were bold and were greatly helped by a favorable external environment. Turkey's reforms—less comprehensive and more gradual, though nonetheless radical—were initiated in much more difficult circumstances, yet were largely successful.

The most important lessons from experience are that the transitional problems of adjustment programs can be considerable and that there is no universal prescription for the right path of adjustment. What is required is "pragmatism" and "flexibility"; these terms cannot be defined a priori, but they can be illustrated by the successes of, for

Box 7.1 Liberalization in Sri Lanka

During the three decades after independence in 1947, government intervention in Sri Lanka's economy increased significantly. After twelve years of ad hoc policymaking, a ten-year plan was introduced in 1959 which placed emphasis on import-substituting industrialization. The early 1970s saw a further significant move toward autarky. The authorities established strict controls on trade and payments to maintain an overvalued currency, controlled many domestic prices, and set up several monopolies in the public sector through nationalization and takeovers.

Between 1971 and 1977 almost all parts of the economy either stagnated or grew only slowly. The rate of saving and investment fell significantly, and unemployment rose. Recent government estimates suggest that policy distortions in 1971–77 reduced the GDP growth rate by about two percentage points a year.

In 1977, with the election of a new government, economic strategy was transformed. The government dismantled most trade and payment controls, relied on tariffs to protect domestic industry, and devalued the exchange rate by 44 percent. In 1979 the authorities ended food rationing and introduced a food stamp scheme for the poor. They removed subsidies on rice, wheat, and most petroleum products; abolished most state trading monopolies and encouraged competition from the private sector; raised interest rates to foster private savings and more active financial markets; and gave new incentives to exports and foreign investment.

The liberalization program initially coincided with unusually high commodity prices for Sri Lanka's traditional exports, which helped pay for extra imports. Paddy production also increased at 7 percent a year, so the volume of foodgrain imports fell by 40 percent between 1977–78 and 1981. The economy grew rapidly, with GDP growth doubling from 3.4 percent a year in 1970–77 to 6.6 percent a year in 1978–81. The rate of investment rose from 14 percent of GDP in 1977 to 34 percent in 1980. With migration of labor to the Middle East, economic growth reduced the unemployment rate from 24 percent in 1977 to 15 percent in 1981.

These achievements have not been costless, however. Devaluation and the reduction of consumer subsidies inevitably raised the inflation rate, as measured by the Colombo cost of living index, from 12 percent in 1978 to 26 percent in 1980. The ending of import controls unleashed pent-up demand for imports in an economy starved of both producer and consumer goods. Some local companies failed to compete with cheap imports (often backed by export subsidies or as part of a dumping strategy), so some jobs were lost and output reduced.

Externally, Sri Lanka started to run large current account deficits after 1979. Its terms of trade deteriorated by more than 30 percent between 1977 and 1981. More liberal imports of motor vehicles and other energy-intensive consumer goods increased the oil import bill. Export performance suffered owing to a 30 percent appreciation in the real effective exchange rate between the end of 1978 and the end of 1981. However, the most serious problem was the government's huge investment program coupled with a declining ratio of taxes to GDP. By 1980 budgetary deficits had increased sharply to 23 percent of GDP, and the balance of payments gap widened to unsustainable levels. In 1981 the government introduced measures to reduce the budget and balance of payments deficits. The sheer size of these deficits means that adjustment will take several years to complete.

---

example, Brazil, Japan, and the Republic of Korea (see Boxes 7.2–7.4). To be effective, such a pragmatic and flexible approach in turn requires institutions capable of designing, evaluating, and adjusting key economic policies. Such institutions are generally weak in developing countries; strengthening them should be a high priority in the 1980s.

Economic management and planning

Through their control of the purse strings, finance ministries have traditionally played a preeminent role in economic management. After 1945, however, the establishment of planning agencies represented a major institutional departure in developing countries. These agencies were intended to provide medium- and long-term perspectives on development, supplementing the short-run preoccupations of finance ministries. They are now commonplace in developing countries. A recent World Bank survey of some eighty countries indicated that four out of five have multiyear development plans; over the past ten years, approximately 200 plan documents have been prepared.

In most countries, however, planning agencies have not lived up to expectations. By the late 1960s there was widespread talk of a "crisis" in planning. Even India, which pioneered the introduction of planning in mixed economies, allowed its plan to lapse between 1966 and 1969 and relied solely on annual budgets. In Yugoslavia two successive plans were abandoned in the early 1960s. In Latin America there was wide agreement by the late 1960s that medium-term planning had little influence either on public sector investments or on economic policy; indeed, Mexico, which had the most impressive development record in the

1950s and 1960s, had no medium-term plan. African planners were also mostly ineffective since they were often excluded from decisionmaking.

In the 1970s the relevance of formal plans was further reduced by dislocations in the world economy. Some countries (thirteen out of thirty-four surveyed recently) managed to achieve or exceed their targets in the first half of the 1970s. Nonetheless, developing countries grew increasingly disillusioned about the performance of their central planning agencies and the usefulness of medium-term plans.

Several factors underlie the limited success of plans. At root, there is an inherent weakness in the "blueprint" approach of planning agencies: available analytical techniques are just not able to cope with the complexity of economic change and to produce plans that are up-to-date, relevant, and comprehensive. Even the less ambitious forms of planning have their weaknesses. For example, investment planning based on input-output models has fallen foul of changing technical coefficients and demand patterns. Similarly, manpower forecasting has been highly inaccurate because of the

Box 7.2 Japan: thematic plans and guiding visions

Since the mid-1950s, Japan has had a series of national economic plans. Each focused on one or two themes within the framework of long-range economic analysis and prospects. The plans indicated the direction of economic development and the contribution expected from individual sectors. The process of preparing the plans provided a forum for identifying and discussing future policy needs. It also enabled private industry to consider its problems in a broader perspective.

The quantitative targets set out in the plans were normally conservative, so (until recently) outturns often far exceeded projections. All plans were revised before the end of the period they were intended to cover. This lack of adherence to detailed plan targets was all to the good inasmuch as the underlying objective was to achieve maximum growth. The higher actual growth rate was the result of buoyant private investment, which the government did not try to limit to the plan target. Moreover, ministries and agencies did not regard their plan targets as strictly binding.

Flexibility and responsiveness at both macro- and microlevel were seen as more important than consistency in macroplanning and tight overall coordination. This flexibility extended to the relation between long-term planning and annual budgeting. The annual budgets, as well as public investment and loan plans, were determined by the Ministry of Finance. Annual budgets played an important role in the process of policymaking by determining the size of total expenditure and its allocation among ministries and major expenditure items. The Ministry of Finance played an important role in economic management through its determined pursuit of a balanced budget.

Another agency which played a key role in economic management was the Ministry of International Trade and Industry (MITI). Unlike many countries in the postwar period, Japan did not nationalize its key industries. Nonetheless, in cooperation with the private sector and other government agencies, MITI contributed significantly in guiding industrial development through its strategic planning and authority (both formal and informal) over investment and production priorities. This was true not only in the promotional phase of the 1950s but also in the liberalizing years of the 1960s and the retrenchment of the 1970s. Instead of drawing up "blueprints" for industrial development and allocating resources accordingly, MITI (in the words of one of its senior officials) "tried to arrive at a vision that may serve as a policy target and to persuade and guide industry towards the vision." In creating these "visions" and executing its policies, MITI sought the opinions of various expert groups and businesses.

In the 1950s the emphasis of MITI policies was on the protection of selected industries from imports, export promotion, fiscal and financial incentives, and the development of technology. In the liberalization phase of the 1960s, protection was gradually and selectively reduced. MITI made detailed studies of the effects of liberalization on industry; the least vulnerable industries were those first exposed to foreign competition. For some industries a detailed timetable of liberalization was drawn up, which seems to have stimulated efficiency. MITI tried to realize economies of scale by arranging mergers where it felt that firms were too small to compete internationally, by encouraging firms in the same industry to specialize, and by indicating those firms which needed to modernize their equipment and expand their plants. Steel, computer, and automobile industries are examples of such MITI-inspired reorganization.

Equally interesting and instructive (for both developed and developing countries) was the MITI approach to structural adjustment in response to more expensive energy in the 1970s. Industries that had become uncompetitive (for example, open-hearth and electric-furnace steelmaking, aluminum refining, synthetic fibers, and shipbuilding) were classed as "depressed industries" and included in a special adjustment program. This program set out, for example, steps to reduce excess capacity, the timing of such reductions, and restrictions on further expansion. Where necessary, the industries were allowed to establish arrangements to maintain orderly markets under the condition of excess supply and were given government financial support to facilitate structural adjustment.

Box 7.3 The Republic of Korea: flexible policies and strong planning

Between the early 1960s and the late 1970s, the Republic of Korea made remarkable economic progress. GNP grew by 10 percent a year, per capita income more than tripled in real terms, and the number of people with incomes below the poverty line fell from about 40 percent of the population to about 10 percent. Among the key factors that contributed to this success were a strong and stable government, single-minded attention to economic growth, a disciplined and socially mobile population, a favorable world environment, and flexible and pragmatic economic policies orchestrated by a central economic authority.

The Economic Planning Board (EPB) was established in 1961, incorporating the Bureau of Budget (transferred from the Ministry of Finance) and the Bureau of Statistics. The EPB was later made responsible for price policy, fair trade administration, project appraisal, and the monitoring and evaluation of project performance. It thus became a "super ministry" overseen by the deputy prime minister, its status indicating the seriousness of the planning effort in the Republic of Korea. The EPB was able to coordinate policies and control conflicts between different economic ministries. Its work was supported by units in each operating ministry that were responsible for both development planning and budgeting.

The government of the Republic of Korea also drew on the views of experts from bodies outside the government, such as industrial associations, financial institutions, research institutes, and universities. They belonged to a number of working groups contributing to the country's economic plan, which in turn reported to the

Deliberation Committee chaired by the prime minister. The Korea Development Institute, which works in close collaboration with EPB, was also a channel through which outsiders contributed advice; it became the research arm of the government for economic policies.

Despite such thorough preparation, the plans were not remarkable for their technical sophistication. Nor were they regarded as sacrosanct: each of the four plans produced since the early 1960s was drastically revised soon after its inception. Individual policies were also changed as circumstances changed. For instance, in 1982 almost 1,000 laws or regulations were either enacted or amended, and about 10 percent of them were revised more than twice in the same year.

The distinguishing characteristic of the Republic of Korea's planning has been the strong emphasis on implementing investment decisions by means of:

• Annual plans. The annual Economic Management Plan is intended to review and evaluate performance in the preceding year and, if necessary, revise policy directions and the list of projects to be implemented. It also reassesses macroeconomic forecasts in the light of changing conditions. It provides guidelines for the government's annual budget and is expected to indicate the stance of government policy toward the private sector.

• The integration of plans into budgets. Responsibility for drawing up the budget rests with the EPB, especially its Bureau of the Budget. In view of growing economic uncertainty and fiscal stringency, the government has recently started some medium-term fiscal plan-

ning so that the budget for a single year may be formulated on realistic assumptions about the availability of resources in future years.

• Monitoring and evaluation. Each responsible government agency is required to monitor the progress of all projects included in the annual plan. The EPB conducts a quarterly evaluation of how the plan is implemented and provides a summary of the results to the president. The EPB is also responsible for consolidating the results of the performance evaluations, including recommended changes in problem projects, and submits a report to the cabinet twice a year.

Central to the Republic of Korea's success was its export promotion policy. Exports were encouraged mainly by incentives, but the way those incentives were determined and then made available was far from automatic. Two institutional mechanisms that were important in the country's export drive were the system of setting export targets and the practice of holding monthly national trade-promotion meetings. These two mechanisms helped translate political resolve into bureaucratic and corporate resolve. They also provided up-to-date information on export performance by firm, product, and market and enabled the government to analyze the reasons for any discrepancies between targets and performance. The government then adjusted its export incentives and targets accordingly. Firms, meanwhile, were kept informed of the government's shifting priorities and policies. More recently export targets are treated more as forecasts than as policy objectives, and the government is emphasizing the liberalization of trade and finance.

---

difficulties of specifying particular skills and of projecting demand over a long period. Moreover, by the nature of their job, many planners have tended to favor big public sector projects and ambitious targets. This bias, sometimes encouraged by foreign aid agencies, has seldom produced the most efficient use of resources.

While the products of planning agencies—the plans themselves—have frequently been ignored,

the process of planning has been useful. It has provided a forum for bringing together different government agencies and different sections of society to think about national development, and it has helped politicians to mobilize public support for development programs. These are considerable virtues. It is now necessary to build on them, so that in the uncertain economic environment of the 1980s the agencies involved in national economic management can work together in a more coordinated and systematic way.

Managing in uncertain times

Given the current uncertainties, comprehensive planning intent on managing quantities (of production and investment) over the medium to long term will be increasingly inappropriate. Instead, emphasis should be put on rationalizing the current policy framework. First and foremost, governments must ensure macroeconomic stability through sound monetary, fiscal, and exchange rate policies.

Within such a framework of macroeconomic stability, it is necessary to correct price distortions in order to provide an environment for the best possible use of resources. Such reorientation—affecting many aspects of policy, from medium-term investment planning to the incentive system—is already taking place in several countries. In the Republic of Korea, for example, the latest plan puts most weight on changing incentives and treats projections for investment and output more as background scenarios to aid decisionmaking than as targets. In both India and Pakistan recent plans give much greater attention than before to prices and incentives.

While attempts to plan overall national investment have generally proved futile, governments clearly need a strong capacity for appraising public investment programs. In many countries the efficiency of public investment would increase significantly if, as a minimum, large projects were carefully vetted. In addition, it is important to aggregate all public sector projects to discover their

Box 7.4 Brazil: flexibility and pragmatism in managing industrialization

Between 1950 and 1980 Brazilian manufacturing grew at an average of almost 10 percent a year, with GNP growth of about 7 percent a year. During this period, per capita income (in 1980 dollars) increased from about $600 to more than $2,000 and, despite continuing problems of poverty in some regions, the overall incidence of poverty declined significantly.

Industrialization was clearly the goal of Brazil's development strategy, although priorities were not set in any systematic or detailed way. Growth followed a typical, and in some sense natural, sequence: first came import substitution of consumer nondurables and then consumer durables; intermediate goods and capital goods followed. The pattern of protection was adjusted flexibly and gradually. Whereas in the 1960s the protection rate was high for consumer goods, medium for intermediate goods, and low for capital goods, by the early 1980s this pattern had been fully reversed.

Brazil's style of growth did not, of course, occur accidentally. Government decisions about exchange rates, tariffs and other import controls, public investments, investment subsidies, and export incentives strongly influenced the allocation of resources. The basic logic followed until the mid-1960s by both private investors and public officials was import substitution: anything imported was potentially a candidate for domestic production. Beyond this, public officials had some ideas about priorities to be given to some sectors, especially in steel, automobiles, and petrochemicals. But indirect promotional policies—such as trade protection and fiscal and credit subsidies—owed their design at least as much to the entrepreneurs who stood to gain or lose from them as to the public officials' view of what was "best" or "efficient" for the nation. Indeed, one reason for the "miracle" growth in the late 1960s and early 1970s was precisely that government listened to the private sector and largely accommodated its wishes.

Consultation and consensus also prevailed during the 1950s, notably in the "Executive Groups" formed to promote growth in five industrial sectors. These groups, made up of senior officials from all relevant agencies, negotiated with private investors to achieve a package that gave the government what it wanted in terms of import substitution, domestic procurement of inputs, and so forth, but that also gave the investors what they needed to be profitable. The government negotiated hard, but the policy package was designed jointly. The automobile industry, one of the five, is a classic example. Costs were high at first, but by the late 1960s at least one firm was producing at internationally competitive costs—perhaps the only one in any developing country at that time. Since then costs and prices have come down in other firms, and today the industry produces competitively and exports a large part of its output.

In the mid-1960s, when the initial phase of import substitution was largely completed, Brazil switched to an export-oriented strategy with major adjustments in its real exchange rate and in financial policy. This was followed by a boom in exports and economic growth that lasted nearly a decade. Since the mid-1970s the government has expanded its share of industry and played a bigger role in the choice of new investment. It has promoted a new wave of import substitution in the few activities where this remained possible. Some sectors (such as steel) may have been overexpanded, and many of the new industries (such as sophisticated machine tools and computers) have complex and rapidly evolving technology; being capital goods, their cost and quality will affect the whole economy. Whether these new activities will become internationally competitive remains to be seen.

implications for financial management over several years. Together, public sector projects can change some basic parameters in the economy and affect the implementation and viability of otherwise sound projects.

Experience during the 1970s has shown that even the most carefully designed policies and investment programs can be confounded by changes in the world economy. In addition, limited knowledge about how quickly economies adjust to policy changes means that rigid adherence to policy prescriptions can be hazardous: Chile has provided an example of this danger. The failure to adjust investment programs to reduced resources has also been costly in countries such as Turkey, Mexico, Yugoslavia, and Venezuela. Governments therefore need to be much more flexible in their policies and programs. To be both flexible and successful, they require better facilities for obtaining and analyzing information on the effect of their policies and programs.

To design adjustment policies and programs, consultation and coordination between policymakers and interest groups is essential. The examples of Brazil, Japan, and the Republic of Korea show that consultation and coordination among different agencies within government and between government and the private sector can provide practically sounder, if analytically less articulate, policies and programs.

For the purposes of sectoral coordination, central ministries—such as finance and planning or any other central coordinating body—need to agree on clear guidelines for such ministries as agriculture, industry, and energy, and then act as a clearinghouse for contacts between them. Similarly, while proposals for policy issues such as agricultural prices, or exchange rates, or interest rates originate in the responsible ministries, some central agency should analyze the links and present political leaders with well-evaluated options on which to base decisions. Governments have found considerable merit in involving academics and businessmen in policy discussions. Their participation, usually through committees, working groups, and conferences, improves official awareness and helps build a consensus on the means and ends of national development. Development research institutes (such as the Korea Development Institute) can provide forums for government and outsiders to exchange ideas.

Combining flexibility with consultation and coordination is not easy: consultation is time-consuming, flexibility implies a quick response. To reconcile these requirements, governments need to be selective in the goals and key instruments they emphasize. In Japan both the national plans and "visions" of the Ministry of International Trade and Industry concentrated on selected themes. In the Republic of Korea export promotion became a focal point for the development effort. In Bangladesh planning was improved when it was directed at such important issues as increasing food production. In Malaysia improvement in the distribution of income and wealth between Malays and non-Malays has been the central theme for the past ten years. In mineral-based economies such as Botswana, planning has focused on converting mineral wealth into human and physical capital, while minimizing the adverse side effects on the rest of the economy.

One way to combine flexibility with consultation is to assign responsibility for coordination to a central authority. In the Republic of Korea planning, budgeting, and policy functions have been integrated under a deputy prime minister, who is also the chairman of a policy committee consisting of various economic ministries. In Brazil and Japan the finance and industry ministries have played an active part in coordinating policies. In Hungary that role has been assumed by an economic policy committee. In both India and Pakistan policy review capacity has recently been strengthened in the planning agencies and in the offices of the prime minister and the president. Although the specific arrangements depend on the circumstances of each country, an authoritative coordinating agency is clearly desirable. Particular attention must always be given to establishing arrangements that successfully integrate planning, budgeting, and performance evaluation.

Improving links between planning, budgeting, and evaluation

In discussions of development planning methods over the past thirty years, the need to strengthen links between budgets and plans has been a constant theme—to little avail. Only one developing country in ten has any system of multiyear budgeting, which is essential if multiyear plans are to be integrated with budgets.

Financial planning and budgeting

While planning agencies have often been preoccupied with the allocation of national resources, they tend to pay too little attention to the availability of these resources and the financing needs of different tiers of government and of state-owned enterprises. Examples abound of public expenditure being out of control because the central authorities have not been aware of the spending programs of different public agencies. Several countries, particularly large federal states such as India and Brazil, are now increasing their efforts to obtain a complete picture of the public sector's financial position.

Planning agencies have also tended to concentrate on new projects rather than on completing half-finished projects and financing the maintenance needs of completed ones. In six out of ten of the World Bank's borrowers in the early 1980s, this bias has assumed serious proportions. In several countries many projects are not being completed because of insufficient funds. This problem can be minimized if, after budgeting for the legitimate needs of existing and completed projects, the amount of "free resources" is calculated systematically before new projects are approved. Botswana's National Development Plan contains projections of the recurrent budget costs arising from each project in the public investment program. These are consolidated into revenue and spending projections for the next three years, which are periodically updated and rolled forward.

To cope with budgetary shortages and uncertainties, finance ministries in many countries have tended to release money only on a monthly or quarterly basis. This has made it difficult for ministries and project managers to plan their operations even a year ahead. Finance ministries have also resorted to across-the-board cuts, which hit high-priority projects as hard as any others. To minimize this damage, some countries have found it useful to identify a "core investment program" that has priority for funding in case of cuts. Even with such provision, however, countries in both the developed and developing world need to revise their investment programs regularly. For most, a three-year horizon is the longest that is practicable, with programs being rolled over each year. With the advent of minicomputers, data processing has opened up new possibilities for consolidating and revising budgetary programs.

Evaluating expenditure

In the past, governments have put too little emphasis on getting value for money from public expenditure. Traditional audits have largely been confined to examining whether the money was spent as authorized. Since the mid-1960s, however, following the program budgeting approach pioneered in the United States, several developing countries have tried to employ concepts and procedures for evaluating the results of public spending. Only slow and intermittent progress has been made. The output of many government services is not clearly definable, let alone measurable. Nor is it easy to evaluate the performance of an individual agency in programs which involve several agencies. And comprehensive evaluation generally takes so long that governments cannot wait for results before deciding whether more money should be spent in the same way. A more promising procedure, adopted in several countries, is selectively to track and evaluate outputs of programs that have a significant influence on the budget (see Box 7.5). In place of annual pro forma "checking," evaluators undertake a thorough investigation of a service or program. The results are then made the basis for efforts to improve performance.

Improving management information

A good information system is essential for all aspects of economic management. Systematic adjustments in policies and programs, necessary in a fast-changing world, are not possible without reliable monitoring of current developments. As a rule, better information—especially about key performance indicators—brings bigger dividends for economic management than do sophisticated techniques of long-term forecasting. Although senior officials may readily agree on the need to improve statistics, genuine commitment (as evidenced by the provision of adequate resources) and sustained efforts are often lacking.

Costs of poor data

The problems of planning without facts have been well documented in Africa, but they are serious in many other countries as well. Lacking sectoral statistics, governments have not been able to address sectoral issues. This proved particularly damaging when oil prices rose sharply in the 1970s, because few developing countries had the data they needed to reassess their energy requirements and to develop conservation programs. For years the lack of good agricultural statistics has seriously handicapped the analysis of agricultural development programs and the formulation of policies. And the whole world has now learned of the dangers of ignorance about a country's financial position. In several countries—notably Indonesia, Mexico, and Turkey—the external debt crisis was compounded by the lack of comprehensive data,

Box 7.5 Government watchdogs: tracking bureaucratic effectiveness

From Russia's inspectors general to the United States' Government Accounting Office, watchdogs have long been appointed to help keep governments honest. Many countries are now emphasizing efficiency as well. Since 1977 Canada has required that federal agencies and departments undertake periodic appraisals of their own efficiency in administering programs and their effectiveness in meeting objectives. In 1978 Malaysia added a unit charged with improving management systems and civil service operations to the already strong project monitoring team in its prime minister's office.

Two other examples, in more detail, are:

• Value-for-money audits in the United Kingdom. A 1982 government report noted that, over a period of three years, the audits had saved $850 million in wages, boosted tax collections by more than $40 million, and reduced social security operating costs by 6 percent. The audits involve rigorous three- to six-month scrutinies carried out by examining officers drawn from the management of the office being investigated. "Ministers and their officials are better equipped than anyone else to examine the use of resources for which they are responsible," said a 1981 note on the program. "The scrutinies, therefore, rely heavily on self-examination; on applying a fresh mind to the policy or activity under scrutiny, unfettered by committee or hierarchy."

A staff of nine in the Management and Personnel Office helps set the ground rules for individual scrutinies, then turns over the task of carrying them out to the examining officers. Each scrutiny is expected to lead to an action document within three months; these show the examining officers' recommendations, the minister's response, the legislative and administrative actions needed for implementation, target dates, and expected savings in money and manpower. They also name the officials responsible for carrying out the recommended reforms.

The government has been impressed enough with the 135 scrutinies so far to extend the system throughout the government. Every department is now required to draw up a financial management plan to aid it in answering the question "Where is the money going and what are we getting for it?" Each must also develop a management information system to track its costs. To involve civil servants in the spirit of reform and "guard against a failure of morale," staff are to be more involved in decisionmaking. Part of the anticipated savings is to be used to "enhance the working environment," and staff-management communications are to be improved, all with the goal of helping the civil service to "sustain its sense of pride in a job worth doing well."

• Program evaluation in India. The Programme Evaluation Organization (PEO) was created to oversee India's Community Development Programme. Its success led to its investigating programs of education, health, rural development, and social welfare. PEO became one of the world's largest evaluation organizations, with more than 200 professional staff and a network of thirty-four field offices. Local evaluation offices have also been established in India's twenty-two states.

PEO is an independent branch of the Planning Commission. It reports to Parliament and provides the Planning Commission with information for forward planning and mid-course revisions to programs. Most PEO reports are made public; their findings are debated in the media and in Parliament. The atmosphere of accountability that PEO has created has encouraged the government to take quick corrective action on program shortcomings. At the project level, the feedback provided by PEO has come to be appreciated rather than feared.

PEO's working methods have changed considerably since the days it limited itself to evaluating completed agriculture and rural development projects. Now it combines sophisticated data gathering and analysis with surveys of intended beneficiaries, particularly those from minority groups. It has developed a training program including courses in cost-benefit analysis, performance budgeting, and statistical sampling and interviewing techniques. Regular regional workshops for senior and supervisory staff have become an important forum for teaching techniques and sharing experiences. PEO programs have also been used to train evaluators from Egypt, Philippines, Nigeria, Malaysia, and Nepal.

---

especially on private debt (which had been growing rapidly). Finally, at the project level, the absence of effective monitoring and evaluation procedures has hampered mid-course correction, and made it difficult to feed back information helpful in the design of future projects.

Benefits of good data

The rewards of a better information system are illustrated by the experience of several countries such as Kenya, Bangladesh, India, and the Republic of Korea. The export-oriented strategy of the Republic of Korea was greatly aided by com-

prehensive and up-to-date statistics on foreign trade. Kenya, through its rural household surveys, gathered estimates of food production and prepared crop forecasts that proved invaluable in the drought of the late 1970s. The authorities were able to act quickly in organizing transport and distribution of supplies to the drought-stricken areas. By contrast, the countries of the Sahel region had poor or nonexistent information on food production, which made it difficult to organize effective drought-relief operations in the 1970s. Improved data on food supplies helped Bangladesh tackle food shortages in 1979 much better than it had done in 1974. And in India the recent centralization of information on movements of railway wagons has helped improve the railways' efficiency, with spin-off benefits for such industries as coal and fertilizers.

Statistical priorities

Since it is expensive to collect information, governments must set themselves clear priorities. This task can be assisted by a medium-term plan for statistical development, as the Malaysian experience has shown. Such plans identify not only what figures are required, but also what is needed to collect them—equipment, manpower, office accommodation, and so on. In many countries, priorities include financial statistics, covering both external debt and government receipts and spending. In several countries, however, even the basic components of the national income accounts and balance of payments are absent or unreliable; as a rule, these should receive priority.

To assist flexible policymaking, governments need to make more use of sample surveys and administrative records. Well-planned and well-designed sample surveys are relatively cheap in comparison to censuses, impose a smaller burden on the statistical office, and can produce thorough and up-to-date information. Kenya has made wide use of such surveys; its Central Bureau of Statistics is now able to provide better historical data as well as current statistics for short-term policymaking, particularly dealing with food and agriculture.

The administrative records of government agencies can also provide valuable information. Although they have weaknesses, administrative records are an inexpensive source of data. The records of different agencies can often be linked in useful ways: in Malaysia, for example, information on family planning acceptors has been combined with records on births to indicate the impact of the family planning program. The usefulness of administrative records can be enhanced if statistical agencies are consulted in the design of administrative forms and the development of appropriate classifications and codes.

All three themes developed in this chapter—coordination of planning efforts, reforms of budgetary systems, and monitoring of projects—entail the processing of large quantities of data. They are therefore all greatly helped by recent advances in microcomputers and associated software (see Box 7.6). Being relatively cheap, portable, resilient, and easy to operate, microcomputers are suitable for work in rural areas and for middle and junior managers who have no special programming skills. However, their full exploitation does depend on accounting systems being rationalized and on the development of appropriate indicators for program monitoring. Both of these changes initially require a substantial investment of skills and time.

Box 7.6   The management information revolution

The value of microcomputers in processing information is well illustrated by their use in Nigeria and Kenya. In Nigeria microcomputers are now handling data from farm management surveys on nine agricultural projects, three of which cover entire states. The first computer was introduced in August 1981 and was in operation two months later. By June 1982 seventeen machines were in use, with another eleven on order. Field staff needed only two weeks' training in operation and preventive maintenance. They now enter data directly onto computer files, so avoiding the need to code and cardpunch large numbers of survey forms for later analysis. Managers now obtain reports within a month of survey completion and they can handle large quantities of data bunched at peak seasons.

Kenya's Ministry of Agriculture adopted microcomputers in 1981 to improve its annual budgeting process. Until then, spending estimates sent to the Finance Ministry were simply the sum of the estimates proposed by operating divisions. Sometimes they amounted to double the previous year's spending on agriculture and twice the likely amount available from the Treasury. As a result, the Finance Ministry was effectively in charge of deciding agricultural priorities. Microcomputers have helped the Ministry of Agriculture regain control of its own budget through:

• Improved management information. With a simplified reporting format, showing budgets, commitments, and spending for different subheads on a series of single summary sheets, the ministry can now calculate expenditure returns within two days of receiving the raw data.

• Clearer ranking of priorities. As with expenditure reports, the ministry has developed a printout format that reduces the annual budget documents from 100 stenciled pages to only 5 pages of summary information. Where budget shortfalls are identified, the computer projects the results of alternative budget cutbacks. When officials decide to reduce spending on a particular activity, the printout immediately summarizes the corresponding reduction in the overall budget deficit, and shows the average percentage cut needed on other activities in order to stay within Treasury ceilings. This kind of control has been made possible by up-to-date expenditure reports, since any requests for more money could immediately be compared with recent performance and inflated requests adjusted accordingly.

8   Managing state-owned enterprises

In all countries—developing and developed, market and socialist—governments are showing increasing concern over the performance of their state-owned enterprises (SOEs). One reason is that SOEs make large and growing claims on the budget. In a sample of twenty-seven developing countries in 1976–79, the net budgetary payment to nonfinancial SOEs averaged more than 3 percent of GDP. Current spending alone—subsidies and other transfers—represented 1.4 percent of GDP. State enterprises are also important foreign borrowers; nonfinancial SOEs accounted for 28 percent of all Eurocurrency borrowing by developing countries in 1980.

Governments, intent on curbing SOE borrowing and getting value for the money they spend, are searching for ways to improve SOE efficiency. In theory, efficiency is highest when an enterprise strives to maximize profits in a competitive market, under managers with the autonomy, motivation, and capability to respond to the challenge of competition. Inefficient enterprises would not be able to compete and would go bankrupt. But SOEs seldom face such conditions. Governments may have established SOEs for reasons quite different from—and often incompatible with—profit maximization. SOEs often operate in noncompetitive markets; the absence of competition is one reason for creating them. Their autonomy is often compromised by government intervention in their operating decisions. Managers may not be held accountable for results or given incentives to improve performance. The way they are selected and rewarded often encourages qualities more appropriate to a central bureaucracy than to a competitive enterprise. Even nonviable SOEs are seldom liquidated.

These special constraints on SOEs need not become an excuse for poor performance. Efficiency can be greatly enhanced by setting clear and attainable objectives, reducing undue interference, holding management accountable for results, designing a framework of incentives, and developing a team of managers with appropriate skills. These are the main topics of this chapter, which ends with a review of the issues involved in liquidating and privatizing SOEs.

The growing fiscal burden

Accounting deficiencies and different ways of classifying SOEs make it difficult to generalize about their financial performance or to assess the return to capital. Available data for SOEs in twenty-four developing countries showed a small operating surplus before depreciation in 1977. However, no account was taken of interest payments, subsidized input prices, taxes, or accumulated arrears. Proper provision for these items and depreciation would show SOEs in many of these countries to be in deficit.

Since SOEs often control some of the largest revenue-earning activities (petroleum and mining, for example), their poor aggregate performance is especially disturbing. Evidence from individual countries indicates low and declining profitability. For example, Turkish public enterprises, which were breaking even in the early 1970s, averaged net losses equivalent to 3.9 percent of GDP during 1977–79. Subsequent policy measures resulted in a profit of 0.1 percent of GDP in 1981 and an estimated 0.5 percent in 1982. Mexican SOEs (excluding the state petroleum company), which earned profits equivalent to 0.3 percent of GDP in 1970, showed a net loss of 1.2 percent of GDP in 1980. Senegal's SOEs, which had been in surplus in the mid-1970s, recorded a deficit in 1977–78 and again in 1979–80, and the number of money-losing companies reached forty-two (out of sixty-eight in 1980). The picture is not entirely black; in India, for example, the gross pretax return on capital employed grew from 7.8 percent (before interest payments) in 1980–81 to 12.2 percent in 1981–82. Low profitability limits the ability of SOEs to self-finance their investments, increasing their dependence on central government resources. Figure

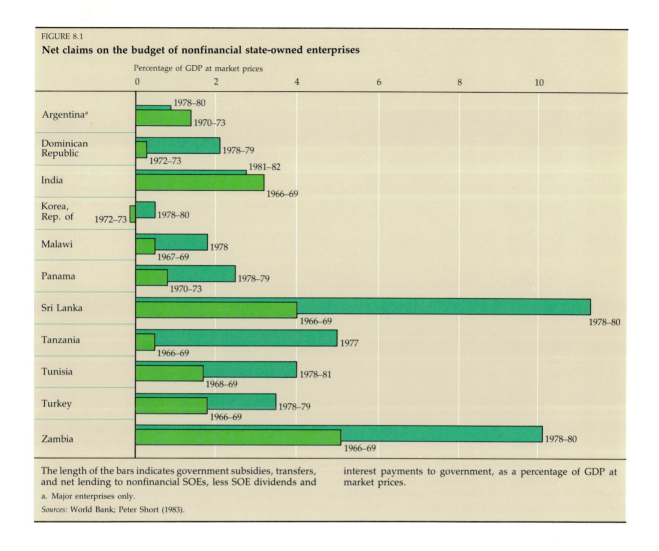

FIGURE 8.1

Net claims on the budget of nonfinancial state-owned enterprises

Percentage of GDP at market prices

The length of the bars indicates government subsidies, transfers, and net lending to nonfinancial SOEs, less SOE dividends and interest payments to government, as a percentage of GDP at market prices.

a. Major enterprises only.

Sources: World Bank; Peter Short (1983).

8.1 shows how the net claims on the budget have grown for a sample of twelve developing countries. These figures include legitimate and desirable equity investments by government, of course, but they also reflect the limited ability of SOEs to generate internal resources.

In an aggregate analysis it is impossible to determine the extent to which these results reflect general economic conditions or price controls and how much they are caused by a failure to minimize costs or maximize productivity. Evidence from individual enterprises indicates substantial room for efficiency gains. A modest improvement in efficiency could have significant effect. For example, a 5 percent increase in SOE revenues plus a 5 percent drop in costs would generate resources amounting to:

• Almost 2 percent of GDP in Turkey, or 10 percent of tax revenues
• Some 1.5 percent of GDP in Tanzania, enough to finance all its spending on health

• As much as 2.2 percent of GDP in Mali—roughly two-thirds of expenditure on education or twice that on health
• Some 1.4 percent of GDP in Bolivia—14 percent of tax revenue or one and a half times the spending on health.

The nature of SOEs

The term "state-owned enterprise" covers all state-owned industrial and commercial firms, mines, utilities, and transport companies, as well as financial intermediaries. The number of SOEs has been on the rise in most countries. Figure 8.2 shows the increase in a sample of eight countries. SOEs are distinguished from the rest of the government because their revenue comes from the sale of goods and services and because they are self-accounting and have a separate legal identity. Beyond that, their circumstances and characteristics may appear to vary widely. A state enterprise might be op-

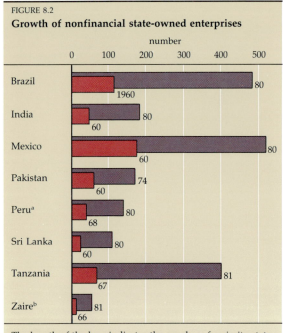

FIGURE 8.2
Growth of nonfinancial state-owned enterprises

number

The length of the bars indicates the number of majority state-owned enterprises in selected countries for specific years. Local government SOEs are not included.

a. Includes minority shareholdings.
b. 100 percent state-owned enterprises only.

lems of SOEs and suggest ways of tackling them. Of course, suggestions have to be tailored to the characteristics of individual firms and countries. A government's approach toward a manufacturing SOE selling in competitive export markets will differ from its treatment of a large, natural monopoly. The former might be required to maximize profits; the latter's prices might be set according to its marginal cost or it might be required to minimize costs. Similarly, the options of countries will vary. In some countries it might be possible to fire poor SOE managers and replace them with better ones. A country with less managerial talent might have no alternative but to try and improve the skills of its less capable managers.

Defining objectives

One of the most important and difficult tasks for governments is to clarify and rank the objectives of their SOEs. Where state enterprises are expected to pursue both commercial and social goals and to answer to many different constituencies, their performance will suffer unless they are given a clear sense of priorities. Without that, their results cannot be measured against expectations, while losses can be too easily attributed to social goals, and poor management thereby concealed.

The cost of noneconomic goals

SOEs are frequently expected to contribute to the broader goals of government policy. The consequences can be perverse, as illustrated by the experience of the Ghana Cocoa Marketing Board (see Box 8.1). For instance, SOE prices may be controlled in order to benefit the poor or to assist counterinflationary policies. But SOE consumers are often large industrial users or wealthy people, so they—not the poor—benefit most. For instance, energy and food subsidies in Egypt in 1979 amounted to more than $4 billion; three-quarters of the subsidies went to the relatively more affluent urban areas and 62 percent of these went to the richer half of the urban population. Furthermore, the costs of subsidies are shifted from the consumer to the taxpayer or, if the deficit is financed through inflationary monetary expansion, to the public at large. Given the regressive nature of taxes in many developing countries and the impact of inflation on the poor, the net result may be to increase income inequalities.

erating in a command economy surrounded by other SOEs, or it may be one of a handful of state firms in a predominantly free market.

In practice, however, SOEs share many qualities. Most economies are a mixture of markets and central controls, and whatever the mixture, the problems of trying to ensure SOE efficiency are strikingly similar. Conflicting objectives, insufficient SOE autonomy, inadequate measures for judging performance, lack of incentives linked to performance, and bureaucratic rather than commercial management styles—all these have prompted attempts at reform in socialist and market economies alike. When such reforms fail, the consequences are also similar. Every economy finds that financial weaknesses in SOEs are transmitted to other public and private firms. They suffer if SOEs command financial resources to which others might ordinarily be entitled, or if they fail to supply promised goods or services.

Increased SOE efficiency typically requires internal improvements—better financial management, more careful inventory control, and a balanced production line, for example. But these reforms will not solve the wider problems of relations between SOEs and government. This chapter will concentrate on these common prob-

Box 8.1 Conflicting objectives: the Ghana Cocoa Marketing Board

Agricultural marketing boards are often subject to conflicting economic and social objectives. Those principally concerned with the domestic market for basic food-stuffs are expected to shield consumers (mostly urban) from scarcities and high food prices while simultaneously protecting farmers' incomes. Boards that deal mainly with export crops are expected both to raise fiscal revenues and to insulate farmers from fluctuations in world prices. Experience in Ghana illustrates what can happen when one conflicting objective becomes dominant.

The Ghana Cocoa Marketing Board (CMB) was established in 1947, following pressures from farmers to eliminate middlemen and traders. Initially CMB's stated objective was to market and export cocoa and to stimulate the activities of smallholders. After ten years of operation, however, CMB's governing legislation had been amended by two other objectives: to protect farmers from extreme fluctuations in world cocoa prices and to tax export earnings. The revenue objec-

tive finally prevailed over the other goals. Producer prices were initially set to cover the board's development and operating costs and to allow it to accumulate reserves. However, the need for government revenues soon predominated: after 1965, the board was no longer permitted to hold reserves. The government's share of sales revenues increased from 3 percent in 1947–48 to almost 30 percent after 1953–54 and reached 60 percent in 1978–79. CMB's share of revenues was set to cover operating costs and rarely exceeded 20 percent; farmers' earnings became a residual.

As a result of this policy and of the overvalued exchange rate, the price received by Ghanaian cocoa farmers has been declining in real terms since the early 1960s. By 1979 producer prices averaged about half their 1963 level, even after taking account of subsidies on seeds and other inputs. Furthermore, the CMB was unable to protect farmers from sharp price fluctuations. The prices they were paid fell by 30 percent in 1949–50, by 17

percent in 1959–60, and by 34 percent in 1965–66.

As cocoa has become less profitable, Ghana's production has plummeted— from a peak of about 540,000 tons in 1965 to about 250,000 tons in 1979. The volume of exports has fallen by almost 80 percent over the same period. An estimated 45,000 tons a year has been smuggled to neighboring countries, a foreign exchange loss equivalent to about 15 percent of the average value of Ghana's exports in 1974–78. By 1979 Ghana had lost its rank as first world producer and exporter of cocoa, which it had held since the early 1960s. Many farmers have switched to other crops, such as maize and rice, which in Ghana yield a net return per hectare about twice that of cocoa. But this switching still involves heavy losses for the country. If farmers were to receive even half the world price for cocoa and no input subsidies, their net return per hectare (at 1979 prices) would be more than seven times that of rice and more than fifty times that of maize.

Similarly, SOEs are often used to expand employment. The excessive wage bills that result can seriously damage an SOE's financial performance while overmanning can be bad for morale. Since SOEs are usually capital-intensive, they can make only a limited contribution to alleviating unemployment. In a survey of seventeen developing countries in 1982, nonfinancial SOEs were responsible for less than 15 percent of modern sector employment, ranging from a low of 5.5 percent in Latin America to a high of 20.4 percent in Africa.

Where noncommercial achievements are expected of SOEs, a government can judge the net gain (or loss) to society only by making these goals explicit and by calculating their costs and benefits. But a strong case can be made for letting an enterprise operate on commercial, profit-seeking lines, and then using its profits to achieve social goals. The profits of an SOE could then be invested to generate new growth and jobs, rather than siphoned into paying the wages of redundant workers. A commercially oriented SOE can be a most effective tool for improving social welfare, as exemplified by the experience of the Kenya Tea Development Authority (KTDA—see Box 8.2).

Setting objectives

In practice it is hard to define targets for SOEs by an assessment of costs and benefits. Often there are strong political motives for keeping objectives fuzzy and not analyzing trade-offs. But since noneconomic goals are frequently given as a reason for poor performance, governments should at least view this excuse with skepticism and require SOE managers to document the financial effects of having to meet such goals.

Some governments have gone further. France and Senegal, for example, have negotiated formal agreements with SOEs to establish a clearer operating framework (see Box 8.3). Under such arrangements, governments pledge to meet their financial obligations and to eschew ad hoc interference; for their part, SOEs accept negotiated performance targets. The agreements help both parties to translate vague intentions into specific tasks. Contracts also make the costs of achieving objectives more transparent, thus allowing a more rational consideration of costs and benefits. Their success rests on substantial political commitment—as well as a readiness of both parties to

Box 8.2 Autonomy, accountability, and incentives: KTDA

The Kenya Tea Development Authority (KTDA) was created as a state-owned enterprise in the early 1960s. It has organized the planting of about 54,000 hectares of tea by some 138,000 smallholders, and has become a major processor and the world's largest exporter of black tea. Thanks to its commercial orientation, KTDA developed an industry that substantially benefits the 1 million members of tea-grower households plus untold numbers of laborers, traders, and others in the economically vibrant tea districts. KTDA achieved these results without operating subsidies, in marked contrast to the generally poor results of smallholder tea schemes in South Asia or elsewhere in East Africa. Its success has had three ingredients:

• Autonomy. KTDA was set up to be a commercial enterprise and was not given many secondary social responsibilities. It has never been financially dependent on the government. Its start-up and development costs were financed largely by external borrowing. Its operating costs are covered by a flat-rate levy deducted from the monthly "first payment" to farmers. (Growers receive a fixed payment per kilogram every month and a second payment based on market prices at the end of each season.) Although the levy has not changed for the past ten years, KTDA has avoided government subsidies by keeping down costs. Good performance and support from growers helped secure independence.

From the outset KTDA had control over all strategic aspects of tea production: credit, extension, propagation, transport, processing, and marketing. With such authority KTDA could tightly control the quality of the tea—often a weakness of smallholder production. KTDA has also moved into factory operations and thus controlled the quality of processed tea.

• Accountability. Since KTDA's objectives were clearly defined, the government was able to develop a set of standards against which its performance could be evaluated. Through its representative on the board, the government holds KTDA responsible for results. Added to this, the tea growers sit on district tea committees and are represented on KTDA's board. Some are also shareholders in KTDA factories or members of factory boards. The growers play an important role since they have strong personal incentives to hold the Authority to high standards. Similarly, KTDA's factory managers, workers, and field staff are held accountable for results by their supervisors; their performance is monitored and evaluated against predetermined standards.

• Incentives. The basic set of incentives for both growers and KTDA is provided by world market prices. KTDA has not tried to insulate itself from that market by building up large reserves (or running deficits). Sustained market pressure is thus used to enhance the drive for premium tea production by demonstrating the direct link between quality and returns.

In recent years KTDA has become vulnerable to the falling trend in world tea prices. Its finances have also been threatened by a drop in output because of drought and some shift by growers to higher-income crops. Furthermore, KTDA is moving from a phase of rapid expansion to one of consolidating its gains, a transition that has been difficult for both public and private enterprises throughout the world.

---

renegotiate if the contracts are threatened by unforeseen economic developments.

Control without interference

SOE autonomy needs to be counterbalanced by some central control. Unless governments monitor the performance of their SOEs and make the main decisions on investment and debt, their macroeconomic management will be undermined, as Brazil's experience has demonstrated (see Box 8.4). Yet central control can itself be poorly organized. All too often, different official agencies intervene in SOE decisions that should be the prerogative of management, and yet government fails to coordinate their action. Too much interference can be combined with too little control. In addition, policy that swings between autonomy and central control can prevent coherent direction of SOEs. The challenge is to design a system that holds management accountable for results while giving it the power to achieve them.

Institutional links between government and enterprise

To try and reduce arbitrary intervention by government, countries have devised institutional arrangements that place government at arms' length from SOEs. Boards of directors or holding companies have been widely used to create a buffer between SOE management and the central bureaucracy, to provide policy direction, and to report on results. Special bureaus, commissions, and ministries have become a popular way of centralizing information and control of SOEs.

These arrangements have a mixed record, showing that institutional changes alone rarely achieve a satisfactory balance between independence and control. Furthermore, arrangements that work well for one country or enterprise may not do so elsewhere. For example, the successful Ethiopian Telecommunications Authority has a politically oriented board of directors dominated by a minister (see Box 8.5)—an arrangement that has proved disastrous in other countries.

To avoid such direct political control, many countries rely on holding companies. Some have proved a useful way of achieving government aims while giving SOEs greater discretion in day-to-day operational matters; others have become counterproductive, substituting one form of ex-ante bureaucratic intervention for another. An added drawback of introducing an extra layer of bureaucracy is that it also uses scarce managerial resources.

On the positive side, the Istituto per la Ricostruzione Industriale (IRI) in Italy has been credited with cooperating with government to achieve its social goals while freeing the individual enterprises to pursue profits. Nevertheless, IRI has been caught between conflicting government aims—such as the directive to make profits and yet support failing subsidiaries to bolster employment. Holding companies can also provide technical assistance and managerial talent. Portugal's holding

---

Box 8.3   Contracts between the state and its enterprises: the experience of France and Senegal

France

The concept of contracts for state enterprises was first introduced in France in the late 1960s to increase both the autonomy and accountability of SOE managers. Initially only two contracts between government and SOEs were signed; four more were added in 1979, and in 1981 the new government announced its intention to negotiate more contracts with the expanded state enterprise sector. By early 1983, eight contracts had been signed and more were being negotiated.

The French experience has been mixed. The first two contracts were overtaken by the 1973 oil shock and subsequent stagflation; although they contained procedures for revisions, these were not adequate to cope with the unprecedented conditions of the mid-1970s. A serious deficiency of the agreements was their failure to specify remedies for nonperformance. The contract with the electricity company provided that the state could suspend the contract if the results were not achieved, but adjustment rather than suspension is often the more appropriate response. The plans were also weakened or opposed by the bureaucracy, which disliked the degree of pricing freedom which contracts would have given SOEs.

Despite these shortcomings, the contracts have helped clarify relations between the state and SOEs. They allowed the implications of government's pricing and subsidy policy to be discussed. The medium-term focus of the contracts (most covered three to five years) required the government to be more consistent in its

policies, particularly in the annual discussions of the enterprises' investment programs. Furthermore, the contracts made the company's results more transparent, by distinguishing between normal operations and social objectives. For example, the railway's contract specified that the company be compensated for losses on passenger lines that it was not allowed to close. Similarly, Air France was compensated for having to operate the Caravelle IIIs and to split operations between two Paris airports.

Senegal

The Senegalese government has negotiated contract plans with five SOEs since 1980, and is in the process of negotiating five more. Although it is too early to draw any firm conclusions, initial results are promising and suggest some lessons for other developing countries.

The preparation of the three-year plans helped in strategic planning for the SOEs. It forced them to identify the sources of their operating deficits, and to articulate medium-term operating and investment goals. Thus, for the first time Air Senegal and the Dakar bus company (SOTRAC) calculated losses per passenger-kilometer on certain services that the government obliged them to operate.

The contracts allowed the government to compare more systematically the cost of social objectives and investment proposals with their benefits. As a result, loss-making air services to certain remote areas were cut back. The government also reconsidered a costly investment in passenger rail equipment after the railway's plan presented a thorough quantification

of its long-term implications for the company's debt service and operating revenues. Ultimately, senior ministers decided to concentrate new investment on freight, rather than passenger, traffic. The government also adopted formulas for regular tariff adjustments linked to increases in the cost of inputs (especially fuel) for most enterprises. It agreed to place limits on staff numbers to protect enterprises from pressures to take on excess or ill-qualified personnel.

Most of the contracts have produced measurable improvements in SOE performance. SOTRAC has been guaranteed regular tariff increases, quarterly payment of a specific subsidy for money-losing suburban lines, and financial support for more buses and a second maintenance terminal. For its part, the company has set strict targets for worker productivity, maintenance, and more efficient fleet utilization—targets which, so far, it has met. Improvements in cash flow alone enabled SOTRAC to eliminate its bank overdraft and 30 percent of its arrears to suppliers in the first year of the contract. The one contract that seems to have failed did so because of the magnitude of the restructuring required to reduce the company's substantial operating deficit.

Initially, the effect of the contracts on the budget and investment program was not adequately assessed. Nor was provision made for monitoring performance with agreed sanctions in the case of noncompliance. The Senegalese government is taking steps to remedy this, including six-month joint reviews of contract execution.

Box 8.4 The control of state-owned enterprises in Brazil

Until 1979 the Brazilian government had no consolidated information on earnings, spending, or debt of its SOEs. It therefore had no way of comparing consolidated public investment with financial resources, so public investment often exceeded the amount of money actually available, thus increasing inflation and the country's foreign debt.

In addition to their own revenues earned on the sale of goods and services, the SOEs received substantial transfers from the government. These included earmarked tax revenues, credits from official financial institutions, inter-enterprise transfers, and loan guarantees. With the multiplication of these extrabudge-

tary funds, control over the economic and financial operations of SOEs was gradually eroded. Projects were started without adequate provision for their financing, and supplementary transfers were often required to prevent large-scale layoffs and defaults to suppliers, contractors, and creditors.

Faced with growing inflationary pressures and a deteriorating balance of payments, in 1979 the government introduced a series of significant reforms. It phased out most of the SOEs' earmarked taxes, and centralized authority over SOE finances in a new agency in the Planning Ministry, the Special Secretariat for Control of the State Enterprises (SEST). SEST

is responsible for approving and monitoring the budgets for 382 SOEs and autonomous institutions. These are summarized in an annual SEST budget authorized by the president. All foreign and domestic credit operations by these SOEs require prior SEST approval, as do any proposals to create, expand, or liquidate any state enterprise. So far the Planning Ministry and SEST have been primarily concerned with setting and enforcing firm-by-firm ceilings. They have not become seriously involved in evaluating SOE investment plans, but this may change as a result of the first multiyear consolidation of government investment programs in 1982.

Box 8.5 Ethiopian Telecommunications Authority

The Ethiopian Telecommunications Authority (ETA) has expanded its telecommunication services rapidly, and in the main cities quality is considered good for a developing country. For example, periodic checks show that less than 2 percent of test calls fail due to congestion or faulty equipment. ETA's telephone service is one of the least expensive in Africa, yet it has generated a good financial rate of return on net assets. This allows it to make a reasonable contribution to its investment; 33 percent of the latest program will be financed internally. Labor productivity is high for a developing country: ETA has 50 staff per 1,000 telephone lines, compared with 75 to 150 staff per 1,000 lines in most African countries.

The Authority is run by a policymaking board and a professional manager. Board members are all government officials; the chairman is the minister of

transport and communications. Its composition gives the board a political, policymaking orientation. The company's general manager, in contrast, is recruited from the ranks of ETA, and is expected to run the company as a commercial operation within the guidelines set by the board. While board membership has changed frequently, there has been reasonable continuity in ETA's top management, with only six general managers since 1952.

The board conveys the government's general objectives to the firm's management, which then draws up a five-year corporate plan for review and amendment by the board. ETA's current plan responds to the priority the Ethiopian government has assigned to increasing rural services. The company also submits an annual budget with quantitative targets; at the end of the year the board compares results against targets, holding

managers accountable and removing them for poor performance.

By channeling its objectives through the board, the government has helped avoid putting conflicting demands on ETA. ETA's board has powers that in many other countries are vested in several different ministries and agencies. It sets tariffs, hires and fires the general manager, and gives final approval to the company's staffing plan, budget, and investment proposals (with the exception of foreign borrowing, which must also be approved by the minister of finance and the planning authorities). The board has not interfered in the daily operations of the company. The general manager can fire incompetent staff, compete for funds in the domestic capital market, and make the necessary decisions to implement the plan.

company, Instituto dos Participacoes do Estado (IPE), for instance, helps subsidiaries negotiate credits if they also agree to undertake reforms. IPE also recruits experts to assist its subsidiaries in improving corporate planning or management information systems. It also provides training and finances outside studies.

Such merits need to be set against less favorable

experiences elsewhere. Pakistan, for example, created a Board of Industrial Management (BIM) in 1973 to direct twelve corporations (with about fifty production units) on the model of Italy's IRI. The reports of two government commissions found that BIM had drastically reduced the production units' operating autonomy and weakened managerial authority. It was therefore abolished in 1978.

A different approach to decentralizing has been tried in several Eastern European countries (East Germany, Bulgaria, Poland, and Romania), where a new administrative level has been put between the ministry and the enterprise. Here again, experience shows that structural changes by themselves are not enough to alter the underlying balance of power. The *centrale* in Romania, for example, were created in 1968 and given certain minor powers over enterprise investments, borrowing, input supply, and marketing. But the ministries continued to intervene directly both in the enterprises and in the day-to-day operations of the centrale.

Some countries have centralized control in government bureaus or specialized ministries. India, for example, created the Bureau of Public Enterprises (BPE) as part of the Ministry of Finance in 1965. In 1979 Brazil set up the Secretariat for the Control of State Enterprises, and in Pakistan the Ministry of Production controls all state-owned manufacturing enterprises. These bodies are responsible for setting performance standards (or expenditure limits in the case of Brazil), evaluating results, and approving debt and investments. The BPE collects and analyzes data on India's SOEs and in 1982 set performance targets with the enterprise managers. It also gives technical assistance and training, does special studies, and provides guidelines in such areas as wage settlements. Central bodies thus obtain valuable information on SOEs, a prerequisite for effectively assessing and controlling performance. However, sometimes they become involved in unnecessary detail; one such body has set standards for factory perimeter fencing. Central bodies can play a vital role in monitoring performance or they can become an annoying bottleneck obsessed with trivia. Their role depends largely on whether a government is concerned with short-term goals, such as implementing austerity programs or curbing SOE abuses, or with the long-run process of changing relations between SOEs and government.

Holding managers accountable for results

There are strong arguments for creating conditions in which SOEs can be instructed to maximize profits and then be judged by that standard. Profit is a composite indicator that applies positive weights (prices) to benefits (outputs) and negative weights to costs (inputs). If the weights are correct, a profit-maximizing firm strives to achieve maximum benefits for minimum costs—the definition of efficiency. For SOEs, this criterion needs modifying for four reasons: many SOEs are monopolies; the profit relevant for society is different from private profits; many SOE objectives conflict with profit maximization; and market prices may be distorted.

These qualifications need not negate the use of profits as a guide to performance.

● Monopoly. The best way to end monopoly power is to introduce competition. Where that is not possible, the prices of a monopoly SOE can be set according to its marginal costs (see discussion in Chapter 6); the SOE can then be instructed to maximize profits. If that produces unacceptably high prices, the enterprise can still be required to minimize costs. Although adjusting administered prices typically involves practical and political problems, the long-run benefits can be substantial.

● Accounting for public profits. Some items (such as interest payments) can be excluded from public profits so as not to encourage SOE managers to waste time on, for example, interest arbitrage, which may be deemed irrelevant to their tasks. Targets can also be set for activities such as investment, maintenance, and research, which might not be compatible with short-run profit maximization or cost minimization.

● Conflicting goals. If the SOE is required to perform noncommercial roles that reduce its profits (such as hiring extra staff to increase employment or setting up a plant in a particular area to promote regional development), the government can reimburse it for the extra costs or reduce its profit target accordingly. Careful calculation is needed of the cost of noncommercial goals: if the subsidy is too high, the incentive for the company to improve its efficiency is reduced.

● Distorted prices. These can be rectified by using shadow prices for assessing SOE results. Shadow prices are calculated to reflect the opportunity costs of an enterprise's inputs and outputs. For example, the price of imported fuel may be held down by a government subsidy, but SOE accounting should value it according to its world price to ensure it is used efficiently.

The results derived from shadow-price accounting can differ widely from conventional profits and losses, as one study of SOEs in Egypt demonstrated. In almost all twenty-seven industries sampled, the financial rate of return calculated on the basis of extensively controlled market prices pointed in opposite directions from the economic rates of return based on shadow prices. Industries producing oils, soaps, and detergents showed a 14.4 percent economic rate of return, yet financial profitability was negative; nonferrous metals earned a

Box 8.6 Performance evaluation in Pakistan

Pakistan's performance evaluation system, launched in 1981, uses "public profitability" as an indicator of performance. "Public profits" are private profits adjusted for those elements not deemed relevant to an SOE. For example, taxes and interest, which are private costs but public benefits, are excluded so as not to encourage SOE managers to devote time to minimizing taxes or to interest arbitrage. Rather, public profitability aims to encourage managers to maximize net economic benefits, judged from a national perspective. Costs of noncommercial objectives (such as the extra cost of purchasing from local suppliers to encourage domestic industry) are deducted before profits are calculated and treated as an "in-kind" dividend to the government.

Since many prices are administered and there are problems of monopoly pricing, market prices may not reflect true economic scarcity. Since SOE managers generally cannot affect prices, it would be unfair to reward or penalize them for the effects of changing prices on profitability. The ideal solution would be to elim-inate the divergence between market prices and real economic costs. Where that is not feasible, a second-best remedy is to use shadow prices that reflect true economic costs. Shadow prices, however, are complex and controversial to administer. Pakistan is therefore judging its SOE managers, for control purposes only, by trends in public profit at constant prices; that is, constructing a quantum index of profits based on quantum indices of inputs and outputs. This is an acceptable approximation of efficiency in performance evaluation (though not in project evaluation), since it is concerned with the trend rather than the level of performance. All enterprises will be judged on the basis of their return to fixed operating assets, or public profitability in constant terms. The performance of any individual firm will be compared with its record over the past five years, to make allowance for the fact that some enterprises operate under greater handicaps than others.

Used in isolation, public profitability would encourage managers to ignore activities with current costs but future ben-efits (such as planning, maintenance, training, or innovation). Government and SOEs will therefore negotiate extra targets for these areas, assigning them weights that vary over time and from one company to another. A firm will first have to show that it can use existing resources efficiently; hence, 90 percent of its initial target may be assigned to public profitability.

At the end of the year the performance of each SOE will then be rated according to how close it came to meeting its composite target. The monitoring and evaluation will be done by the Experts Advisory Cell, a semi-autonomous agency responsible to the Ministry of Production but financed by a levy on the SOEs themselves. The Cell has been able to maintain a remarkable degree of independence and, because it is outside the civil service system, to attract a specialist staff. At a review meeting with the Cell, managers will be able to present an explanation of their results. The government proposes to reward good performance with a salary bonus.

15.5 percent financial rate of return, but the economic return was negative. Not only would it be misleading to judge an SOE on the basis of its financial performance, but a manager reacting to financial signals under these circumstances would make the wrong economic decision. Shadow prices can be complex to calculate and administer, so the best solution is to move market prices closer to them by removing distortions wherever feasible.

While these four refinements have been extensively analyzed in theoretical work, their application has proven practically and politically difficult. Some countries are moving to overcome these problems. One system for judging the performance of manufacturing SOEs in Pakistan is described in Box 8.6. The Republic of Korea and Venezuela have also initiated similar projects that will tackle the more complex problem of evaluating enterprises responsible to different ministries.

Information on performance

Assessing SOE performance requires a regular flow of reliable information. But in many developing countries the internal management information systems of SOEs are deficient or nonexistent. SOEs (as well as private companies) are not audited according to uniform standards; more than seventy developing countries have no accounting standards. Trained accountants are scarce, because in many developing countries (outside Latin America) accounting became part of the university curricula only after 1960. Even now there are often no uniform standards of training.

These weaknesses are gradually being rectified. Many francophone West African countries have tried to adapt France's accounting model to their needs. This program—the OCAM *plan comptable*, started almost twenty years ago—has met with mixed success. But its application has been too inflexible, with too much reliance on expatriate experts and too little attention paid to local accounting capabilities. In Senegal the accountancy profession has proposed a two-tiered system, with annual external audits conforming to internationally accepted procedures required for all companies above a certain size and "limited review audits" for all other companies. The latter would be stricter than the current standard but less comprehensive (and cheaper) than full-scale audits.

The development of uniform and credible accounting requires a trained body of practitioners as well as a system to set and review standards and to qualify accountants. This foundation can be built up by designating responsibility within the government for the development of accounting; establishing accounting standards backed by an appropriate legal framework; assessing staff needs and designing training for bookkeepers and accountants; and fostering a professional association that could assume responsibility for enforcing standards.

Formal accountancy procedures are not the only way managers can improve the information on which they base their actions. Improvements can also be obtained through a management audit, which requires the firm to establish and adhere to a basic information system and routine control procedures. As with a financial audit, an outside auditor would check that these procedures function properly and generate reliable data that management and government can compare with targets. Many large accounting firms can now assist enterprises in setting up and using management-auditing systems.

A somewhat similar management tool is the action plan, designed to focus efforts on improving efficiency and monitoring results. The experience of the Bolivian railways illustrates how action plans work in practice. The railway had three action plans between 1973 and 1979, with objectives that ranged from reorganizing workshops and repairing rolling stock to rehabilitating and maintaining track. Monitored targets included the average percentage of total cars and locomotives in operating condition during the year, the number of staff, the turnaround time for maintenance, and the amount of track to be rehabilitated. Action plans specify the measures to be used to achieve the targets (such as training or allocation of foreign exchange for the purchase of spare parts) and the timing.

Pressure from competition, the public, and clients

Governments cannot always arrange for their SOEs to be exposed to competition. Many state firms are monopolies producing goods and services that are not traded internationally or that the government prefers to produce domestically for reasons of national security or public interest. In other cases, the economy may be too small to support another domestic producer. Where it is possible to do so, however, exposing SOEs to competition can be a simple and effective way to promote their efficiency. And if managers are required to pursue noncommercial goals for political or social reasons, competition will help to quantify the costs of those goals. Thus Peru recently reduced tariffs and eliminated import quotas to force industries to compete with imports.

Another possibility is to split large public monopolies into smaller competing units, especially if the monopoly did not benefit from economies of scale. In Hungary, for example, at least 130 new enterprises were established by breaking up horizontal trusts and large state firms. For competition to be fully effective in promoting efficiency, these measures must be accompanied by pricing freedom. Privileged access to subsidized credit and inputs would have to end. Also, managers must be given discretion to respond to competitive pressures, which may mean reducing staff or ending unprofitable services. The enterprise might also have to be reimbursed for the extra costs of meeting social goals.

Organized public pressure is another way of encouraging SOE efficiency. Britain, for example, has consumer councils. Although they have no executive powers, they monitor the service provided by public monopolies and act as a proxy for market forces. The Electricity Consumer Council examines not just tariffs but also power cuts, delays in connections or repairs, and responsiveness of staff to customer inquiries and complaints.

Clients can also induce efficiency; accountability to growers was an important factor in the success of the Kenya Tea Development Authority. SOEs can be required to publish timely annual reports and accounts, to be tabled in Parliament or made publicly available. Chile, for example, recently required state companies to publish their financial balances in the newspapers.

Appropriate managerial incentives and skills

Institutional success is often attributed to the presence of "a good manager." Competent staff are no doubt essential for any efficient enterprise. They do not operate in a vacuum. They need incentives to attract and motivate them, and the power to be effective.

Incentives linked to results. Some of the most effective rewards are nonpecuniary—recognition, greater responsibility, promotion, and national honors. Autonomy can also be a strong incentive for SOE managers. For example, the threat of losing its independence motivated the management of the Kenya Tea Development Authority. By the same token, managers need to know that they face penalties for poor performance, such as losing their jobs.

As for pecuniary incentives, few countries have used performance bonuses or profit sharing to motivate top management. An exception is Mexico, which distributes 7 percent of SOE profits to all employees in proportion to their salaries. In Hungary, ministries judge the size of bonuses to senior SOE managers by reference to such factors as profitability, exports, development of new products, and punctuality of deliveries. Many more countries award performance bonuses to workers, and their experience reveals some of the difficulties involved. Bonuses run the risk of becoming so automatic and large that they are treated as part of everybody's salary; they are not easily related to the actions and decisions of individual managers. To be effective, profit-sharing schemes require that managers affect profits and that profits be a fair guide to performance. Otherwise managers of SOEs in which profits are inherent in their operating conditions—such as many petroleum or electricity companies—would be enriched, while a manager who stems chronic losses might go unrewarded.

Appropriate managerial skills. The skills of a public enterprise manager need to be closer to those of his private sector counterpart than to those of a government bureaucrat. Nevertheless, in some countries managers are part of the civil service, or at least subject to its pay scale. Even where this is not the case, their pay seldom matches private salaries. Although the prestige and challenge of running what are often the largest corporations in the country may sometimes compensate for lower pay, low salaries tend to deter skilled managers and increase staff turnover. To give one of many examples, salaries in a Turkish public utility averaged one-third those of the private sector in 1981 and the company has had seven general managers in the past ten years. In addition, good SOE managers who face frequent unjustified interventions, or whose achievements go unnoticed for want of a system to evaluate them, tend to become disgruntled and leave.

The growing number of SOEs has contributed to a chronic shortage of managers in many sub-Saharan African and South Asian countries, a shortage sometimes exacerbated by programs for rapid indigenization. Many senior posts are left vacant or are filled by unqualified staff. For example, in Tanzania half of the ten large agricultural SOEs had no financial manager in 1980. In the Nigerian Electric Power Authority, thirty-five of eighty-seven higher management posts were vacant in 1981. The lack of competent middle managers often leads general managers to take over lower supervisory functions. In a centralized system they may also be the only point of contact with outsiders. The organization thus becomes too dependent on its chief executive.

The shortage of managers also contributes to a high rate of turnover, as competent people are shifted around to head troubled SOEs. A study of nine countries in sub-Saharan Africa found that the average tenure of SOE general managers in the 1970s was less than two years. Even countries without a managerial shortage change SOE managers with damaging frequency if selection of top managers is based on nepotism or political patronage. To counteract this, some countries (such as India and Brazil) have set up management selection boards to nominate candidates on merit alone. Continuity of top management is especially important in a company's formative years. Furthermore, continuity allows a good chief executive time to attract and retain talented middle managers. For example, the Hindustan Machine Tool Company, one of the most successful Indian SOEs, was also one of the few public corporations in India to have the same chief executive for almost fifteen years.

In certain specialized areas (mining in Zaire, for example), management contracts with expatriate firms have helped alleviate the shortage of managers. Another step is to give priority to managerial development in SOEs. In the past, more attention has been paid to technical expertise for SOEs than to their managerial requirements. Although SOE management training does not lend itself to centralized direction, governments can encourage SOEs to earmark funds for training. Some of the largest have their own management training centers but most rely on business schools, management consultants, expatriate advisers, and foreign suppliers or collaborators.

"Twinning" an SOE with its counterpart in another country has proved an effective way of transferring know-how and training staff. Companies offering technical assistance as twins are not exclusively from North America and Europe. Among many examples from developing countries are the Port of Singapore, the National Irrigation Agency of the Philippines, and the Tunisian Water Au-

Box 8.7 TANESCO: a study in institution building

The Tanzania Electric Supply Company Limited (TANESCO) was founded as a private company in 1931 and acquired by the government of Tanzania in 1964. It now operates as an SOE under the sponsorship of the Ministry of Water and Energy. TANESCO has more than 6,000 employees and produces about 98 percent of the country's electricity consumption.

Management continuity and a firm commitment to staff training have been critical to TANESCO's development. Over the past twenty-eight years, it has had only four general managers, and many of its senior staff have been with the company for at least ten years. The proportion of Tanzanians in senior posts has risen from 20 percent in 1964 to 85 percent in 1980. In 1968, TANESCO established its own technical training institute, which was developed with assistance from the Swedish International Development Agency. European and Indian expatriate staff provided on-the-job training. By 1974, after the first stage of the company's literacy program, all employees were able to read and write. Between 1976 and 1981 TANESCO sent fifty staff overseas to obtain engineering degrees. The first Tanzanian general manager, who was appointed in 1973 and retired in 1981, used foreign management consultants to reorganize the utility on functional lines and expanded the programs for training and staff development.

The "twinning" of TANESCO and the Electricity Supply Board of Ireland (ESB) in 1977 had a decisive influence on the development of the company's managers. During the first year of the scheme, about twenty TANESCO staff members were given from three to twelve months' training in Dublin followed by a brief period of on-the-job training with ESB or in similar utilities in the United Kingdom and the United States. Both "twins" took great care to design a training program that fitted TANESCO's needs. When the trainees returned to Tanzania, their shared experience in Ireland helped them to work better as a team.

---

thority. The more-developed SOE may temporarily provide its twin with some of its own staff as advisors and trainers, may make periodic visits to give technical assistance, or may employ the staff of its twin at its own facility for on-the-job training (see Box 8.7).

The administrative burden placed on SOE managers may be partly caused by their diversion to extraneous activities. For example, in Peru the management of a public fishing plant also runs a hotel. While diversification can be profitable and logical, it is often done for the wrong reasons and, by straining resources, damages the SOE's mainstream activities.

Liquidation

By saving the economy the burden of nonviable enterprises, liquidations act as a major force for efficiency. Because of the financial and social consequences, however, governments are reluctant to let big firms close, whether they are in the public or the private sector. Even among small firms, SOEs are seldom liquidated. But the costs of keeping nonviable companies alive are considerable—fiscal drain, administrative demands, and waste of potentially productive resources. To take an extreme case, in Peru a freeze-drying plant owned by the state was built without adequate study of the market or its suppliers of raw materials. From the start, the firm's production costs exceeded its revenues. It was shut down and reopened on several occasions. Finally, in 1980 and after fifteen years of losses, it was liquidated.

This case also illustrates the need for a proper legal framework to allow speedy liquidation. Peruvian law makes it almost impossible to dismiss workers (in both the public and private sectors). Although the company offered its staff a bonus over and above required severance pay to leave, for more than six months after the plant was shut down a small group of workers continued to report for work each day to receive their wages. Until all the staff had left, the assets could not be sold.

Liquidation and other forms of divestment give the government the flexibility to put resources to more productive use. Since these gains have to be weighed against short-term costs, vested interests often deny the state the possibility of even considering the option—to the long-run detriment of the economy.

Divestiture

Selling state-owned enterprises is another way of easing their administrative and financial burden on the state. A number of governments, including Bangladesh, Brazil, Chile, Italy, Jamaica, Republic of Korea, Pakistan, Peru, Philippines, United Kingdom, and Zaire, have divested or are planning to divest SOEs. Generally, however, the number and importance of the enterprises sold is not large.

After an initial attempt to promote industrialization through state ownership, the Japanese government in the 1880s sold many state firms, including fifty-two factories, ten mines, and three shipyards. Between 1974 and 1980, Chile sold some 130 state enterprises, with a value of more than $500 million. (In addition, more than 250 enterprises nationalized between 1971 and 1973 were returned to their former owners.) Despite these measures, in 1979 the eight largest Chilean companies (in terms of net worth) were still publicly owned.

Other privatizing programs have been far more limited. Brazil created a commission for divestiture in 1981: by mid-1982 it had sold ten enterprises and was in the process of selling another thirty-six, while ten other SOEs have been legally dissolved. Jamaica has set up a divestiture committee which has sold three enterprises and leased four hotels. Pakistan denationalized some 2,000 rice, flour, and cotton mills, while Bangladesh returned 35 jute and 23 textile mills to the private sector.

Although divestiture can produce important net gains to society when the costs of public operation outweigh the benefits, it has been hard to implement. It is politically sensitive and prompts charges of corruption. In addition, governments often try to sell only their money losers, for which there are few buyers. Even profitable nationalized companies may be hard to sell. An informal survey of the potential market for Peruvian SOEs found that likely buyers were reluctant to purchase even fairly small companies. The reasons given included fear of renationalization and concern about extensive government regulation of formerly public firms. These perceptions may mean governments have to accept a lower price than the market value for a similar private firm. Both Chile and Japan sold most of their state firms on attractive terms.

Another reason divestiture is so difficult in developing countries is the absence of a strong capital market. Public companies are often large and domestic investors may not be able to raise enough capital to buy them. And selling large SOEs to oligopolists who already dominate the private sector might reduce competition. It could also result in unhealthy ties between financial institutions and industry, further reducing the flexibilty of capital markets.

Efforts to develop the stock market, and schemes that appeal to small savers through their pension funds, could make it easier for governments to divest. Spreading ownership more widely and divesting only gradually can improve the chances of privatization; it may even reduce the attendant political controversy. Leasing can also be a promising route to divestiture: a private manager might be brought in to run a potentially profitable enterprise for a share of the profits and an option to buy.

Agenda for reform

This chapter has suggested ways of improving SOE efficiency, concentrating on the problems that are common to most SOEs in most countries. Judging from what is known about the ideal conditions for operating efficiently, it has examined how the reality of SOEs differs from the theoretical ideal. By recognizing the SOEs' special circumstances and constraints, it is possible to develop an agenda for reform that would correct some of their main weaknesses:

• Setting clear-cut and attainable objectives is the inescapable first step toward improved SOE performance. The costs of noncommercial constraints placed on SOEs should be calculated and weighed against the benefits to society.

• Once constraints have been identified and costed, governments can instruct many SOEs to maximize their profits, taking into account other objectives that reduce profits by reimbursing the companies or lowering their profit targets.

• Where there are price distortions, shadow pricing offers a way to assess SOE performance consistent with economic efficiency. The better alternative is to move to market pricing (or marginal cost pricing where market pricing is not feasible). This would encourage greater efficiency by giving the correct market signals to managers and consumers. Although market pricing typically entails short-run political problems and costs, the long-run benefits are substantial.

• Negotiated agreements, such as contracts or corporate plans, can help put relations between SOEs and government on a more constructive plane. In particular, two-way contracts can help win SOE management over to the idea of reform by laying out benefits as well as responsibilities.

• Once government has laid down objectives, managers can be made responsible for choosing the methods of achieving them.

• Systems for monitoring and evaluating performance are needed to transform good intentions into results. By promoting domestic and international competition and encouraging consumers and other customers to make their views known, governments can add to the pressures for good SOE performance. Some of the most powerful incentives are nonpecuniary (recognition, prestige, awards).

• Managerial ability is a key to the success of SOE reform. Managerial incentives linked to performance are important in motivating top managers. Compensation and training should be geared to create a corps of competent SOE managers with appropriate skills. Efforts should also be directed at encouraging continuity of senior staff.

• The managerial and fiscal burden of SOEs can be reduced by liquidating nonviable enterprises as well as by selective sales. These should not be treated as instant solutions, but rather as integral parts of the process of replacing the burden of central administration by decentralized market forces.

With strong political backing, this agenda is feasible. In any administrative system there are strong vested interests opposed to change. Opposition to reform may come from managers of powerful SOEs or senior government bureaucrats fearing loss of power, labor unions fearing job cuts, SOE clients fearing an end to subsidized outputs, suppliers fearing reduced SOE spending, or even from SOE competitors (some private companies profit nicely when prices or incentives for a sector are geared to allow an inefficient SOE to survive).

Since these elements are interrelated, a piecemeal approach is unlikely to achieve the desired results. Without clear objectives there can be no standards by which to judge performance; without accountability few governments would increase SOE autonomy; autonomy becomes license without performance evaluation; incentives can be linked to performance only if there is a meaningful way to measure results; performance evaluation makes sense only if managers have the autonomy to influence outcomes; without performance evaluation there is no way to distinguish good managers from bad. Developing a framework to guide SOEs toward efficiency is thus a lengthy, complex process that requires commitment, persistence, and flexibility on the part of state authorities and enterprise management.

9 Project and program management

The growing number of development projects and programs has strained the managerial capacity of governments in all developing countries. This trend is likely to continue in the 1980s as population increases and expectations rise. While there is no general formula for avoiding management strains, experience has revealed ways of easing them.

The requirements of project management vary widely according to the nature of the project and the number of objectives and agencies involved. In particular, management techniques appropriate for physical projects (building and maintaining infrastructure, operating industrial plants and utilities) differ significantly from those needed in people-centered development (small farmer agriculture, education, family planning, health and nutrition; and infrastructure and housing projects where beneficiaries participate in design, construction, or maintenance). In general, methods in physical projects are well understood: constructing and operating an oil refinery may not be simple, but the technology is well specified and can be applied in different countries and cultures. The main managerial requirements are to train and motivate staff and to strengthen operational control. Because performance can be measured in terms of physical output, there is much scope for reinforcing government efforts by using private contractors.

In contrast, less is known about how to change patterns of behavior so that people adopt new farming methods or birth control, because cultural influences predominate. These uncertainties about people-centered development are combined with less managerial control, since success depends on stimulating peoples' voluntary participation. Management therefore requires experimentation, flexibility, and a willingness to work closely with program beneficiaries to learn about, and respond to, local needs. Governments often find programs involving the poorest are the most difficult to make effective. The answer to this dilemma is not to give up, but to build steadily on experience.

The first two sections of this chapter contrast the management approaches needed in physical and in people-centered development. The final section reviews the management problems that arise when projects and programs involve several implementing agencies. Again, there is a contrast between physical projects, which can rely on contracts between agencies, and people-centered programs, which need continuous informal contacts among field staff.

Managing physical development

Construction projects enjoy a big advantage—the availability of technical solutions; and suffer from two common weaknesses—the easiest solutions are not always the most economically efficient, and financial constraints can delay projects and starve them of resources for maintenance.

• *Well-defined technology.* Fertilizer plants, refineries, dams, highways, and other projects are broadly alike in that they are built according to well-defined methods. Technical problems can still arise, of course, but the techniques for solving them are generally available to management. Where skills are lacking domestically, they are universal enough to be imported. For example, a scheme in southern Sudan to build the large Roseires dam used designs by French and British consultants, and was managed by an Italian contractor. Despite its remote location and consequent transport difficulties, the dam was built in five years instead of six, and for 97 percent of the estimated cost.

• *Economic efficiency.* The fastest and easiest operational solutions are not necessarily ideal in economic terms, however. Developing countries with abundant labor ought in theory to avoid capital-intensive construction techniques, yet they often lack the capacity to manage large labor forces. Nor do some countries do much to encourage the development of such a capacity. For example, a key criterion for promotion of government engineers is often their experience in managing machinery. Such biases can be reduced by the creation of labor-based construction departments offering security and prospects of promotion, as Honduras did for highway construction in 1976.

- *Financial constraints.* New construction is often smoothly implemented because it is politically attractive and therefore given financial priority. Nonetheless, delays are still common, and not simply because of bureaucratic procurement procedures or supply problems. Budgetary shortfalls also occur, and are made more damaging because many construction projects—dams, roads, factories—are indivisible. They cannot be scaled down or modified in response to financial constraints. It is therefore particularly important that governments make realistic provision for construction projects in their budgets (discussed in Chapter 7).

Operating physical projects

Chapter 8 explored in detail the problems raised when managers of physical projects are set several (often conflicting) goals by government. Yet even when managers have clear goals and real autonomy, physical projects generally cause more trouble during their operating, than during their construction, phase: the troubled history of Togo's CIMAO clinker plant, built with only trivial time and cost overruns, is an example. Problems arise partly because commitment to operating efficiency is harder to sustain than commitment to the short-term goal of completing a building. But it is also because, unlike one-time construction projects that can be managed with foreign technical assistance where necessary, continuous production or service operations must depend on local managers. Their expertise can be developed only over long periods.

Skilled top management is often seen as the key to operating success, yet outstanding senior managers are scarce and cannot run large institutions single-handed. The case of PUSRI in Indonesia (see Box 9.l) illustrates the importance of a long-term development' strategy for training middle management and workers, and for building physical and financial control systems to monitor performance. The managerial task also varies from project to project. Some—textiles, cement, power and chemical plants, for example—have relatively simple technologies, needing relatively few skilled staff. Others—such as steel production—are harder to manage because they involve many processes in which human skills are critical and error costly. Managing large work forces is difficult in any country, but developing countries face special

---

Box 9.1   PUSRI: a long-term strategy for management development

PUSRI, Indonesia's largest fertilizer company, has an international reputation for efficiency in both construction and production. Its two most recent expansions, supported by foreign aid and totaling $135 million, were completed in 1977, one month and four months ahead of schedule. Efficient cost control and higher-than-anticipated capacity utilization in the early years of production helped to produce rates of return significantly higher than initial appraisal forecasts. PUSRI's success at home has led to a contract to train Bangladesh nationals in fertilizer production, and to a joint venture with Kellogg to build plants in other developing countries.

An outstanding general manager helped get PUSRI off the ground in 1959. But the company's subsequent success was due to its strong and stable technical and middle management team and to effective financial control systems. While PUSRI's training program draws on expertise from abroad and from local universities, its emphasis is on technical, financial, and marketing skills immediately relevant to employees' day-to-day tasks. Production directors regularly lecture in the classroom, and much of the training takes place on the job.

PUSRI pays special attention to developing skills in financial management, since there is no specialized accounting education in Indonesia. Foreign consultants were brought in to establish cost centers and to improve procurement, management information systems, capital budgeting, and financial planning. This attention to financial management goes far beyond the needs of the official government audit, which is concerned mainly with compliance with regulations. It has ensured the company's financial success, and thus a prestige that helps to attract and retain competent staff. PUSRI has also earned the confidence of government, which ensures its continued autonomy.

The company's personnel policy sees training and incentives as part of a single package. Incentives come partly in the form of fringe benefits—housing, transport, and medical facilities—which may be as important to employees as their basic salaries. But the company also uses training schemes as an incentive in themselves. Training is not limited to PUSRI staff; other fertilizer companies in Indonesia put their technicians and managers through PUSRI courses. The prospect of career advancement outside the company encourages PUSRI staff to seek further training to upgrade their skills. By consciously training more staff than it can handle, PUSRI has turned staff "wastage" into a valuable incentive.

problems. They often need to train many people from scratch—for example, more than 3,000 in the Vinh Phu pulp and paper project in Viet Nam, which was constructed with assistance from Sweden. And managers may need to overcome cultural barriers in getting workers to adapt to the discipline demanded by production lines.

Operating performance is also affected by the number of links joining the individual enterprise to the rest of the economy. To operate efficiently, the Vinh Phu paper plant depends on forest plantations, water treatment and power plants, local schools and health centers, and road, rail, and river transport. Many of these services are outside the control of the project's managers.

Having few customers or suppliers greatly simplifies project operation. PUSRI's performance, for example, is helped by the fact that it depends for resources on only one key supplier (the national oil company), and for revenues on output prices set by the Indonesian government. By contrast, organizations that depend on charges levied on many users, such as Sao Paulo's successful water supply and sewage company, need to place high priority on the development of financial and accounting systems to charge and collect from thousands of consumers.

Managing large maintenance programs

While production and service operations tend to be less efficient than project construction, maintenance operations are typically less efficient than either. This is partly because successful maintenance provides no visible result, and so can seem dispensable. Maintenance and rehabilitation programs depend on continuing budgetary support, but are often neglected in favor of new projects (discussed in Chapter 7)—a "capital bias" that is shared by foreign development agencies.

Large, dispersed maintenance programs are particularly hard to supervise and control from the center. Experience with highway maintenance illustrates three ways of responding to these difficulties:

• Force account operations (whereby government departments carry out maintenance themselves) can counter the lack of a profit motive with improved training and personal reward systems. Training programs in Kenya, Zaire, Brazil, Ethiopia, Nigeria, and the Dominican Republic have introduced "training production units." In place of classroom instruction, one or more stretches of road are given to each training unit which then has sole responsibility for their maintenance. Trainees therefore learn their skills in the field, and their performance is judged by the results they achieve.

Although large programs are bound by low civil service pay norms, trained staff can often be motivated through prompter payment linked more closely to performance. For example, wages paid ten days late have been associated with a 25 per-

---

Box 9.2 Contracting maintenance to the private sector

Argentina has many private contractors who have taken over maintenance of about half the national road network since 1979. Other countries have moved less rapidly, often to ease the costs of transition. In Brazil, for example, the federal highway authority reduced the extent of roads it directly maintained by almost 75 percent between 1970 and 1980. In Yugoslavia, with more than twenty years of experience of universal subcontracting, as few as five inspectors and one director control maintenance for a road network of 4,700 kilometers in Slovenia. Slovenia's entire road authority (including planning, construction, maintenance, operations, and safety) consists of only 185 people.

It is difficult to make direct comparisons of the cost-effectiveness of private versus public sector operations, since the latter seldom account for indirect costs such as interest. Nevertheless, the limited evidence available favors contracting. In Brazil, cost-plus contracts are still the primary method of contracting, though they give little incentive to contractors to control their costs. They also involve government in supervising quantities used, as well as inspecting results. Competition for contracted work has been keen: of a sample of 180 cost-plus tenders, 45 percent attracted six or more bids each, more than two-thirds, at least three bids. And in one region of Brazil, where the public sector operation is considered one of the most efficient, and where government accounts for in-

direct costs, it has been possible to make a comparison; for the same work, private contractors were 37 percent cheaper.

One main reason contractors are cheaper is their flexibility. They gear up more easily for peak demand and slim down faster when demand slackens. As a result, the capacity utilization of equipment is between 70 and 90 percent for private contractors, while force account operations average 40 to 50 percent. Since force accounts treat labor and equipment as fixed costs, even a small reduction in a project's budget significantly reduces output, because the cutback is in variable costs—fuel and other materials essential to the project.

Two examples of how projects can be delayed:

- In a West African country, local managers do not have the authority to buy even small supplies of materials for their project. Authority rests with a traveling paymaster who makes short and unannounced visits, and will release funds only to the purchasing field officer in person. As a result, field staff spend up to a third of their time waiting for the paymaster rather than carrying out their duties, and supplies are held up for as long as six months.

- One East African agricultural project was hampered by an unreliable postal and telephone service; lacking a telex or a photocopier, it could distribute multi-

ple copies of forty-page bid documents only through laborious retyping and a series of fourteen-hour bus journeys to the capital city.

Such stories are common, and result in delays costing hundreds of times the value of the missing local good or service. The solution lies in matching disbursement authority and resources with responsibility for implementation. For example, Mexico's rural development program (PIDER) shifted disbursement authority from Mexico City to state governments in 1977. Each state set up PIDER accounts, and payments to contractors were authorized locally after checking field supervision reports against a contractor's or agency's invoice. The new

payment process was much faster and thereby resulted in some cost savings: contractors were often willing to lower prices when they were not obliged to wait months to be paid.

In Morocco the Ministry of Agriculture has decentralized its procurement process in line with a shift in responsibility for agricultural development programs to its regional and provincial offices. Local management has been strengthened by staff engineers from the center, who have received in-service procurement training. Field staff familiar with local problems now have the capacity to support and supervise local contractors.

---

cent drop in productivity in Lesotho. Cumbersome payment procedures as well as budgetary problems are often at fault. In Honduras, for example, before the system was simplified, several departments and two different ministries were involved in paying highway construction workers, who each had to collect five different stamps and signatures before being paid each month. Cutting this kind of red tape can greatly improve force account performance.

- Contracting to private companies. This can reduce the management load on highway departments and increase cost-effectiveness (see Box 9.2). Experience in countries as diverse as Brazil, Yugoslavia, Argentina, and Kenya suggests that the prospects for subcontracting are promising. While much depends on the capacity of the private sector in each country, the availability of such work spurs the growth and skills of private contractors.

- Using local communities to maintain local roads. An important example is the "lengthman" system for rural road maintenance, successfully used in Kenya, Colombia, and elsewhere. Under this system, maintenance workers are hired as part-time contractors responsible for from one-half to two kilometers of road in their area. Roads are inspected once a month, and contractors paid only if maintenance is adequate. Community concern—the contractor is known to many who use the road he maintains—reinforces formal supervision. Dependence on machines and transport is reduced to an absolute minimum, as is administration once

the system is established. However, as with all labor-intensive methods, the demands on management are heavy while the system is being set up, and technical assistance is often required.

These three strategies are not mutually exclusive. Colombia, for example, is experimenting with all three. Argentina maintains contract and force account operations side by side. Use of both public and private sectors can encourage efficiency through competition; and it makes price-fixing and other forms of corruption more difficult. Contracting maintenance automatically involves decentralized management, which can simplify dispersed operations by dividing them into smaller tasks. Colombia's force account operation has used the same strategy for its feeder-road program. Since 1980 the organization's twenty-four regional offices have increased their responsibility for programming, evaluation, and execution of works; the central agency's role is now limited to logistic support and overall planning, technical, financial, and administrative control.

Delegation by contract to the private sector guarantees financial resources and reduces bureaucratic controls. Within the government, however, decentralization of responsibility is often not accompanied by a complementary grant of resources and authority. Successful decentralization necessarily involves limited but genuine local autonomy, as in the Mexican rural development program and the Moroccan irrigation program (see Box 9.3). But if decentralization is to be controllable—and, equally important, if it is to be politically acceptable to central government—its essential complement is the strengthening of central monitoring systems. This is a priority for both physical and people-centered development programs.

Managing people-centered development

Programs to improve the productivity and welfare of the poor—who in many countries do not share even a common language with government administrators—have always posed special problems. In the 1980s increasing concern about the cost and replicability of programs is leading to greater involvement of beneficiaries in the construction, maintenance, and financing of local projects that hitherto either were provided and run by government or were simply unavailable.

People-centered programs are particularly hard to manage because of the degree of uncertainty involved. First, goals can be abstract ("community self-reliance," for example) and performance not quantifiable in terms of construction time and costs or profits and losses. Second, there is little knowledge of how to design suitable programs, because they involve changing human behavior patterns that vary among cultures and localities. Third, the success of a project depends on whether people want the services it offers: project managers therefore often have to create demand. The task of management is thus more one of experimenting and learning than of implementing known procedures, as is the case with physical development.

Responding to local needs

Learning about local communities requires social skills not needed in physical development—skills still neglected by governments in developing countries and by foreign aid agencies. Relative lack of success in people-centered programs, coupled with a growing sociological awareness, has led to greater recognition of their complexity and uncertainty. This has encouraged a gradual move away from traditional "blueprint planning," in which an initial learning and design phase is separated from implementation and operation.

In blueprint planning, learning is accomplished largely through surveys and pilot projects. The former have important drawbacks. Although microcomputers promise speedier data processing, surveys remain complex and time-consuming to organize. The large amount of data they generate is often turned into usable information too late for practical planning. Even when they are timely, large-scale surveys are better suited to quantitative analysis of people's assets and production, for example, than to the qualitative assessment of social relations and attitudes required for program design.

Pilot projects—learning by doing, but on an initially small scale—anticipate implementation problems in a way surveys cannot. Provided they are done by the agencies that will later be responsible for operations, and use procedures that are replicable on a large scale, they can greatly increase responsiveness to local needs and bureaucratic realities. Pilot projects make sense particularly for agencies (including donors) required to justify future spending with firm and tested proposals.

They do not solve all the problems of running big programs, however. These programs need to be adjusted over time in response to varying local needs and environmental conditions. More recent planning methods have therefore moved toward a continuous learning and design process during implementation. Rather than design one initial replicable plan, the aim is to develop a flexible system for producing local plans in conjunction with local people. Managing the link between bureaucracy and people therefore becomes centrally important.

For foreign development agencies, as for recipient bureaucracies, the need to shift away from blueprint planning is challenging and not entirely welcome. Pressures to "move money" encourage focusing on the appraisal, commitment, and construction phases of projects rather than on their operation. This focus is reinforced by donors' strong preferences for financing capital and foreign exchange rather than recurrent and local costs. These pressures, coupled with an interest in quick, visible, and preferably measurable results, have encouraged donors to take a short-term view of the development process. They have often paid insufficient attention to institutional factors. They have also badly underestimated the persistence needed to mobilize the rural poor, to make full use of local skills and experience, to sort out competing interests and objectives, and to try alternative ways of expanding income and employment. While some external agencies have acquired a longer-term perspective through multiple projects with individual institutions, others must be more prepared to look at their relations with developing countries in a time frame of decades rather than of two or three years.

For governments, greater participation of local communities has both drawbacks and advantages. On the one hand, it adds to the management burden of government at the project design stage. Also, where communities are highly stratified, participation may bring to the surface tensions between local interest groups: local elites, which dominate "community" organizations, may oppose the involvement of disadvantaged groups and take over programs to serve their own ends. In addition, field staff may not be enthusiastic if working for local communities is thought to incur loss of authority and status, as well as inconvenience.

On the other hand, some form of partnership with local communities in the design of programs is essential, if plans are to meet beneficiaries' needs and encourage contributions of money and labor. Without such contributions, programs may never be viable or, once started, may not be sustained. The widespread success of "sites and services" schemes during the 1970s indicates that communities are prepared to shoulder much of the financial and managerial burden of development if design technologies and levels of service are appropriate and affordable.

There are different ways of involving local communities, of course. In the Philippines, a new approach being tested by the National Irrigation Administration treats local organization and autonomy as a major goal of development, desirable in its own right (see Box 9.4). In contrast, the Training and Visit (T&V) System of agricultural extension pays less attention to community organization, though it stresses responsiveness to the needs of beneficiaries (see Box 9.5). T&V's framework of routine procedures, tight supervision, and lack of emphasis on community mobilization have eased its adoption in traditional development bureaucracies. Suitably adapted, T&V's management principles have great potential for increasing access to basic services (for example, in primary health care and certain types of education). In these areas, the morale of field staff is often low because they have unclear goals and are poorly supervised, supported, and trained.

While the financial burden of T&V and similar systems falls entirely on government, the costs can be minimized by using part-time paraprofessionals recruited from the communities they are to serve and trained in basic skills. In eastern Senegal, for example, herdsmen from traditional communities have been trained as "barefoot vets" responsible

Box 9.4   NIA: learning a participatory approach to irrigation development

The traditional focus of irrigation development on technical design and construction has often led to long periods of inefficient operation while water management skills are developed. Since 1976 the National Irrigation Administration (NIA) in the Philippines has been experimenting with a different way of promoting small irrigation schemes.

NIA is developing water users' associations before the systems are built and involving farmers in their planning and construction. The result is irrigation systems that better meet local needs and a strong and representative farmers' organization ready to aid in water allocation as soon as the irrigation scheme has been built. Instead of farmers participating in NIA schemes, the emphasis is increasingly on NIA participation in the farmers' own efforts. The new approach has been directed by a Communal Irrigation Committee of senior NIA officials. They are supported by social scientists from several research institutions, both in the Philippines and abroad.

Social scientists participated heavily in the initial pilot project in central Luzon, which concentrated on developing an approach to irrigation that made sense to the villagers. This first phase—"learning to be effective"—differed from conventional pilot projects in that its aim was not to produce a technology to be packaged and applied elsewhere. Its primary purpose was for NIA to learn how to work with local people to develop their own capacity to manage irrigation.

The second phase—"learning to be efficient"—began with two new projects in central Luzon. Many problems encountered in the first project were anticipated and avoided so that construction could start sooner. A researcher was stationed in each of the two sites throughout this phase, providing monthly reports on the activities and concerns of the farmers, the community organizers, and the engineers. In 1980 the program entered its third phase, "learning to expand." One project was established in each of the nation's twelve administrative regions, and in 1981 each region added two more. In 1982 participatory projects were begun in each of sixty-six provinces, and by 1983 the participatory approach had become the standard for communal irrigation assistance throughout the country.

Many NIA staff have found greater job satisfaction working with farmers, and farmers, for their part, watch that the money they contribute to construction is well spent. They observe the opening of bids and help check the quantity and quality of materials and find the lowest prices for locally purchased goods. Working in partnership has added a new dimension of accountability—downward to farmer clients, as well as upward in the bureaucratic hierarchy.

Box 9.5   The Training and Visit System of agricultural extension

Training and Visit (T&V) has been adopted as the extension method in more than forty agricultural projects in about twenty countries, and has influenced many others. It has four broad principles:

- Concentration. Village-level workers (VLWs) spend their time learning from and advising farmers; they are not expected to deliver supplies, to organize credit, or to make reports. In India, where T&V has been adopted by thirteen states, moving to a single line of command and responsibility required extensive reform of a system that previously gave VLWs a multipurpose role in community development.
- Simplicity. VLWs are trained every two weeks, with emphasis on what is important for farmers to know about the current stage of cultivating their most important crops. This ensures the relevance of VLW work and does not overburden them with more information than they can handle.
- Regularity. There are rigid schedules for farm visits, training, and supervision,

usually based on a two-week cycle. VLWs spend eight days a fortnight visiting eight separate farmers' groups, returning fortnightly to each group on the same day of the week. This means that farmers know when and where to find extension advice, and can hold the VLW accountable if he does not keep to his schedule. The regular schedule also means that extension supervisors know where all staff will be on any given day. Each supervising extension officer has no more than eight people under him, so that he can visit each of them not less than once a fortnight. Group training for VLWs, also rigidly scheduled, is carried out fortnightly in the field by specialists and agricultural extension officers. In addition, monthly training workshops are held, which are attended by extension specialists, researchers, and supervisors. At these workshops, forthcoming advice is refined and disseminated and farmers' reactions are reviewed.
- Communication. T&V recognizes the importance of effective communication

links between researchers, extension staff, and farmers. Face-to-face meetings, held as far as possible in farmers' fields, replace the common emphasis on time-consuming and unproductive written reporting. This allows quick and effective feedback and adjustments where necessary. VLWs do no more than keep a simple diary of key messages and farmers' reactions for their own reference. Meetings with farmers, in which supervisors participate, are the main means not only of monitoring field staff performance but also of defining priorities for agricultural research.

None of the individual management principles of T&V is new. What distinguishes T&V is that it has combined mutually reinforcing management principles into a clearly defined system for managing activities which are geographically scattered and constantly changing. Consistent commitment from senior officials has been critical to sustained success.

---

for vaccinations and simple medical treatment, leaving fully trained (and scarce) veterinarians to handle more complex cases.

Political backing

Commitment to the mass provision of services in rural areas is difficult to sustain against the vested interests that favor urban elites. This is true even where the dominant political doctrine stresses the importance of local communities: in 1965, Mao Zedong summed up China's struggle to achieve responsive primary health care with his exclamation that "the Ministry of Public Health is not a Ministry of Public Health for the people, so why not change its name to the Ministry of Urban Health, the Ministry of Gentlemen's Health, or even to the Ministry of Urban Gentlemen's Health?"

Governments find it particularly hard to redirect their bureaucratic efforts to serve local communities when corruption affects the attitudes of field staff (see Box 9.6). For that reason, programs that do not involve money changing hands have a great

advantage. The T&V scheme is one example: extension workers have nothing to do with the provision of agricultural inputs such as seed and fertilizer—their service emphasizes professionalism and pride in performance. By contrast, in irrigation management, which is responsible for repair works and rationing a valuable commodity (water), other approaches must be considered. Morocco and India have experimented with burying irrigation pipes to reduce the chances of their being tampered with: the extra capital cost can be more than justified by higher agricultural production.

Corruption can also be checked by community participation in the design, operation, and financing of programs, since this increases the accountability of field staff to local people. In some irrigation schemes in Asia, for example, farmers can give part of their water charges to managers as a performance bonus. Information can also be a powerful weapon for increasing accountability. This was shown by Kenya's decision in 1978 to publish high school examination results comparing the performance of schools and districts. Political and official interest was thereby awakened and resulted in awards for successful schools; in 1980 and 1981, schools markedly improved their performance.

Alternatives to government action

Physically and psychologically remote from the poor, bureaucracies are often unable to respond to popular needs, even when money and manpower are not a constraint. Their work can become more effective by making greater use of the skills of nongovernment organizations (NGOs) and the commercial private sector. In many countries, small private traders, moneylenders, and truckers already provide farmers with convenient and flexible support services. Their potential disadvantages—monopoly pricing and diseconomies of small scale, for example—are not always assessed against the often greater inefficiencies of government services, especially when the latter are given a monopoly. One alternative to state services is the "pump-priming" of private sector activity—and of increased competition—through the provision of credit. Other examples include the provision of extension advice by private traders in agriculture and village midwives in health; and the substitu-

tion of private tubewells for lumpy government investments in dams.

The work of NGOs is sometimes hard to coordinate with big government programs. Yet the contribution of both foreign and indigenous NGOs is often underestimated by official bodies. NGOs in the industrial countries of the OECD alone transferred some $2 billion to developing countries in 1981. NGOs have developed technologies from windmills and water handpumps to beekeeping, and services from primary health care to farm credit. An NGO which began a self-help housing project in El Salvador in 1968 (see Box 9.7) has now helped to build more than 4,300 houses with about 7,000 more under construction. In Bangladesh, the combined efforts of NGOs in promoting nonfarm rural employment are greater than those of government. The effectiveness of NGOs is the result of many factors: commitment to poverty relief; freedom from bureaucratic procedures and attitudes; scarce funds, which force concentration on priorities and replicable technologies; and their small size, which makes it easier to understand and respond to the needs of local communities.

Box 9.6   Field staff incentives: private profit versus public service

The perverse incentives that can determine field staff behavior have been thoroughly documented in the case of an irrigation program. The program managers have two main sources of illicit income—the annual maintenance budget and the farmers. By long-established convention, 8.5 percent of the price of a maintenance contract is shared among irrigation staff—2.5 percent to the senior engineer (in charge of an area of 80,000 to 400,000 acres), 1 percent to the clerical staff and draughtsmen, 5 percent to be split between the works supervisor and the junior engineer (in charge of 30,000 to 100,000 acres). This minimum kickback is supplemented by "savings"—the contractor uses less material or carries out less work than specified, and the money saved is split between irrigation officers and the contractor. The size of these savings is negotiable, but is normally at least 15 percent of the value of the contract, sometimes as much as 40 percent.

By custom, senior engineers receive further payments on top of the 2.5 per-

cent of each maintenance contract. They expect 5 percent of each irrigation area's total works budget (including the amount spent on field staff salaries). Since junior engineers generally cannot find this money from their works budget alone, they raise some of it from farmers. In return for an assurance of water for the whole season, villages whose water supply is uncertain make a flat-rate payment. They may also make one-time payments for more active intervention by irrigation staff depending on weather conditions and the immediate need for water. In relation to incomes, the scale of such corruption is large: for junior engineers, it is often more than three times their annual salary, and for senior engineers more than eight times. Since appointments to these posts are valuable, they are bought rather than decided on merit. Senior engineer posts cost from three to well over ten times annual salary, depending on productivity and hence on the farmers' ability to pay.

Systematic corruption means that budgets, already short of money, do not pro-

vide the construction and maintenance they are intended to. Staff have an incentive to disrupt water supplies in order to increase farmers' uncertainty and hence their willingness to pay bribes. As for farmers, villages which can afford the biggest bribes get the most water, to the detriment both of equity and of farm production over the irrigation system as a whole.

Safeguards against corruption are needed at every level. Politically, the accountability of officials to ministers, and ministers to the general public, is a well-tried way to minimize abuse. For programs, pressure on corrupt managers can also be increased by making clients (especially the poor) more aware of their rights. One Asian irrigation scheme has worked out detailed individual rights—how much water will be supplied and when. Rights are displayed on large boards at the canals or pumps, and water-measuring devices that all farmers can understand are provided. Organizing beneficiaries to act collectively can also increase farmers' leverage.

Box 9.7 Housing for the poor: tapping local initiative in San Salvador

In 1968 a small group of people organized by a priest and a Peace Corps volunteer helped to rehouse thirty families who were victims of flooding in San Salvador. Two years later, with the backing of local businessmen, La Fundacion Salvadorena de Desarrollo y Vivienda Minima (FSDVM) was registered as a nonprofit foundation. Expanding with external financial support, by 1980 FSDVM had become a major producer of low-income, institutionally financed dwellings in El Salvador. Since then the deteriorating political and economic situation in the country has reduced FSDVM's effectiveness.

FSDVM's approach to housing was a radical departure from government programs, which traditionally had concentrated on building houses that most of the population could not afford. FSDVM's basic house cost $2,800 in 1982, including land and administrative overhead, with credit repayment for families over twenty years. In addition, FSDVM allowed people to work on their houses in place of down payments, so that about three-quarters of all urban families could afford FSDVM housing.

FSDVM emphasized appropriate technology, close contact with participating communities, and learning by doing. Houses were built in affordable stages, with top priority given to secure land tenure and services. Potential homeowners helped reduce costs through mutual help with construction at weekends, and so laid the foundation for community groups capable of self-management. Participation in decisionmaking involved beneficiaries in defining and solving their own problems at every stage of the program. As civil unrest grew, community workgroups became more difficult to organize, and some basic construction was taken over by small contractors; nevertheless, homeowners continued to help each other with finishing work.

Before external factors intervened, FSDVM's repayment record was excellent: in July 1980, arrears on loans were only 2.3 percent of the total outstanding. The Foundation's low reserves made repayments essential for the program to continue, so all those involved were motivated to build economically and to collect debts. More important, FSDVM saw its work not just as an end in itself, but as a means of organizing and increasing the self-reliance of the urban poor. The sense of community created during construction encouraged social responsibility and a willingness to pay.

Mass urban and rural services

The sheer scale of many people-centered programs makes heavy demands on management. Urbanization in particular will pose formidable challenges for the developing countries, since they will contain most of the world's large cities by the end of the century (see Figure 9.1). The more successful metropolitan development agencies, such as Calcutta's (established in 1971), have recognized the weaknesses of central control over detailed planning and operations and have helped to strengthen a local government tier in closer touch with local needs. For the metropolitan authorities, this has meant politically difficult decisions to relinquish executive control and operating budgets. They have correspondingly strengthened their work in capital budgeting, long-range planning, coordination, and fiscal management.

The Indonesian government's successful family planning program has also decentralized day-to-day managerial authority, involved local politicians, and strengthened central monitoring. Regional managers are largely free to set spending and performance targets, but officials in Jakarta insist on a realistic relationship between planned and past spending, and strict adherence to budget ceilings. Performance is monitored monthly on one-page forms that are collated rapidly at the center, and the results are immediately made available in clinics, districts, and provinces. Each administrative center receives a report ranking all subordinate units by performance, which then influences the allocation of finance the following year.

Monitoring systems, essential if field managers are granted greater autonomy, serve two purposes—to maintain central control and to motivate local managers. Applied intelligently, they can produce big improvements in performance—even in their first year of operation, to judge by a new monitoring system for rural health care in the Indian state of Maharashtra. If monitoring is to be effective, the right balance must be struck between sufficiency and simplicity, so that monitoring does not divert managers from implementing programs. Often more could be done to develop simple indicators that relate inputs to outputs, and to widen the use of monitoring systems as management incentives.

Managing multiagency programs

As governments have grown more aware of the interdependence of development efforts, their projects and programs have become increasingly integrated. They often involve many institutions and functions, posing challenging and sometimes overwhelming problems of interagency coordination. These problems have been widespread in the complex "new-style" projects favored by the foreign development agencies from the early 1970s.

In some cases, it is a mistake to attempt an ambitious integration of programs. Coordinating the work of agencies with different interests and power takes time and scarce managerial skills, and can founder in bureaucratic politics. Between agencies, coordination poses the same managerial problem as people-centered development: how to involve those outside a manager's direct control.

Where effective coordination cannot be assured, complex programs can often be simplified by delinking them, or reducing the number of components. Many of the world's most successful people-centered programs were developed with a single purpose: population planning in Indonesia, T&V in India, tea development in Kenya, and rural education in Mexico, for example. The Kenyan government plans to divide its ambitious integrated agricultural development program into a series of administratively separate projects—in extension, smallholder credit, livestock, and so on. Such decisions recognize that it may often be important for services to be available simultaneously, but not always essential that they be integrated administratively.

The need for coordination can also be minimized by reducing the number of program components. A recent scheme to rehabilitate watersheds in the Indian Himalayas intentionally avoided burdening

management with responsibility for education, village electricity, health care, and roads—much needed though all of these are. Instead, it concentrated on farming and fuelwood development, which are critical both to local living standards and to the success of measures for soil conservation and reforestation. Similarly, Ethiopia's Minimum Agricultural Package Project concentrated on a few key tasks replicable on a large scale with limited managerial resources.

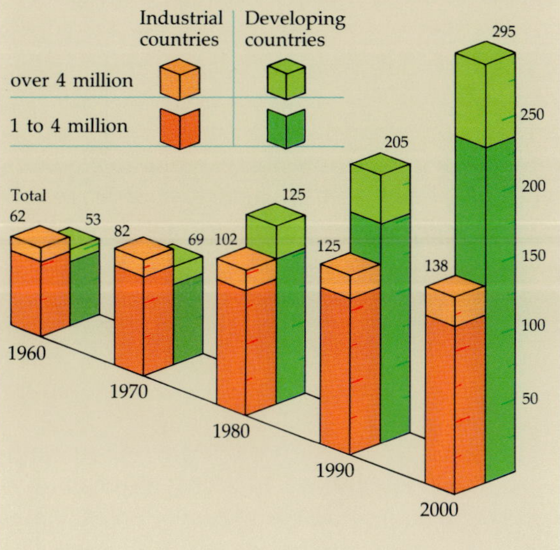

Coordinating action

For some projects and programs, integration is essential. Mines and factories, for example, often cannot operate without parallel transport investments. In agriculture, new seeds will produce high yields only if they have enough water and fertilizer. Even where integration is not critical, it may offer significant benefits. Farmers will be more willing to adopt new agricultural methods if they have access to credit, ready markets, and transport. Innovation is also stimulated by education, while better health means less working time lost. Similarly, in urban areas, health services are of limited use without complementary water and waste services.

Establishing cooperation. Where managerial resources can handle the complexities of integrated development, three strategies for coordination have been commonly adopted:

• Special management units with their own budgets and resources set up parallel to, and administratively isolated from, existing agencies. While convenient for foreign development agencies interested in short-term results, these are often not in the interests of long-term institutional development (see Box 9.8). They may also lead to bureaucratic proliferation that complicates the tasks of managing budgets and planning investment.

• Contracts and written understandings between agencies. In the case of power supplies, for example, some companies in India have required guarantees of continuous electricity before they will build new factories. In general, however, contracts are hard to enforce unless tasks are clear and performance quantifiable—rarely the case in people-centered development. Written understandings are more flexible than formal contracts. Several Latin American countries have a tradition of *convenios* between public agencies for the provision of services. For example, the Brazilian State of Minas Gerais has successfully coordinated a rural development program involving thirty-nine agen-

FIGURE 9.1

Number of cities with populations of more than one million, 1960–2000

97

Box 9.8 Project management units: integration in isolation

Parallel project units can increase the speed at which projects are implemented—by avoiding bureaucratic procedures and the need to negotiate the cooperation of independent line agencies. But they may also have long-term disadvantages. Such was the experience with the Thaba Bosiu Rural Development Project in Lesotho. The project's management unit was created in 1973 to integrate road development and soil conservation, with supplies, credit, advice, and marketing services to about 12,000 farmers. The unit was set up to compensate for administrative weakness in the Ministry of Agriculture, and proved effective while the project was being implemented. But its success was partly due to above-average local staff attracted by salaries higher than civil service norms. When the project was completed, the staff could not be integrated into the Ministry of Agriculture because of salary differentials. When the project unit was finally dissolved, few if any institutional benefits were left.

A more extreme version of this weakness can be seen in Sierra Leone, where a series of integrated agricultural projects, each with a separate management unit, has proliferated to cover 80 percent of the country. The result has been a weakened Ministry of Agriculture with a field staff demoralized by competition from the project management units; no clear lines of authority from headquarters to the field; and an inability to plan rational development in agriculture. The government is now planning a gradual reintegration of ministry and units.

Project units have however proved useful vehicles for developing and demonstrating new technologies, and can be effective in the long-term if their eventual merger with a "parent" institution is carefully planned from the outset. One example is the introduction of the "sites and services" concept in urban housing. Although the special management unit of a pilot project in Zambia was disbanded after the project was completed, the cheapness (and hence replicability) of its approach had been so well demonstrated that it was taken up by conventional housing institutions. A similar unit in Kenya was successfully merged with the Housing Department of the Nairobi City Council. Only when project unit staff are motivated by the prospect of a long-term career, will they be prepared to work for salaries compatible enough with the parent institution for eventual merging of the unit to be possible.

---

cies within a convenio framework. In practice, convenios tend to be renegotiable arrangements. Their value lies less in the enforceability of the contract than in the joint planning and negotiating process before signature.

• Informal cooperation. Most projects require voluntary cooperation from agencies over which project managers have influence but no direct control. Integration then becomes a matter of negotiation between those who have certain rewards and sanctions at their disposal, and agencies with varying commitment to program goals. Three broad lessons emerge from the many failures and few successes. Where integration has worked well, coordination has been planned at the project design stage, rather than left to emerge during implementation; attention has been given to the people and processes involved in building and maintaining consensus, rather than simply to organograms and structures; and coordinating mechanisms have been designed at the appropriate hierarchical levels.

The importance of early involvement is demonstrated in all successful integrated programs. Agencies will have more incentive to identify with a project and contribute to it if they have helped to formulate goals, cooperated in design, and agreed on their implementation tasks. Their roles can then usefully be publicized: in two urban development schemes in Mexico and Liberia, agencies took part in one- or two-day "project launch workshops" to which politicians and press were invited, and in which project goals and agency responsibilities were set out. Public visibility provided recognition—and the pressure of increased accountability to communities.

Project plans often emphasize formal coordinating structures in organograms, rather than the composition of coordinating committees and the power of their members. A common problem associated with liaison committees is the nomination of senior officials who are too busy to attend regular meetings, and who therefore delegate this task to junior staff lacking the authority to deal with problems. Getting things done depends on compromise between the power, knowledge, and regular availability of committee members. Coordinating committees can be made more effective by balancing agency staff with representatives of the beneficiaries and other political groups. This can improve bureaucratic accountability as well as involve interest groups with the power to support or subvert program goals.

The appropriate level for effective coordination depends on the activity involved. Production of standardized services, for example, needs liaison at the top of the hierarchy. Electric power in Colombia is coordinated by one central company which operates the national grid; when a joint effort is needed, it pools the financial resources of regional companies to develop hydroelectric schemes. People-centered programs, by contrast, require coordinating links further down the hierarchy. Since such programs focus on local needs, strong local liaison is particularly important.

Maintaining cooperation. To be effective, coordination needs to be maintained when a program is in operation. Cooperation can be encouraged by sharing information and by joint budgeting, both geared to performance criteria. The effectiveness of coordinating committees depends as much on the quality of information available to them, as on the power and abilities of their members. Diagrams (known as critical path charts) showing the links and lead times of all projects have been used to monitor slum improvement and sites and services programs in Madras and have helped reduce construction time by a third. All project participants know immediately if any of them are falling short of their commitment, and this knowledge prompts corrective action.

Budgeting can also help to maintain cooperation. Colombia's integrated rural development program (see Box 9.9) has used its programming

and budgeting system to transform the attitudes of agencies which had jealously guarded their independence. Budgets are now jointly agreed, and later adjusted on the basis of performance; this encourages each agency to make its promised contributions. Budgeting units such as those in Colombia differ from the special management units described in Box 9.8 in that they do not have an independent implementing capacity.

Some lessons learned: a summary

This chapter has illustrated how management can adapt to the demands of different tasks. While approaches vary according to the activity involved, many successful projects and programs share certain qualities:

• The development of management skills through on-the-job training and incentives. On-the-job training—emphasized by PUSRI in fertilizer production, TANESCO in the case of a utility, training production units in road maintenance, and in the Training and Visit system of extension—is relevant and avoids diverting staff from productive work. Different incentives have been used to retain and motivate staff: apart from financial rewards, they include promotion prospects and sta-

---

Box 9.9 Integrated rural development in Colombia

Colombia's rural development program uses its planning and budgeting system to coordinate the activities of eight departmental administrations (the provincial level of government), four central line ministries and their provincial representatives, eight other government agencies, and about 2,500 *veredas* (communities of 50 to 100 families) in 226 municipalities where small farmers predominate. It has brought clinics and schools, water supply, electricity, and rural roads to more than a million people; more than 100,000 farmers have been trained; agricultural production has increased; and about 1,000 hectares of forest land have been replanted by smallholders. This program is being extended to another 126 municipalities and eventually will have nationwide coverage.

Programming and budgeting is initiated and coordinated by the National Planning Office, which annually prepares budgetary guidelines and selection criteria for investments. Programming then proceeds from the bottom up. Vereda assemblies select priority investments and activities. Their proposals are examined by technical, municipal, and provincial committees, which include representatives of line agencies and beneficiaries as well as local and regional government. National planning officials working with provincial governments help to combine individual budgets into an overall program. This program is then presented to an interministerial committee, which need not get involved in bilateral negotiations with individual agencies. Instead, it judges the budgets against the objectives and achievements of the program.

Thereafter, the program is coordinated in two ways. First, national planning officials at the provincial level can suspend disbursements to any agency whose performance, judged by field visits and monthly financial statements, is deemed unsatisfactory. Second, beneficiaries can ask for changes through the local and municipal committees; on their recommendation, the provincial representative of the National Planning Office can authorize program and budget adjustments without prior approval from the national management unit.

To use the budget as a coordinating device, the Colombian program departs from budgeting procedures standard in many countries. First, budgetary and disbursement authority is vested in an independent unit. Second, money is allocated to agencies on the basis of their previous year's performance (this requires a rapid reporting system). Third, money is released in tranches according to performance instead of being automatically disbursed when the project has been designed.

bility of tenure (PUSRI); collegial management styles (NIA in the Philippines and T&V); and public ranking and recognition of performance (Indonesia's population program and Kenya's examination system). Management development policies often have their main payoff in the longer term, so a continuous commitment to them is a precondition of success.

- The use of external resources—the private sector, nongovernment organizations, and program beneficiaries. This involves corresponding changes in management—such as the ability to supervise contractors (road maintenance in Argentina and Yugoslavia), and to enlist the help of beneficiaries (NIA and FSDVM). It also means changing technical designs to meet the needs of clients and ensure wider replicability.

- Managerial autonomy coupled with the development of management information systems. Successful organizations have made individual management groups the basic unit for measuring performance (PUSRI's cost centers and the Indonesian population program's field units). Timely reporting of results has given managers the encouragement of recognition and the pressure of possible sanctions (Colombia's monitoring and budgeting system for rural development). Reporting results to beneficiaries and the general public is also an important and much-neglected performance incentive.

- A simplified management task, through isolating priorities, defining individual and agency roles, and dividing big programs into smaller tasks and management teams. Clarity and concentration count, whether in choosing a single program goal or limiting extension advice to a few key messages (T&V); agreeing on a set of goals and roles in multiagency programs (the Minas Gerais integrated program); or developing relevant skills (on-the-job training). Successful schemes have also developed those management functions that are critical to particular tasks—for example, PUSRI's emphasis on financial management systems and, in people-centered programs, the focus on learning, adapting to local conditions, and managing the link between bureaucracy and beneficiary.

This chapter has been concerned with initiatives that are within the discretion of agency managers. However, such initiatives often require support in areas beyond the control of individual managers. First and foremost, political commitment determines the adequacy of money and the competence and security of senior staff—the preconditions of a sustained management-development effort. Second, project-level efforts to improve personnel management cannot compensate for a sectoral or national shortage of skills, or for national personnel practices that need reform; these issues are discussed in Chapter 10. Third, some structural and procedural improvements—decentralization and coordination, for example—may also be possible only in the context of national measures; these issues are taken up in Chapter 11.

10 Managing the public service

Earlier chapters have proposed various measures for improving the performance of the public sector. Success in implementing these measures is largely determined by a government's ability to staff and manage its public service. That in turn depends partly on attractive salaries and career prospects in the public service and partly on political leaders' being committed to high standards of performance and integrity. Even then, public servants often have to work through and with institutions that have been established only recently—and in conditions that may not be conducive to efficiency. In many developing countries, public servants have a more challenging task than their counterparts in developed countries.

This chapter is divided into three sections. The first traces the growth of public employment and the skill shortages faced by the public service; the second, the role of training in overcoming them; and the third identifies improvements needed in personnel management. A concluding note stresses the importance of cultural and political factors in reforming a country's management practices. The chapter has three main findings:

• Public employment in developing countries has grown rapidly in recent years in response to the demand for improved public services. But often there is overstaffing at lower levels, accompanied by shortages of professional and technical staff. These shortages are exacerbated by the "brain drain."

• Public service training needs to be made more relevant to the demands of the job. This requires forging closer links between trainers and trainees and between training and career development, as well as developing local training materials and programs.

• A strong civil service requires a personnel office that actively manages rather than passively administers personnel policies. Strengthening personnel management demands, above all, improving the management capabilities of personnel offices and giving them the status they need to carry

out policy reforms. Other policy measures include establishing career schemes for occupational groups, instituting an effective system of performance evaluation, and avoiding big salary differentials between the private sector and the civil service.

Availability and distribution of skills

The labor force in developing countries is expected to grow by 588 million people between now and the year 2000. Finding productive work for them, and for the millions who are already unemployed or underemployed, is a fundamental challenge of development. Although developing countries have made remarkable progress in education and training, most still have large reserves of unskilled labor alongside severe shortages of skilled people. This imbalance is most acute in the public sector, which provides a high percentage of modern sector employment. Governments are under strong political and social pressure to employ more people, while facing strong competition from the private sector for technical and professional staff.

Growth in public employment

Recent data for about seventy-five countries show that as countries grow richer public employment increases on a per capita basis but declines as a share of nonagricultural employment. The industrial market economies have about twice as many public employees per 1,000 people as the developing countries, but public employment in developing countries has grown three to four times faster in recent years (see Box 10.1). This often makes the state the dominant employer, particularly of professional and technical personnel. In Kenya, for example, a 1976 study revealed that roughly 70 percent of these people were employed by the government.

This rapid growth partly reflects the demand for more public services. For example, the number of primary school pupils in developing countries in-

Box 10.1   Trends in public service employment

According to recent ILO data from a sample of countries, public service employment in some developing countries increased three to four times faster than in developed countries in the mid- and late 1970s and two to three times faster than the population at large. In most cases this was to be expected, given the small public service with which many developing countries started at independence. While public employment fell in some developed countries (such as Canada and the United Kingdom) between 1976 and 1980, it increased in all the developing countries surveyed.

In industrial countries the share of public employment in total employment has risen gradually, from 12 percent in 1960 to 18 percent in 1979. On a per capita basis, these countries now have more than twice the number of government employees as the developing countries.

This disparity is largely explained by agriculture's high share of the labor force in developing countries (more than 70 percent in low-income economies and 40 to 45 percent in middle-income economies, compared with barely 5 percent in industrial market economies); and agriculture is almost entirely in the private sector. A different picture emerges when agriculture is excluded. In a sample of twenty-eight developing countries, an average of 27 percent of salaried jobs in the nonagricultural sectors were in government, compared with 20 percent in industrial countries. In India the rate was

as high as 54 percent; followed by Liberia, 53 percent; Benin, 50 percent; and Tanzania, 46 percent. In developed countries the ratio ranged from a low of 9 percent in Japan to a high of 30 percent in Sweden.

Grouped by different levels of government, the figures show that state and local government account for 60 percent of total government employment in industrial countries compared with 14 percent in developing countries. In the African countries surveyed, less than 7 percent of government employment is at the local level.

Growth in government employment

Average annual growth rate

(percent)

15 — Zaire

— Mexico
— Burundi

— Nigeria
10 — Ecuador

— Cameroon

— Egypt
— Thailand

5 — Kenya   — Sweden
— Bolivia   — Australia
— Philippines   — Denmark
— India   — Belgium
— Turkey   — France
                  — Germany, Fed. Rep.
                  — United States
0 — Argentina   — Japan
                  — United Kingdom
                  — Canada

Points on the graph indicate average annual growth rates for developing countries on the left and for industrial countries on the right. For most countries listed, the period covered is 1976-80 and government employment includes only central and local government employees.

Sources: ILO; World Bank.

Share of government in nonagricultural employment

(percent)

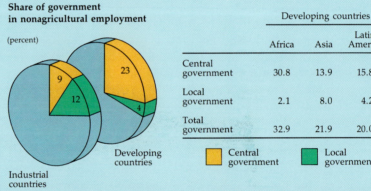

Industrial countries

Developing countries

	Developing countries		
	Africa	Asia	Latin America
Central government	30.8	13.9	15.8
Local government	2.1	8.0	4.2
Total government	32.9	21.9	20.0

■ Central government   ■ Local government

The pie chart compares unweighted averages for sixteen industrial countries with those for twenty-eight developing countries. The developing countries are grouped by region in the table. The data for this figure and the one below are based on the findings of a survey conducted in 1982 by the IMF; they cover the period between the late 1970s and the early 1980s.

Number of government employees per 1,000 inhabitants

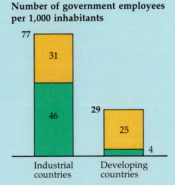

Industrial countries   Developing countries

	Developing countries		
	Africa	Asia	Latin America
Central government	18	26	30
Local government	2	4	8
Total government	20	30	38

■ Central government   ■ Local government

The bars compare unweighted averages for sixteen industrial countries with those for thirty-one developing countries. The developing countries are grouped by region in the table.

creased from about 117 million in 1960 to more than 236 million in 1975, requiring a proportional growth in the number of teachers. Another principal reason for the rapid growth in public employment is the understandable desire of governments to improve tribal, ethnic, or regional representation, or to use public payrolls as a means for combating unemployment. The governments of such countries as Egypt, Ivory Coast, Mali, Mauritius, and Sri Lanka have at various times explicitly acted as "employer of last resort," particularly of university graduates. In Egypt, according to an ILO estimate, overstaffing was almost 42 percent of total civil service employment in 1976. A consultant's recent study of two ministries in a West African country classified as redundant 6,000 out of 6,800 headquarters' staff. In some oil-producing countries, governments have hired extra staff as a way of distributing oil revenues.

A clear distinction must be drawn between manning the public service with competent staff and using it to tackle unemployment. For the latter, temporary public works (or food-for-work) programs are cheaper and more effective than indiscriminate increases in public employment. Overstaffing imposes a financial burden on the state, undermines morale, and obstructs efficient management. Several countries have therefore started to reduce the number of staff members, in part prompted by recession and fiscal stringency. Among industrial countries, the Federal Republic of Germany, United States, Japan, United Kingdom, and Canada have recently trimmed or curtailed the growth of their public service. Among developing countries, Turkey's government stopped hiring in 1980 and has since maintained strict control over staff. In Yugoslavia the government is encouraging older federal officials to retire early, and Egypt is trying to limit the growth of staff at lower levels.

Skill shortages

In most developing countries, overstaffing at lower grades coexists with severe shortages of senior professional and technical people—shortages that can often be made good only by employing expatriates. More than half the technical assistance received by developing countries is used to finance expatriates, while much of the rest goes for the overseas training of developing country nationals (see Box 10.2). This imbalance of skills is particularly severe in African countries: at independence, more than three quarters of the jobs for university graduates were held by expatriates. Since then this ratio has been steadily reduced.

While skill shortages are hard to quantify, the World Bank finds that two-thirds of its borrowing countries face serious difficulties in filling certain posts in the public sector, particularly for engineers, managers, accountants, economists, and doctors. These difficulties are compounded by a tendency for the more experienced staff to quit the public service in search of better jobs. In about half the countries, the outflow from government is mostly toward employment abroad; in the other half, mostly toward the domestic private sector. Vacancy rates derived from manpower surveys also provide partial evidence of shortages. A 1977 survey in Nigeria, for example, found a 22 percent vacancy rate for modern sector occupations; rates for scientists, secondary school teachers, and other professionals all exceeded 40 percent.

Shortages are most severe in local government. In Nigeria a third of the primary school teachers possessed no qualifications beyond a primary school leaving certificate and most worked in rural areas. This bias extends to technical assistance personnel. For understandable reasons, rural institutions everywhere find it hard to lure staff away from the attractions of urban life.

In many developing countries, skill shortages in the public service are as much qualitative as quantitative. This stems from the uneven quality of secondary and higher education in most developing countries, the strong demand from the private sector for good graduates, and the fact that government salaries are too low to attract or retain enough capable individuals. All these problems are made worse by emigration.

The brain drain

For many developing countries the export of labor and skills makes an important contribution to their balance of payments. But, given the shortage of professional and technical people in many developing countries, their emigration often has serious consequences for development management. The brain drain has some harmful effects even in the few instances in which there appears to be a relative abundance of skilled people (such as doctors and engineers in urban India), since emigrants are then replaced by people who might otherwise have worked in rural areas. Some countries undoubtedly benefit substantially from their emigrants, whose remittances more than offset the cost of their education. For most developing countries,

Box 10.2 Technical cooperation in development

Between one-fifth and one-quarter of official aid flows goes to financing technical cooperation for the purpose of transferring knowledge and skills to developing countries. Although the figures are not complete, they suggest that total disbursements of technical assistance in 1981 were some $7–8 billion, mostly in the form of grants. More than half ($4.6 billion) was provided by OECD countries on a bilateral basis, most of the rest by the UNDP, $730 million; other UN agencies, $540 million; and the World Bank, $510 million. The International Monetary Fund (IMF) and the regional banks were also important sources of official technical assistance, as were the countries of Eastern Europe and some of the developing countries, such as China and India. Private voluntary agencies too had technical assistance programs (more than $40 million for the Ford Foundation alone), and developing-country governments contributed heavily to meeting local costs.

The biggest recipient of technical assistance was sub-Saharan Africa, accounting for 30 percent of the UNDP's field expenditures in 1981 and 40 to 50 percent of the disbursements of OECD countries. Other big recipients were Bangladesh, Brazil, Egypt, India, Indonesia, Morocco, Peru, Philippines, and Thailand. Saudi Arabia and other Middle Eastern oil exporters obtain considerable amounts of (reimbursable) technical assistance from a variety of sources, including the World Bank.

More than half the recorded spending on technical cooperation is used to finance expatriate staff. Overseas training of developing-country nationals accounts for about one-tenth of the total outlays of both OECD countries and the UNDP; OECD countries provide roughly 110,000 fellowships a year and the UNDP, 10,000. Technical cooperation aid is also used to provide equipment (particularly in fields of high technology), design and feasibility studies, economic and social surveys, and research.

In recent years there has been a steady growth of technical cooperation between developing countries (TCDC). Of the 10,000 experts serving in the field in 1981 under programs financed by the UNDP, 37 percent came from developing countries compared with fewer than 25 percent in the early 1970s. The UNDP can now use up to 10 percent of its funds for TCDC. Bilateral technical assistance is still mostly tied—provided by people or organizations in the donor country—but some donors such as Sweden are financing training and other technical assistance from third countries.

Technical assistance from DAC countries, 1981
(millions of dollars)

Recipients	France[a]	Germany, Fed. Rep.	Japan	Netherlands	United Kingdom	United States	Other DAC	Total
Europe	8.6	60.0	3.5	6.3	3.4	2.0	15.0	98.8
Africa north of Sahara	161.9	37.7	10.9	5.1	9.1	200.0	36.1	460.8
of which								
Egypt	6.6	19.9	5.6	3.8	8.8	183.0	7.0	234.7
Morocco	66.2	7.6	1.5	0.2	0.1	9.0	15.0	99.6
Africa south of Sahara	449.5	286.3	41.7	94.8	162.8	213.0	371.3	1,619.4
of which								
Kenya	2.2	16.7	9.4	12.5	25.0	13.0	33.5	112.3
Senegal	72.3	6.8	0.9	1.7	0.5	18.0	7.5	107.7
Sudan	1.7	25.9	1.8	13.5	9.1	16.0	5.6	73.6
Tanzania	0.5	28.3	4.0	15.5	18.9	15.0	64.4	146.6
Zaire	13.4	9.7	2.2	2.3	0.2	7.0	81.3	116.1
North and Central America	11.4	43.0	19.5	21.2	17.3	66.0	31.9	210.3
South America	23.3	132.4	52.4	44.7	13.7	16.0	30.0	312.5
Middle East	22.1	46.3	13.1	12.3	12.4	48.0	12.3	166.5
South Asia	4.4	77.8	31.6	26.5	39.0	55.0	54.9	289.2
of which								
Bangladesh	0.2	15.0	6.8	8.5	9.2	38.0	20.9	98.6
India	2.1	30.0	2.5	11.1	14.6	1.0	16.2	77.5
Far East	19.3	83.0	137.1	39.8	18.2	53.0	84.8	435.2
of which								
Indonesia	4.7	25.4	37.3	25.1	7.3	32.0	23.5	155.3
Thailand	1.9	11.2	32.2	4.4	3.5	7.0	10.6	70.8
Oceania	12.2	5.1	6.6	2.0	22.5	6.0	24.3	78.7
Unspecified	110.3	106.9	21.5	68.5	133.9	306.0	168.5	915.6
Total	823.0	878.5	337.9	321.2	432.3	965.0	829.1	4,587.0

a. Excluding French assistance of $687 million to its overseas territories.
Source: DAC Secretariat.

however, emigration faces them with the difficult (and usually urgent) task of finding replacements (see Box 10.3).

Small countries tend to be hardest hit by shortages of trained manpower, but the impact can be serious even for relatively large countries. A recent study of the Philippines estimates that, with present enrollment rates and no emigration, it will take the country about sixteen years to produce the physicians it needs. But if the present emigration rate among physicians continues, twenty-six years will be needed. A World Bank study of migration in the Middle East reached similar conclusions: in 1975 the number of trained people leaving nine Arab countries to work in neighboring oil-producing countries constituted 13 percent of the home countries' professional and technical manpower. If present trends continue to 1985, more than two-thirds of Sudanese professional and technical workers are likely to be employed elsewhere in the Middle East.

The nature of the brain drain varies from country to country. When emigration of skilled people is balanced by a flow of more experienced returning migrants and trained expatriates, no serious problems arise. If the underlying cause of emigration is political, a change in the political climate may encourage migrants to return. If the brain drain is caused by the pull of higher salaries, however, reversing it is costly and should only be attempted on a selective basis. The Sri Lankan government, for example, launched a program in 1979 to encourage professionals to stay or return home by revising its pension system, easing exchange controls so that people could finance the education of their children abroad, and making it possible for senior staff to return at appropriate levels in the public service. Guaranteeing jobs for those who might return and recruiting abroad for important public service positions have also been effective measures. In the 1970s, with a similar approach, the Republic of Korea was successful in attracting back Korean scientists trained abroad.

Other steps can also be taken to slow the brain drain, though some may compromise basic human rights. A survey of developing country students in Canada, France, and the United States showed that they were much more likely to return home if they signed a pledge or deposited a money bond before their departure. Some countries have imposed heavy emigration taxes and passport fees on trained people to discourage them from leav-

Box 10.3   Brain drain: who gains?

No comprehensive estimate of the size of the brain drain is available, though it is undoubtedly very large. Most studies focus on a single country of destination and examine its gains against the losses suffered by the countries from which people emigrated. Less attention has been given to the foreign exchange earnings from remittances, and almost none at all to the enhanced incomes enjoyed by the migrants.

One study by the United States government estimated that the United States saved $883 million in 1972 in educational costs, against a loss suffered by the developing countries of $320 million—the amount spent on educating these immigrants. According to a Canadian study, the replacement costs of the human capital transferred to Canada during 1967–73 ranged from C$1.0 billion to C$2.4 billion at 1968 prices—roughly ten times greater than the value of Canada's spending on aid for education and tech-

nical assistance during the same period. A third study, conducted by UNCTAD in 1975, puts the income gains of Canada, the United Kingdom, and the United States in 1961–72 at $44 billion more than the income lost by the developing countries. The imputed capital value of skilled migration in 1961–72 as a percent of official aid during the same period is reported to be 272 percent for Canada, 56 percent for the United Kingdom, and 50 percent for the United States.

The balance of these figures changes when migrants' remittances are included. A recent World Bank study of thirty-two labor-exporting developing countries shows that these countries recorded remittances of about $23 billion in 1978, equivalent to about 10 percent of the value of their exports of goods and services. Within this total, the share contributed by professional and technical people is not known, although there is some evidence for a few individual coun-

tries. While professional and technical workers constituted only 4 percent of Pakistani emigrants to the Middle East in 1979, they earned about 17 percent of total emigrant income and their per capita remittances averaged $4,500 a year—more than twice that of unskilled workers. Professionally trained Bangladeshis returned even more—those working in the Middle East in 1978 sent home about 60 percent of their salaries, an average of about $9,800 each at 1979 prices.

None of these calculations take into account the losses in output that may be suffered by the exporting country as a result of its losing skilled technicians and managers. There are several well-documented examples—Guyana's bauxite and electric utility institutions and Turkey's electricity, coal, and petroleum authorities—of just how serious such losses can be.

Box 10.4 High returns to secondary education

The 1980 *World Development Report* described how even limited education can raise the productivity and incomes of poor people. A new World Bank study of 4,000 primary and secondary school graduates in Kenya and Tanzania compared workers' wages with the number of years they had spent in school (their credentials) and their literacy and numeracy skills. The study concluded that skills accounted for almost 50 percent more of increased earnings than did credentials.

Although, on average, secondary education equipped students with better skills and, as a result, they earned more than those with only primary education, the study showed that, in both countries, primary school graduates with strong literacy and numeracy skills earned appreciably more than secondary graduates with weak skills. Thus, Kenyan primary graduates scoring in the top 10 percent of the skills tests earned an average of 1,109 Kenyan shillings a month compared with 864 shillings for the bottom 10 percent of secondary graduates. In Tanzania the most skilled primary graduates averaged 747 Tanzanian shillings a month; the lowest scoring secondary graduates, 681 shillings.

The findings applied equally to blue- and white-collar occupations, since the returns to skills achievement were just as high in nonmanual occupations. For technicians, machinists, and fork-lift drivers, as much as for accountants, clerks, and secretaries, basic literacy and numeracy skills apparently increased their productivity enough for employers to pay more for their services. In sum, secondary education paid in both countries, particularly for students who learned their lessons well.

The study has important economic implications for Kenya and Tanzania. Two decades ago both countries had similar secondary school enrollments and total population. By 1978 secondary enrollment was 350,000 in Kenya but only 60,000 in Tanzania. Because of this difference in enrollments, Kenya's labor force is more skilled than Tanzania's. The difference in skill, in turn, contributed to differences in the growth of wages, labor productivity, and output. Average wages, which fifteen years ago were roughly equal in both countries, are now nearly twice as high in Kenya. Tanzania's policy of moderating wage differentials accounts for some of the difference in earnings between the two countries; but Kenya's greater abundance of skills acquired in school accounts for as much as a third of that difference.

---

ing. Developed countries can aid these efforts by enforcing visa rules for certain categories of temporary immigrants (for example, "exchange visitors" to the United States) that require visitors to leave on completion of their studies.

While a slowing of the brain drain can make it easier for the public service to retain its staff, it will still face competition from the domestic private sector. In some Asian countries, where lifetime employment in one organization is the norm, labor mobility is low. But in several Middle Eastern countries, many university graduates start their careers in the public sector and later move to the private sector. In such countries as Kenya and Nigeria, where graduates are scarce and private businesses have grown rapidly, the public sector is continually faced with the danger of losing its senior staff.

Governments are in constant competition with the private sector for competent staff. Care must be taken to balance the needs of the public and private sectors. Highly successful government recruitment may risk choking off the supply of skills to the private sector. The long-run solution to this problem lies in producing more skills of all kinds—which means increasing the responsiveness of the formal educational system to trends in the labor market. Recent research confirms the strong association between education and economic growth noted in *World Development Report 1980* (see Box 10.4). But the immediate shortages remain and can be met partly through job-related training and more imaginative personnel policies.

Public service training

Training is widely advocated but often poorly executed. Before 1950 most developing countries had only limited training facilities. Over the next thirty years, aid donors directed large quantities of aid to training public officials in developing countries and to building training institutions inside and outside governments:

- Five regional and intergovernmental training institutions have been established in Africa, Asia, and Latin America—three under UN auspices—to support public service training.
- The United Nations, the United States government, and the Ford Foundation are estimated to have spent roughly $250 million in support of institutions for training in public administration alone during 1951–62.
- The industrial market economies are currently granting $500–600 million a year for training of developing country nationals, including the award of roughly 110,000 overseas fellowships.

• Training schemes financed by the UN Development Programme in 1981 amounted to more than $70 million, including the award of 11,500 overseas fellowships to developing-country nationals.

• World Bank spending on project-related training increased from $38 million in 1976 to $187 million in 1981.

According to a survey by the International Association of Schools and Institutes of Administration, there were 276 government institutions, university departments, and independent institutes providing public administration and management training in 91 developing countries in 1980. This is four times the number listed in a United Nations report for 1960. In Malaysia the number of people attending courses at such institutes increased from 1,000 in 1960 to 9,000 in 1980. For the Indian central government, the corresponding expansion has been from 1,500 to 7,000. In the Philippines nearly 20,000 officials participated in a special program for middle-ranking administrators in the five years after it was inaugurated in 1972. These are examples of a general trend in all developing countries.

Coverage and gaps

Despite its growth, training still receives less emphasis in developing countries than in public sector organizations in industrialized countries, or private enterprises, or multinational corporations. The US and Japanese governments, for instance, offer training opportunities to nearly a quarter of their employees every year. All IBM managers get at least forty hours of mandatory training a year, and Siemens and Unilever annually spend the equivalent of 5 percent of their payrolls on training. By contrast, most developing countries spend much less (the Indian central government spent roughly 0.5 percent in 1968). In Malaysia, which puts greater emphasis on training than do most developing countries, only 4 percent of federal and state employees received some form of training in 1978. In India only one senior civil servant in five is likely to have some in-service training during his entire career; in Turkey only one in seven has received any instruction in public administration. Local government officials typically fare even worse. Though they account for 20 to 30 percent of all government employees, only 10 to 15 percent of total government budget for training is allocated to them.

A dominant characteristic of public service training in most developing countries is its concentration on pre-entry and immediate post-entry courses for administrative elites, to the neglect of in-service training and the needs of lower-level staff. In India, Malaysia, Pakistan, and the Philippines, among others, new entrants to the senior administrative ranks go on courses lasting from nine months to two years. Several francophone countries in Africa have followed the French national administration schools in offering two-year pre-entry training courses for top civil servants.

The few reliable studies of training in developing countries show that the quality of most public service training is low. This is primarily because it is usually treated as a discrete event, rather than as one element in a comprehensive program of organizational improvement. Too often, little effort has been made to adapt training programs borrowed from abroad or to generate indigenous ones. As a result, most programs are classroom-based and tend to teach the skills that trainers know rather than building upon the knowledge that trainees already possess. Many programs rely on stylized examples rather than on trying to solve real problems. And few offer rotational assignments that are tied to a training and career development plan, and that attempt to broaden civil servants' outlooks and help them develop their skills in different jobs and organizations.

Policy improvements

The weaknesses of training can be tackled in four interrelated ways:

• The use of training policies and plans. A recent review of training in developing countries shows that most have no policies and plans for public service training, although some (such as India, Kenya, Malaysia, Philippines, and Zimbabwe) have made notable attempts to fill this vacuum. Plans should specify the nature and purpose of training for different categories of personnel, and should be based on a systematic assessment of training needs and the effectiveness of past programs. The experience of the World Bank's Economic Development Institute in Niger, Tunisia, and other countries shows how important it is to judge training by its relevance to the actual problems facing the public service. Field-testing can therefore be valuable: one such test, conducted in Zambia in 1974 by the African Center for Administrative Training and Research for Development, showed that the training curriculum designed by the headquarters staff dealt with less than 30 percent of the subjects in which rural project managers felt they needed instruction. To ensure a more accurate assessment of training needs, it can be helpful to put training budgets under the control of line managers.

• Better use of existing training facilities. Some courses—pre-entry programs for top civil servants, for example—can be shortened to make room for training staff in other grades and to give high fliers better in-service instruction. More use could also be made of institutions such as universities and management training centers. The latter have themselves some lessons to offer in getting the most out of their facilities. The best of them—such as the Indian Institute of Management, Ahmedabad (IIMA), the Asian Institute of Management in the Philippines (AIM), Malaysia's National Institute of Public Administration (INTAN), and the Central American Institute of Business Administration (INCAE) in Nicaragua—have several features in common. They enjoy autonomy in planning and implementing their own strategies; they have integrated their training with research and consultancy, so helping to forge close links with their clients; and they have benefited from stable

leadership. Many of these qualities are embodied in INTAN in Malaysia (see Box 10.5).

• Stronger links between training and career development. If training improves the skills required for career advancement, trainees will be encouraged to take it seriously. But if promotion policies and staff reports make no reference to training, public servants will know that it is dispensable. Governments also need to pay attention to the career prospects of the trainers themselves. In most countries, civil service training bodies (unlike their military counterparts) lack status, and instructors have few opportunities for career development. There are several ways of correcting this bias. A senior civil servant of recognized merit can be brought in to head the training organization. Overseas assignments and consultancy opportunities can be given to successful instructors. After a period in training institutions, staff can be given regular civil service jobs, which would bring them more closely in touch with operational work and stimulate new ideas for training.

• More international cooperation on training. Regional institutes and international agencies can

Box 10.5   Malaysia's INTAN: training that works

Malaysia's National Institute of Public Administration (INTAN) was created in 1972 to train all grades among Malaysia's 200,000 federal and local government staff. Its role is linked to the Government's New Economic Policy, which lays stress on improving public sector employment and promotion opportunities for ethnic Malays. INTAN's staff of seventy now trains some 15,000 government employees a year. Its growth has not been without problems, which it is seeking to overcome through various internal reforms.

INTAN's director is a senior civil servant whose personal prestige underscores the seriousness with which the government views its work. The institute is located in Malaysia's central personnel agency, but has operational and budgetary autonomy. An advisory council of senior representatives from government ministries and the state governments provides advice and feedback from INTAN's institutional clients. In many departments INTAN's courses are often seen as an integral part of career devel-

opment. Each trainee's performance is formally assessed, and in some cases certain courses have to be completed successfully before a public servant can be promoted. For some jobs, this pattern is reversed—people are selected for the training needed for promotion only if they have performed well at their jobs.

For a relatively young institution, INTAN has developed a wealth of training methods. Early feedback from participants in rural and people-centered programs showed that classroom lectures were not an effective way of training, so INTAN quickly devised courses that included extensive field work. When ministers complained about releasing staff for the longer courses, the institute divided its instruction into a series of shorter courses instead. The institute often tests trainees to see how well its programs have been absorbed, and supervisors as well as trainees are asked to evaluate the impact of programs on job performance.

For top administrators, INTAN provides seminars and workshops, usually for not more than four days, on impor-

tant policy questions. Senior officials are given advanced management training, while the middle ranks are offered specialized programs in subjects such as finance and personnel management. Recruits in most branches of government are given introductory courses and programs designed to teach special skills, many of which lead to diplomas. Junior staff are given two- or three-week skill-development courses. The institute also undertakes "action-training" programs for entire organizational units, and it has combined its programs with ministerial training departments and the University of Malaya.

INTAN has also devoted time to training and expanding its own staff. It has a large enough budget to be able to offer competitive salaries, and its own prestige also helps recruitment. Instructors are required to have previous experience in government, and they benefit from a systematic staff development plan that allows further training (in Malaysia and abroad) and advancement within INTAN itself.

Box 10.6 Improving the relevance of training

In their efforts to improve the relevance of training, instructors are making increasing use of four promising approaches:

• Action learning, pioneered by the National Coal Board in the United Kingdom and then used in many public and private organizations throughout the world. Managers work individually or in teams to solve a practical problem. They may spend time in a lecture room with a tutor or consultant, but there is no "trainer" who is teaching "trainees." Experiments with action learning have been made with OECD assistance in Egypt, with British assistance in India, with the Ford Foundation's support in the Philippines and Bangladesh, and with USAID involvement in a number of countries including Ghana, Jamaica, and Tanzania. Initial results have been most encouraging.

• Integrated Training Programs, developed by the Economic Development Institute of the World Bank. This method combines short courses with project-related technical assistance. Experimental

programs in Niger and Tunisia have encouraged participants to assess their own training needs, trained instructors, and made selective use of outside consultants to provide technical knowledge.

• Performance Improvement Planning (PIP), favored by the ILO and the UN, has been applied to public enterprises in Bangladesh, Dominican Republic, Ecuador, Nigeria, Somalia, Sri Lanka, Syria (where public enterprises and their supervising ministries participated in the same exercise), and Zambia. Typically, the program begins with diagnostic workshops in which senior managers identify problems faced in their organizations and devise solutions. Consultants and management specialists play only a catalytic role. Instead of passively attending lectures, participants collectively set targets and prepare plans for pursuing them. Follow-up action is specific and immediate, sometimes leading to dramatic improvements. One airline turned a large loss into a substantial profit within a year, and a postal and telecom-

munications corporation far exceeded its targets for new telephone connections.

• Modular training, also used by the ILO, has been effective in upgrading supervisory skills and knowledge quickly. The training program consists of thirty-four modules covering various aspects of management such as finance and cost control, maintenance, purchasing, and salary and wage administration. Specialized packages have also been developed for public works and cooperative management. Some of these modules are now available in fourteen languages. The modules allow the users to choose topics that are relevant to their organizations and to incorporate local cases and problems into the prepackaged materials. The effectiveness of modular training can be enhanced if trainees, after trying to implement what they have learned, are brought back to the training institution to discuss their results and to work out their own strategies for further action.

help satisfy the need for specialized kinds of training. The UN Development Administration Division and the ILO have concentrated on doing this. Assistance in training instructors can be valuable, especially for small developing countries that may not be able to afford their own schemes. Aid donors can also involve local training institutions with project-related training activities; and they can do more in support of research and development in public management training, especially if it is adapted to the needs of particular countries (see Box 10.6).

Personnel policies and management

In most governments, personnel departments play a relatively passive (sometimes even negative) role, administering an ingrained system of rules rather than developing policies for improving public sector management. In addition to planning and overseeing public service training, a more positive approach would include:

• Building effective career-development systems

• Improving public sector pay and conditions
• Linking incentives more closely to performance
• Better management of expatriates.

To institute such a program, the status of the personnel function in government should be raised and the managerial capacity of the personnel offices should be strengthened. This requires a sustained effort, as Bangladesh's experience has demonstrated (see Box 10.7).

In a number of countries responsibility for personnel matters is widely diffused. In such cases it is difficult to talk of a single civil service; almost every ministry has its own personnel department and policies for staff recruitment, promotion, and training. Although some governments have created centralized personnel agencies, much more can be done to streamline their operations and give them the status, resources, and authority they need to be effective. At the local government level, improvements in personnel management often require either horizontal integration of personnel systems with other local authorities or vertical integration with the national government structure.

Box 10.7 Personnel reform in Bangladesh: persistence pays

On gaining independence in 1971, Bangladesh faced the task of creating a national administration out of parts of the Civil Service of Pakistan (CSP) and the former provincial East Pakistan Civil Service (EPCS). In March 1972 an Administrative and Services Reorganization Committee was appointed, with broad terms of reference. After a year's work the Committee proposed the establishment of a unified grading structure, with a number of pay scales matching different levels of qualifications, skills, and responsibilities. The Committee also recommended developing a personnel management system based on merit, long-term career planning, a general training policy, and coordination of institutionalized training.

For political reasons, the report was largely ignored. During 1971–76 the government recruited heavily. People were put in jobs with scant regard to their aptitude or skills, often as a reward for their service during the war of liberation. The recommendations of a National Pay Commission were also largely overlooked. Of the nearly 2,000 pay scales in existence, only those of the lower grades were rationalized.

In 1976 a new government set up the Pay and Services Commission (PSC). Its recommendations, though mostly accepted by the government, were disliked by public employees: frequent strikes and demonstrations nearly paralyzed the administration. This time, however, the government persisted. After protracted discussions the PSC's main proposals were gradually put into effect. The pay structure was transformed into twenty-one grades and scales of pay, and remains in place today. The government also set up a Senior Policy Pool to try to equalize the status of former CSP and EPCS officers. A unified career service called the Bangladesh Civil Service was created in 1980.

The government has introduced other reforms over the past five years. It has taken several steps to slow the growth of the public service by a freeze on hiring for certain jobs, delaying appointments, and reducing the number of reserved positions. A National Training Council (NTC) is now responsible for formulating training policies and plans and for monitoring overall progress. A Training and Career Planning unit has been set up in the Establishment Division, to serve as the secretariat to the NTC and to ensure close links between training and appointments. Almost 40 percent of Class I officers and about 20 percent of supervisory and support staff are expected to be trained over the next five years. A Management Services Wing is expected to provide guidance on organizational and procedural reforms and a Personnel Management Information System is being established to help ensure promotion based on merit.

Strengthening of management and policy analysis capabilities of personnel offices requires competent specialists. Although training of existing staff can help, improving the status and career prospects of personnel specialists is needed. In addition, administrators of line agencies can usefully be seconded to personnel offices to expand their awareness and commitment to personnel policies, as well as to keep the personnel office in close touch with client departments. Such exchanges are likely to generate an increased demand for better personnel management from the line managers responsible for implementing personnel policies.

The installation of efficient information systems is also badly needed. In many countries personnel records are maintained manually, are updated infrequently, and are too cumbersome for the aggregate analysis needed for formulating policies, determining staffing and training requirements, and monitoring policy implementation. As discussed in Chapter 7, recent advances in microcomputers provide new and relatively cheap opportunities for installing systems for quick and accurate information storage, retrieval, and processing. Most developed countries have computerized personnel information systems and several developing countries are setting up systems for analyzing personnel-related data, and for making comparisons across departments and organizations. Such systems are essential for carrying out manpower planning for the public sector and for assessing staffing and training needs more accurately.

Career development

Motivation and training will both be helped if public servants have a clear idea of their career paths and of how promotion depends on achievement. For general administration, many developing countries have adopted the British or French models of a career civil service recruited by competitive examination, divided horizontally into classes, and generally closed to experienced outsiders. More open and diversified systems based on American practice are usually to be found in Latin America. About half the developing countries have established separate career paths for specialists, most commonly for accountants and tax administrators. A system that allows staff to move between the public and private sectors has obvious advantages, since it encourages new ideas and firsthand experience of managerial techniques.

Frequent shuffling of civil servants can be harmful, however. In more than a third of the developing countries, principal economic decisionmakers—the secretary of finance, national planning director, and central bank governor—have each been changed three or more times during the past five years. This problem is not limited to senior staff: in one developing country, the commercial, technical, financial, and administrative managers of the national railways were changed four to six times each during a three-year period. In another country, the top staff in a population field project were changed at least three times in five years.

Rapid and unplanned promotions are also a major problem. Some governments have promoted young and inexperienced civil servants into the upper grades, primarily to fill new posts arising from the growth of the public service, or to take over from expatriates. Changes of government can also cause disruptive growth: in Turkey, for example, the number of senior civil servants increased by 146 percent between 1976 and 1978, a period of frequent political changes, compared with an increase of 23 percent for lower grades.

Japan and France have dealt with promotion bottlenecks by moving some civil servants in their fifties out of administrative jobs to staff or advisory posts. Last year China decided to ease bottlenecks by introducing a standard retirement age—sixty for department directors and vice-ministers, sixty-five for ministers. Such measures are particularly relevant when there are no serious shortages of skilled people, and young professionals need to feel that their paths are not blocked for years on end.

Salaries and conditions

To join the public service and stay there, staff need salary and nonsalary benefits that compete with alternative job opportunities. This is particularly important for those with unusual skills: public service compensation, though adequate—and sometimes excessive—for junior staff, too often fails to attract and retain senior professionals.

The reward of any job goes far beyond the straightforward question of salaries. They are relatively easy to compare, however, and the scattered evidence from developing countries indicates that, for senior staff, government pay is usually lower than in the private modern sector. Moreover, many governments, for political and equity reasons, have raised salaries of junior staff more quickly than those of top civil servants, thus reducing the incentive for people to stay in the

civil service once they have reached a certain grade. Countries such as Jordan have experienced a flight of skilled civil servants to the local private sector and to nearby oil-producing states. The same thing has happened in Turkey, where salaries for new university graduates are about two and a half times higher in the private sector, and even higher for many experienced professional and technical staff. By contrast, qualified public servants in some large Latin American countries, such as Brazil and Mexico, are relatively well paid, as evidenced by the difficulties faced by international organizations in recruiting staff from these countries.

Apart from pay, individuals value government service for its other benefits—such as status, interest, and security of tenure. For this reason, complete equality between public and private sector pay is generally neither necessary nor desirable. Singapore and Malaysia, where public sector salaries are regularly adjusted for changes in the cost of living, are two of the few developing countries that appear to have maintained parity. In Nigeria, the restructuring of public sector salaries by the Udoji Commission in 1975 resulted in virtual parity, but the private sector quickly restored its competitive pull for skills in short supply. For most governments it would be prohibitively expensive to match private sector salaries across the board. To do so would simply push up private sector wages and would also widen the gap between public officials and the mass of the population. Average government pay in many developing countries ranges from four to ten times per capita income; for OECD countries, the corresponding ratio is 1.8.

Nor are public servants short of nonsalary "perks." Most governments provide their senior staff with substantial benefits such as housing, cars, directorship fees, medical care, and education. This encourages civil servants to seek new benefits while protecting those they already have, often with damaging results. In one African country, for example, the daily travel allowance is so generous that middle- and high-ranking officials spend a third or more of each year traveling abroad, leaving the business of running the government to their subordinates. In an Asian country an overnight allowance was given to agricultural extension agents if their work took them more than twenty-five kilometers from their duty station: consequently, the agents were rarely seen by farmers living within the twenty-five-kilometer radius.

Some governments also try to retain important officials by giving them discretionary allowances and benefits. In theory, this gives added flexibility for rewarding high performers; in practice, it creates tensions between superiors and subordinates and can easily degenerate into corruption. Discretionary benefits are best given to whole groups whose skills are in short supply—statisticians or computer specialists, for example. To ensure that an imbalance does not arise between public and private sector salaries, regular (and preferably internal) reviews of public servants' pay should be conducted. Such reviews should take into account nonpecuniary benefits resulting from public employment and should eliminate or modify perks that produce perverse results.

Linking incentives with performance

While greater rewards do not automatically produce better performance, it is helpful to establish some link between the two. This is seldom easy to do because public bureaucracies are expected to serve social and political objectives that are inherently hard to quantify. In addition, informal social relations between managers and their subordinates are often so strong that, even where "output" can be measured, supervisors are reluctant to jeopardize loyalties and friendships.

These considerations notwithstanding, several developing countries (including India, Kenya, and the Philippines) are starting to devise appraisal systems that link promotion and pay increases to individual performance. This requires, first, strengthening the capacity of personnel offices to work out such systems. Second, red tape can often be reduced. To take an extreme example, a single promotion decision in one developing country was found to require fifty-four operations, twenty reviews or inspections, and seventy-three movements of documents from one place to another. For an employee in a provincial office, an additional forty-one steps were required. Third and most important, promotion on merit requires the backing of political and bureaucratic leaders and the public at large.

Even with such advantages, performance appraisal systems are difficult to implement objectively. In view of this, developing countries should install them only gradually, while laying stress on nonmaterial rewards for good performance. In some countries where there is strong loyalty among employers and employees, staff may require fewer pecuniary incentives. Research shows that rewarding performance with enhanced prestige or considerate supervisory behavior is often an effective way of motivating staff. The same is true of job enlargement—giving people greater responsibility and chal-

lenge. Finally, productivity and job satisfaction can often be improved if employees are involved in designing the organization of their work—as demonstrated by recent field experiments in India, Norway, and Tanzania.

Better management of expatriates

According to a recent World Bank study, there are at least 80,000 expatriates (including teachers) working for public agencies under official aid programs in sub-Saharan Africa alone. More than half the estimated $7 billion to $8 billion spent annually by donors on technical assistance goes to finance expatriate personnel, with costs being shared with host governments. At one extreme, volunteers—who constitute about one in ten of the technical assistance staff financed under Development Assistance Committee (DAC) bilateral aid—cost about $10,000 a year, perhaps less. At the other extreme, the cost of management assistance supplied by North American or European consulting firms can run as high as $15,000 to $16,000 per man-month.

Donors and recipients tend to approach technical assistance from different standpoints. Donors are naturally inclined to push such assistance as a ready solution to what they see as administrative shortcomings in the institutions to which they are lending. Recipient governments may be less convinced of the need for outside help; indeed, local officials often see the recruitment of expatriates as a threat to their own positions and promotion prospects. The proferred assistance may nevertheless be grudgingly accepted for fear that rejection may lead to the aid program being reduced.

This conflict of interest can then be compounded. Local staff may not be consulted on exactly what kind of assistance they need. Salary differentials and differences in lifestyle can cause frictions. Personal qualities highly prized in the donor country may be unsuitable in a different culture. Experts chosen for their technical skills are often inept at training, and recipient governments anyhow usually prefer to use them as doers rather than as instructors.

For all these reasons, better management of expatriates should be a priority both for donor agencies and for recipient governments. Recipients need to establish clear priorities, specify the objectives to be met by expatriates, and adopt a more determined approach to managing and coordinating technical assistance staff. Donors need to accept a more equal partnership with recipients, which means working through a country's institutions and procedures rather than bypassing them. The Bank's experience indicates that when the "psychological distance" between expatriates and their local counterparts is minimized, the value of technical assistance is much enhanced.

The selection of technical staff is also of great importance. For donors, the poor quality of some of their staff can often be attributed to their not having tenure. Development agencies tend to recruit the majority of their field staff on fixed-term contracts, and dispense with them first if budgets have to be cut. Attempts to establish a permanent corps of specialists for service in developing countries have rarely been successful, because staff are not offered promising career prospects. France and Sweden have instead encouraged the secondment of staff from regular public and private employment for service overseas. Canada, the United Kingdom, and the United States have formed private organizations of retired executives to carry out short-term consultancy work in developing countries (see Box 10.8). A similar scheme has recently been launched in the Federal Republic of Germany.

While expatriates often have much to contribute, local consultants should not be neglected. Some donor agencies, such as the UNDP and the World Bank, have declared their preference for national rather than expatriate consultants when both are equally competent. Some of the more advanced developing countries can already offer considerable consulting expertise. A recent study of management consulting in India, for example, lists eight large private consultancies that have been set up by industrial firms and chartered accountants, between them employing more than 750 professionals. In addition, India has numerous small firms and individual consultants, four publicly financed management institutes, the business faculties of various universities, and numerous public sector industrial and technical consulting bodies that provide advisory services to small businesses.

A concluding note: the cultural dimension

It is easy to prescribe what is needed for successful management of the public service. It is much less easy to adapt these requirements to the cultural and political environment of individual countries. Unless management techniques are designed to take explicit account of these cultural influences, however, they will fall far short of their potential. Although practices evolved in developed countries can be used in many developing countries, they need to be tailored to local realities. And it is just as important to identify and develop indigenous management principles.

Whenever an institution is considering changes in its management practices, its internal balance of power is inevitably threatened. Those who are least likely to benefit from a change may agree to it in principle, but then offer covert resistance during implementation. Opposition is usually greater the more alien an idea seems and the more it appears to have been imported indiscriminately. Once installed, however, success or failure in implementing the practice largely depends on its suitability to the local cultural environment.

Some new techniques (for example, quantitative information-based scheduling, accounting, budgeting, and inventory control) have been introduced and implemented successfully in many developing countries. But those that rest heavily on assumptions about the behavior of individuals (for example, management-by-objectives, organization development, and "matrix" management) have either failed or been implemented only after considerable adaptation. A study of administrative change in one Asian country concluded that attempts to introduce Western management practices (such as position classification, performance budgeting, participatory learning, and team re-search) that ran counter to local values or political interests, were either rejected outright or failed eventually. Similarly, in Nigeria, the Udoji Commission's recommendation to install management-by-objectives throughout the government has never been realized.

Such experiences have reinforced the view that "qualitative" management practices are harder to transfer than those that are more "quantitative," though the latter also need to be adapted to local conditions. Japan's success in using American-based quantitative techniques, while developing its own qualitative management approach, is the best example of how discrimination can bring considerable rewards. Such a course calls for initiating or expanding programs to adapt foreign techniques and to identify and develop promising indigenous practices, which can be undertaken by universities, management training institutes, and special units within government.

11   Reorienting government

Many of the management problems identified in this Report can be corrected only by changing the way that central bureaucracies are organized and managed. Recognizing this, developing countries have made numerous attempts to reform their bureaucracies in recent years. Few have succeeded in improving public sector efficiency, partly because of the unfavorable political climate and partly because of the institutions that many countries inherited at independence. This chapter reviews the lessons from their experience and emphasizes the need for reforms to change both official procedures and administrative structures. It also suggests that governments should target administrative reforms selectively, as well as keep up the pressure for general improvements. It is usually more fruitful to concentrate political and administrative effort on radical change in a few critical areas than to spread it ineffectually by attempting comprehensive reforms.

The historical and political context

Developing strong and efficient public institutions requires considerable investment in human skills, and a readiness to experiment with organizational structures to find those that best fit the societies they are intended to serve. It took today's industrialized countries more than a century to develop reasonably effective institutions (see Box 11.1). Many developing countries are attempting to compress that process into a few decades. It is not surprising that disappointments and political strains have often occurred.

Developing countries also have to contend with unprecedentedly rapid population growth and technical change, a more integrated and competitive world economy (which multiplies the consequences of mistakes as well as of success), and high political and economic expectations among their peoples. Creating the managerial skills and institutions to cope with these demands is an exceptional challenge. In countries where general educational levels are low, poverty severe, and institutional experience limited, the task will also need sustained external assistance, although the main contribution will always be a national one.

Current institutional problems should not obscure the notable progress made by developing countries. African countries have within a generation established the entire framework of national institutions and staffed those institutions with their own citizens. Some Latin American countries, whose institutional structures long served predominantly rural oligarchies, have expanded their administrations to cope with the demands of rapid urban and industrial growth. East Asia has developed sophisticated economies along with a more modest, but still impressive, growth in government capabilities.

Nevertheless, many countries have equated institutional development with a proliferation of bureaucracy, particularly in the public sector. However understandable this process was in historical circumstances, it now needs reexamining. The cost of developing the public sector has been considerable; the results often disappointing. Inside and outside governments, people are increasingly aware that recent strategies of institutional modernization have not delivered on their promises.

The alternatives are not simple, however. Many countries brought some of their key industries into public ownership to assert national control; change in their status or their mode of operation is often politically sensitive. Economic efficiency therefore has to be balanced against considerations of practical politics, national sovereignty, and social policy. Similarly, appointment-by-merit in the public service is a principle that might have to be modified to take account of a country's ethnic or religious tensions. In many cases, therefore, "inefficiency" is less the fault of bureaucrats than the consequence of demands—legitimate or otherwise—that the political system places on the bureaucracy's limited capacities.

That said, there are powerful groups that favor

Box 11.1 Institutional development in industrialized countries

In the industrialized world, little more than a century separates the tolerably effective bureaucracies of today from administrations in which corruption and incompetence were the rule rather than the exception. No country made progress in the same way, but certain features stand out. First, most of the large leaps in administrative reform (which were often followed by periods of consolidation) enjoyed strong political sponsorship. In Britain the Northcote-Trevelyan reforms, which established the essence of a merit-based, nonpolitical bureaucracy, were part of the wide-ranging political changes between 1832 and 1884 that consolidated middle-class ascendancy over the aristocracy. In Japan the leaders of the Meiji Restoration after 1868 wished to build a modernizing administration

across the country—and did so, in part by creating state enterprises that for a time dominated such industries as shipbuilding, railroads, mining, and armaments. In the United States the basis of modern administration was laid in the nineteenth century and then expanded during the 1930s as part of the New Deal political response to the Depression.

Second, administrative development also had immediately practical concerns. It was prompted by the growth of national economies and the rapid development of markets, just as it was in developing countries. The state undertook the essential tasks for economic development—organizing infrastructure; standardizing currencies, weights, and measures; strengthening commercial laws; and so on. From the late nineteenth cen-

tury onward, it was also active in educating the labor force and in influencing working conditions through child labor laws and safety standards. The other side of the coin, of course, was the way the state used its power, especially in the early stages of industrialization, to suppress trade unions.

The growth of the public sector has produced its own problems: unequal access to services provided by the state, rising administrative costs (and often diminishing effectiveness), and the growth of self-serving bureaucracies allied to political elites. These weaknesses are paralleled in some respects in the private sector, as large corporations are seen by many to be less adaptable in the face of changing technological and competitive conditions.

---

bureaucratic growth and oppose changes that would improve efficiency. Where the public sector provides a large proportion of modern employment (as it does in many developing countries), change may be opposed whenever it seems to threaten employees' livelihoods. Overstaffed bureaucracies and cumbersome procedures often have even more powerful beneficiaries—those who control the flow of patronage or who profit from the corruption that comes from administrative restrictions (see Box 11.2). Where institutional development outside the state is limited, as in much of Africa, or where political organizations that could oppose and expose inefficiencies are suppressed (as they often are), it is harder than ever to improve government performance.

Managing administrative change

Previous attempts at bureaucratic reform have sometimes succeeded in establishing new administrative structures but have often failed to improve efficiency or change bureaucratic behavior (see Box 11.3). This suggests that governments need to choose their candidates for reform carefully and then concentrate their efforts on them. Far from being mere tinkering, such an approach should be seen as the best way of achieving a long-term strategy for institutional development. It requires a political commitment to those strategic

goals—a commitment that is difficult to sustain, particularly since it must contend with bureaucratic inertia and resistance. But in many countries this combination of selective radicalism and incremental change will achieve more than plunging into wholesale reform of the entire administration, and can gradually build support for change by showing results.

Persistence is fundamental to bureaucratic reform. This requires a permanent capacity—though not necessarily a single agency—to provide analysis and operational support for reforms. If that capacity exists, governments will be better placed to seize the occasional opportunity to make fundamental reforms because the preparatory and technical work will have been done. The experience of developing countries indicates that public service commissions, central personnel agencies, and the like are inappropriate overseers of administrative reform, being too limited in scope and preoccupied with detail. Institutes of public administration tend to be too remote from power, though they can help to diagnose the kind of reform that is needed. In several smaller developing countries, technical offices concerned with organization and methods or management services have been useful instruments of reform, but are rarely able to deal with the larger structural and performance issues.

Experience has also shown how persistence

can pay off. Japan's Administrative Management Agency has a formidable reputation for keeping government staff numbers firmly under control, and for requiring ministries to carry through their own reorganizations. In Brazil the Ministry of Debureaucratization has simplified and reduced paperwork and red tape, by starting at the point where the bureaucracy encounters the public, and then working back to make administrative structures suit the requirements of their job. Thailand has a systematic and effective program of reforms (see Box 11.4). None of these countries tries to deal with all administrative problems and none of them would claim complete success. Instead, they concentrate on a limited range of objectives and persist with them. It is probably wise, as the Thai experience illustrates, to link reforms to the budgetary process so that leaders can impose their priorities on the administration and redirect its activities.

In many developing countries it makes sense to base reforms on two broad principles: first, reducing the management intensity of development, rather than adding new managerial burdens to an already overextended bureaucracy; second, instituting reforms that make the bureaucracy more responsive, both to political authority and to the public at large.

Economizing on management

Countries have tried to reduce the burden on public sector managers in three main ways: rationalizing economic management, improving central coordination, and decentralizing government activities.

Rationalizing economic management

Chapter 5 suggested that many countries could improve their economic performance if governments intervened less in markets. The managerial benefits would also be considerable, since officials would have fewer economic instruments to administer, and less occasion to devise corrective bureaucratic mechanisms necessitated by inappropriate controls. By simplifying agricultural producer prices, for example, governments would re-

---

Box 11.2 Corruption

All societies have corrupt features in the sense that some public money is illicitly diverted for private gain. The particular circumstances of developing countries—rapid social and economic change, strong kinship ties, new institutions, overlapping and sometimes conflicting views about proper public behavior—may be peculiarly conducive to corruption.

Corruption takes place in transactions between private individuals or firms and public officials; thus, it is the misuse of public funds and the failure of public trust that is of particular concern. Corruption seriously undermines the effectiveness of government.

• Over time corruption tends to corrode popular confidence in public institutions. This makes it harder to raise the standards of public service, deflects public debate away from economic performance toward this single issue, and in extreme cases prompts (or at least provides a justification for) violent changes in government.

• "Rent-seeking" can become an ob-

sessive preoccupation. Public officials will do nothing without bribes, and many people are unproductively employed in securing their favors or buying their silence. Corruption can thus become an institution's raison d'être, rather than a minor aspect of its activities. In extreme cases, such as in countries which are major exporters of illegal drugs, administration in entire regions and arms of government may become perverted by corruption.

• Corruption tends to favor those with economic or institutional power.

• Some corruption is on such a scale that it has major economic consequences: it may stimulate the illegal export of capital or result in large projects being awarded to contractors (often multinational companies) according to the size of their bribes rather than the quality of their performance.

The eradication of corruption as a feature of public life depends on the gradual creation of a political and public climate favoring impartial institutions, as well as

on specific actions by government. Many governments from time to time have initiated anticorruption drives. However, such efforts tend to be shortlived and ineffective, since they often concentrate on punitive measures and even closer—but still unworkable—controls, instead of designing interventions so as to minimize the opportunities or incentives for corruption. For example, corruption can be limited by avoiding administratively created scarcities (as some centrally planned economies are doing by effectively sanctioning a "second economy"); by reducing controls on international trade and payments; and by improving the incentives and accountability of officials in the areas where regulations or administrative discretion remain. Corruption is usually better fought by a combination of fewer, better-paid officials controlling only what really needs to be (and can effectively be) controlled in the full light of public scrutiny, than by occasional anticorruption "campaigns."

Box 11.3 Experiences with comprehensive administrative reform

Most developing countries that have attempted comprehensive administrative reform have done so primarily in response to political demands rather than on the initiative of the bureaucracy itself. At independence, governments were concerned with replacing expatriate public employees. They also wanted to gear the public service to promoting their ambitious programs of economic development. The Indian reform exercises in the 1950s and 1960s, for example, were prompted by the view that a more responsive and decentralized administration was needed to spearhead planning. Kenya's Ndegwa Commission in the late 1960s focused particularly on Africanizing the civil service and its role vis-a-vis the burgeoning private economy. In Latin America some postwar reforms have been closely tied to changes in economic management. Bolivia, Brazil, and Honduras, for example, linked their administrative reform programs in the 1960s and 1970s to national economic plans and planning agencies. The political impetus for radical change was sometimes given added thrust by new (and often military) governments in such countries as Chile,

Ghana, Indonesia, Republic of Korea, Mali, Pakistan, Peru, Philippines, and Thailand.

Most of the major reform efforts—in both developed and developing countries—have had only limited impact. Sometimes the political commitment withered as governments fell or achieved their political goals in other ways. Particularly in Latin America, reforms that were linked to planning ambitions languished as planning itself became largely irrelevant to government decisionmaking. In the numerous instances where bureaucrats were responsible for implementing proposed reforms, they chose those that enhanced their status and ignored or emasculated the rest. Examples from developed countries of limited follow-through after official enquiries included the Fulton Committee (United Kingdom), the Glassco Commission (Canada), and the Coombs Commission (Australia). India's experience has been similiar. Over thirty years, a succession of committees, reports, and recommendations have tended to produce changes in detail while leaving broad structures intact. In Pakistan between independ-

ence and the end of the 1960s, twenty-eight major reports running to 3,621 pages were produced by administrative reform committees with a collective membership of 146. None achieved the main objectives of reform. For some African countries—Kenya and Nigeria, for example—the most important practical outcome of reform initiatives was a substantial increase in the pay and perquisites of the bureaucracy. The pay proposals of Nigeria's Udoji Commission (1974) were so radical as to have immediate inflationary and political effects on society at large, while its other recommendations were largely ignored.

To overcome these obstacles, reform requires the sustained support of political leaders. Without that, reforms will be undermined by those most directly affected—civil servants themselves—or be ensnared by the legal and constitutional framework of public service laws (a particular problem in Latin America and the Middle East). Political leaders intent on reform should therefore concentrate on a few priorities at a time, pursuing these to completion before attempting other changes.

---

duce the need for managing subsidy programs for credit and fertilizer. The feasibility of such adjustments depends not only on economic and political choices but also on effective institutions to design and evaluate policies.

Improving coordination

All governments need to coordinate the activities of their different departments to avoid duplication and confusion. But to save rather than waste managerial resources, coordination needs to take place at the right level—to provide incentives for officials and agencies to cooperate and to ensure that it generates useful information for decisionmaking. This much has become clear as a result of current stabilization and adjustment programs in many countries. Governments found that they lacked the means of monitoring foreign debt and of controlling budgets. Although they have responded in different ways, all have been concerned with coordinating their policy changes.

Facing a crisis in 1979, the Turkish government set up four coordinating committees in the prime minister's office to implement the country's adjustment program. One committee dealt with trade regimes and economic aid; a second, with monetary and credit policies—especially pricing and exchange rate policies; a third reviewed foreign investment applications; and the fourth handled investment policies and export incentives. In the Ivory Coast an interministerial committee was set up in 1981 to monitor the economic recovery program supported by a World Bank structural adjustment loan and to oversee the budget. Jamaica has given high priority to concerting action among the ministries and public agencies responsible for energy policy. In other developing countries (for example, Sudan, Thailand, and Uganda), senior committees have concentrated on establishing priorities for the public investment program to take account of new financial stringencies.

Although such coordinating committees have been valuable in emergencies, they are rarely a long-term solution to management problems. All too often, top-level "coordination" is merely part of the pathology of overcentralization. Decisions are routinely referred up the hierarchy, and ministers are absurdly overstretched "coordinating" everything in their portfolios or negotiating over details with their cabinet colleagues. Ecuador, for instance, was recently estimated to have almost 200 coordinating boards, committees, and commissions. The minister of finance was a member of forty-five of these bodies and was required personally to attend meetings of twelve of them. Co-ordination can degenerate into mere "bureau-shuffling": the recent tendency in some Middle Eastern countries to put groups of ministries under a number of vice-prime ministries has not noticeably improved their performance, and has sometimes produced further conflicts and coordination difficulties. The failure of planning (discussed in Chapter 7) is partly a consequence of expecting planning agencies to act as coordinating "over-lords" of economic policy even though crucial information, political influence, and operational responsibilities remained with ministries that had

Box 11.4 Thailand's approach to institutional reform

Rapid economic growth and progress against poverty have made Thailand one of the success stories of the developing world over the past two decades. Yet the country has had many apparent institutional disadvantages: political instability, bureaucratic fragmentation and duplication, poor coordination among government agencies, centralized decisionmaking, and rigid administrative controls.

Thailand has been greatly helped by the dynamism of its private sector and by a broad consensus on the main goals of development, despite frequent changes in political leadership. A third critical factor has been the capacity to institute administrative changes, however partial and imperfect, which have recognized and corrected institutional deficiencies at crucial junctures when failure to do so would have had a serious effect on development. That capacity has existed, with varying effectiveness, for the country since King Chulalongkorn established ministries, provinces, salaried officials, and other features of modern public administration in Thailand. Indeed, the Thai bureaucracy has for long played a central stabilizing role, despite its shortcomings, in the midst of considerable political instability.

The many deficiencies that remain, however, have been highlighted by Thailand's recent difficulties in dealing with an expanding fiscal deficit and deteriorating balance of payments while trying to maintain its development momentum. As part of its structural adjustment pro-

gram, the government is therefore making extensive institutional changes. Its strategy is now more systematic and far-reaching than in the past, and the pace and priorities of reform are being carefully chosen.

Part of the current initiative for reform comes from within the bureaucracy itself. As in other countries, however, there are limits to internally sponsored reforms, and a perceived need to reinforce and extend the reform process from outside by gradually developing the bureaucracy's public accountability through the political system.

The aim of the Royal Thai Government is to improve overall efficiency of public resource management. On the revenue side, a number of measures are being taken to increase resource mobilization. These range from strengthening the fiscal planning capacity of the Ministry of Finance, decentralizing and computerizing the operations of the Revenue Department, reorganizing the Customs and Excise departments, and establishing a training institute for tax officials to expanding land survey and property valuation capabilities to augment local government revenues from land and property taxes.

Simultaneously, major efforts are being made to rationalize public expenditure programs. All of the core agencies—the Budget Bureau, the National Economic and Social Development Board, and the Civil Service Commission in the Prime Minister's Office, the Ministry of Finance, and the Office of the Auditor

General—have embarked on programs of closely interconnected reforms. These include the introduction of modern program budgeting mechanisms to link annual budget appropriations more effectively to national policy objectives and program priorities as well as to the new fiscal plans and rolling three-year investment and borrowing programs; improvements in policy analysis, planning, and project appraisal at national, sectoral, agency, and subnational levels; changes in government accounting and management information systems to render them compatible with the requirements of program budgeting and multiyear fiscal and investment planning; greater delegation of expenditure authority to line managers and provincial governors in order to expedite program implementation and to decentralize the impact of public expenditures; the streamlining of procurement procedures applicable to externally funded projects; and the development of program monitoring and performance auditing systems. Parallel measures are being taken to strengthen the organization and management of the public service and to institutionalize the promotion of further long-term administrative reforms. These measures include the establishment of a civil service staff college, the development of indigenous management advisory capabilities, the planned rotation of senior government officials, and the launching of a major study of public service salaries and fringe benefits.

nothing to gain and much to lose from cooperation. Such a coordinating role is possible only if planning agencies influence budget allocations.

In the field, the lessons from coordination efforts reviewed in Chapter 9 are clear and widely applicable. Where effective coordination cannot be assured, the need for it may be reduced by simplifying development programs and shedding or postponing their least manageable components. Otherwise, collaboration may be improved by joint project planning and the negotiation of contracts between agencies, and by strengthening financial control so that funds are released only when agencies deliver on previous commitments. In some countries—for example, India, Kenya, and Malaysia—senior district officials, such as district commissioners and collectors, have proved effective coordinators. They enjoy considerable authority within the government and the local community, yet do not threaten each ministry's control of its plans and budgets.

If government feels a strong need to coordinate, it could well be a sign that other things in its structure and activities have gone wrong. Perhaps it is trying to do too much. Its decisions may have been inefficiently overcentralized. Departments may be jealously guarding their "territory." Or officials may not be responding to the requirements of policy and of their clients. Whatever the reason, governments have to decide whether elaborate coordination will improve their effectiveness or simply postpone other kinds of improvements in, for example, cabinet decisionmaking, policy analysis, and budgetary control.

Decentralizing government activities

The need for coordination is reduced when government managers transfer those functions they cannot manage efficiently to other levels of government, public enterprises, local communities, or the private sector. Decentralization is conventionally defined as one of three things: (a) "deconcentration"—transferring resources and decisionmaking from headquarters to other branches of central government; (b) "devolution"—to autonomous units of government such as municipalities and local governments; and (c) "delegation"—to organizations outside the regular bureaucratic structure, such as public corporations and regional development authorities, or even to nongovernmental bodies such as farmer cooperatives, credit associations, and trade unions. In practice, the three forms are often combined: responsibilities for

executing development projects might be given to provincial officers of central government (deconcentration) to work with local government (devolution) and with community groups (delegation).

The most common form of decentralization in developing countries has been deconcentration. In Indonesia, for example, the centrally funded provincial and village development programs enable provincial and district planning units to plan and execute schemes for increasing rural productivity and incomes. In Thailand funds are now provided to *tambon* councils to identify and manage small projects. Pakistan has created *markaz* councils—under the supervision of project managers—which coordinate the credit, marketing, and other development activities of central government with those of local agricultural cooperatives and private businesses. Bangladesh is stregthening its *thana*-level administrators to undertake local development activities. In Tunisia each of the country's provincial governments receives a block grant for spending on locally generated projects under the national rural development program (see Box 11.5). Few countries "deconcentrated" as radically as Tanzania did—with mixed results—in the 1970s, when many ministries' functions and staff were transferred from Dar es Salaam to provincial centers.

Delegation has also been used extensively in developing countries—especially by creating state-owned enterprises (SOEs). And governments have resorted to special agencies to tackle specific problems, though this may do little more than encourage bureaucratic proliferation. Mexico is a striking example: apart from having more than 600 SOEs, it has approximately 100 "decentralized organizations." Governed by federal administrative laws, they provide social services such as pensions, health, education, and research. Mexico also has some 800 independent councils and commissions dealing with issues from the development of arid areas to electricity rate-setting to the promotion of tourism. Another characteristic form of delegation is the regional development authority. It is often established to supervise irrigation development, as in much of Asia, or to open up underdeveloped regions—for example, the Amazon basin in Brazil.

Recent trends have not favored devolution as a decentralization technique. After independence, Africa's political leaders tended to see local government as incompetent, profligate, and politically divisive, so its functions and revenues were whittled away. In countries of the francophone administrative tradition, local government was in any

Box 11.5 Tunisia's rural development program

Tunisia's Rural Development Program has been run for almost a decade with modest success. It works as follows: each of the twenty *gouvernorats* (provinces of limited autonomy) receive a block grant, presently about $1.75 million a year. The generally poorer inland gouvernorats receive $3.5 million. The money must be spent on locally generated and supervised projects, with those that promote community development and employment being favored. All project proposals must be backed by a detailed sched-ule required by the central Ministry of Planning, and money can be spent only if it has been approved by the central government. The vetting is not simply a formality: some proposals have been turned down.

Representatives of the technical ministries in the gouvernorats identify projects, study their feasibility and potential payoff, harmonize them with central government projects in the region, and supervise their implementation. Officials can respond quickly and flexibly to local opportunities and local crises. The generally excessive demands on the program's limited funds have their positive side: gouvernorat officials have been forced to learn how to justify projects on the basis of their quality. Through this successful pilot program, more money has been made available and experience gained for the far-reaching proposals for decentralization and regional planning which the government is now considering.

case part of an administrative hierarchy, with relatively little autonomy. This bias against devolution may now be changing. In countries as diverse as Chile, Nigeria, Papua New Guinea, and Sudan, governments have started to devolve responsibilities to reformed local government institutions. The change may reflect two developments: first, the growing desire to find new ways of mobilizing local resources; and second, the recognition that local government employees could be used more efficiently than they have been.

By itself, however, devolution can do little to compensate for a general shortage of technical and administrative skills. If other tiers of government have difficulty obtaining qualified staff, local government will find it even harder: in developing countries, its salaries are typically only half those paid by central government. Nor can local government enjoy genuine autonomy when, as usually happens, it depends on central grants for the bulk of its budget. The revival of local government therefore depends on vigorous action to raise more local revenues. Evidence from such countries as the Yemen Arab Republic and the Republic of Korea suggests that, where local government is strongly established, it can tap revenue sources that escaped the net of the central authorities. However, property taxes—on which local governments tend to depend for a large part of their revenues—are inherently difficult to administer. The central government may be able to help in this task, as it has done in Thailand, for example.

Decentralizing has also taken the form either of privatization (discussed in Chapter 8) or of involving communities in the execution of projects. In some countries delegation to users and interest groups has effectively become national policy. In China, for example, the Production Responsibility System combines moves toward private production with the transfer of authority downward from state and commune levels (see Box 5.3). In India the dairy cooperatives formed under the national Operation Flood program are the local agents of the National Dairy Development Board, but are elected by, and responsible to, their village membership. In Kenya the self-help movement has used informal taxation, community development groups, and the women's movement to play a significant role in secondary and technical education and rural health care.

Despite difficulties in evaluating the evidence on decentralization, some lessons can be drawn. First, decentralizing has been most common where governments felt reasonably secure. Weak governments cannot afford to decentralize—except in desperation, which rarely works—and weakening governments try to pull control into the center rather than spread it outward. Second, decentralization is probably best seen as an incremental process of building up the capacity of organizations to assume greater responsibilities. In most countries that have decentralized on any scale, access to services has improved for people in previously neglected communities, the capacity of local administrative and political leadership has increased, and new perspectives and interests have been introduced into the policymaking process. Third, the most successful decentralizing efforts have been carefully designed and uncomplicated to administer, have specified clearly the responsibilities of different participants, and have started on a small scale. Fourth, for decentralization to

Box 11.6 Decentralization in a socialist economy: Hungary

Like other socialist states of Asia and Europe, Hungary initially adopted, largely unmodified, the system of centralized physical planning practiced in the Soviet Union. By squeezing consumption and extracting substantial surpluses from agriculture, Hungary quickly raised its rate of industrial investment. It also made impressive social progress, reducing infant mortality and improving educational standards.

The shortcomings of central planning became increasingly apparent as industrialization advanced and consumers' expectations rose. Lacking omniscience, the planners found that their targets for output, employment, and investment conflicted with the availability of resources and the need to improve technology and the quality of finished products. Prices did not reflect scarcities, so Hungary was being denied the chance to maximize its output and exports by specializing.

Responding to these problems, Hungary began to experiment with economic decentralization in agriculture in 1957. Farmers were allowed to choose how much produce they would sell to state buying organizations, and were given an incentive to join collectives because they would then be paid higher prices. Over the next ten years, Hungary became self-sufficient in foodstuffs and managed a net export surplus. This success helped persuade the political leadership to rely more on market mechanisms in other sectors. After long debate and preparation, in 1968 Hungary initiated its New Economic Mechanism, which changed the fundamentals of its economic planning.

Although the national plans remained important for determining broad economic strategy (about 45 percent of investment over the past decade was decided by the central authorities), they were to be implemented chiefly through the use of economic regulators, such as taxes, subsidies, interest rates, and the exchange rate. Prices of industrial and (to a lesser extent) agricultural goods were partially liberalized. Enterprises were given more freedom to decide on wages and investment. Workers were free to seek the employment of their choice, and firms to hire the most promising applicants. Profitability became a more important performance indicator than physical output, while central allocation of credit became a key mechanism for ensuring that firms' decisions were consistent with macroeconomic objectives. For big investments, firms generally had to compete for loans to supplement their retained profits, plus part of depreciation allowances (normally 60 percent) that they also retained. However, companies have still often invested more than the authorities had anticipated, forcing them to change the regulators in an effort to control aggregate demand.

By 1973 the New Economic Mechanism had achieved several of its objectives, particularly by making prices the main instrument for decentralizing decisions. But the reforms had not changed the industrial structure—which had become highly concentrated during the 1960s, thereby limiting domestic competition. Furthermore, even when company managers had considerable autonomy in principle, ministries and state agencies retained informal control over their decisions. Since managers of large enterprises could also exert pressures on central bodies, special favors were often bargained for, reducing competitive pressures.

Between the end of 1972 and 1978, links between domestic and international prices weakened and the role of prices in economic decisions declined. This was partly in response to urban workers' discontent with increasing income differentials, and partly to try and insulate the Hungarian economy from unfavorable international changes. As a result, efficiency suffered and Hungary did not improve its international competitiveness. It maintained GDP growth at an average of almost 6 percent a year, but largely by relying heavily on foreign borrowing.

In 1978, faced with the prospect of more expensive petroleum and other raw materials from its socialist trading partners, and the impossibility of indefinite reliance on foreign loans to maintain growth, Hungary decided to accelerate its economic reforms. The government took measures to link domestic and international prices more closely and to unify the exchange rate. Central intervention in enterprises has been reduced, and the government has divided large state firms into several smaller units to promote competition. Wages are to be linked more closely to productivity and profits, and unprofitable enterprises are supposed to be closed down. It is still early to judge the impact on economic efficiency of this new phase, especially in bleaker international trading conditions. But it is remarkable that pressure for economic decentralization has recurred in Hungary as the only means seen to be available to promote economic efficiency.

---

work, there has to be a real political willingness to relinquish some central financial powers. Local organizations need money and, in the long term, revenue-raising powers as well. The responsibility of raising and spending money can galvanize local people; without it, they feel dependent and frustrated.

This last point raises broader questions about the purpose of decentralization. Where governments are simply divesting themselves of activities that they cannot manage, the transfer of ownership itself confers the autonomy that is needed to make decentralization work. A change of ownership may not be the real objective, however. Governments may be decentralizing as a way of obtaining the greater efficiency that is possible with market mechanisms. In socialist countries, for example, the main thrust of decentralization has been to increase the autonomy of enterprises and to expand market and quasi-market relationships rather than to privatize ownership (although the latter has also occurred to a small extent—see Box 11.6). In many developing countries, managerial economies in the public sector may be realized by simplifying objectives and increasing the autonomy of managers to carry them out. This is particularly important in SOEs, as Chapter 8 showed; managers spend much of their time coping with problems created by central government, and sponsoring ministries get involved in details instead of concentrating on strategic policy issues.

Decentralization should therefore be seen as part of a broader market-surrogate strategy, designed to make public enterprises and bureaucracies more responsive to their ministers and to their clientele, and to achieve a closer connection between inputs and outputs. But a balance clearly has to be struck. Governments often need greater central control over some activities—as they do today over budgets and foreign debt, for example. And some functions will always be subject to close central supervision for political and other reasons. However, improving some kinds of central control can lay the groundwork for decentralizing other kinds of government activity—particularly the delivery of rural and social services and routine maintenance and administration. Since good senior managers and administrators are scarce almost everywhere, it is always worth examining the scope for dividing up development tasks to make greater use of junior managers. They may be less sophisticated but they are also more abundant.

Making bureaucracies responsive

All these avenues for management-saving reform—rationalizing the policy framework, improving coordination, and decentralization—need to be supported by corresponding changes in the way public employees regard their work. In many countries, that means improving the accountability of individual employees and of the bureaucracy at large.

Improving accountability

As criticism of bureaucracy has mounted in both developed and developing countries, administrative reform has increasingly been seen as an issue of accountability. This has both external and internal dimensions.

Political responsibility for the conduct of public business—especially the spending of public money—is at the heart of external accountability.

In many countries it needs strengthening by, for example, prompter publication of accounts and increased power and staff for auditing agencies. However, there is little point in establishing the principle of accountability if political leaders do not enforce it. Enforcement is clearly much less likely in countries where the political process does not extend far beyond the state apparatus itself. Elsewhere, a clear political commitment, even if mainly symbolic, can have salutary effects. In Malaysia, for example, all public servants (including the prime minister) have to punch a time clock when they arrive at, and leave, work.

One way to strengthen accountability—and also to give managers a dispassionate view of particular agencies' competence and problems—is to develop performance (or "value for money") auditing of government bodies. Since monitoring is costly, it needs to be done selectively and in collaboration with the bodies concerned (while taking care to avoid being "captured" by them). There may also be opportunities to improve performance by making the bureaucracy accountable to its "users." The Brazilian debureaucratization process has something of this approach in its concentration on the everyday encounters between state and citizen. Where agencies are operating with organized community or user groups, they may become answerable to them—especially if the clienteles can be given some market power. Chapter 8 gave the example of Kenya's Tea Development Authority, where small tea growers can switch to other crops if they are dissatisfied with the Authority's performance.

External pressures must be complemented by internal accountability—officials being individually accountable to their superiors. This can seldom be done, however, without managerial responsibilities being decentralized to the appropriate operational level. Most large private companies give managers specific responsibilities and the budgets and staff to go with them—and then judge them on their results. Public bureaucracies, by contrast, have been slow to give their managers similar freedom—just as governments have been reluctant to increase the autonomy of public enterprises.

The connection between autonomy and accountability matters most in SOEs. As Chapter 8 made clear, before SOE managers can be held accountable for performance, their goals have to be established, preferably by negotiation; they must have reasonable control over the means of achieving them; and government must be capable of monitoring their achievements. Performance agreements—contracts specifying conditions that can then be monitored—are among the most promising mechanisms, although they are not without problems.

Budgetary reform can also help improve internal accountability in the bureaucracy itself, as Chapter 7 indicated. The example of Kenya's Ministry of Agriculture, for instance, showed how budgetary procedures and allocations can be brought closer to the way programs are managed. These changes are always difficult to implement—but the alternative can often be worse. In Liberia, for example, it can still take a senior official in a rural area three or four months to buy a few bags of cement from a local merchant. He also needs eleven signatures on the purchase order and at least one trip to the capital, Monrovia—for expenditure that is already approved in the budget. In such circumstances, nobody is really accountable; the system tends to breed irresponsibility and corruption.

Individual accountability can sometimes be encouraged by organizing the internal workings of agencies so that units can offer market-like services to each other. Yugoslavia, for example, has decentralized management accountability in its railway system, so that separate units for traffic, traction, workshops, track, and so on buy and sell services between each other. Similar structural pressures are part of the Training and Visit System, with extension workers being encouraged to put pressure on agricultural specialists to come up with more relevant advice, because that is what farmers are asking of them.

Finally, this Report has emphasized that better management is at root a question of people: individual incentives in both private and public sectors are therefore a vital part of any strategy of reform. Accountability needs to be buttressed by careful changes in the material and nonmaterial rewards which public organizations extend to their employees—as discussed in Chapter 10.

Conclusions

The approach to reform discussed in this Report has emphasized that ends should influence means:

much depends on what governments are trying to achieve, and on what reforms will best fit the administrative system of individual countries. Nonetheless, it is worth repeating that all countries need specific capacity to plan and execute organizational reforms in the public sector—for better policy analysis, to improve the management of public enterprises and the design of development projects, and to improve accountability and incentives. That capacity is probably best located close to particular targets of reform rather than combined in a single grand "reform agency." Whatever the precise arrangements, experience suggests some guidelines for effectiveness:

• Administrative reforms should concentrate on a few strategic institutions or functions, rather than be dispersed (and ineffective) across the board.

• Governments can simultaneously keep up pressures for gradual system-wide improvements, particularly by incremental changes which increase official accountability and which reduce excessive coordination requirements or unproductive centralization.

• Reform needs careful administrative planning and continuity in implementation—close attention to detailed procedures as well as the overall policy thrust.

• Nonbureaucratic interests must be included in the reform process to keep up pressure for accountability, to ensure that external criteria of efficiency and service are observed, and to see that the viewpoint of ordinary people is taken into account.

• There should be incentives for officials and agencies to help devise and execute reforms: otherwise their suspicion or hostility can quickly undermine results.

Any realistic agenda of reform requires a balance between society's objectives and the limitations and interests of the bureaucracy. Progress is more likely if reforms take account of that reality—by assessing the administrative impact of policy changes, by reducing the more unproductive and burdensome bureaucratic interventions, and by providing officials with incentives to adopt improvements rather than resist them.

12 Concluding themes

For three years worldwide development has been stunted by recession. While population continues to grow inexorably, production and trade have lagged, unemployment has risen, much industrial capacity has remained idle, and the standard of living in Africa and Latin America has declined.

In some industrial countries there are now signs of recovery. But business confidence has been badly shaken, investment is sluggish, and large debts overhang many countries. Global recovery cannot, by itself, produce accelerated, equitable growth in low-income countries, and there is a danger that continued recession in developing countries will undermine the pace of economic recovery in the industrial countries.

The World Bank's assessment suggests that a 4 to 5 percent GDP growth rate annually over the next decade is feasible for the developing countries as a group. What is needed to achieve this result is a concerted national and international effort to ensure that recovery from the current recession is strong and lasting, and that individual economies are restructured to meet the changed economic conditions.

Policy reforms are needed so all economies can conform better to their comparative advantage, keep wages in line with productivity, and remove price distortions. These will be much easier to accomplish if pressures toward increased protectionism are resisted and existing barriers to trade begin to be rolled back, permitting the return to a rapidly expanding world trade, including increasing trade among developing countries.

But if the developing countries are to return to the growth rates of the 1960s and 1970s, net capital flows of *all* kinds must continue to increase, not as rapidly as in the 1970s, but by 10 percent or more in nominal terms (see Table 3.7). International private capital is essential to the development process, in the form of both direct investment and commercial lending. The liquidity problems of some major borrowers have shaken confidence in international lending with the perverse effect of reducing the availability of commercial capital even to some developing countries that have managed to perform well through the current crisis; this has resulted in postponed investment, curtailed inputs, and slowed development.

In this context the role of international financial institutions is extremely important. The IMF's recently expanded capacity will help ensure that resources are available to meet urgent short-term balance of payments crises. But the restoration of growth requires that flows from multilateral development banks be expanded as well. They have proven to be effective intermediaries between private markets and developing-country borrowers, and yet their current lending levels fall far short of what can be done. Substantially increased lending in support of sound development programs is essential to regain and sustain the development momentum in middle-income borrowers.

The poorest developing countries—especially those in sub-Saharan Africa—have been hardest hit by the current prolonged recession. They are particularly dependent on flows of concessional resources (ODA). Yet only 35 to 40 percent of ODA is channeled to the low-income countries; measures should be taken to raise this share. IDA loans are the most important component of ODA and are focused entirely on the poorest countries. An essential international action to ameliorate the crisis and restore some forward movement for these countries would be completion of the currently delayed IDA VI replenishment and early agreement on a substantially increased IDA VII.

The present debt difficulties of the developing countries are the culmination of trends over several years—especially the effect of higher energy prices and expanding commercial bank lending combined with inappropriate domestic policies. These difficulties were exacerbated to the point of crisis by the prolonged recession that has caused export earnings to fall and by unprecedently high real interest rates. All arrangements to help individual countries to avoid default depend in the first instance on the sustained recovery of the industrialized countries, and ultimately on the borrowing countries putting in place successful adjustment programs. With ample underutilized capacity, economic recovery will produce many benefits—cutting unemployment, reducing the pressure for protection, easing the debt problem, and facilitating structural adjustments.

The restructuring strategy in developing countries should aim at correcting price distortions and at overcoming institutional weaknesses that have contributed to the low productivity of investment in recent years. These and other measures discussed in Part II would assist countries to exploit more effectively their comparative advantage. For them to bear full fruit, however, the world economy must regain the momentum it achieved in 1976–78. Without that, the developing countries' prospects are bleak indeed.

Over the longer term the challenge for developing countries is to use their limited resources more efficiently and more equitably. Every government faces this challenge: whatever the political objectives, the goal is to find the most cost-effective means of achieving them. Evidence abounds of how much can be gained from greater efficiency. Price distortions alone may slow down GDP growth by as much as two percentage points a year. Other substantial losses result from poor investment decisions, project delays, inadequate maintenance of plant and machinery, and failure to make full use of human skills and energy. And in most countries, the consequences of these inefficiencies are felt most by those who have least—the poor.

In an effort to accelerate development, governments have become increasingly active. In the process many have often been badly overextended and hence have contributed to inefficiency. This Report has suggested ways to strengthen public management and, more generally, the incentives for all enterprises to operate more efficiently. Governments could also share more of the burden of promoting development with other organizations—private firms, community associations, and the like.

This Report has stressed the importance of government policy in the adjustment process—particularly in correcting price distortions and exploiting comparative advantage. Whatever the state's role as producer and owner, its role as regulator is everywhere of prime importance in establishing incentives for efficiency.

Good management of the economy depends on well-functioning public institutions as well as on the correct choice of policies, which has been the main theme of Part II. The role of the public sector has to be tailored to the human and financial resources available, and these are almost everywhere overstretched. Hence the importance of relying on markets to do what experience has shown that markets generally do best. That still leaves the government responsible for macroeconomic policy, for managing public revenues and expenditures, and for running public enterprises and public services. Equipping the public service to carry out these tasks well is challenge enough.

Though diverse, the experience of developing countries in managing development has revealed four broad conclusions:

• Policy and institutional reform are complementary. Policies are relevant only if there is the institutional capacity to carry them out, while strong institutions are ineffective—even counterproductive—if the policy framework discourages efficiency.

• The implied rejection of "blueprints" in tackling the complexities of development is not a counsel of despair. The chief lesson to be drawn from experience is the importance of building into every strategy and program an effective learning process. This is as true for programs of structural adjustment and administrative reform as it is for new initiatives in rural development.

• Public bureaucracies would be more effective if they paid less attention to form and more to substance. This means agencies' preparing fewer grand plans and instead undertaking more analyses of the actions needed to achieve government's central goals. It means restructuring traditional budgeting to identify the costs of specific programs. It means transforming auditing into a system of selective performance evaluation that relates the cost of inputs to the value of outputs. And, at the field level, it means officials' looking outward to serve their clients rather than inward to satisfy predetermined bureaucratic procedures. All these changes imply more vigorous attention to issues of accountability, cost-effectiveness, and incentives.

• On administrative reform, governments can achieve more through persistent but selective efforts at change, step by step, rather than through major reforms that threaten many entrenched interests simultaneously and are therefore often neutralized by them. The correct time horizon for institutional development is decades rather than years.

Yet the very pressures that push governments into an activist role are those that drive them to seek quick solutions. Too often a program has hardly started before fashions change, support is withdrawn, the approach changed, and a new program started. Institutional reform will be successful only if it is pursued with vision, tenacity, and strong political leadership.

Technical appendix

This technical appendix discusses the sources of data in Chapter 2 and the main reasons for disparities between sources and across years between this *World Development Report* and previous Reports. It also outlines the procedure used for making projections in Chapter 3 and notes some of the major changes in these projections compared with those presented in the 1982 Report. This appendix should be read in conjunction with the Introduction to the World Development Indicators and Technical notes.

Historical data

The World Bank assembles its data from a variety of national sources, and the information reported by other international organizations, including the International Monetary Fund (IMF), the United Nations agencies, the Organisation for Economic Co-operation and Development (OECD), the General Agreement on Tariffs and Trade Secretariat, and the Bank for International Settlements. Staff estimates are used to fill data gaps.

Comparisons of Report data with those of other international organizations, such as the IMF, is complicated by differences in country groupings and in underlying statistical concepts—in each case owing to different analytical requirements and varying access to source material. Continuous efforts are made to reduce these differences.

For balance of payments data the Bank mainly relies on the IMF. For countries included in the Bank's country groupings, but not reporting to the Fund, the Bank staff obtains estimates from the country authorities. For a few other countries, IMF data are adjusted on the basis of information derived from the Bank's country economic work. Also, the statistical conventions used by the Bank occasionally differ from those of the Fund. For example, while the Bank values all gold holdings at the London Clearing House price, the Fund values gold holdings for some countries according to that country's convention and for other countries at the world market price. The Bank's country groupings differ from those of the Fund because, for its analytical work, the Bank needs to make different distinctions among groups of developing countries with different economic structures.

Historical data are revised from one Report to the next for several reasons:

- Country authorities constantly revise data
- Country authorities re-base their country statistics to different years, often changing measured rates of growth
- The membership of country groupings is adjusted to reflect changes in income levels which are largely the basis for country classification.

Historical data may be subject to substantial revision even for periods far into the past. The growth rate for China during 1960–73, for example, increased from 4.7 percent reported in the 1982 Report to 5.5 percent reported in the 1983 Report; this change was based on additional benchmark data for different years supplied by the Chinese government. For high-income oil-exporting countries between 1960 and 1973 GNP growth was changed from 8.6 percent to 10.7 percent because of changes in the oil prices used by country authorities to value national output, and because of their revisions of estimates of investment income.

As countries improve their statistical collection techniques and the scope of data coverage, such revisions are made by statistical agencies in all countries. Historical data for the industrial countries for the period 1960–73 have been revised every year as at least one country in that group has revised data for that period. The United States, for example, from time to time revises components of its national accounts as far back as 1929. In addition to such revisions, the periodic changing of the base year changes the weights used in computing indices and, therefore, measured GNP growth.

Membership in country groupings is varied to reflect changes in relative levels of economic development. Declines in income, for example, led to shifting Ghana from the middle-income to low-income developing-country category. A rise in income and continued growth of industry, on the other hand, moved Spain from the middle-income developing-country group to the industrial-country group.

Projections

Table 3.1 was derived by first projecting potential industrial-country output growth, industrial-country demand for developing-country exports, and potential industrial-country lending to developing countries. These are then used to arrive at individual developing-country and regional projections consistent within a global framework.

Projecting industrial-country growth

To obtain the projections of potential industrial-country output at full employment, assumptions are made about industrial-country labor force growth and technical progress. The industrial-country labor force is assumed to grow 0.7 percent a year between 1980 and 2000, based on existing population size and age structure, with some rise in the female labor force participation rate, and no change in migration regulations. Technical progress for all industrial countries is assumed to advance at the historical rate experienced in the United States, so that potential per capita income growth for the industrial countries as a whole falls to 2.8 percent over the forecast period from 3.6 percent experienced between 1960 and 1980. Domestic capital formation is projected to be lower than in the past in view of diminished projected profit opportunities arising from reduced labor force growth and technical progress. The High case assumes a continuation of past trends in reducing differences in technologies, so that less prosperous industrial countries experience more rapid rates of per capita GDP growth than the average industrial country. Under the High case, more rapid technical progress would permit repeating the 3.6 percent annual rate of per capita GDP growth witnessed between 1960 and 1980; capital formation would, accordingly, be higher. The Low case assumes that all industrial countries experience the rate of technical progress experienced by those industrial countries with the lowest rate of per capita growth, thereby lowering rates of capital formation and reducing industrial-country per capita growth to 1.8 percent a year.

Combining the projected labor force growth rate of 0.7 percent a year with the three rates of growth of per capita output associated with the different technical progress and capital formation assumptions—1.8 percent, 2.8 percent, and 3.6 percent—forms the "cone" of Low, Central, and High industrial-country potential output growth rates of 2.5 percent, 3.5 percent, and 4.3 percent for capacity GDP that lie behind the projections of actual output shown in Table 3.1.

Actual industrial-country output presently lies far below its potential. While the potential output projection does set a ceiling for industrial-country output, it does not provide any information on the rate (or direction) of growth of actual OECD output when below the ceiling. In projecting actual output for 1983 and 1984, the Bank follows the forecast of the OECD published in mid-1983. As an institution specializing in long-term development and adjustment and making longer-term loans, the Bank concentrates on longer-term projections. Therefore, the time horizon is shifted periodically to cover eight to twelve years into the future. For this Report, it was shifted from 1990 to 1995. The Bank makes no independent projection of short-term industrial-country developments, but reviews the upside and downside risks surrounding the short-term forecasts of the OECD and the Fund, and assesses their implications for developing countries.

When, as is now the case, all short-term forecasts envisage a level of output well below potential, the Bank projects a rate of growth over the longer term (3.8 percent from 1984 to 1990) which brings the industrial countries gradually back to full employment and capacity output; after that, growth is assumed to fall to the Central case capacity rate of growth of 3.6 percent. That projected rate of recovery is about the average based on postwar cyclical experience; recoveries from relatively deep recessions tend to be somewhat faster. The rate of recovery was assumed to be faster in the High case and slower in the Low case projections.

Since potential output depends on technical progress and labor force growth, not demonstrably sensitive to recession over the longer term, the projection of potential industrial-country income levels for 1990 to 1995 is unchanged from the previous Report. The more severe the recession, therefore, the larger the gap between potential and actual output and the greater the possible recovery of output growth after the recession. The increase in projected growth rates for the industrial countries—this year's Central case is 3.7 percent whereas last year's High case was 3.6 percent—reflects the severity of the present recession rather than a revision of expectations about long-term potential growth.

Projecting developing-country growth

Given the projected industrial-country growth and the projected rate of inflation, the Bank projects real and nominal developing-country exports of primary products in detail by individual commodities. It constructs aggregate projections of trade in manufactured goods. These projections show the exports of developing countries to the industrial countries both in aggregate and by developing-country region of origin.

The Bank computes a notional "potential lending" by industrial countries; this is partly based on past shares of net foreign lending in total industrial-country GNP and shares of foreign assets in total industrial-country assets. A separate procedure projects high-income oil-exporting country lending, combining the previous projection of oil exports with a projection of imports. Given the assumed underlying long-term real interest rate of 3 percent (plus a 150 basis point spread to developing countries), trial debt service ratios are computed based on the projected exports and trial growth rates in developing countries. If the ensuing lending path produces debt service ratios within historical experience, the lending path is considered feasible.

The composition of net capital flows by type of investment is projected with a variety of techniques. It is sensitive to data revisions, which can be quite large for some time series. Direct foreign investment, for example, showed a growth rate in the 1981 Report of 13.6 percent over the period 1970–80; but subsequent revisions in estimates of the 1980 level of direct foreign investment raised that growth rate to 18.5 percent. In view of this upward revision in historical growth rates, the projected growth rates were raised in this Report to 11 percent, up from the range of 5 percent to 7.5 percent shown in the 1982 Report.

Given the above global framework, the Bank's regional economists prepare projections of regional economic growth based on detailed country economic analysis. These regional projections are then reconciled with the Bank's aggregate projections of net capital flows, trade, and debt service payments. The end result is the Central case scenario. The High and Low cases are obtained by projecting high and low OECD growth paths and simulating the effects of these changes on developing countries by using a general equilibrium system developed, in cooperation with the Bank, by the Centre d'Economie Mathematique et d'Econometrie of l'Universite Libre de Bruxelles.

Bibliographical note

This Report has drawn on a wide range of World Bank work as well as on external research. Selected sources used in each chapter are briefly noted below, and then listed alphabetically by author. They are divided into two groups. The first consists of a set of background papers commissioned for this Report; their primary purpose is to synthesize the relevant literature and Bank work. (Thus not all the sources cited in these papers are listed separately.) Those issued as World Bank Staff Working Papers are available from the Bank's Publications Sales Unit. The views they express are not, however, necessarily those of the World Bank or of this Report. The second group consists of external publications and World Bank sources, which include sector policy papers, ongoing economic analysis and research, and project sector and economic work on individual countries.

Selected sources, by chapter

Chapters 2 and 3

These chapters draw heavily on the Bank's data files and on published statistics from other official agencies including the IMF, OECD, GATT, and United Nations organizations. The basic projections are the product of the World Bank's *Global Framework* as explained by Cheetham, Gupta, and Schwartz. The sensitivity analysis is the result of simulations undertaken with the Brussels global development model described in Waelbroeck and Associates. The trade discussion draws on Hughes and Krueger's study of protectionism and the report of the group of experts commissioned by the Commonwealth Secretariat.

Chapters 4 and 5

Public finance data were derived from IMF sources. Short's study and World Bank files are the main sources of information on SOEs. General discussions of the impact of state regulations on the

economy can be found in Balassa; Bhagwati; Choksi; and Krueger. Rhee, Pursell, and Ross-Larson, as well as Shinohara, Yanagihara, and Kim's work for the World Bank, provided insights into the role of the state in the Republic of Korea and Japan.

Chapters 6 and 7

The discussion of price distortions and their impact on growth draws on the extensive literature that has developed on the subject over the past two decades. In addition to the earlier *World Development Reports*, key sources were the writings of Balassa; Bhagwati; Krueger; Fry; Little; and McKinnon.

On planning, the key references are Waterston and Lewis. A review of the crisis in planning in the late 1960s is provided by Faber and Seers. Issues on budgetary policy are examined in Caiden and Wildavsky, and the experience of budgetary reforms reviewed in Baudrillart and Poinsard.

Boxes on Japan and the Republic of Korea draw on the background papers by Shinohara and Kim respectively. Other boxes draw on material prepared mostly by Bank staff but also by some outside experts.

Chapter 8

The analysis of SOE problems is based primarily on the Bank's extensive operational experience, supplemented by materials published by UNIDO, APDAC, and individual governments. Works by Choksi and materials edited by Baumol; Jones; Shepherd; and Vernon provide a useful overview of SOE problems. The chapter also draws on Jones' work on the cost of noneconomic objectives and Bank-sponsored research on performance evaluation systems in Pakistan. The statistics on SOEs, like those in Chapter 5, are predominantly from Short's research for the IMF, as well as UNIDO publications and World Bank data.

Chapter 9

This chapter is based much more on Bank operational experience than on published research. While the Bank's evaluations of individual projects are unpublished, they are summarized in a series entitled *Annual Review of Project Performance Audit Reports*, which is available from the Bank's Publications Sales Unit. Box 9.4 outlines a learning process approach to development more fully described in Korten, and Box 9.5 on the Training and Visit System of extension is amplified in Benor and Harrison.

Relevant Bank Staff Working Papers include Esman; Heaver; and Smith, Lethem, and Thoolen. Other publications include Chambers; Honadle and Klauss; Paul; and Tendler.

Chapter 10

The analysis of growth in public employment is based on World Bank country studies and data compiled by ILO. Figures on the composition of public service employment reported in Box 10.1 are derived from Heller and Tait. Material on skill shortages stems primarily from World Bank reports and the discussion of brain-drain issues from UNCTAD studies and World Bank reports. Figures on technical cooperation were compiled from data provided by DAC Secretariat and other donor agencies.

The discussion of public service training is based primarily on Paul and secondarily on reports by the UN, ILO, USAID, Ford Foundation, Commonwealth Secretariat, and the World Bank's Economic Development Institute. The treatment of career development and salaries and incentives is based predominantly on World Bank materials and UN reports. The section on management of expatriates is based on information gathered from the major donor agencies and on Lethem and Cooper. Finally, the note on the cultural dimension relies, among others, on Kubr and Wallace; and Stifel, Coleman, and Black. A full set of references for the chapter is listed in Ozgediz.

Chapter 11

There is a great deal of published material on the evolution of institutions in industrialized countries: Heady; Pempel; and Williamson discuss much of the relevant literature for the public and private sectors. The discussion of administrative reform draws on a number of reports by government commissions in developing countries, on World Bank country studies, on Caiden and Siedentopf; on the UN Development Administration Division studies; and on others. Material on coordination is drawn primarily from World Bank sources, as is the discussion of experiences in Thailand and Hungary. Background papers on decentralization (Rondinelli, Nellis, and Cheema), on local government (Cochrane), and on corruption (Gould and Amaro-Reyes) provided material on these themes for this chapter. The section on accountability is based on World Bank sources.

Background papers

Agarwala, Ramgopal. *Price Distortions and Growth in Developing Countries*. World Bank Staff Working Paper no. 575. Washington, D.C., 1983.

———. *Planning in Developing Countries: Lessons of Experience*. World Bank Staff Working Paper no. 576. Washington, D.C., 1983.

Cochrane, Glynn. *Policies for Strengthening Local Government in Developing Countries*. World Bank Staff Working Paper no. 582. Washington, D.C., 1983.

Gordon, David. *Development Finance Companies, State and Privately Owned: A Review*. World Bank Staff Working Paper no. 578. Washington, D.C., 1983.

Gould, David J., and Jose A. Amaro-Reyes. *Corruption and Administrative Performance: Examples from Developing Countries*. World Bank Staff Working Paper no. 580. Washington, D.C., 1983.

Knight, Peter T. *Economic Reform in Socialist Countries: The Experiences of China, Hungary, Romania, and Yugoslavia*. World Bank Staff Working Paper no. 579. Washington, D.C., 1983.

Kubr, Milan, and John Wallace. *Successes and Failures in Meeting the Management Challenge: Strategies and Their Implementation*. World Bank Staff Working Paper no. 585. Washington, D.C., 1983.

Lethem, Francis J., and Lauren Cooper. *Managing Project-Related Technical Assistance: The Lessons of Success*. World Bank Staff Working Paper no. 586. Washington, D.C., 1983.

Ozgediz, Selcuk. *Managing the Public Service in Developing Countries: Issues and Prospects*. World Bank Staff Working Paper no. 583. Washington, D.C., 1983.

Paul, Samuel. *Training for Public Administration and Management in Developing Countries: A Review*. World Bank Staff Working Paper no. 584. Washington, D.C., 1983.

Rondinelli, Dennis A., John R. Nellis, and G. Shabbir Cheema. *Decentralization in Developing Countries: A Review of Recent Experience.* World Bank Staff Working Paper no. 581. Washington, D.C., 1983.

Shinohara, Miyohei, Toru Yanagihara, and Kwang Suk Kim. *The Japanese and Korean Experiences in Managing Development.* Ed. Ramgopal Agarwala. World Bank Staff Working Paper no. 574. Washington, D.C., 1983.

Shirley, Mary M. *Managing State-Owned Enterprises.* World Bank Staff Working Paper no. 577. Washington, D.C., 1983.

Other sources

Balassa, Bela, and Associates. *Development Strategies in Semi-industrial Economies.* Baltimore, Md.: Johns Hopkins University Press, 1982.

Balassa, Bela. "Disequilibrium Analysis in Developing Economies: An Overview." *World Development* (December 1982), pp. 1027–38.

———. *Policy Reform in Developing Countries.* London: Oxford University Press, 1977.

Baudrillart, Wenceslas, and Robert Poinsard. *20 Years of Budgetary Reform: a tentative international stocktaking.* General Report of the Working Group on Integrated Budgeting Systems, International Congress of Administrative Sciences. Brussels, 1982.

Basu, Prahlad Kumar, and Alec Nove. *Public Enterprise Policy on Investment, Pricing, Returns.* Kuala Lumpur: Asian and Pacific Development Administration Center, 1979.

Baumol, William J., ed. *Public and Private Enterprise in a Mixed Economy.* New York: St. Martin's, 1980.

Benor, Daniel, and James Q. Harrison. *Agricultural Extension: The Training and Visit System.* Washington, D.C., World Bank, 1977.

Bhagwati, Jagdish. *Anatomy and Consequences of Trade Control Regimes.* New York: National Bureau of Economic Research, 1978.

———. "The Brain Drain." Tripartite World Conference on Employment, Income Distribution, and Social Progress and the International Division of Labour. Background Papers, volume 2. Geneva: International Labour Office, 1976.

Caiden, Gerald E., and Heinrich Siedentopf, eds. *Strategies for Administrative Reform.* Lexington, Mass.: Lexington Books, 1982.

Caiden, Naomi, and Aaron Wildavsky. *Planning and Budgeting in Poor Countries.* New York: Wiley, 1974.

Cairncross, Alec, and Associates. *Protectionism: Threat to International Order.* London: Commonwealth Secretariat, 1982.

Chambers, Robert. *Managing Rural Development.* Uppsala: Scandinavian Institute of African Studies, 1974.

Cheetham, Russell J., Syamaprasad Gupta, and Antoine Schwartz. *The Global Framework.* World Bank Staff Working Paper no. 355. Washington, D.C., 1979.

Choksi, Armeane M. *State Intervention in the Industrialization of Developing Countries: Selected Issues.* World Bank Staff Working Paper no. 341. Washington D.C., 1974.

Duncan, Ronald, and Ernst Lutz. "Penetration of Industrial Country Markets by Agricultural Products from Developing Countries." *World Development.* Forthcoming.

Esman, Milton J. *Paraprofessionals in Rural Development: Issues in Field-level Staffing for Agricultural Projects.* World Bank Staff Working Paper no. 573. Washington, D.C., 1983.

Faber, Mike, and Dudley Seers, eds. *The Crisis in Planning.* Two volumes. London: Chatto and Windus for Sussex University Press, 1972.

Fry, Maxwell J. "Savings, Investment, Growth and the Cost of Financial Repression." *World Development*, vol. 8, no. 4 (April 1982), pp. 317–27.

Galbis, V. "Financial Intermediation and Economic Growth in Less-Developed Countries: A Theoretical Approach." *Journal of Development Studies*, January 1977.

General Agreement on Tariffs and Trade (GATT). *International Trade in 1982 and Current Prospects.* Press release. March 4, 1983.

Heady, Ferrel. *Public Administration: A Comparative Perspective.* New York: Dekker, 1979.

Heaver, Richard A. *Bureaucratic Politics and Incentives in the Management of Rural Development.* World Bank Staff Working Paper no. 537. Washington, D.C., 1982.

Heller, Peter S., and Alan A. Tait. *Government Employment and Pay: Some International Comparisons.* Washington, D.C.: International Monetary Fund. Forthcoming.

Honadle, George, and Rudi Klauss. *International Development Administration: Implementation Analysis for Development Projects.* New York: Praeger, 1979.

Hughes, Helen. "External Debt Problems of Developing Countries." Paper presented at the 13th Pacific Trade and Development Conference on Energy and Structural Change in the Asia and Pacific Region, Manila, Philippines, January 24-28, 1983. Washington, D.C.: World Bank.

Hughes, Helen, and Anne O. Krueger. "Effects of Protection in Developed Countries on Developing Countries' Exports of Manufactures." Washington, D.C.: World Bank, 1983.

International Labour Office. *General Report.* Third Session of the Joint Committee on the Public Service. Geneva, 1983.

Jones, Leroy P. "Public Enterprise for Whom? Perverse Distributional Consequences of Public Operational Decisions." Paper presented at the Conference on Problems and Policies of Industrialization in an Open Economy, Bogazici University, Istanbul, Turkey, August 20–24, 1981.

Jones, Leroy P., ed. *Public Enterprise in Less Developed Countries*. New York: Cambridge University Press, 1982.

Korten, David C. "Community Organization and Rural Development: A Learning Process Approach." *Public Administration Review*, September–October, 1980.

Krueger, Anne O. "Liberalization Attempts and Consequences." Washington, D.C.: National Bureau for Economic Research, 1978.

———. *Trade and Employment in Developing Countries*. Chicago: University of Chicago Press, 1982.

Lewis, William Arthur. *Development Planning: The Essentials of Economic Policy*. London: Allen and Unwin, 1966.

Lindauer, David. *Public Sector Wages and Employment in Africa: Facts and Concepts*. World Bank Studies in Employment and Rural Development no. 68. Washington, D.C., 1981.

Little, Ian Malcolm David. *Economic Development: Theory, Policy, and International Relations*. New York: Basic Books, 1982.

Magee, Stephen P. "Factor Market Distortions, Production, and Trade: A Survey." *Oxford Economic Papers*, vol. 25, no. 1 (March 1973), pp. 1–43.

McKinnon, Ronald Ian. *Money and Capital in Economic Development*. Washington, D.C.: Brookings Institution, 1973.

Paul, Samuel. *Managing Development Programs: The Lessons of Success*. Boulder, Col.: Westview, 1982.

Pempel, T. J. *Policy and Politics in Japan*. Philadelphia: Temple University Press, 1982.

Redwood, John, and John Hatch. *Controlling Public Industries*. Oxford: Basil Blackwell, 1982.

Rhee, Yung Whee, Gary Pursell, and Bruce Ross-Larson. "Promoting Exports: Institutions, Technology, and Marketing in Korea." Washington, D.C: The World Bank, Development Research Department, January 1983.

Sadique, Abu Sharaf H. K., ed. *Public Enterprise in Asia: Studies on Coordination and Control*. Kuala Lumpur: Asian Center for Development Administration (APDAC), 1976.

Serageldin, Ismail, James Socknat, Stace Birks, Bob Li, and Clive Sinclair. *Manpower and International Labor Migration in the Middle East and North Africa*. New York: Oxford University Press, 1983.

Shepherd, William G., ed. *Public Enterprise: Economic Analysis of Theory and Practice*. Lexington, Mass.: Lexington Books, 1978.

Short, Peter. *Appraising the Role of Public Enterprises: An International Comparison*. IMF Occasional Paper Series. Washington, D.C., 1983.

Smith, William E., Francis J. Lethem, and Ben A. Thoolen. *The Design of Organizations for Rural Development Projects— A Progress Report*. World Bank Staff Working Paper no. 375. Washington, D.C., 1980.

Stifel, Lawrence D., James S. Coleman, and Joseph E. Black, eds. *Education and Training for Public Sector Management in Developing Countries*. New York: The Rockefeller Foundation, 1977.

Tendler, Judith. *Turning Private Voluntary Organizations into Development Agencies: Questions for Evaluation*. Program Evaluation Discussion Paper no. 12. Washington, D.C.: US Agency for International Development, 1982.

United Nations. *Changes and Trends in Public Administration and Finance for Development—Second Survey—1977–79*. Sales No. E.82.II.H.1. New York, 1982.

United Nations Conference on Trade and Development. *The Feasibility of Measuring International Flows of Human Resources*. UNCTAD Secretariat Study no. TD/B/c.6/AC.8/2. Geneva, 1982.

United Nations Industrial Development Organization. Papers presented at the Expert Group Meeting on the Changing Role and Function of the Public Industrial Sector in Development in Vienna, Austria, October 5–9, 1981.

Vernon, Raymond, and Yair Aharoni, eds. *State-Owned Enterprise in the Western Economies*. New York: St. Martin's, 1981.

Waelbroeck, Jean, J. M. Burniaux, G. Carrin, and Jan Gunning. "General Equilibrium Modeling of Global Adjustment." World Bank Staff Working Paper. Forthcoming.

Waterston, Albert. *Development Planning: Lessons of Experience*. Baltimore, Md.: Johns Hopkins University Press, 1965.

Williamson, Oliver E. "The Modern Corporation: Origins, Evolution, Attributes." *Journal of Economic Literature*, vol. 19, no. 4 (December 1981).

Annex

World
Development
Indicators

Contents

Key

In each table, countries are listed in their group in ascending order of income per capita. The reference numbers indicating that order are shown in the alphabetical list of countries below.

Figures in the colored bands are summary measures for groups of countries. The letter w after a summary measure indicates that it is a weighted average; the letter m, that it is a median value; the letter t, that it is a total.

.. Not available.

(.) Less than half the unit shown.

All growth rates are in real terms.

Figures in italics are for years or periods other than those specified.

Afghanistan	9	Hong Kong	91	Peru	60
Albania	118	Hungary	119	Philippines	49
Algeria	80	India	17	Poland	122
Angola	50	Indonesia	41	Portugal	83
Argentina	84	Iran, Islamic Republic of	75	Romania	120
Australia	107	Iraq	76	Rwanda	16
Austria	105	Ireland	99	Saudi Arabia	96
Bangladesh	5	Israel	92	Senegal	36
Belgium	110	Italy	101	Sierra Leone	27
Benin	25	Ivory Coast	63	Singapore	93
Bhutan	2	Jamaica	62	Somalia	18
Bolivia	43	Japan	104	South Africa	86
Brazil	81	Jordan	72	Spain	100
Bulgaria	121	Kampuchea, Democratic	1	Sri Lanka	24
Burma	8	Kenya	35	Sudan	32
Burundi	14	Korea, Democratic Republic of	69	Sweden	116
Cameroon	56	Korea, Republic of	74	Switzerland	117
Canada	108	Kuwait	97	Syrian Arab Republic	71
Central African Republic	26	Lao People's Democratic Republic	3	Tanzania	19
Chad	4	Lebanon	79	Thailand	48
Chile	85	Lesotho	42	Togo	33
China	21	Liberia	40	Trinidad and Tobago	94
Colombia	66	Libya	95	Tunisia	67
Congo, People's Republic of	58	Madagascar	28	Turkey	70
Costa Rica	68	Malawi	11	Uganda	13
Cuba	57	Malaysia	77	Union of Soviet Socialist Republics	123
Czechoslovakia	124	Mali	10	United Arab Emirates	98
Denmark	113	Mauritania	37	United Kingdom	103
Dominican Republic	64	Mexico	82	United States	112
Ecuador	61	Mongolia	65		
Egypt, Arab Republic of	46	Morocco	52	Upper Volta	15
El Salvador	47	Mozambique	31	Uruguay	88
Ethiopia	6	Nepal	7	Venezuela	89
Finland	106	Netherlands	109	Viet Nam, Socialist Republic of	20
France	111	New Zealand	102		
German Democratic Republic	125	Nicaragua	53	Yemen Arab Republic	38
Germany, Federal Republic of	114	Niger	29	Yemen, People's Democratic Republic of	39
Ghana	34	Nigeria	54	Yugoslavia	87
Greece	90	Norway	115	Zaire	12
Guatemala	59	Pakistan	30		
Guinea	22	Panama	78	Zambia	45
Haiti	23	Paraguay	73	Zimbabwe	55
Honduras	44				

Introduction

The World Development Indicators, produced as a by-product of the World Bank's statistical and analytical work, provide information on the main features of social and economic development. Over time, the World Bank has developed standard data formats for operational use, and its data bank has become increasingly geared to the provision of statistical inputs for internal information and decision papers. The broad range of internationally comparable statistical information is intended to be suitable for cross-economy analysis.

Most of the data collected by the World Bank are on its developing member countries. Because comparable data for developed market economies are readily available, these are also included in the indicators. Data for nonmarket economies, a few of which are members of the World Bank, are included if available in a comparable form.

Every effort has been made to standardize concepts, definitions, coverage, timing, and the evaluation of the basic data to ensure the greatest possible degree of comparability. Since the publication of the first World Development Indicators in 1978, considerable progress has been made, through the use of more uniform definitions and concepts, toward making the data more internationally comparable. Although the number of indicators included in this edition is greater than in the first edition, it is believed that the quality of the data has been substantially improved.

The indicators in Table 1 give a summary profile of economies. The data in other tables fall into the following broad areas: national accounts, agriculture, industry, energy, external trade, external debt, aid flows, other external transactions, demography, labor force, urbanization, social indicators, defense and social expenditure, and income distribution. Two of these tables appear for the first time this year, one on agriculture and food, the other on terms of public borrowing. The first is now included because of the importance of the agricultural sector and food aid in developing economies; the second, because of growing attention to the external obligations of developing countries.

Most of the information used in computing the indicators was drawn from the data files and publications of the World Bank, the International Monetary Fund, and the United Nations and specialized agencies.

For ease of reference, ratios and rates of growth are shown; absolute values are reported only in a few instances. Most growth rates were calculated for two periods: 1960–70 and 1970–81, or 1970–80 if data for 1981 were not available. All growth rates are in real terms and were computed, unless noted otherwise, by using the least-squares method. Because this method takes all observations in a period into account, the resulting growth rates reflect general trends that are not unduly influenced by exceptional values. Table entries in italics indicate that they are for years or periods other than those specified. All dollar figures are US dollars.

Some of the differences between figures shown this year and last year reflect not only updating but also revisions to historical series. They also reflect revisions to the estimates of population on the basis of new information from surveys and the 1980 round of censuses.

The economies included in the World Development Indicators are classified by GNP per capita. This classification is useful in distinguishing economies at different stages of development. Many of the economies included are also classified by dominant characteristics—to distinguish oil importers and exporters and to distinguish market and nonmarket industrial economies. The groups used in the tables are 34 low-income developing economies with a GNP per capita of less than $410 in 1981, 60 middle-income developing economies with a GNP per capita of $410 or more, 4 high-income oil exporters, 19 industrial market economies, and 8 East European nonmarket economies. Note that because of the paucity of data and the differences in the method for computing national income, estimates of GNP per capita are available only for nonmarket economies that are members of the World Bank.

The format of this edition generally follows that used in previous years, but some of the economies have been reclassified to reflect changes in their income levels.

In each group, economies are listed in ascending order of income per capita, and that order is used in all tables. The alphabetical list in the key shows the reference number of each economy. Countries with populations of less than a million are not reported in the tables, largely for lack of comprehensive data. The technical notes for Table 1 show some basic indicators for 34 small countries that are members of the United Nations, the World Bank, or both.

Summary measures—totals, median values, or weighted averages—were calculated for the economy groups only if data were adequate and meaningful statistics could be obtained. Because China and India heavily bias the summary measures for all low-income economies, summary measures are separately shown for China and India and for other low-income economies. And because trade in oil affects the economic characteristics and performance of middle-income economies; summary measures are also shown for oil importers and for oil exporters. In this year's edition, the large group of middle-income economies is also divided into lower and upper categories to give greater meaning to the summary measures.

The weights used in computing the summary measures are described in the technical notes. The letter w after a summary measure indicates that it is a weighted average; the letter m, that it is a median value; the letter t, that it is a total. The median is the middle value of a data set arranged in order of magnitude. Because the coverage of economies is not uniform for all indicators and because the variation around central tendencies can be large, readers should exercise caution in comparing the summary measures for different

Groups of economies

The colors on the map show what group a country has been placed in on the basis of its GNP per capita and, in some instances, its distinguishing economic characteristics. For example, all low-income countries, those with a GNP per capita of less than $410, are colored yellow. The groups are the same as those used in the 27 tables that follow, and they include only the 125 countries with a population of more than 1 million.

- Low-income economies
- Middle-income oil importers
- Middle-income oil exporters
- High-income oil exporters
- Industrial market economies
- East European nonmarket economies

- Not included in the Indicators

indicators, groups, and years or periods.

Readers should also exercise caution in comparing indicators across economies. Although the statistics are drawn from sources generally considered the most authoritative and reliable, some of them, particularly those describing social features and income distribution, are subject to considerable margins of error. In addition, variations in national statistical practices mean that the data in certain instances are not strictly comparable. The data should thus be construed only as indicating trends and characterizing major differences between economies.

The technical notes should be referred to in any use of the data. These notes outline the methods, concepts, definitions, and data sources. The bibliography gives details of the data sources, which contain comprehensive definitions and descriptions of concepts used.

This year's edition again includes five world maps. The first map shows country names and the groups in which economies have been placed. The maps on the following pages show population, adult literacy, life expectancy at birth, and the share of agriculture in gross domestic product (GDP). The Eckert IV projection has been used for these maps because it maintains correct areas for all countries, though at the cost of some distortions in shape, distance, and direction. The maps have been prepared exclusively for the convenience of the readers of this book; the denominations used, and the boundaries shown, do not imply on the part of the World Bank and its affiliates any judgment on the legal status of any territory or any endorsement or acceptance of such boundaries.

The World Development Indicators are prepared under the supervision of Ramesh Chander.

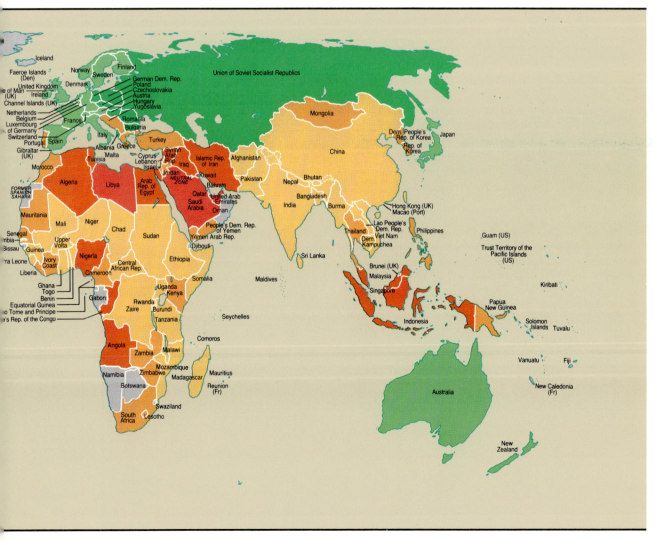

Population and GNP per capita

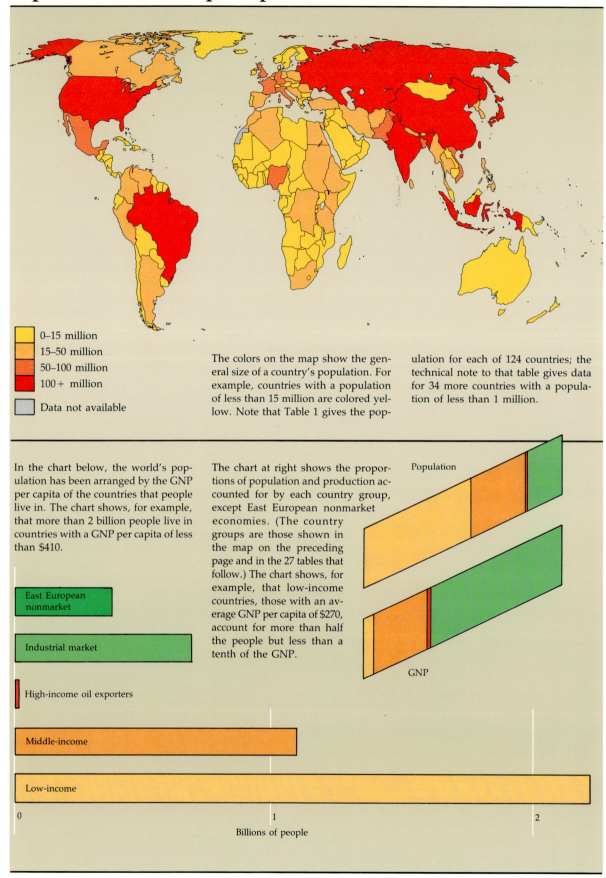

0–15 million
15–50 million
50–100 million
100 + million

Data not available

The colors on the map show the general size of a country's population. For example, countries with a population of less than 15 million are colored yellow. Note that Table 1 gives the population for each of 124 countries; the technical note to that table gives data for 34 more countries with a population of less than 1 million.

In the chart below, the world's population has been arranged by the GNP per capita of the countries that people live in. The chart shows, for example, that more than 2 billion people live in countries with a GNP per capita of less than $410.

The chart at right shows the proportions of population and production accounted for by each country group, except East European nonmarket economies. (The country groups are those shown in the map on the preceding page and in the 27 tables that follow.) The chart shows, for example, that low-income countries, those with an average GNP per capita of $270, account for more than half the people but less than a tenth of the GNP.

Population

GNP

East European nonmarket

Industrial market

High-income oil exporters

Middle-income

Low-income

0   1   2

Billions of people

Adult literacy

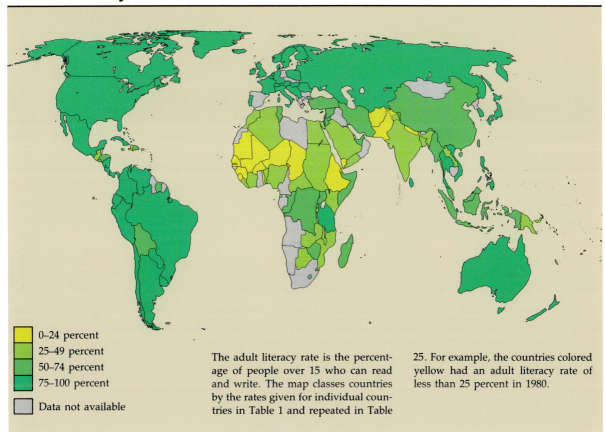

0–24 percent
25–49 percent
50–74 percent
75–100 percent
Data not available

The adult literacy rate is the percentage of people over 15 who can read and write. The map classes countries by the rates given for individual countries in Table 1 and repeated in Table 25. For example, the countries colored yellow had an adult literacy rate of less than 25 percent in 1980.

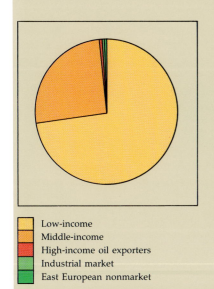

Low-income
Middle-income
High-income oil exporters
Industrial market
East European nonmarket

The chart at left shows where the world's illiterate adults live—mostly in low-income countries, which account for half the world's people.

The chart at right shows how the proportion of illiterate and literate adults changed in developing countries between 1960 and 1980. The height of the cylinders reflects the total number of adults in developing countries in each of the two years. So, while the proportion of literate adults has increased—from 39 percent to 56 percent—the number of literate adults has increased even more—from 480 million to 1.2 billion.

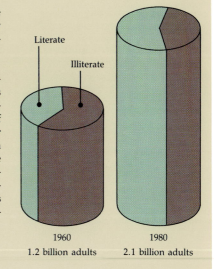

Literate

Illiterate

1960
1.2 billion adults

1980
2.1 billion adults

Life expectancy

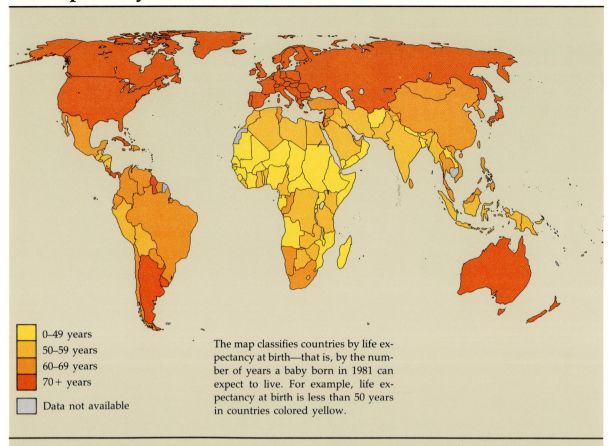

0–49 years
50–59 years
60–69 years
70+ years

Data not available

The map classifies countries by life expectancy at birth—that is, by the number of years a baby born in 1981 can expect to live. For example, life expectancy at birth is less than 50 years in countries colored yellow.

The chart at right shows how life expectancy has increased since 1960 for the various country groups. For example, life expectancy in the low-income countries has increased 17 years, from 41 for a baby born in 1960 to 58 for one born in 1981. Table 23 shows how individual countries have fared in relation to the average for their country group.

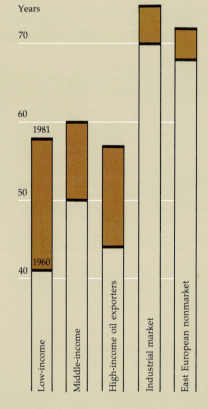

Years

70

1981

60

50

1960

40

Low-income
Middle-income
High-income oil exporters
Industrial market
East European nonmarket

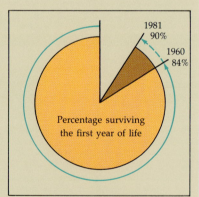

1981
90%
1960
84%

Percentage surviving
the first year of life

The chart above shows that the proportion of infants surviving the first year of life has increased from 84 percent in low-income countries in 1960 to 90 percent in 1981.

Share of agriculture in GDP

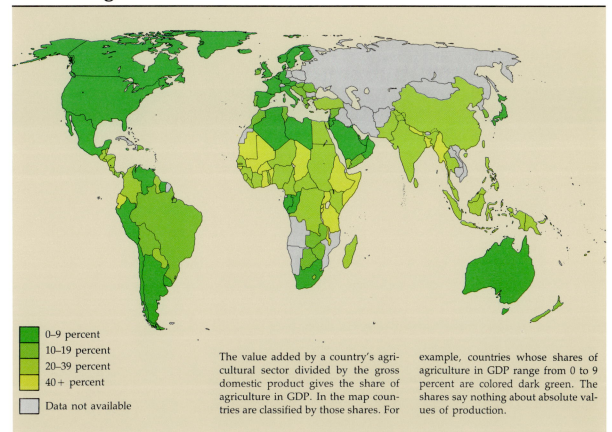

- 0–9 percent
- 10–19 percent
- 20–39 percent
- 40+ percent
- Data not available

The value added by a country's agricultural sector divided by the gross domestic product gives the share of agriculture in GDP. In the map countries are classified by those shares. For example, countries whose shares of agriculture in GDP range from 0 to 9 percent are colored dark green. The shares say nothing about absolute values of production.

The chart at right shows the weighted average of agriculture's share in GDP for each group of countries. For example, the weighted average for low-income countries is 37 percent, that for industrial countries 3 percent. This difference shows that as GNP per capita goes up, the share of agriculture in GDP goes down. It is not that the agricultural sector gets smaller, but that the industrial and services sectors get larger.

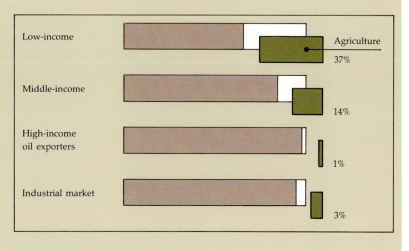

Low-income — Agriculture 37%

Middle-income — 14%

High-income oil exporters — 1%

Industrial market — 3%

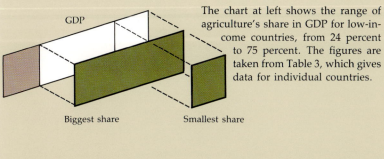

GDP

Biggest share   Smallest share

The chart at left shows the range of agriculture's share in GDP for low-income countries, from 24 percent to 75 percent. The figures are taken from Table 3, which gives data for individual countries.

Table 1. Basic indicators

	Population (millions) Mid-1981	Area (thousands of square kilometers)	GNP per capita — Dollars 1981	GNP per capita — Average annual growth (percent) 1960–81[b]	Average annual rate of inflation[a] (percent) 1960–70[c]	Average annual rate of inflation[a] (percent) 1970–81[d]	Adult literacy (percent) 1980[e]	Life expectancy at birth (years) 1981
Low-income economies	2,210.5 t	31,020 t	270 w	2.9 w	3.5 m	11.2 m	52 w	58 w
China and India	1,681.5 t	12,849 t	280 w	3.5 w	. .	. .	56 w	61 w
Other low-income	529.0 t	18,171 t	240 w	0.8 w	3.3 m	11.6 m	40 w	50 w
1 Kampuchea, Dem.	. .	181			3.8		. .	
2 Bhutan	1.3	47	80	0.1	. .	. .	. .	45
3 Lao, PDR	3.5	237	80		. .	. .	44	43
4 Chad	4.5	1,284	110	−2.2	4.6	7.4	15	43
5 Bangladesh	90.7	144	140	0.3	3.7	15.7	26	48
6 Ethiopia	32.0	1,222	140	1.4	2.1	4.1	15	46
7 Nepal	15.0	141	150	0.0	7.7	9.3	19	45
8 Burma	34.1	677	190	1.4	2.7	10.7	66	54
9 Afghanistan	16.3	648	. .	. .	11.9	5.0	20	37
10 Mali	6.9	1,240	190	1.3	5.0	9.7	10	45
11 Malawi	6.2	118	200	2.7	2.4	10.3	25	44
12 Zaire	29.8	2,345	210	−0.1	29.9	35.3	55	50
13 Uganda	13.0	236	220	−0.6	3.2	41.2	52	48
14 Burundi	4.2	28	230	2.4	2.8	11.6	25	45
15 Upper Volta	6.3	274	240	1.1	1.3	9.5	5	44
16 Rwanda	5.3	26	250	1.7	13.1	13.4	50	46
17 India	690.2	3,288	260	1.4	7.1	8.1	36	52
18 Somalia	4.4	638	280	−0.2	4.5	12.6	60	39
19 Tanzania	19.1	945	280	1.9	1.8	11.9	79	52
20 Viet Nam	55.7	330	. .	. .	. .	. .	87	63
21 China	991.3	9,561	300	5.0			69	67
22 Guinea	5.6	246	300	0.2	1.5	4.6	20	43
23 Haiti	5.1	28	300	0.5	4.0	10.0	23	54
24 Sri Lanka	15.0	66	300	2.5	1.8	13.1	85	69
25 Benin	3.6	113	320	0.6	1.9	9.4	28	50
26 Central African Rep.	2.4	623	320	0.4	4.1	12.6	33	43
27 Sierra Leone	3.6	72	320	0.4	. .	12.2	15	47
28 Madagascar	9.0	587	330	−0.5	3.2	10.6	50	48
29 Niger	5.7	1,267	330	−1.6	2.1	12.2	10	45
30 Pakistan	84.5	804	350	2.8	3.3	13.1	24	50
31 Mozambique	12.5	802	. .	. .	. .	. .	33	. .
32 Sudan	19.2	2,506	380	−0.3	3.7	15.9	32	47
33 Togo	2.7	57	380	2.5	1.3	8.9	18	48
34 Ghana	11.8	239	400	−1.1	7.6	36.4	. .	54
Middle-income economies	1,128.4 t	41,108 t	1,500 w	3.7 w	3.0 m	13.1 m	65 w	60 w
Oil exporters	506.5 t	15,036 t	1,250 w	3.8 w	3.0 m	13.8 m	58 w	57 w
Oil importers	621.9 t	26,072 t	1,670 w	3.7 w	3.0 m	13.0 m	72 w	63 w
Lower middle-income	663.7 t	19,302 t	850 w	3.4 w	2.8 m	11.1 m	59 w	57 w
35 Kenya	17.4	583	420	2.9	1.6	10.2	47	56
36 Senegal	5.9	196	430	−0.3	1.7	7.9	10	44
37 Mauritania	1.6	1,031	460	1.5	2.1	9.0	17	44
38 Yemen Arab Rep.	7.3	195	460	5.5	. .	15.6	21	43
39 Yemen, PDR	2.0	333	460	. .	. .	. .	40	46
40 Liberia	1.9	111	520	1.2	1.9	8.9	25	54
41 Indonesia	149.5	1,919	530	4.1	. .	20.5	62	54
42 Lesotho	1.4	30	540	7.0	2.7	10.5	52	52
43 Bolivia	5.7	1,099	600	1.9	3.5	23.0	63	51
44 Honduras	3.8	112	600	1.1	2.9	9.1	60	59
45 Zambia	5.8	753	600	0.0	7.6	8.4	44	51
46 Egypt	43.3	1,001	650	3.5	2.6	11.1	44	57
47 El Salvador	4.7	21	650	1.5	0.5	10.8	62	63
48 Thailand	48.0	514	770	4.6	1.8	10.0	86	63
49 Philippines	49.6	300	790	2.8	5.8	13.1	75	63
50 Angola	7.8	1,247	. .	. .	. .	. .	. .	42
51 Papua New Guinea	3.1	462	840	2.5	4.0	8.6	32	51
52 Morocco	20.9	447	860	2.4	2.0	8.2	28	57
53 Nicaragua	2.8	130	860	0.6	1.8	14.2	90	57
54 Nigeria	87.6	924	870	3.5	4.0	14.2	34	49
55 Zimbabwe	7.2	391	870	1.0	1.3	10.1	69	55
56 Cameroon	8.7	475	880	2.8	4.2	10.6	. .	50
57 Cuba	9.7	115	. .	. .	. .	. .	95	73
58 Congo, People's Rep.	1.7	342	1,110	1.0	5.9	11.8	. .	60
59 Guatemala	7.5	109	1,140	2.6	0.3	10.4	. .	59
60 Peru	17.0	1,285	1,170	1.0	10.4	34.3	80	58
61 Ecuador	8.6	284	1,180	4.3	6.1	14.1	81	62
62 Jamaica	2.2	11	1,180	0.8	4.0	16.8	90	71
63 Ivory Coast	8.5	322	1,200	2.3	2.8	13.0	35	47
64 Dominican Rep.	5.6	49	1,260	3.3	2.1	9.1	67	62

148

	Population (millions) Mid-1981	Area (thousands of square kilometers)	GNP per capita Dollars 1981	GNP per capita Average annual growth (percent) 1960–81[b]	Average annual rate of inflation[a] (percent) 1960–70[c]	Average annual rate of inflation[a] (percent) 1970–81[d]	Adult literacy (percent) 1980[e]	Life expectancy at birth (years) 1981
65 Mongolia	1.7	1,565	..	..	..	..	..	64
66 Colombia	26.4	1,139	1,380	3.2	11.9	22.4	81	63
67 Tunisia	6.5	164	1,420	4.8	3.6	8.2	62	61
68 Costa Rica	2.3	51	1,430	3.0	1.9	15.9	90	73
69 Korea, Dem. Rep.	18.7	121	..	..	..	..	..	66
70 Turkey	45.5	781	1,540	3.5	5.6	32.7	60	62
71 Syrian Arab Rep.	9.3	185	1,570	3.8	2.6	12.0	58	65
72 Jordan	3.4	98	1,620	..	..	..	70	62
73 Paraguay	3.1	407	1,630	3.5	3.1	12.4	84	65
Upper middle-income	**464.7 t**	**21,806 t**	**2,490 w**	**4.2 w**	**3.0 m**	**18.6 m**	**76 w**	**65 w**
74 Korea, Rep. of	38.9	98	1,700	6.9	17.5	19.8	93	66
75 Iran, Islamic Rep. of	40.1	1,648	..	..	−0.5	20.1	50	58
76 Iraq	13.5	435	..	..	1.7	..	..	57
77 Malaysia	14.2	330	1,840	4.3	−0.3	7.4	60	65
78 Panama	1.9	77	1,910	3.1	1.6	7.6	85	71
79 Lebanon	2.7	10	..	..	1.4	14.6	..	66
80 Algeria	19.6	2,382	2,140	3.2	2.7	13.4	35	56
81 Brazil	120.5	8,512	2,220	5.1	46.1	42.1	76	64
82 Mexico	71.2	1,973	2,250	3.8	3.5	19.1	83	66
83 Portugal	9.8	92	2,520	4.8	3.0	17.0	78	72
84 Argentina	28.2	2,767	2,560	1.9	21.4	134.2	93	71
85 Chile	11.3	757	2,560	0.7	33.0	164.6	..	68
86 South Africa	29.5	1221	2,770	2.3	3.0	12.8	..	63
87 Yugoslavia	22.5	256	2,790	5.0	12.6	19.4	85	71
88 Uruguay	2.9	176	2,820	1.6	51.1	60.2	94	71
89 Venezuela	15.4	912	4,220	2.4	1.3	12.5	82	68
90 Greece	9.7	132	4,420	5.4	3.2	14.8	..	74
91 Hong Kong	5.2	1	5,100	6.9	2.4	18.4	90	75
92 Israel	4.0	21	5,160	3.6	6.2	45.5	..	73
93 Singapore	2.4	1	5,240	7.4	1.1	5.2	83	72
94 Trinidad and Tobago	1.2	5	5,670	2.9	3.2	18.7	95	72
High-income oil exporters	**15.0 t**	**4,012 t**	**13,460 w**	**6.2 w**	**..**	**18.2 m**	**32 w**	**57 w**
95 Libya	3.1	1,760	8,450	4.7	5.2	17.3	..	57
96 Saudi Arabia	9.3	2,150	12,600	7.8	..	24.3	25	55
97 Kuwait	1.5	18	20,900	−0.4	..	18.2	60	70
98 United Arab Emirates	1.1	84	24,660	..	..	..	56	63
Industrial market economies	**719.5 t**	**30,935 t**	**11,120 w**	**3.4 w**	**4.3 m**	**9.9 m**	**99 w**	**75 w**
99 Ireland	3.4	70	5,230	3.1	5.2	14.2	98	73
100 Spain	38.0	505	5,640	4.2	8.2	16.0	..	74
101 Italy	56.2	301	6,960	3.6	4.4	15.7	98	74
102 New Zealand	3.3	269	7,700	1.5	3.6	12.9	99	74
103 United Kingdom	56.0	245	9,110	2.1	4.1	14.4	99	74
104 Japan	117.6	372	10,080	6.3	5.1	7.4	99	77
105 Austria	7.6	84	10,210	4.0	3.7	6.1	99	73
106 Finland	4.8	337	10,680	3.6	6.0	12.0	100	75
107 Australia	14.9	7,687	11,080	2.5	3.1	11.5	100	74
108 Canada	24.2	9,976	11,400	3.3	3.1	9.3	99	75
109 Netherlands	14.2	41	11,790	3.1	5.4	7.6	99	76
110 Belgium	9.9	31	11,920	3.8	3.6	7.3	99	73
111 France	54.0	547	12,190	3.8	4.2	9.9	99	76
112 United States	229.8	9,363	12,820	2.3	2.9	7.2	99	75
113 Denmark	5.1	43	13,120	2.6	6.4	10.0	99	75
114 Germany, Fed. Rep.	61.7	249	13,450	3.2	3.2	5.0	99	73
115 Norway	4.1	324	14,060	3.5	4.4	8.8	99	76
116 Sweden	8.3	450	14,870	2.6	4.3	10.0	99	77
117 Switzerland	6.4	41	17,430	1.9	4.4	4.8	99	76
East European nonmarket economies	**380.8 t**	**23,422 t**	**..**	**..**	**..**	**..**	**99 w**	**72 w**
118 Albania	2.8	29	..	..	..	..	..	70
119 Hungary	10.7	93	2,100 [a]	5.0	..	2.9	99	71
120 Romania	22.5	238	2,540 [a]	8.2	−0.2	..	98	71
121 Bulgaria	8.9	111	..	..	..	..	..	73
122 Poland	35.9	313	..	..	..	..	98	73
123 USSR	268.0	22,402	..	..	..	..	100	72
124 Czechoslovakia	15.3	128	..	..	..	..	..	72
125 German Dem. Rep.	16.7	108	..	..	..	..	..	73

a. See the technical notes.   b. Because data for the early 1960s are not available, figures in italics are for periods other than that specified.
c. Figures in italics are for 1961–70, not 1960–70.   d. Figures in italics are for 1970–80, not 1970–81.   e. Figures in italics are for years other than those specified. See the technical notes.

Table 2. Growth of production

	GDP		Agriculture		Industry		Manufacturing		Services	
	1960–70[a]	1970–81[b]	1960–70[a]	1970–81[b]	1960–70[a]	1970–81[b]	1960–70[a]	1970–81[b]	1960–70[a]	1970–81[b]
Low-income economies	4.6 w	4.5 w	2.2 m	2.3 m	6.6 m	3.6 m	5.4 m	2.9 m	4.2 m	4.6 m
China and India	4.5 w	4.8 w	1.8 m	2.4 m	8.3 m	6.4 m	. .	. .	5.2 m	4.8 m
Other low-income	4.7 w	3.6 w	2.7 m	2.3 m	6.6 m	3.2 m	5.9 m	2.8 m	4.2 m	4.6 m
1 Kampuchea, Dem.	3.1	. .	. .	. .	. .	. .	. .	. .	. .	. .
2 Bhutan	. .	. .	. .	. .	. .	. .	. .	. .	. .	. .
3 Lao, PDR	. .	. .	. .	. .	. .	. .	. .	. .	. .	. .
4 Chad	0.5	. .	. .	. .	. .	. .	. .	. .	. .	. .
5 Bangladesh	3.7	4.2	2.7	2.4	8.0	9.0	6.6	11.2	4.2	5.3
6 Ethiopia	4.4	2.2	2.2	0.9	7.4	1.8	8.0	2.8	7.8	4.2
7 Nepal	2.5	2.1	. .	. .	. .	. .	. .	. .	. .	. .
8 Burma	2.6	4.8	4.1	4.7	2.8	5.6	3.4	4.6	1.5	4.7
9 Afghanistan	2.0	3.9	. .	3.2	. .	3.2	. .	2.8	. .	5.3
10 Mali	3.3	4.6	. .	4.0	. .	2.4	. .	. .	. .	5.9
11 Malawi	4.9	5.6	. .	. .	. .	. .	. .	. .	. .	. .
12 Zaire	3.4	−0.2	. .	1.5	. .	−0.8	. .	−2.3	. .	−0.4
13 Uganda	5.6	−1.6	. .	−0.8	. .	−9.8	. .	−9.3	. .	−0.7
14 Burundi	4.4	3.2	. .	2.2	. .	8.5	. .	5.9	. .	3.5
15 Upper Volta	3.0	3.6	. .	1.4	. .	2.9	. .	3.4	. .	5.8
16 Rwanda	2.7	5.3	. .	. .	. .	. .	. .	. .	. .	. .
17 India	3.4	3.6	1.9	1.9	5.4	4.4	4.7	5.0	4.6	5.2
18 Somalia	1.0	3.9	−0.6	. .	3.4	. .	4.0	. .	4.2	. .
19 Tanzania	6.0	5.1	. .	5.5	. .	2.2	. .	2.9	. .	5.4
20 Viet Nam	3.8	. .	. .	. .	. .	. .	. .	. .	. .	. .
21 China	5.2	5.5	1.6	2.8	11.2	8.3	. .	. .	5.7	4.4
22 Guinea	3.5	3.0	. .	. .	. .	. .	. .	. .	. .	. .
23 Haiti	0.2	3.4	−0.6	1.1	0.2	7.1	−0.1	7.6	1.1	3.5
24 Sri Lanka	4.6	4.3	3.0	3.0	6.6	4.2	6.3	2.1	4.6	5.0
25 Benin	2.6	3.3	. .	. .	. .	. .	. .	. .	. .	. .
26 Central African Rep.	1.9	1.6	0.8	2.3	5.4	4.0	5.4	−4.3	1.8	(.)
27 Sierra Leone	4.3	1.9	. .	2.4	. .	−3.6	. .	3.7	. .	4.5
28 Madagascar	2.9	0.3	. .	0.3	. .	0.3	. .	. .	. .	0.4
29 Niger	2.9	3.1	3.3	−3.0	13.9	11.4	. .	. .	(.)	6.9
30 Pakistan	6.7	4.8	4.9	2.6	10.0	5.5	9.4	4.4	7.0	6.1
31 Mozambique	. .	. .	. .	. .	. .	. .	. .	. .	. .	. .
32 Sudan	1.3	4.1	. .	2.3	. .	3.2	. .	1.5	. .	6.0
33 Togo	8.5	3.2	. .	1.5	. .	6.2	. .	−10.4	. .	3.2
34 Ghana	2.1	−0.2	. .	0.0	. .	−2.2	. .	−1.0	. .	0.4
Middle-income economies	6.0 w	5.6 w	3.4 m	3.0 m	7.4 m	6.8 m	6.7 m	5.9 m	5.5 m	6.1 m
Oil exporters	6.3 w	6.2 w	3.3 m	3.4 m	7.4 m	7.6 m	7.4 m	8.7 m	4.8 m	7.2 m
Oil importers	5.8 w	5.4 w	3.5 m	2.9 m	7.0 m	5.9 m	6.5 m	5.6 m	5.7 m	5.7 m
Lower middle-income	5.0 w	5.6 w	3.0 m	3.2 m	6.8 m	7.4 m	7.1 m	5.8 m	5.3 m	6.0 m
35 Kenya	5.9	5.8	. .	4.2	. .	8.5	. .	9.5	. .	6.0
36 Senegal	2.5	2.0	2.9	2.6	4.4	4.1	6.2	2.0	1.7	0.9
37 Mauritania	6.7	1.7	1.4	3.1	14.1	−4.0	9.2	4.6	7.4	5.2
38 Yemen Arab Rep.	. .	8.7	. .	3.6	. .	13.9	. .	12.1	. .	11.7
39 Yemen, PDR	. .	. .	. .	. .	. .	. .	. .	. .	. .	. .
40 Liberia	5.1	1.3	. .	4.0	. .	−0.7	. .	5.6	. .	1.4
41 Indonesia	3.9	7.8	2.7	3.8	5.2	11.2	3.3	13.9	4.8	9.5
42 Lesotho	5.2	8.4	. .	4.3	. .	12.9	. .	9.6	. .	9.2
43 Bolivia	5.2	4.4	3.0	2.9	6.2	3.7	5.4	5.3	5.4	5.2
44 Honduras	5.3	3.8	5.7	1.9	5.4	4.9	4.5	4.7	4.8	4.6
45 Zambia	5.0	0.4	. .	1.8	. .	−0.4	. .	0.3	. .	1.2
46 Egypt	4.3	8.1	2.9	2.9	5.4	7.6	4.8	8.7	4.7	11.8
47 El Salvador	5.9	3.1	3.0	2.3	8.5	3.3	8.8	2.4	6.5	3.3
48 Thailand	8.4	7.2	5.6	4.5	11.9	9.9	11.4	10.3	9.1	7.5
49 Philippines	5.1	6.2	4.3	4.9	6.0	8.4	6.7	6.9	5.2	5.3
50 Angola	. .	. .	. .	. .	. .	. .	. .	. .	. .	. .
51 Papua New Guinea	6.7	1.9	. .	. .	. .	. .	. .	. .	. .	. .
52 Morocco	4.4	5.2	4.7	(.)	4.2	5.8	4.2	5.4	4.4	6.4
53 Nicaragua	7.3	0.8	7.8	2.7	10.4	2.1	11.4	2.8	5.8	−0.8
54 Nigeria	3.1	4.5	−0.4	−0.4	14.7	6.0	9.1	12.4	2.3	7.4
55 Zimbabwe	4.3	1.8	. .	. .	. .	. .	. .	. .	. .	. .
56 Cameroon	3.7	6.3	. .	3.9	. .	9.4	. .	5.3	. .	6.8
57 Cuba	. .	. .	. .	. .	. .	. .	. .	. .	. .	. .
58 Congo, People's Rep.	2.3	5.1	1.8	2.1	7.4	13.6	7.4	−1.8	1.1	2.2
59 Guatemala	5.6	5.5	4.3	4.3	7.8	7.3	8.2	5.9	5.5	5.4
60 Peru	4.9	3.0	3.7	0.3	5.0	3.4	5.7	2.9	5.3	3.5
61 Ecuador	. .	8.6	. .	2.9	. .	12.5	. .	10.8	. .	8.7
62 Jamaica	4.4	−1.2	1.5	0.5	4.8	−3.6	5.7	−2.6	4.6	(.)
63 Ivory Coast	8.0	6.2	4.2	4.7	11.5	9.3	11.6	5.8	9.7	5.8
64 Dominican Rep.	4.5	6.3	2.1	3.2	6.0	7.6	5.0	6.1	5.0	6.7

150

	Average annual growth rate (percent)									
	GDP		Agriculture		Industry		Manufacturing		Services	
	1960–70[a]	1970–81[b]	1960–70[a]	1970–81[b]	1960–70[a]	1970–81[b]	1960–70[a]	1970–81[b]	1960–70[a]	1970–81[b]
65 Mongolia	..	..	..	..	..	..	..	..	..	..
66 Colombia	5.1	5.7	3.5	4.7	6.0	4.7	5.7	5.7	5.7	6.8
67 Tunisia	4.7	7.3	2.0	4.1	8.2	9.3	7.8	11.7	4.5	7.5
68 Costa Rica	6.5	5.2	5.7	2.2	9.4	7.4	10.6	7.1	5.7	5.2
69 Korea, Dem. Rep.	..	..	..	..	..	..	..	..	..	..
70 Turkey	6.0	5.4	2.5	3.2	9.6	6.1	10.9	5.5	6.9	6.2
71 Syrian Arab Rep.	4.6	10.0	..	8.2	..	9.8	..	8.2	..	10.8
72 Jordan	..	..	..	..	..	..	..	..	..	..
73 Paraguay	4.2	8.8	..	7.0	..	11.0	..	8.1	..	9.1
Upper middle-income	**6.4** w	**5.6** w	**4.0** m	**2.6** m	**8.8** m	**4.5** m	**7.8** m	**6.3** m	**7.1** m	**6.5** m
74 Korea, Rep. of	8.6	9.1	4.4	3.0	17.2	14.4	17.6	15.6	8.9	8.2
75 Iran, Islamic Rep. of	11.3	..	4.4	..	13.4	..	12.0	..	10.0	..
76 Iraq	6.1	..	5.7	..	4.7	..	5.9	..	8.3	..
77 Malaysia	6.5	7.8	..	5.2	..	9.3	..	11.1	..	8.5
78 Panama	7.8	4.6	5.7	2.0	10.4	4.1	10.5	2.7	7.6	5.3
79 Lebanon	4.9	−5.4	6.3	..	4.5	..	5.0	..	4.8	..
80 Algeria	4.3	6.9	0.1	3.9	11.6	7.6	7.8	11.6	−1.1	6.4
81 Brazil	5.4	8.4	..	5.2	..	9.1	..	8.7	..	8.3
82 Mexico	7.6	6.5	4.5	3.4	9.4	7.4	10.1	7.1	7.3	6.6
83 Portugal	6.2	4.4	1.3	−0.8	8.8	4.4	8.9	4.5	5.9	6.0
84 Argentina	4.3	1.9	1.8	2.5	5.8	1.4	5.6	0.7	3.8	2.2
85 Chile	4.4	2.1	3.1	3.0	4.4	0.7	5.5	(.)	4.6	2.9
86 South Africa	6.3	3.7	..	..	..	..	..	..	..	..
87 Yugoslavia	5.8	5.7	3.3	2.6	6.2	6.8	5.7	7.1	6.9	5.6
88 Uruguay	1.2	3.1	1.9	1.2	1.1	3.5	1.5	4.3	1.0	2.9
89 Venezuela	6.0	4.5	5.8	3.4	4.6	2.7	6.4	5.3	7.3	5.9
90 Greece	6.9	4.4	3.5	1.7	9.4	4.5	10.2	5.5	7.1	5.2
91 Hong Kong	10.0	9.9	..	−3.0	..	..	..	10.1	..	..
92 Israel	8.1	4.0	..	..	..	..	..	..	..	..
93 Singapore	8.8	8.5	5.0	1.7	12.5	9.0	13.0	9.7	7.7	8.5
94 Trinidad and Tobago	4.0	5.5	..	−1.8	..	4.0	..	1.3	..	6.9
High-income oil exporters	..	**5.3** w	..	**7.1** m	..	**3.1** m	..	**9.2** m	..	**12.2** m
95 Libya	24.4	2.3	..	10.5	..	3.1	..	14.7	..	17.1
96 Saudi Arabia	..	10.6	..	5.3	..	10.2	..	6.5	..	12.2
97 Kuwait	5.7	2.3	..	7.1	..	−2.2	..	9.2	..	9.6
98 United Arab Emirates	..	..	..	..	..	..	..	..	..	..
Industrial market economies	**5.1** w	**3.0** w	**1.4** m	**1.6** m	**5.7** m	**2.9** m	**5.9** m	**3.1** m	**4.6** m	**3.6** m
99 Ireland	4.2	4.0	0.9	..	6.1	..	..	..	4.3	..
100 Spain	7.1	3.2	..	2.1	..	3.9	..	6.0	..	4.5
101 Italy	5.5	2.9	2.6	1.3	6.6	2.9	8.0	3.7	5.1	3.2
102 New Zealand	3.6	2.0	..	..	..	..	..	..	..	..
103 United Kingdom	2.9	1.7	2.2	1.6	3.1	0.4	3.3	−0.5	2.8	2.5
104 Japan	10.4	4.5	2.1	0.2	13.0	5.6	13.6	6.5	10.2	4.2
105 Austria	4.6	3.5	1.2	1.9	5.4	3.2	5.2	3.4	4.4	3.9
106 Finland	4.3	3.1	0.5	0.0	5.2	3.3	6.1	3.7	5.0	3.6
107 Australia	5.6	3.3	2.0	..	5.9	..	5.5	..	4.0	..
108 Canada	5.6	3.8	2.5	1.8	6.3	2.9	6.8	3.2	5.5	4.3
109 Netherlands	5.2	2.7	2.8	3.9	6.8	2.0	6.6	2.6	5.1	3.7
110 Belgium	4.7	3.0	−0.5	0.7	5.5	3.1	6.2	3.0	4.6	3.5
111 France	5.5	3.3	1.6	0.5	7.1	2.7	7.8	3.2	5.0	4.2
112 United States	4.3	2.9	0.5	1.6	4.6	2.3	5.3	2.9	4.4	3.3
113 Denmark	4.5	2.1	0.1	2.6	5.2	1.1	5.2	3.1	4.6	2.5
114 Germany, Fed. Rep.	4.4	2.6	1.5	1.3	4.8	..	5.4	2.1	4.2	2.5
115 Norway	4.3	4.5	0.7	2.2	5.5	5.0	4.8	1.3	5.0	4.5
116 Sweden	4.4	1.8	0.8	−1.1	6.2	0.8	5.9	0.7	3.9	2.7
117 Switzerland	4.3	0.7	..	..	..	..	..	..	..	..
East European nonmarket economies	..	..	..	..	..	..	..	..	..	..
118 Albania	..	..	..	..	..	..	..	..	..	..
119 Hungary[c]	5.3	5.0	3.2	2.9	6.3	5.8	6.5	5.9	5.8	5.0
120 Romania[c]	8.6	9.1	1.7	4.9	12.8	9.2	..	..	..	..
121 Bulgaria	..	..	..	..	..	..	..	..	..	..
122 Poland	..	..	..	..	..	..	..	..	..	..
123 USSR	..	..	..	..	..	..	..	..	..	..
124 Czechoslovakia	..	..	..	..	..	..	..	..	..	..
125 German Dem. Rep.	..	..	..	..	..	..	..	..	..	..

a. Figures in italics are for 1961–70, not 1960–70.   b. Figures in italics are for 1970–80, not 1970–81.   c. Services include the unallocated share of GDP.   d. Based on net material product.

Table 3. Structure of production

	GDP (millions of dollars)		Distribution of gross domestic product (percent)							
			Agriculture		Industry		(Manufacturing)[a]		Services	
	1960[b]	1981[c]	1960[b]	1981[c]	1960[b]	1981[c]	1960[b]	1981[c]	1960[b]	1981[c]
Low-income economies			48 w	37 w	25 w	34 w	11 w	16 w	27 w	29 w
China and India			48 w	33 w	28 w	39 w	. .	. .	24 w	28 w
Other low-income			48 w	45 w	12 w	17 w	9 w	10 w	40 w	38 w
1 Kampuchea, Dem	. .	. .	. .	. .	. .	. .	. .	. .	. .	. .
2 Bhutan	. .	. .	. .	. .	. .	. .	. .	. .	. .	. .
3 Lao, PDR	. .	. .	. .	. .	. .	. .	. .	. .	. .	. .
4 Chad	180	. .	52	. .	12	. .	4	. .	36	. .
5 Bangladesh	3,170	11,910	58	54	7	14	5	8	35	32
6 Ethiopia	900	3,870	65	50	12	16	6	11	23	34
7 Nepal	410	2,420	. .	. .	. .	. .	. .	. .	. .	. .
8 Burma	1,280	5,770	33	47	12	13	8	10	55	40
9 Afghanistan	1,190	3,230	. .	. .	. .	. .	. .	. .	. .	. .
10 Mali	270	1,120	55	42	10	11	5	6	35	47
11 Malawi	170	1,420	58	43	11	20	6	13	31	37
12 Zaire	130	5,380	30	32	27	24	13	3	43	44
13 Uganda	540	9,390	52	75	12	4	9	4	36	21
14 Burundi	190	880	. .	56	. .	16	. .	9	. .	28
15 Upper Volta	200	1,080	55	41	16	16	9	12	29	43
16 Rwanda	120	1,260	80	46	7	22	1	16	13	32
17 India	29,550	142,010	50	37	20	26	14	18	30	37
18 Somalia	160	1,230	71	. .	8	. .	3	. .	21	. .
19 Tanzania	550	4,350	57	52	11	15	5	9	32	33
20 Viet Nam	. .	. .	. .	. .	. .	. .	. .	. .	. .	. .
21 China	42,770	264,340	47 [d]	35	33 [d]	46	. .	. .	20 [d]	20
22 Guinea	370	1,670	. .	37	. .	33	. .	4	. .	30
23 Haiti	270	1,590	. .	. .	. .	. .	. .	. .	. .	. .
24 Sri Lanka	1,500	4,120	32	28	20	28	15	16	48	44
25 Benin	160	850	55	44	8	13	3	7	37	43
26 Central African Rep.	110	690	51	37	10	13	4	6	39	50
27 Sierra Leone	. .	1,040	. .	31	. .	20	. .	6	. .	49
28 Madagascar	540	2,890	37	35	10	14	4	. .	53	51
29 Niger	250	1,710	69	30	9	32	4	8	22	38
30 Pakistan	3,500	25,160	46	30	16	26	12	17	38	44
31 Mozambique	. .	. .	. .	. .	. .	. .	. .	. .	. .	. .
32 Sudan	1,160	7,540	. .	38	. .	14	. .	6	. .	48
33 Togo	120	880	55	24	16	27	8	7	29	49
34 Ghana	1,220	21,260	41	60	10	12	. .	7	49	28
Middle-income economies			24 w	14 w	30 w	38 w	20 w	22 w	46 w	48 w
Oil exporters			27 w	13 w	26 w	40 w	15 w	17 w	47 w	47 w
Oil importers			23 w	14 w	33 w	36 w	22 w	25 w	44 w	50 w
Lower middle-income			36 w	22 w	25 w	35 w	15 w	17 w	39 w	43 w
35 Kenya	730	6,960	38	32	18	21	9	13	44	47
36 Senegal	610	2,330	24	22	17	26	12	15	59	52
37 Mauritania	90	630	44	28	21	24	3	7	35	48
38 Yemen Arab Rep.	. .	2,770	. .	28	. .	16	. .	6	. .	56
39 Yemen, PDR	. .	570	. .	13	. .	28	. .	14	. .	59
40 Liberia	220	930	. .	36	. .	27	. .	8	. .	37
41 Indonesia	8,670	84,960	50	24	25	42	. .	12	25	34
42 Lesotho	30	320	. .	31	. .	21	. .	5	. .	48
43 Bolivia	460	7,900	26	18	25	27	15	14	49	55
44 Honduras	300	2,380	37	32	19	25	13	17	44	43
45 Zambia	680	3,430	11	18	63	32	4	18	26	50
46 Egypt	3,880	23,110	30	21	24	38	20	32	46	41
47 El Salvador	570	3,550	32	26	19	20	15	15	49	54
48 Thailand	2,550	36,810	40	24	19	28	13	20	41	48
49 Philippines	6,960	38,900	26	23	28	37	20	25	46	40
50 Angola	. .	. .	. .	. .	. .	. .	. .	. .	. .	. .
51 Papua New Guinea	230	2,580	49	. .	13	. .	4	. .	38	. .
52 Morocco	2,040	14,780	23	14	27	34	16	18	50	52
53 Nicaragua	340	2,590	24	20	21	33	16	26	55	47
54 Nigeria	3,150	70,800	63	23	11	37	5	6	26	40
55 Zimbabwe	780	6,010	18	18	35	37	17	27	47	45
56 Cameroon	550	6,270	. .	27	. .	20	. .	8	. .	53
57 Cuba	. .	. .	. .	. .	. .	. .	. .	. .	. .	. .
58 Congo, People's Rep.	130	1,870	23	9	17	53	10	5	60	38
59 Guatemala	1,040	8,660	. .	. .	. .	. .	. .	. .	. .	. .
60 Peru	2,410	23,260	18	9	33	41	24	25	49	50
61 Ecuador	970	13,430	26	12	20	38	16	11	54	50
62 Jamaica	700	2,960	10	8	36	37	15	15	54	55
63 Ivory Coast	570	8,670	43	27	14	23	7	12	43	50
64 Dominican Rep.	720	6,650	27	18	23	27	17	15	50	55

152

	GDP (millions of dollars)		Distribution of gross domestic product (percent)							
			Agriculture		Industry		(Manufacturing)[a]		Services	
	1960[b]	1981[c]	1960[b]	1981[c]	1960[b]	1981[c]	1960[b]	1981[c]	1960[b]	1981[c]
65 Mongolia	..	..	..	..	..	..	..	..	..	..
66 Colombia	3,780	32,970	34	27	26	31	17	21	40	42
67 Tunisia	770	7,100	*24*	16	*18*	37	*8*	14	*58*	47
68 Costa Rica	510	2,630	26	23	20	28	14	20	54	49
69 Korea, Dem. Rep.	..	..	..	..	..	..	..	..	..	..
70 Turkey	8,820	53,910	41	23	21	32	13	23	38	45
71 Syrian Arab Rep.	890	15,240	..	19	..	31	..	26	..	50
72 Jordan	..	2,550	..	8	..	30	..	14	..	62
73 Paraguay	300	5,260	36	28	20	26	17	17	44	46
Upper middle-income			18 *w*	10 *w*	33 *w*	39 *w*	23 *w*	24 *w*	49 *w*	51 *w*
74 Korea, Rep. of	3,810	65,750	37	17	20	39	14	28	43	44
75 Iran, Islamic Rep. of	4,120	..	29	..	33	..	11	..	38	..
76 Iraq	1,580	..	17	..	52	..	10	..	31	..
77 Malaysia	2,290	24,770	36	23	18	36	9	18	46	41
78 Panama	420	*3,490*	23	10	21	21	13	10	56	69
79 Lebanon	830		12	..	20	..	13	..	68	..
80 Algeria	2,740	41,830	16	6	35	55	8	11	49	39
81 Brazil	14,540	*210,660*	16	*13*	35	*34*	26	*27*	49	*53*
82 Mexico	12,040	238,960	16	8	29	37	19	22	55	55
83 Portugal	2,340	21,290	25	12	36	44	29	35	39	44
84 Argentina	12,170	153,330	16	9	38	38	32	25	46	53
85 Chile	3,910	32,860	9	7	35	35	21	22	56	58
86 South Africa	6,980	74,670	12	7	40	53	21	23	48	*40*
87 Yugoslavia	9,860	63,350	24	12	45	43	36	30	31	45
88 Uruguay	1,110	9,790	19	8	28	33	21	26	53	59
89 Venezuela	7,570	67,800	6	6	22	45	..	15	72	49
90 Greece	3,110	33,390	23	17	26	31	16	20	51	52
91 Hong Kong	950	27,220	4	..	39	..	27	..	57	..
92 Israel	2,030	17,440	11	5	32	36	23	26	57	*59*
93 Singapore	700	12,910	4	1	18	41	12	30	78	58
94 Trinidad and Tobago	470	6,970	8	2	46	52	24	13	46	46
High-income oil exporters			..	1 *w*	..	76 *w*	..	4 *w*	..	23 *w*
95 Libya	310	27,400	..	2	..	71	..	3	..	27
96 Saudi Arabia	..	115,430	..	1	..	78	..	4	..	20
97 Kuwait	..	24,260	..	(.)	..	71	..	4	..	29
98 United Arab Emirates	..	30,070	..	*1*	..	77	..	4	..	22
Industrial market economies			6 *w*	3 *w*	40 *w*	36 *w*	30 *w*	25 *w*	54 *w*	61 *w*
99 Ireland	1,770	16,590	22	..	26	..	..	..	52	..
100 Spain	11,430	185,080	..	7	..	36	..	29	..	57
101 Italy	37,190	350,220	13	6	41	42	31	29	46	53
102 New Zealand	3,940	25,010	..	11	..	31	..	23	..	58
103 United Kingdom	71,440	496,580	3	2	43	33	32	20	54	65
104 Japan	44,000	1,129,500	13	4	45	43	34	30	42	53
105 Austria	6,270	66,240	11	4	46	39	35	37	43	57
106 Finland	5,010	48,940	17	7	34	36	23	25	49	57
107 Australia	16,370	171,070	12	5	40	..	28	..	48	..
108 Canada	39,930	282,500	5	4	34	32	23	19	61	64
109 Netherlands	11,580	140,490	9	4	46	33	34	24	45	63
110 Belgium	11,280	96,940	7	2	41	37	30	25	52	62
111 France	60,060	568,560	10	4	39	35	29	25	51	61
112 United States	505,300	2,893,300	4	3	38	34	29	23	58	63
113 Denmark	5,960	58,260	11	4	31	32	21	19	58	64
114 Germany, Fed. Rep.	72,100	708,540	6	2	53	46	41	..	41	49
115 Norway	4,630	57,140	9	5	33	41	21	15	58	54
116 Sweden	13,950	112,420	7	3	40	31	27	21	53	66
117 Switzerland	8,550	94,260	..	..	..	..	..	..	..	..
East European nonmarket economies			..	..	..	..	..	..	..	..
118 Albania	..	..	..	..	..	..	..	..	..	..
119 Hungary[e]	..	22,560	28	18	39	48	..	..	33	34
120 Romania	..	48,412	..	13	..	60	..	..	..	27
121 Bulgaria	..	..	..	..	..	..	..	..	..	..
122 Poland	..	..	..	..	..	..	..	..	..	..
123 USSR	..	..	..	..	..	..	..	..	..	..
124 Czechoslovakia	..	..	..	..	..	..	..	..	..	..
125 German Dem. Rep.	..	..	..	..	..	..	..	..	..	..

a. Manufacturing is a part of the industrial sector, but its share of GDP is shown separately because it typically is the most dynamic part of the industrial sector.   b. Figures in italics are for 1961, not 1960.   c. Figures in italics are for 1980, not 1981.   d. Based on net material product.
e. Based on constant price series. Services include the unallocated share of GDP.

Table 4. Growth of consumption and investment

	Average annual growth rate (percent)					
	Public consumption		Private consumption		Gross domestic investment	
	1960–70[a]	1970–81[b]	1960–70[a]	1970–81[b]	1960–70[a]	1970–81[b]
Low-income economies	4.5 m	3.3 m	3.2 m	3.5 m	4.6 m	4.3 m
China and India	..	..	3.1 m	4.2 m	7.6 m	5.5 m
Other low-income	4.6 m	3.1 m	3.2 m	3.5 m	4.3 m	3.7 m
1 Kampuchea, Dem.	2.6		3.2		0.3	
2 Bhutan	..	..	..	..	..	..
3 Lao, PDR	..	..	..	..	..	..
4 Chad	4.4	..	−0.7	..	2.3	..
5 Bangladesh	c	c	3.4	4.2	11.1	2.9
6 Ethiopia	4.7	3.4	4.7	3.4	5.7	−0.3
7 Nepal	..	..	..	..	..	..
8 Burma	c	c	2.8	4.2	3.6	8.9
9 Afghanistan	c	..	2.0	..	−1.0	..
10 Mali	6.2	7.3	2.8	4.8	4.9	3.5
11 Malawi	4.6	2.2	4.1	5.5	15.4	2.8
12 Zaire	8.5	−0.2	3.5	−3.4	9.6	7.3
13 Uganda	c	c	5.6	−0.9	7.5	−16.4
14 Burundi	19.2	3.1	3.2	3.3	4.3	16.7
15 Upper Volta	..	7.1	..	3.5	..	3.7
16 Rwanda	1.1	11.8	4.3	3.2	3.5	14.9
17 India	−0.2	4.2	3.7	3.2	5.3	4.9
18 Somalia	3.7	..	0.4	..	4.3	..
19 Tanzania	c	c	6.7	6.5	9.8	3.7
20 Viet Nam	..	..	..	..	..	..
21 China	c	c	2.5	5.2	9.8	6.0
22 Guinea	..	..	..	..	..	..
23 Haiti	c	c	−1.0	5.0	1.7	9.1
24 Sri Lanka	c	c	2.1	2.7	6.6	9.4
25 Benin	1.7	2.4	4.9	3.3	4.2	11.0
26 Central African Rep.	2.2	−2.9	3.0	2.4	1.3	−7.5
27 Sierra Leone		−1.9	..	3.5	..	−1.2
28 Madagascar	3.0	1.3	1.9	−0.6	5.4	−1.1
29 Niger	2.0	2.6	3.9	2.8	3.0	7.3
30 Pakistan	7.3	4.7	7.1	5.3	6.9	3.2
31 Mozambique	..	..	..	..	..	..
32 Sudan	12.1	c	−1.6	6.9	−1.3	5.2
33 Togo	6.7	9.9	7.6	4.1	11.1	9.1
34 Ghana	7.1	4.7	1.7	−0.8	−3.1	−1.4
Middle-income economies	6.2 m	6.6 m	5.2 m	5.5 m	7.7 m	7.9 m
Oil exporters	6.3 m	10.6 m	4.8 m	7.4 m	4.2 m	10.5 m
Oil importers	6.0 m	6.4 m	5.4 m	4.6 m	8.8 m	6.6 m
Lower middle-income	5.8 m	6.6 m	4.8 m	5.5 m	7.9 m	8.2 m
35 Kenya	10.0	9.2	2.9	6.2	10.3	1.9
36 Senegal	−0.2	5.9	3.2	2.8	1.1	1.9
37 Mauritania	(.)	9.0	2.6	3.2	−2.0	6.4
38 Yemen Arab Rep.	..	10.8	..	10.0	..	24.6
39 Yemen, PDR	..		..		..	
40 Liberia	5.6	2.2	0.7	4.2	−3.9	3.3
41 Indonesia	0.9	12.3	4.1	8.9	4.6	14.0
42 Lesotho	(.)	15.4	6.5	11.6	20.7	19.3
43 Bolivia	8.9	6.6	3.8	6.0	9.6	0.9
44 Honduras	5.3	7.1	4.8	4.1	10.2	8.3
45 Zambia	11.0	0.8	6.8	1.9	10.6	−10.8
46 Egypt	c	c	6.7	6.0	3.1	16.2
47 El Salvador	6.4	5.6	6.1	4.1	3.5	2.4
48 Thailand	9.7	9.3	7.0	6.2	15.8	7.5
49 Philippines	5.0	6.6	4.7	4.8	8.2	10.1
50 Angola	..	..	..	..	..	..
51 Papua New Guinea	6.0	−1.2	5.7	3.1	23.2	−3.7
52 Morocco	4.4	14.2	4.1	4.3	8.8	9.2
53 Nicaragua	2.2	9.8	7.6	0.7	10.9	−1.2
54 Nigeria	10.0	11.0	0.6	6.3	7.4	10.0
55 Zimbabwe	..	..	..	..	..	..
56 Cameroon	6.1	3.0	2.7	6.2	9.3	9.2
57 Cuba	..	..	..	..	..	..
58 Congo, People's Rep.	5.4	2.3	1.0	1.7	2.7	8.7
59 Guatemala	4.7	6.7	4.7	5.1	7.9	7.1
60 Peru	6.3	5.6	7.1	3.0	1.0	3.1
61 Ecuador	..	13.7	..	7.5	..	10.4
62 Jamaica	8.6	5.9	3.0	−1.4	7.8	−9.6
63 Ivory Coast	11.8	10.1	8.0	5.8	12.7	12.1
64 Dominican Rep.	1.9	2.2	6.3	6.0	11.4	9.6

	Average annual growth rate (percent)					
	Public consumption		Private consumption		Gross domestic investment	
	1960–70[a]	1970–81[b]	1960–70[a]	1970–81[b]	1960–70[a]	1970–81[b]
65 Mongolia	. .	. .	. .	. .	. .	. .
66 Colombia	5.5	5.2	5.5	6.6	4.5	6.6
67 Tunisia	5.2	9.0	3.2	8.2	4.2	10.8
68 Costa Rica	8.0	5.9	6.0	4.2	7.1	6.7
69 Korea, Dem. Rep.	. .	. .	. .	. .	. .	. .
70 Turkey	6.7	6.4	5.1	3.7	8.8	8.1
71 Syrian Arab Rep.	. .	16.0	. .	12.1	. .	16.7
72 Jordan	. .	. .	. .	. .	. .	. .
73 Paraguay	6.9	6.6	5.3	7.8	6.8	19.8
Upper middle-income	**6.8** m	**6.5** m	**5.4** m	**5.8** m	**7.5** m	**7.2** m
74 Korea, Rep. of	5.5	7.8	7.0	7.1	23.6	12.2
75 Iran, Islamic Rep. of	16.0	. .	10.0	. .	12.2	. .
76 Iraq	8.1	. .	4.9	. .	3.0	. .
77 Malaysia	7.5	10.2	4.2	7.3	7.5	10.4
78 Panama	7.8	5.2	6.7	4.6	12.4	1.0
79 Lebanon	5.9	. .	4.4	. .	6.2	. .
80 Algeria	1.5	11.4	2.3	9.2	−0.2	11.8
81 Brazil	3.7	6.9	5.4	8.7	6.1	7.9
82 Mexico	8.8	8.3	7.0	6.0	9.9	9.0
83 Portugal	7.7	8.3	5.5	3.8	7.7	2.3
84 Argentina	1.1	4.8	4.5	1.1	4.0	2.5
85 Chile	5.1	2.2	3.7	0.8	9.9	3.0
86 South Africa	7.0	4.9	6.2	0.6	9.4	3.2
87 Yugoslavia	0.6	4.3	9.5	5.8	4.7	5.9
88 Uruguay	4.4	3.9	0.7	1.3	−1.8	10.6
89 Venezuela	6.3	. .	5.0	. .	7.6	. .
90 Greece	6.6	6.6	7.1	4.1	10.4	1.3
91 Hong Kong	8.6	9.9	8.6	9.9	6.9	14.1
92 Israel	13.8	3.0	7.4	5.3	5.7	−0.4
93 Singapore	12.6	6.3	5.4	6.8	20.5	7.2
94 Trinidad and Tobago	c	c	4.8	8.7	−2.3	10.6
High-income oil exporters	. .	**13.2** m	. .	**18.5** m	. .	**17.5** m
95 Libya	. .	15.6	. .	18.5	. .	10.7
96 Saudi Arabia	. .	c	. .	18.8	. .	42.6
97 Kuwait	. .	10.8	. .	13.1	. .	17.5
98 United Arab Emirates	. .	. .	. .	. .	. .	. .
Industrial market economies	**4.2** m	**3.5** m	**4.3** m	**3.0** m	**5.8** m	**0.9** m
99 Ireland	3.9	5.6	3.8	2.8	9.0	4.6
100 Spain	3.8	5.2	7.0	3.6	11.3	1.2
101 Italy	4.1	2.8	6.1	2.8	3.7	0.9
102 New Zealand	3.6	3.3	3.3	1.9	3.2	−0.6
103 United Kingdom	2.2	2.3	2.4	1.6	5.1	(.)
104 Japan	6.2	4.5	9.0	4.2	14.6	3.1
105 Austria	3.3	3.9	4.3	3.6	5.9	2.6
106 Finland	5.0	5.1	4.0	2.7	4.1	(.)
107 Australia	7.1	5.2	5.0	3.0	6.7	1.8
108 Canada	6.2	2.5	4.9	4.5	5.8	4.1
109 Netherlands	2.8	2.7	5.9	3.3	7.4	−0.9
110 Belgium	5.7	4.8	3.8	3.6	6.0	0.8
111 France	4.0	3.2	5.3	4.1	7.7	1.4
112 United States	4.2	2.0	4.4	3.2	5.0	1.9
113 Denmark	5.9	4.0	4.1	1.9	5.9	−1.8
114 Germany, Fed. Rep.	4.1	3.5	4.6	2.8	4.1	1.3
115 Norway	6.2	4.1	3.7	5.0	5.0	−0.3
116 Sweden	5.4	3.3	3.5	1.9	5.3	−0.6
117 Switzerland	4.8	1.8	4.3	1.4	3.9	−1.0
East European nonmarket economies						
118 Albania	. .	. .	. .	. .	. .	. .
119 Hungary	c	4.5	3.1	3.7	7.8	4.9
120 Romania	. .	. .	. .	. .	11.2	8.2
121 Bulgaria	. .	. .	. .	. .	. .	. .
122 Poland	. .	. .	. .	. .	. .	. .
123 USSR	. .	. .	. .	. .	. .	. .
124 Czechoslovakia	. .	. .	. .	. .	. .	. .
125 German Dem. Rep.	. .	. .	. .	. .	. .	. .

a. Figures in italics are for 1961–70, not 1960–70. b. Figures in italics are for 1970–80, not 1970–81. c. Separate figures are not available for public consumption, which is therefore included in private consumption.

Table 5. Structure of demand

	Distribution of gross domestic product (percent)											
	Public consumption		Private consumption		Gross domestic investment		Gross domestic saving		Exports of goods and nonfactor services		Resource balance	
	1960[a]	1981[b]	1960[a]	1981[b]	1960[a]	1981[b]	1960[a]	1981[b]	1960[a]	1981[b]	1960[a]	1981[b]
Low-income economies	8 w	11 w	78 w	74 w	19 w	24 w	18 w	21 w	7 w	9 w	−1 w	−3 w
China and India	..	..	77 w	74 w	21 w	26 w	20 w	25 w	4 w	8 w	−1 w	−2 w
Other low-income	10 w	11 w	81 w	84 w	12 w	14 w	10 w	7 w	15 w	12 w	−2 w	−7 w
1 Kampuchea, Dem.	..	..	..	..	..	..	..	..	..	..	..	..
2 Bhutan	..	..	..	..	..	..	..	..	..	..	..	..
3 Lao, PDR	..	..	..	..	..	..	..	..	..	..	..	..
4 Chad	13	..	82	..	11	..	5	..	23	..	−6	..
5 Bangladesh	6	8	86	90	7	17	8	2	10	7	1	−15
6 Ethiopia	8	15	81	81	12	10	11	4	9	13	−1	−6
7 Nepal	..	c	..	92	..	14	..	8	..	..	..	−6
8 Burma	c	c	89	83	12	24	11	17	20	9	−1	−7
9 Afghanistan	c	..	87	..	16	..	13	..	4	..	−3	..
10 Mali	12	26	79	80	14	16	9	−6	12	18	−5	−22
11 Malawi	16	10	88	80	10	22	−4	10	21	22	−14	−12
12 Zaire	18	16	61	59	12	33	21	25	55	36	9	−8
13 Uganda	9	c	75	97	11	3	16	3	26	1	5	(.)
14 Burundi	3	16	92	79	6	19	5	5	13	9	−1	−14
15 Upper Volta	10	15	94	96	10	16	−4	−11	9	13	−14	−27
16 Rwanda	10	17	82	75	6	23	8	8	12	12	2	−15
17 India	7	10	79	70	17	23	14	20	5	7	−3	−3
18 Somalia	8	..	86	..	10	..	6	..	13	..	−4	..
19 Tanzania	9	14	72	78	14	22	19	8	31	14	5	−14
20 Viet Nam	..	..	..	..	..	..	..	..	..	..	..	..
21 China	c	c	76	72	23	28	24	28	4	9	1	(.)
22 Guinea	..	19	..	67	..	11	..	14	..	34	..	3
23 Haiti	c	c	93	99	9	13	7	1	20	14	−2	−12
24 Sri Lanka	13	7	78	81	14	28	9	12	44	31	−5	−16
25 Benin	16	13	75	89	15	35	9	−2	12	31	−6	−37
26 Central African Rep.	19	13	72	90	20	9	9	−3	23	26	−11	−12
27 Sierra Leone	..	11	..	91	..	13	..	−2	..	17	..	−15
28 Madagascar	20	16	75	77	11	15	5	7	12	13	−6	−8
29 Niger	9	9	79	76	13	27	12	15	9	22	−1	−12
30 Pakistan	11	11	84	82	12	17	5	7	8	12	−7	−10
31 Mozambique	..	..	..	..	..	..	..	..	..	..	..	..
32 Sudan	8	c	80	100	12	13	12	(.)	16	9	(.)	−12
33 Togo	8	17	88	68	11	31	4	15	19	25	−7	−16
34 Ghana	10	11	73	85	24	6	17	4	28	4	−7	−2
Middle-income economies	11 w	14 w	70 w	66 w	20 w	25 w	19 w	22 w	17 w	23 w	−1 w	−3 w
Oil exporters	11 w	15 w	70 w	61 w	18 w	26 w	19 w	24 w	21 w	23 w	1 w	−2 w
Oil importers	11 w	14 w	70 w	69 w	21 w	25 w	19 w	21 w	15 w	23 w	−2 w	−4 w
Lower middle-income	10 w	13 w	76 w	68 w	15 w	25 w	14 w	19 w	15 w	23 w	−1 w	−6 w
35 Kenya	11	21	72	63	20	25	17	16	31	25	−3	−9
36 Senegal	17	22	68	83	16	17	15	−5	40	29	−1	−22
37 Mauritania	25	29	71	62	38	38	4	9	15	49	−34	−29
38 Yemen Arab Rep.	..	20	..	101	..	44	..	−21	..	6	..	−65
39 Yemen, PDR	..	..	..	..	..	..	..	..	..	..	..	..
40 Liberia	7	21	58	62	28	18	35	17	39	51	7	−1
41 Indonesia	12	11	80	66	8	21	8	23	13	28	(.)	2
42 Lesotho	17	26	108	163	2	21	−25	−89	12	13	−27	−110
43 Bolivia	7	10	86	77	14	13	7	13	13	13	−7	(.)
44 Honduras	11	14	77	68	14	24	12	18	22	32	−2	−6
45 Zambia	11	28	48	57	25	23	41	15	56	36	16	−8
46 Egypt	17	19	71	64	13	30	12	17	20	34	−1	−13
47 El Salvador	10	15	79	75	16	12	11	10	20	31	−5	−2
48 Thailand	10	12	76	65	16	28	14	23	17	25	−2	−5
49 Philippines	8	8	76	67	16	30	16	25	11	19	(.)	−5
50 Angola	..	..	..	..	..	..	..	..	..	..	..	..
51 Papua New Guinea	28	26	71	63	13	28	1	11	16	38	−12	−17
52 Morocco	12	c	77	92	10	23	11	8	24	21	1	−15
53 Nicaragua	9	21	79	73	15	24	12	6	24	21	−3	−18
54 Nigeria	6	12	87	65	13	29	7	23	15	25	−6	−6
55 Zimbabwe	11	18	67	67	23	22	22	15	..	..	−1	−7
56 Cameroon	..	7	..	71	..	21	..	22	..	32	..	1
57 Cuba	..	..	..	..	..	..	..	..	..	..	..	..
58 Congo, People's Rep.	23	12	98	50	45	32	−21	38	21	62	−66	6
59 Guatemala	8	8	84	81	10	17	8	11	13	17	−2	−6
60 Peru	9	13	64	73	25	19	27	14	20	17	2	−5
61 Ecuador	11	15	78	61	14	26	11	24	16	22	−3	−2
62 Jamaica	7	21	67	67	30	16	26	12	34	50	−4	−4
63 Ivory Coast	10	18	73	62	15	27	17	20	37	34	2	−7
64 Dominican Rep.	13	8	68	78	12	24	19	14	24	18	7	−10

	Public consumption		Private consumption		Gross domestic investment		Gross domestic saving		Exports of goods and nonfactor services		Resource balance	
	1960[a]	1981[b]	1960[a]	1981[b]	1960[a]	1981[b]	1960[a]	1981[b]	1960[a]	1981[b]	1960[a]	1981[b]
65 Mongolia	..	..	..	..	..	..	..	..	..	..	..	..
66 Colombia	6	8	73	68	21	28	21	24	16	12	(.)	−4
67 Tunisia	17	15	76	62	17	31	7	23	20	42	−10	−8
68 Costa Rica	10	15	77	60	18	28	13	25	21	44	−5	−3
69 Korea, Dem. Rep.	..	..	..	..	..	..	..	..	..	..	..	..
70 Turkey	11	11	76	70	16	25	13	19	3	11	−3	−6
71 Syrian Arab Rep.	..	22	..	69	..	24	..	9	..	18	..	−15
72 Jordan	..	30	..	86	..	41	..	−16	..	54	..	−57
73 Paraguay	8	7	76	74	17	29	16	19	18	7	−1	−10
Upper middle-income	12 w	15 w	67 w	65 w	22 w	25 w	21 w	24 w	18 w	23 w	−1 w	−1 w
74 Korea, Rep. of	15	12	84	66	11	26	1	22	3	39	−10	−4
75 Iran, Islamic Rep. of	10	..	69	..	17	..	21	..	19	..	4	..
76 Iraq	18	..	48	..	20	..	34	..	42	..	14	..
77 Malaysia	11	21	62	53	14	32	27	26	54	53	13	−6
78 Panama	11	21	78	56	16	29	11	23	31	40	−5	−6
79 Lebanon	10	..	85	..	16	..	5	..	27	..	−11	..
80 Algeria	15	16	60	45	42	37	25	39	31	34	−17	2
81 Brazil	12	c	67	81	22	20	21	19	5	9	−1	−1
82 Mexico	6	15	76	62	20	25	18	23	10	13	−2	−2
83 Portugal	11	16	76	77	19	27	12	8	17	27	−7	−19
84 Argentina	9	15	70	62	22	26	21	23	9	7	−1	−3
85 Chile	9	13	79	75	14	22	12	12	14	18	−2	−10
86 South Africa	9	13	64	50	22	29	27	37	30	36	5	8
87 Yugoslavia	19	15	49	56	37	32	32	29	14	23	−5	−3
88 Uruguay	9	13	79	75	18	15	12	12	14	15	−6	−3
89 Venezuela	14	14	53	56	21	25	33	30	32	30	12	5
90 Greece	12	18	77	66	19	25	11	14	9	20	−8	−11
91 Hong Kong	7	8	87	68	18	30	6	24	82	111	−12	−6
92 Israel	18	36	68	59	27	20	14	5	14	43	−13	−15
93 Singapore	8	10	95	57	11	42	−3	33	163	212	−14	−9
94 Trinidad and Tobago	9	c	61	60	28	30	30	40	37	45	2	10
High-income oil exporters	..	21 w	..	22 w	..	26 w	..	58 w	..	69 w	..	32 w
95 Libya	..	26	..	26	..	34	..	48	..	60	..	14
96 Saudi Arabia	..	23	..	18	..	26	..	59	..	68	..	33
97 Kuwait	..	15	..	39	..	17	..	46	..	71	..	29
98 United Arab Emirates	..	11	..	17	..	28	..	72	..	78	..	44
Industrial market economies	15 w	17 w	63 w	61 w	21 w	22 w	22 w	21 w	12 w	20 w	1 w	−1 w
99 Ireland	12	22	77	62	16	30	11	16	32	63	−5	−14
100 Spain	7	12	72	70	18	20	21	18	10	17	3	−2
101 Italy	13	18	62	63	25	21	25	19	14	27	(.)	−2
102 New Zealand	11	17	68	60	23	25	21	23	22	29	−2	−2
103 United Kingdom	17	22	66	58	19	17	17	20	21	28	−2	3
104 Japan	8	10	59	58	33	31	33	32	11	15	(.)	1
105 Austria	13	18	59	56	28	26	28	26	25	42	(.)	(.)
106 Finland	13	18	58	55	30	28	29	27	23	34	−1	−1
107 Australia	10	17	65	60	29	26	25	23	15	15	−3	−3
108 Canada	14	20	65	55	23	25	21	25	18	28	−2	(.)
109 Netherlands	13	18	62	61	27	18	29	21	48	58	2	3
110 Belgium	13	20	69	66	19	18	18	14	33	65	−1	−4
111 France	13	16	62	67	23	21	25	17	15	22	2	−4
112 United States	17	18	64	64	18	19	19	18	5	10	1	−1
113 Denmark	13	28	62	56	26	16	25	16	32	36	−1	(.)
114 Germany, Fed. Rep.	14	21	57	56	27	23	29	23	19	30	2	(.)
115 Norway	13	19	59	47	30	26	28	34	41	48	−2	8
116 Sweden	16	30	60	52	25	19	24	18	23	31	−1	−1
117 Switzerland	9	13	62	63	29	26	29	24	29	37	(.)	−2
East European nonmarket economies	..	..	..	..	..	..	..	..	..	..	..	..
118 Albania	..	..	..	..	..	..	..	..	..	..	..	..
119 Hungary	c	10	74	61	28	30	26	29	..	39	..	−1
120 Romania	..	..	..	..	..	33	..	..	..	28	..	(.)
121 Bulgaria	..	..	..	..	..	..	..	..	..	..	..	..
122 Poland	..	..	..	..	..	..	..	..	..	..	..	..
123 USSR	..	..	..	..	..	..	..	..	..	..	..	..
124 Czechoslovakia	..	..	..	..	..	..	..	..	..	..	..	..
125 German Dem. Rep.	..	..	..	..	..	..	..	..	..	..	..	..

Distribution of gross domestic product (percent)

a. Figures in italics are for 1961, not 1960.   b. Figures in italics are for 1980, not 1981.   c. Separate figures are not available for public consumption, which is therefore included in private consumption.

Table 6. Agriculture and food

		Value added in agriculture (millions of 1975 dollars)		Volume of cereal imports (thousands of metric tons)		Food aid in cereals (thousands of metric tons)		Fertilizer consumption (per hectare of arable land)		Average index of food production per capita (1969–71 = 100)
		1970	1981[a]	1974	1981	1974[b]	1981[b]	1970[c]	1980	1979–81
Low-income economies		22,884 t	27,052 t	5,659 t	3,827 t	180 w	560 w	111 w
China and India		14,437 t	18,934 t	1,582 t	472 t	230 w	766 w	111 w
Other low-income		8,447 t	8,118 t	4,077 t	3,355 t	78 w	166 w	111 w
1	Kampuchea, Dem.	. .	. .	223	150	226	133	13	27	45
2	Bhutan	. .	. .	23	30	0	1	0	11	107
3	Lao, PDR	. .	. .	53	50	13	2	4	78	110
4	Chad	246	211	50	14	13	14	7	3	96
5	Bangladesh	9,475	11,100	1,719	1,079	2,130	737	142	463	94
6	Ethiopia	1,128	1,300	118	207	59	228	4	40	85
7	Nepal	1,012	1,068	19	12	0	45	30	97	84
8	Burma	1,479	2,528	26	14	14	0	34	100	102
9	Afghanistan	. .	. .	5	965	10	75	24	63	97
10	Mali	260	352	281	102	114	50	29	60	88
11	Malawi	221	. .	17	113	(.)	17	52	141	96
12	Zaire	397	497	343	538	(.)	77	8	13	87
13	Uganda	1,926	1,543	37	37	16	57	13	1	86
14	Burundi	239	310	7	19	6	12	5	8	100
15	Upper Volta	217	262	99	71	0	51	3	40	94
16	Rwanda	. .	394	3	16	19	15	3	1	104
17	India	29,097	35,407	5,261	1,523	1,582	435	114	309	103
18	Somalia	357	. .	42	432	110	330	31	23	65
19	Tanzania	842	1,352	431	265	148	237	30	69	91
20	Viet Nam	. .	. .	1,854	1,150	6	142	512	407	112
21	China	42,900	59,400	9,176	17,411	. .	37	418	1,546	116
22	Guinea	. .	520	63	134	49	34	18	2	87
23	Haiti	. .	. .	83	233	25	84	4	4	89
24	Sri Lanka	841	1,148	951	669	271	226	496	770	148
25	Benin	. .	217	8	93	9	11	33	17	96
26	Central African Rep.	120	152	7	14	1	3	11	5	102
27	Sierra Leone	192	231	72	58	10	12	13	10	81
28	Madagascar	691	722	114	268	7	26	56	29	94
29	Niger	440	322	155	89	75	11	1	8	93
30	Pakistan	3,258	4,273	1,274	305	619[b]	277[b]	168	495	105
31	Mozambique	. .	. .	62	368	34	155	27	90	73
32	Sudan	1,435	1,778	125	305	50	195	31	65	102
33	Togo	145	178	6	62	0	4	3	30	90
34	Ghana	2,281	2,500	177	256	43	94	9	43	74
Middle-income economies				41,308 t	73,513 t	2,342 t	4,884 t	212 w	457 w	110 w
Oil exporters				17,941 t	34,822 t	1,074 t	2,561 t	145 w	394 w	108 w
Oil importers				23,367 t	38,691 t	1,268 t	2,323 t	249 w	489 w	112 w
Lower middle-income				16,947 t	29,389 t	1,582 t	3,840 t	170 w	357 w	109 w
35	Kenya	700	1,184	15	534	2	173	224	262	85
36	Senegal	491	514	341	458	28	153	20	36	76
37	Mauritania	117	146	115	182	48	106	6	108	77
38	Yemen Arab Rep.	221	390	158	509	0	4	1	35	96
39	Yemen, PDR	. .	. .	149	252	38	29	0	98	102
40	Liberia	142	201	42	111	3	26	55	92	95
41	Indonesia	7,896	12,168	1,919	1,978	301	382	119	630	118
42	Lesotho	34	61	49	95	14	44	17	154	86
43	Bolivia	348	488	207	253	22	55	13	16	102
44	Honduras	306	390	52	144	31	36	160	139	80
45	Zambia	278	351	93	295	1	84	71	157	92
46	Egypt	2,683	3,716	3,877	7,287	610	1,865	1,282	2,324	90
47	El Salvador	328	396	75	123	4	50	1,048	892	104
48	Thailand	3,591	5,666	97	221	0	21	76	162	129
49	Philippines	3,682	6,149	817	1,071	89	85	214	337	122
50	Angola	. .	. .	149	244	0	25	45	48	81
51	Papua New Guinea	336	461	71	155	. .	. .	76	148	97
52	Morocco	1,725	1,541	891	2,758	75	120	130	335	81
53	Nicaragua	265	324	44	67	3	58	184	358	87
54	Nigeria	9,061	8,707	389	2,441	7	0	3	57	91
55	Zimbabwe	375	. .	56	21	. .	18	466	655	92
56	Cameroon	732	1,125	81	106	4	9	28	51	101
57	Cuba	. .	. .	1,622	2,094	. .	. .	1,539	1,653	106
58	Congo, People's Rep.	93	131	34	56	2	2	112	8	82
59	Guatemala	. .	. .	138	186	9	14	224	507	116
60	Peru	2,232	2,349	637	1,245	37	116	297	325	84
61	Ecuador	628	888	152	317	13	4	123	277	97
62	Jamaica	206	227	340	459	1	37	886	661	90
63	Ivory Coast	876	1,480	172	619	4	0	71	137	110
64	Dominican Rep.	667	981	252	427	16	76	354	421	99

	Value added in agriculture (millions of 1975 dollars)		Volume of cereal imports (thousands of metric tons)		Food aid in cereals (thousands of metric tons)		Fertilizer consumption (per hectare of arable land)		Average index of food production per capita (1969–71 = 100)
	1970	1981[a]	1974	1981	1974[b]	1981[b]	1970[c]	1980	1979–81
65 Mongolia	..	..	28	173	..	5	18	86	92
66 Colombia	2,848	4,630	503	694	28	5	310	537	122
67 Tunisia	480	899	307	960	1	99	82	135	124
68 Costa Rica	338	461	110	177	1	1	1,086	1,500	110
69 Korea, Dem. Rep.	..	..	1,108	720	..	..	1,484	3,255	134
70 Turkey	7,691	10,777	1,276	299	70	9	166	412	112
71 Syrian Arab Rep.	595	1,484	339	971	47	39	67	220	163
72 Jordan	..	97	171	619	63	84	20	104	74
73 Paraguay	419	899	71	68	10	11	58	33	111
Upper middle-income			24,361 *t*	44,124 *t*	760 *t*	1,044 *t*	252 *w*	555 *w*	113 *w*
74 Korea, Rep. of	3,995	5,610	2,679	7,687	234	678	2,466	3,757	126
75 Iran, Islamic Rep. of	3,739	..	2,076	3,236	..	..	76	359	112
76 Iraq	1,172	..	870	2,275	1	0	35	169	89
77 Malaysia	2,049	3,554	1,017	1,244	1	0	436	1,051	139
78 Panama	290	345	63	89	3	2	391	533	102
79 Lebanon	..	..	354	692	21	39	1279	764	109
80 Algeria	952	1,464	1,816	3,261	54	29	174	320	81
81 Brazil	8,737	14,932	2,485	5,571	31	3	169	678	125
82 Mexico	8,501	12,649	2,881	6,602	..	0	246	517	106
83 Portugal	2,242	2,025	1,860	3,942	0	255	411	730	74
84 Argentina	3,523	4,313	0	10			24	32	116
85 Chile	440	557	1,737	1,392	331	28	317	210	97
86 South Africa	..	..	127	476			425	779	104
87 Yugoslavia	3,655	4,840	992	454			766	1,045	117
88 Uruguay	385	404	70	44	31	0	392	424	104
89 Venezuela	1,362	1,918	1,270	2,378			165	642	104
90 Greece	2,851	3,521	1,341	685			858	1,342	123
91 Hong Kong	183	155	657	801			..	..	71
92 Israel	..	..	1,176	1,700	53	10	1,394	1,987	103
93 Singapore	100	123	682	1,258	(.)	0	2,667	5,500	148
94 Trinidad and Tobago	80	65	208	327	..	..	640	506	69
High-income oil exporters			1,327 *t*	5,715 *t*			59 *w*	378 *w*	..
95 Libya	126	388	612	942			64	374	141
96 Saudi Arabia	331	551	482	4,100			44	352	..
97 Kuwait	20	37	101	386			0	4,400	..
98 United Arab Emirates	..	..	132	287			0	2,692	..
Industrial market economies			65,494 *t*	65,420 *t*			985 *w*	1,258 *w*	112 *w*
99 Ireland	..	..	631	598			3,573	6,182	115
100 Spain	7,945	9,762	4,675	6,012			595	810	125
101 Italy	14,093	15,820	8,100	7,088			962	1,701	112
102 New Zealand	..	..	92	62			8,875	10,177	107
103 United Kingdom	5,386	6,744	7,541	4,366			2,521	2,936	122
104 Japan	24,218	24,825	19,557	24,420			3,849	3,721	91
105 Austria	1,806	2,018	165	99			2,517	2,491	112
106 Finland	3,188	3,009	222	524			1,931	2,039	103
107 Australia	4,351	5,916	2	8			246	277	117
108 Canada	6,743	8,371	1,513	1,393			192	432	109
109 Netherlands	3,173	4,721	7,199	5,228			7,165	7,888	116
110 Belgium[d]	1,929	2,204	4,585	6,083			5,686	4,990	109
111 France	17,077	17,957	654	1,746			2,424	3,008	117
112 United States	46,300	59,800	460	188			800	1,116	116
113 Denmark	1,641	2,365	462	509			2,254	2,364	111
114 Germany, Fed. Rep.	11,567	13,870	7,164	4,995			4,208	4,714	110
115 Norway	1,409	1,859	713	686			2,471	3,010	117
116 Sweden	3,133	3,080	301	216			1,639	1,624	117
117 Switzerland	..	..	1,458	1,199			3,842	4,576	119
East European nonmarket economies			18,543 *t*	58,774 *t*			635 *w*	1,050 *w*	107 *w*
118 Albania	..	..	48	4			745	1,249	106
119 Hungary	1,619	2,240	408	180			1,485	2,624	132
120 Romania	..	..	1,381	2,590	0		559	1,165	147
121 Bulgaria	..	..	649	1,016			1,446	1,984	116
122 Poland	..	..	4,185	7,218		0	1,715	2,356	96
123 USSR	..	..	7,755	43,713			437	809	102
124 Czechoslovakia	..	..	1,296	1,128			2,402	3,347	114
125 German Dem. Rep.	..	..	2,821	2,925			3,202	3,252	129

a. Figures in italics are for 1980 not 1981.   b. Figures are for the crop years 1974/75 and 1980/81.   c. Average for 1969–71.   d. Includes Luxembourg.

Table 7. Industry

		Distribution of manufacturing value added (percent; 1975 prices)					Value added in manufacturing (millions of 1975 dollars)	
		Food and agriculture 1980[a]	Textiles and clothing 1980[a]	Machinery and transport equipment 1980[a]	Chemicals 1980[a]	Other manufacturing 1980[a]	1970	1980[a]

1	Kampuchea, Dem.	..	..	..	..	..	..	..
2	Bhutan	..	..	..	..	..	..	..
3	Lao, PDR	..	..	..	..	..		
4	Chad	..	..	..	..	..	37	27
5	Bangladesh	26	40	4	16	14	647	1,197
6	Ethiopia	..	..	..	..	..	236	335
7	Nepal	..	..	..	..	..		
8	Burma	..	..	..	..	..	287	429
9	Afghanistan	..	..	..	..	..		
10	Mali	..	..	..	..	..	44	55
11	Malawi	50	11	..	..	39	56	
12	Zaire	44	20	..	10	26	186	162
13	Uganda	..	..	..	..	..	222	90
14	Burundi	..	..	..	..	..	23	43
15	Upper Volta	..	..	..	..	..	67	94
16	Rwanda	58	..	..	..	42	..	100
17	India	13	19	20	13	35	10,202	15,909
18	Somalia	..	..	..	..	..	42	
19	Tanzania	..	..	..	..	..	190	237
20	Viet Nam	..	..	..	..	..		
21	China	..	..	..	..	..	..	..
22	Guinea	..	..	..	..	..	..	44
23	Haiti	38	12	..	1	49		
24	Sri Lanka	..	..	..	..	..	556	679
25	Benin	..	..	..	..	..	..	43
26	Central African Rep.	..	..	..	..	..	54	39
27	Sierra Leone	..	..	..	..	..	25	34
28	Madagascar	27	41	2	11	19	295	353
29	Niger	..	..	..	..	..	54	165
30	Pakistan	..	..	..	..	..	1,492	2,270
31	Mozambique	..	..	..	..	..		
32	Sudan	..	..	..	..	..	266	284
33	Togo	..	..	..	..	..	30	14
34	Ghana	31	..	..	..	69	601	490

35	Kenya	30	11	12	8	39	165	501
36	Senegal	52	14	..	7	27	276	348
37	Mauritania	..	..	..	..	..	21	30
38	Yemen Arab Rep.	..	..	..	..	..	25	83
39	Yemen, PDR	..	..	..	..	..		
40	Liberia	27	..	..	..	73	25	41
41	Indonesia	29	8	7	11	45	1,517	5,546
42	Lesotho	..	..	..	..	..	5	12
43	Bolivia	..	..	..	..	..	237	389
44	Honduras	46	13	1	7	33	137	213
45	Zambia	14	20	12	13	41	319	381
46	Egypt	..	..	..	..	..	1,835	4,204
47	El Salvador	..	..	..	..	..	252	321
48	Thailand	..	..	..	..	..	1,675	4,355
49	Philippines	39	11	10	8	32	2,816	5,519
50	Angola	..	..	..	..	..		
51	Papua New Guinea	..	..	..	..	..	71	132
52	Morocco	32	12	9	9	38	1,138	1,960
53	Nicaragua	..	..	..	..	..	262	334
54	Nigeria	25	18	13	13	31	1,191	3,598
55	Zimbabwe	21	18	10	10	41	511	717
56	Cameroon	..	..	..	..	..	201	342
57	Cuba	36	16	..	17	31		
58	Congo, People's Rep.	..	..	..	..	..	114	65
59	Guatemala	..	..	..	..	..		
60	Peru	27	14	10	11	38	2,911	4,048
61	Ecuador	29	14	10	7	40	322	872
62	Jamaica	..	..	..	..	..	428	339
63	Ivory Coast	..	..	..	..	..	398	732
64	Dominican Rep.	72	4	1	5	18	483	931

	Distribution of manufacturing value added (percent; 1975 prices)					Value added in manufacturing (millions of 1975 dollars)	
	Food and agriculture 1980[a]	Textiles and clothing 1980[a]	Machinery and transport equipment 1980[a]	Chemicals 1980[a]	Other manufacturing 1980[a]	1970	1980[a]
65 Mongolia	22	31	..	5	42	..	..
66 Colombia	32	15	12	12	29	1,800	3,293
67 Tunisia	23	15	9	16	37	222	727
68 Costa Rica	..	..	..	..	..	261	540
69 Korea, Dem. Rep.	..	..	..	..	..	..	..
70 Turkey	24	12	13	12	39	3,678	6,056
71 Syrian Arab Rep.	25	31	..	3	41	575	1,318
72 Jordan	..	..	..	..	..	..	191
73 Paraguay	31	12	8	4	45	183	398
Upper middle-income							
74 Korea, Rep. of	17	22	17	12	32	2,346	9,843
75 Iran, Islamic Rep. of	..	..	..	..	..	2,601	..
76 Iraq	..	..	..	..	..	522	..
77 Malaysia	22	8	17	6	47	941	2,780
78 Panama	51	11	2	6	30	252	319
79 Lebanon	..	..	..	..	..	..	..
80 Algeria	..	10	28	10	38	1,030	3,030
81 Brazil	14	10	28	10	38	18,819	44,733
82 Mexico	19	9	19	12	41	14,592	29,084
83 Portugal	13	20	20	10	37	3,496	5,905
84 Argentina	12	11	27	13	37	10,693	12,637
85 Chile	15	5	16	11	53	1,881	2,107
86 South Africa	15	11	16	11	47	..	..
87 Yugoslavia	15	14	20	8	43	6,579	13,300
88 Uruguay	26	23	11	8	32	725	1,034
89 Venezuela	25	7	8	9	51	3,419	5,718
90 Greece	20	26	9	9	36	2,540	4,594
91 Hong Kong	..	..	..	..	..	1,620	4,030
92 Israel	13	12	25	8	42	..	..
93 Singapore	5	4	53	5	33	827	2,323
94 Trinidad and Tobago	13	4	9	7	67	404	480
High-income oil exporters							
95 Libya	..	..	..	..	..	154	632
96 Saudi Arabia	3	..	..	..	97	1,726	3,378
97 Kuwait	8	..	..	17	75	369	915
98 United Arab Emirates	..	..	..	..	..	..	..
Industrial market economies							
99 Ireland	22	10	12	12	44	..	..
100 Spain	12	15	17	10	46	18,331	33,396
101 Italy	10	15	26	9	40	..	..
102 New Zealand	26	11	15	5	43	..	..
103 United Kingdom	13	8	34	10	35	58,677	56,530
104 Japan	8	6	33	8	45	118,403	234,036
105 Austria	14	9	23	7	47	9,112	13,532
106 Finland	12	8	22	8	50	5,636	8,635
107 Australia	17	8	22	8	45	20,207	..
108 Canada	14	7	21	8	50	25,748	36,232
109 Netherlands	18	4	26	15	37	18,684	24,245
110 Belgium	17	8	28	13	34	14,386	19,650
111 France	16	8	32	9	35	75,800	107,805
112 United States	11	6	32	12	39	382,200	436,900
113 Denmark	23	6	26	7	38	5,858	8,095
114 Germany, Fed. Rep.	9	6	35	11	39	149,113	184,741
115 Norway	15	4	27	7	47	5,322	6,373
116 Sweden	10	3	34	6	47	16,743	18,817
117 Switzerland	15	9	21	16	39	..	..
East European nonmarket economies							
118 Albania	..	..	..	..	..	..	..
119 Hungary	10	10	29	10	41	3,244	5,700
120 Romania	12	15	33	12	28	..	..
121 Bulgaria	24	15	15	6	40	..	..
122 Poland	5	19	32	8	36	..	..
123 USSR	12	11	28	6	43	..	..
124 Czechoslovakia	8	9	35	9	39	..	..
125 German Dem. Rep.	18	10	32	9	31	..	..

a. Figures in italics are for 1979, not 1980.

Table 8. Commercial energy

		Average annual energy growth rate (percent)				Energy consumption per capita (kilograms of coal equivalent)		Energy imports as a percentage of merchandise exports	
		Energy production		Energy consumption					
		1960–74[a]	1974–80	1960–74[a]	1974–80	1960[b]	1980	1960	1980[c]
Low-income economies		5.0 w	5.6 w	4.9 w	5.0 w	218 w	368 w	11 w	43 w
China and India		4.6 w	5.6 w	4.6 w	5.2 w	252 w	450 w	..	..
Other low-income		14.7 w	6.5 w	9.0 w	2.0 w	58 w	107 w	10 w	43 w
1	Kampuchea, Dem.	..	..	−5.1	44.0	19	128	9	..
2	Bhutan	..	..	..	..	..	..	..	..
3	Lao, PDR	..	9.3	13.8	16.2	16	127	..	..
4	Chad	..	..	..	..	8	22	23	..
5	Bangladesh	..	11.8	..	6.9	..	49	..	27
6	Ethiopia	14.1	2.5	22.7	−1.6	5	25	11	42
7	Nepal	26.8	0.7	15.2	2.1	3	13	..	43
8	Burma	5.6	11.9	4.3	5.8	60	87	4	..
9	Afghanistan	38.8	−3.1	10.4	5.1	23	83	12	..
10	Mali	40.4	7.0	10.2	4.7	10	31	13	..
11	Malawi	..	2.7	..	2.9	..	59	..	24
12	Zaire	3.0	13.2	6.5	0.1	82	107	3	..
13	Uganda	5.2	−8.3	8.9	−8.4	39	34	5	..
14	Burundi	..	35.2	1.8	6.8	11	16	..	14
15	Upper Volta	..	..	7.8	12.7	5	33	38	52
16	Rwanda	..	4.6	8.2	9.6	15	28	..	..
17	India	4.9	4.5	5.5	4.6	114	210	11	43
18	Somalia	..	..	9.7	12.8	16	85	4	12
19	Tanzania	10.6	12.4	13.6	−1.3	17	69	..	47
20	Viet Nam	0.0	6.6	11.3	−1.3	95	148	..	..
21	China	4.5	5.8	4.4	5.3	340	618	..	..
22	Guinea	16.0	0.5	17.8	1.6	17	83	7	..
23	Haiti	..	12.9	10.1	12.7	16	88	..	47
24	Sri Lanka	10.1	6.9	4.9	2.2	177	201	8	47
25	Benin	..	..	10.1	1.7	38	70	16	..
26	Central African Rep.	14.1	4.0	7.7	7.7	30	46	12	26
27	Sierra Leone	..	..	0.8	0.4	212	166	11	..
28	Madagascar	6.7	−6.3	11.0	−0.2	40	74	9	..
29	Niger	..	..	14.9	14.1	5	54	6	55
30	Pakistan	9.4	6.9	5.1	4.6	143	224	17	..
31	Mozambique	3.2	47.9	6.4	−2.9	111	103	11	..
32	Sudan	29.6	12.8	12.9	−4.2	58	101	8	32
33	Togo	3.1	66.9	12.9	20.7	22	203	10	43
34	Ghana	36.9	2.9	12.5	1.9	104	268	7	..
Middle-income economies		12.5 w	−2.4 w	7.9 w	4.8 w	462 w	987 w	9 w	23 w
Oil exporters		13.5 w	−3.7 w	6.1 w	4.6 w	423 w	760 w	5 w	7 w
Oil importers		7.8 w	3.7 w	8.7 w	4.9 w	493 w	1,172 w	13 w	34 w
Lower middle-income		23.2 w	3.6 w	8.2 w	5.4 w	218 w	504 w	8 w	22 w
35	Kenya	9.6	13.3	9.3	2.3	57	208	18	63
36	Senegal	..	..	1.7	−0.5	555	364	8	55
37	Mauritania	..	..	20.9	4.8	18	199	39	..
38	Yemen Arab Rep.	..	..	12.9	13.9	7	62	..	591
39	Yemen, PDR	..	..	−12.8	9.9	..	..	..	..
40	Liberia	31.8	−5.8	19.6	0.1	96	502	3	25
41	Indonesia	8.5	5.9	4.3	9.0	129	266	3	8
42	Lesotho	..	..	..	..	..	..	..	..
43	Bolivia	17.1	−2.1	6.9	7.7	169	452	4	1
44	Honduras	29.4	12.4	8.9	2.4	149	292	10	20
45	Zambia	..	1.7	..	2.9	..	733	..	..
46	Egypt	9.4	23.2	2.6	10.6	287	595	12	2
47	El Salvador	5.1	20.7	7.8	7.0	145	357	6	24
48	Thailand	28.3	−2.5	16.3	6.5	63	370	12	44
49	Philippines	3.0	26.2	9.7	4.4	159	380	9	41
50	Angola	35.4	−1.6	11.5	1.1	85	255	6	..
51	Papua New Guinea	12.3	10.4	21.8	4.4	36	332	7	..
52	Morocco	2.0	4.8	7.6	6.8	173	368	9	41
53	Nicaragua	26.4	−10.4	10.3	−0.4	181	362	12	42
54	Nigeria	36.6	0.7	9.3	9.3	29	169	7	1
55	Zimbabwe	..	−2.4	..	−0.2	..	778	..	..
56	Cameroon	1.1	52.3	5.3	7.1	79	154	7	14
57	Cuba	21.2	5.0	4.4	4.2	920	1,361	..	..
58	Congo, People's Rep.	15.8	7.0	6.2	24.7	130	458	25	3
59	Guatemala	9.9	7.0	6.3	4.5	180	308	12	25
60	Peru	3.6	17.3	6.7	3.4	433	807	4	2
61	Ecuador	19.4	4.5	8.6	13.3	216	692	2	..
62	Jamaica	−0.7	−1.1	9.6	−5.2	654	1,440	11	46
63	Ivory Coast	9.7	10.2	14.7	4.6	73	248	5	11
64	Dominican Rep.	1.8	−4.7	14.6	−0.8	158	517	..	51

162

	Average annual energy growth rate (percent)				Energy consumption per capita (kilograms of coal equivalent)		Energy imports as a percentage of merchandise exports	
	Energy production		Energy consumption					
	1960–74[a]	1974–80	1960–74[a]	1974–80	1960[b]	1980	1960	1980[c]
65 Mongolia	10.4	12.2	7.4	10.2	529	1,452	. .	. .
66 Colombia	3.5	1.3	6.3	4.8	519	970	3	14
67 Tunisia	71.9	6.0	10.2	9.2	173	652	15	33
68 Costa Rica	9.5	6.7	10.4	7.0	311	829	7	24
69 Korea, Dem. Rep.	9.4	3.2	9.6	3.5	1,179	2,864	. .	. .
70 Turkey	7.5	3.1	9.8	5.0	258	779	16	126
71 Syrian Arab Rep.	86.0	4.0	11.4	11.9	233	964	16	50
72 Jordan	. .	. .	6.9	12.6	185	627	79	73
73 Paraguay	. .	10.4	8.9	9.6	80	300	. .	41
Upper middle-income	**8.8** w	**−4.5** w	**7.7** w	**4.5** w	**798** w	**1,677** w	**10** w	**23** w
74 Korea, Rep. of	6.3	3.2	15.0	10.7	208	1,563	70	38
75 Iran, Islamic Rep. of,	14.6	−17.4	6.4	−2.1	1,185	1,210	1	. .
76 Iraq	5.0	6.6	5.3	8.7	598	1,221	(.)	. .
77 Malaysia	36.8	24.1	4.1	7.7	616	881	2	13
78 Panama	14.7	40.0	18.6	−5.4	468	1,623	. .	125
79 Lebanon	12.7	−0.3	8.0	−3.1	665	1,153	68	. .
80 Algeria	11.1	4.4	6.4	11.4	321	814	14	2
81 Brazil	8.3	7.5	8.8	6.6	385	1,102	21	53
82 Mexico	5.8	16.7	7.4	7.8	786	1,684	3	3
83 Portugal	4.5	8.8	7.7	6.5	536	1,822	17	48
84 Argentina	6.5	3.7	5.6	3.5	1,177	2,161	14	14
85 Chile	3.9	0.6	6.1	0.1	833	1,137	10	24
86 South Africa	3.8	10.0	6.8	4.3	1,762	3,204	9	(.)
87 Yugoslavia	5.0	3.5	7.5	4.5	858	2,402	8	40
88 Uruguay	3.7	8.5	2.1	2.1	1,020	1,160	35	45
89 Venezuela	1.1	−3.7	5.2	−0.3	3,014	3,039	1	1
90 Greece	14.3	8.2	11.7	5.4	516	2,605	26	48
91 Hong Kong	. .	. .	10.1	6.4	649	1,881	5	6
92 Israel	41.8	−52.9	10.9	2.5	1,006	2,813	17	38
93 Singapore	. .	. .	10.1	6.6	2,111	8,544	17	36
94 Trinidad and Tobago	2.8	2.8	2.1	4.8	6,497	7,312	35	29
High-income oil exporters	**16.6** w	**2.8** w	**13.5** w	**17.2** w	**. .**	**. .**	**. .**	**(.)** w
95 Libya	29.0	4.9	12.5	30.0	288	3,549	83	(.)
96 Saudi Arabia	14.0	4.4	14.6	10.5	1,271	6,764	. .	(.)
97 Kuwait	4.5	−2.8	2.9	3.4	. .	. .	. .	(.)
98 United Arab Emirates	37.9	1.8	70.0	22.5	. .	. .	. .	. .
Industrial market economies	**4.0** w	**1.8** w	**5.4** w	**0.8** w	**4,540** w	**7,495** w	**12** w	**29** w
99 Ireland	−0.1	4.7	5.0	4.6	1,868	3,770	17	19
100 Spain	3.0	6.1	9.4	3.3	900	2,944	22	63
101 Italy	2.3	−0.4	8.1	0.6	1,452	3,725	18	35
102 New Zealand	5.7	3.0	6.2	0.8	2,759	4,816	7	23
103 United Kingdom	−1.0	11.4	2.0	−0.2	4,750	5,363	14	14
104 Japan	−1.4	3.7	10.9	2.2	1,354	4,649	18	54
105 Austria	1.4	0.7	5.3	2.5	2,482	5,102	12	22
106 Finland	3.3	4.5	9.9	1.6	1,501	6,351	11	32
107 Australia	11.0	3.0	5.8	2.8	4,020	7,214	12	13
108 Canada	8.7	1.1	5.9	2.4	7,560	13,153	9	11
109 Netherlands	16.1	0.3	9.1	1.0	3,078	8,068	15	25
110 Belgium	−7.2	4.5	5.4	1.7	3,853	7,431	11	19
111 France	−1.3	2.8	5.7	1.8	2,858	5,368	16	32
112 United States	3.5	0.9	4.2	1.6	8,408	11,626	8	38
113 Denmark	−19.8	25.3	6.0	2.6	2,748	5,746	15	26
114 Germany, Fed. Rep.	−0.6	0.0	4.4	0.9	3,859	6,053	7	22
115 Norway	6.8	21.3	5.8	4.4	5,058	11,928	15	16
116 Sweden	3.6	4.9	4.9	1.0	4,623	7,971	16	26
117 Switzerland	4.2	2.6	6.0	1.3	2,718	5,223	10	14
East European nonmarket economies	**6.6** w	**4.1** w	**5.3** w	**4.1** w	**2,884** w	**6,217** w	**. .**	**. .**
118 Albania	9.7	2.4	12.5	3.8	528	1,800	. .	. .
119 Hungary	2.7	2.7	4.9	4.4	1,710	4,094	13	17
120 Romania	5.9	0.2	7.9	5.5	1,537	4,775	. .	. .
121 Bulgaria	3.3	3.4	9.7	5.0	1,362	5,957	7	. .
122 Poland	4.0	2.8	4.3	4.3	3,108	5,799	. .	20
123 USSR	7.6	4.7	5.6	4.2	2,896	6,422	4	. .
124 Czechoslovakia	1.2	1.6	3.4	3.1	3,862	6,847	. .	19
125 German Dem. Rep.	0.6	2.0	2.2	2.0	4,609	7,412	. .	. .

a. Figures in italics are for 1961–74, not 1960–74.   b. Figures in italics are for 1961, not 1960.   c. Figures in italics are for 1979, not 1980.

Table 9. Growth of merchandise trade

	Merchandise trade (millions of dollars)		Average annual growth rate[a] (percent)				Terms of trade (1975 = 100)	
			Exports		Imports			
	Exports 1981[b]	Imports 1981[b]	1960–70	1970–81[c]	1960–70	1970–81[c]	1978	1981[b]
Low-income economies	42,444 t	60,117 t	4.9 m	−0.7 m	5.3 m	2.4 m	109 m	87 m
China and India	29,624 t	36,567 t	. .	. .	. .	. .	. .	. .
Other low-income	12,820 t	23,550 t	5.0 m	−0.8 m	5.4 m	1.9 m	110 m	88 m
1 Kampuchea, Dem.	. .	. .	. .	. .	. .	. .	. .	. .
2 Bhutan	. .	. .	. .	. .	. .	. .	. .	. .
3 Lao, PDR	9	85	. .	. .	. .	. .	. .	. .
4 Chad	141	137	5.9	−7.2	5.1	−3.8	111	101
5 Bangladesh	791	2,594	6.5	−0.7	7.1	5.1	99	79
6 Ethiopia	374	738	3.6	−0.8	6.2	(.)	158	69
7 Nepal	63	195	. .	. .	. .	. .	. .	. .
8 Burma	455	373	−11.6	1.3	−5.7	−2.8	110	123
9 Afghanistan	263	484	2.5	5.3	0.8	8.9	107	112
10 Mali	154	370	2.9	7.1	−0.4	7.4	110	102
11 Malawi	284	359	11.6	5.9	7.6	2.4	108	82
12 Zaire	662	672	−1.8	−3.1	5.5	−11.9	100	74
13 Uganda	317	395	4.9	−9.8	6.2	−9.1	144	106
14 Burundi	71	167	. .	. .	. .	. .	. .	. .
15 Upper Volta	75	338	14.6	7.3	8.0	7.6	106	98
16 Rwanda	147	191	15.8	0.4	8.0	10.7	180	107
17 India	8,064	15,001	3.2	4.6	−0.9	3.2	108	66
18 Somalia	200	199	2.4	6.7	2.6	3.2	109	98
19 Tanzania	566	1,140	3.4	−8.1	6.0	−1.2	121	113
20 Viet Nam	153	791	. .	. .	. .	. .	. .	. .
21 China	21,560	21,566	. .	. .	. .	. .	. .	. .
22 Guinea	428	351	. .	. .	. .	. .	. .	. .
23 Haiti	333	587	. .	. .	. .	. .	. .	. .
24 Sri Lanka	1,036	1,803	4.6	−1.5	−0.2	1.4	151	80
25 Benin	36	886	5.0	−7.0	7.5	5.0	101	84
26 Central African Rep.	136	88	8.1	1.9	4.5	−1.9	116	104
27 Sierra Leone	277	238	0.4	−4.4	1.9	−1.6	112	73
28 Madagascar	335	494	5.4	−2.5	4.1	−3.1	117	87
29 Niger	297	449	6.0	23.4	11.9	13.4	106	88
30 Pakistan	2,880	5,342	8.3	3.0	5.3	4.0	97	75
31 Mozambique	457	774	6.0	−15.0	7.9	−16.7	84	77
32 Sudan	658	1,529	2.2	−5.2	0.6	4.2	86	88
33 Togo	344	597	10.5	1.5	8.5	10.3	97	63
34 Ghana	878	1,184	0.2	−7.1	−1.5	−5.0	193	75
Middle-income economies	337,172 t	405,729 t	5.4 m	4.1 m	6.4 m	4.8 m	98 m	87 m
Oil exporters	146,227 t	148,221 t	3.9 m	2.5 m	2.8 m	9.5 m	95 m	133 m
Oil importers	190,945 t	257,508 t	7.0 m	4.3 m	7.6 m	3.2 m	101 m	73 m
Lower middle-income	98,497 t	122,588 t	5.2 m	3.0 m	6.5 m	4.1 m	98 m	77 m
35 Kenya	1,144	1,946	7.2	−1.9	6.5	−1.8	144	99
36 Senegal	416	1,035	1.2	−1.4	2.3	2.5	97	68
37 Mauritania	259	265	50.6	−0.3	4.6	3.2	81	72
38 Yemen Arab Rep.	39	1,699	. .	. .	. .	. .	. .	. .
39 Yemen, PDR	421	1,096	. .	. .	. .	. .	. .	. .
40 Liberia	531	448	18.4	1.2	2.9	−1.5	88	63
41 Indonesia	22,259	13,271	3.4	6.5	2.0	11.9	95	154
42 Lesotho	. .	. .	. .	. .	. .	. .	. .	. .
43 Bolivia	909	825	9.6	−1.9	8.0	7.0	129	153
44 Honduras	760	949	10.7	4.2	11.6	1.9	102	75
45 Zambia	1,044	1,032	2.3	−0.2	9.8	−6.8	89	67
46 Egypt	3,233	8,839	3.2	0.4	−0.9	9.4	83	86
47 El Salvador	792	986	5.5	0.7	6.3	2.3	129	80
48 Thailand	6,918	10,014	5.2	11.8	11.4	4.9	87	62
49 Philippines	5,722	7,946	2.2	7.7	7.2	2.6	98	68
50 Angola	1,744	1,640	9.0	−12.7	11.5	0.2	103	152
51 Papua New Guinea	851	1,116	. .	. .	. .	. .	. .	. .
52 Morocco	2,242	4,356	2.5	2.2	3.4	5.4	74	63
53 Nicaragua	529	731	9.7	0.2	10.5	−1.3	113	76
54 Nigeria	18,727	18,776	6.5	0.5	1.7	17.8	102	190
55 Zimbabwe	663	704	. .	. .	. .	. .	81	94
56 Cameroon	1.079	1,428	7.0	4.9	9.3	6.9	168	90
57 Cuba	1,128	1,897	4.0	1.2	5.4	1.6	72	65
58 Congo, People's Rep.	1,040	791	5.1	16.8	−1.0	6.7	82	96
59 Guatemala	1,281	1,774	9.0	5.0	7.1	5.2	134	77
60 Peru	3,255	3,803	2.0	4.6	3.8	0.5	90	72
61 Ecuador	2,562	2,332	2.9	5.7	11.6	9.3	107	136
62 Jamaica	974	1,473	4.6	−6.7	8.1	−6.5	107	75
63 Ivory Coast	2,586	2,434	8.7	5.1	9.7	5.7	150	78
64 Dominican Rep.	1,188	1,450	−2.3	3.8	10.0	2.2	49	49

	Merchandise trade (millions of dollars)		Average annual growth rate[a] (percent)				Terms of trade (1975 = 100)	
			Exports		Imports			
	Exports 1981[b]	Imports 1981[b]	1960–70	1970–81[c]	1960–70	1970–81[c]	1978	1981[b]
65 Mongolia	..	..	..	..	..	..	..	..
66 Colombia	3,190	5,181	2.2	1.6	2.5	6.5	145	127
67 Tunisia	2,209	3,924	4.2	4.0	2.3	9.2	81	104
68 Costa Rica	968	1,198	9.5	4.0	10.0	2.2	125	87
69 Korea, Dem. Rep.	..	..	..	..	..	..	..	..
70 Turkey	4,703	8,911	..	1.2	..	2.0	95	67
71 Syrian Arab Rep.	2,103	4,663	3.3	5.2	4.1	12.6	99	130
72 Jordan	732	3,149	10.1	21.2	3.6	13.9	74	61
73 Paraguay	296	506	5.4	6.8	7.6	6.6	110	72
Upper middle-income	238,675 t	283,141 t	5.4 m	7.0 m	5.9 m	4.7 m	97 m	89 m
74 Korea, Rep. of	21,254	26,131	33.4	22.0	20.6	10.9	105	67
75 Iran, Islamic Rep. of	10,169	12,634	12.5	–13.4	11.6	10.5	94	217
76 Iraq	9,372	18,907	5.4	–2.1	1.4	23.6	94	209
77 Malaysia	12,884	13,132	5.8	6.8	2.3	7.1	109	101
78 Panama	315	1,540	10.2	–1.9	10.5	–4.3	93	93
79 Lebanon	1,107	3,946	14.4	1.9	5.1	3.3	101	88
80 Algeria	14,056	11,505	3.5	1.0	–1.1	12.0	96	196
81 Brazil	23,172	24,007	5.0	8.7	4.9	2.9	108	56
82 Mexico	20,033	24,168	2.8	15.3	6.4	9.5	92	89
83 Portugal	4,147	9,799	9.6	..	14.2	..	..	..
84 Argentina	6,304	9,425	3.5	9.4	0.4	3.2	77	71
85 Chile	3,952	6,364	0.7	9.8	4.8	3.5	88	61
86 South Africa	22,670	21,485	5.4	7.2	8.2	–1.4	80	73
87 Yugoslavia	10,929	15,817	7.7	4.5	8.8	4.6	104	99
88 Uruguay	1,215	1,599	2.2	4.3	–2.9	3.6	124	87
89 Venezuela	20,959	10,645	1.1	–7.0	4.4	9.6	92	212
90 Greece	4,292	8,677	10.8	10.8	10.8	4.7	98	88
91 Hong Kong	21,737	24,680	12.7	9.7	9.2	12.1	103	100
92 Israel	5,416	7,777	10.8	9.6	8.8	2.2	101	68
93 Singapore	20,967	27,608	4.2	12.0	5.9	9.9	102	..
94 Trinidad and Tobago	3,725	3,115	4.9	–4.9	3.2	–5.8	96	129
High-income oil exporters	174,131 t	68,249 t	11.0 m	–1.5 m	11.0 m	20.8 m	94 m	208 m
95 Libya	16,391	15,414	67.5	–7.5	15.4	15.7	94	213
96 Saudi Arabia	120,240	35,244	11.0	4.5	11.2	33.5	94	205
97 Kuwait	16,561	8,042	5.2	–9.4	10.7	16.0	92	210
98 United Arab Emirates	20,939	9,549	..	4.5	5.5	25.6	96	189
Industrial market economies	1,210,104 t	1,290,415 t	8.5 m	5.4 m	9.5 m	4.4 m	100 m	90 m
99 Ireland	7,706	10,603	7.1	8.4	8.3	6.4	104	90
100 Spain	20,337	33,159	11.5	..	18.5	..	99	87
101 Italy	75,215	91,022	13.6	6.7	9.7	3.6	101	86
102 New Zealand	5,563	5,684	4.6	3.9	2.9	1.7	114	107
103 United Kingdom	102,807	101,991	4.8	6.6	5.0	3.6	107	105
104 Japan	152,016	143,287	17.2	9.0	13.7	3.9	112	79
105 Austria	15,845	21,048	9.6	7.3	9.6	6.7	97	88
106 Finland	14,015	14,202	6.8	4.8	7.0	2.5	92	84
107 Australia	21,767	23,768	6.5	3.8	7.2	5.2	92	92
108 Canada	69,907	66,010	10.0	4.2	9.1	5.5	93	95
109 Netherlands	68,732	65,921	9.9	5.0	9.5	3.5	100	96
110 Belgium[d]	55,705	62,464	10.9	4.6	10.3	5.3	96	90
111 France	100,497	120,924	8.2	6.6	11.0	6.5	101	90
112 United States	233,739	273,352	6.0	6.5	9.8	4.4	95	86
113 Denmark	16,317	17,874	7.1	4.9	8.2	2.5	101	87
114 Germany, Fed. Rep.	176,043	163,934	10.1	5.8	10.0	5.5	101	86
115 Norway	18,220	15,652	9.1	7.0	9.7	4.3	92	129
116 Sweden	28,630	28,824	7.7	2.2	7.2	4.2	93	87
117 Switzerland	27,043	30,696	8.5	4.2	9.0	4.5	108	102
East European nonmarket economies	150,270 t	146,968 t	9.4 m	6.7 m	8.6 m	6.1 m	..	..
118 Albania	..	..	..	..	..	..	..	..
119 Hungary	8,893	8,854	9.7	8.2	9.1	6.1	98	96
120 Romania	12,610	12,458	9.4	..	8.8	..	..	..
121 Bulgaria	1,848	2,633	14.4	11.6	12.9	8.7	..	..
122 Poland	13,182	15,224	–0.3	6.7	–0.4	6.0	101	98
123 USSR	79,003	72,960	9.7	5.6	7.1	8.3	..	..
124 Czechoslovakia	14,876	14,658	6.7	6.4	7.0	5.1	..	..
125 German Dem. Rep.	19,858	20,181	8.3	..	8.6	..	..	..

a. See the technical notes. b. Figures in italics are for 1980, not 1981. c. Figures in italics are for 1970–80, not 1970–81. d. Includes Luxembourg.

Table 10. Structure of merchandise exports

	Fuels, minerals, and metals		Other primary commodities		Textiles and clothing		Machinery and transport equipment		Other manufactures	
Percentage share of merchandise exports										
	1960[a]	1980[b]	1960[a]	1980[b]	1960[a]	1980[b]	1960[a]	1980[b]	1960[a]	1980[b]
Low-income economies	9 w	18 w	70 w	37 w	15 w	18 w	(.) w	4 w	6 w	23 w
China and India	..	20 w	..	30 w	..	18 w	..	5 w	..	27 w
Other low-income	8 w	9 w	83 w	62 w	4 w	21 w	(.) w	2 w	5 w	6 w
1 Kampuchea, Dem.	0	..	100	..	0	..	0	..	0	..
2 Bhutan	..	..	..	..	..	..	..	..	..	..
3 Lao, PDR	..	..	..	..	..	..	..	..	..	..
4 Chad	3	..	94	..	0	..	0	..	3	..
5 Bangladesh	..	(.)	..	34	..	49	..	(.)	..	17
6 Ethiopia	0	8	100	92	0	(.)	0	(.)	0	(.)
7 Nepal	..	(.)	..	69	..	24	..	0	..	7
8 Burma	4	..	95	..	0	..	0	..	1	..
9 Afghanistan	(.)	..	82	..	14	..	3	..	1	..
10 Mali	0	..	96	..	1	..	1	..	2	..
11 Malawi	..	(.)	..	90	..	5	..	4	..	1
12 Zaire	42	..	57	..	0	..	0	..	1	..
13 Uganda	8	..	92	..	0	..	0	..	(.)	..
14 Burundi	..	(.)	..	99	..	(.)	..	(.)	..	1
15 Upper Volta	0	(.)	100	89	0	2	0	2	(.)	7
16 Rwanda	..	..	..	..	..	..	..	..	..	..
17 India	10	7	45	34	35	22	1	7	9	30
18 Somalia	0	1	88	98	0	(.)	8	(.)	4	1
19 Tanzania	(.)	10	87	74	0	8	0	1	13	7
20 Viet Nam	..	..	..	..	..	..	..	..	..	..
21 China	..	25	..	28	..	16	..	5	..	26
22 Guinea	42	..	58	..	0	..	0	..	0	..
23 Haiti	0	..	100	..	0	..	0	..	0	..
24 Sri Lanka	(.)	16	99	65	0	11	0	1	0	7
25 Benin	10	..	80	..	7	..	(.)	..	3	..
26 Central African Rep.	12	(.)	86	74	(.)	(.)	1	(.)	1	26
27 Sierra Leone	15	..	20	..	0	..	0	..	65	..
28 Madagascar	4	9	90	84	1	2	1	2	4	3
29 Niger	..	..	100	..	0	..	0	..	0	..
30 Pakistan	0	7	73	43	23	37	1	2	3	11
31 Mozambique	0	..	100	..	0	..	0	..	0	..
32 Sudan	0	1	100	96	0	1	0	2	0	(.)
33 Togo	3	58	89	32	3	4	0	3	5	3
34 Ghana	7	..	83	..	0	..	0	..	10	..
Middle-income economies	30 w	36 w	59 w	27 w	3 w	9 w	1 w	10 w	7 w	18 w
Oil exporters	48 w	78 w	48 w	15 w	1 w	2 w	(.) w	2 w	3 w	3 w
Oil importers	15 w	12 w	68 w	34 w	5 w	13 w	2 w	14 w	10 w	27 w
Lower middle-income	20 w	44 w	76 w	38 w	1 w	5 w	(.) w	2 w	3 w	11 w
35 Kenya	1	34	87	50	0	1	0	3	12	12
36 Senegal	3	39	94	46	1	1	1	3	1	11
37 Mauritania	4	..	69	..	1	..	20	..	6	..
38 Yemen Arab Rep.	..	(.)	..	49	..	6	..	25	..	20
39 Yemen, PDR	..	75	..	25	..	(.)	..	(.)	..	(.)
40 Liberia	45	59	55	38	0	(.)	0	1	0	2
41 Indonesia	33	76	67	22	0	1	(.)	(.)	(.)	1
42 Lesotho	..	..	..	..	..	..	..	..	..	..
43 Bolivia	..	86	..	11	..	(.)	..	1	..	2
44 Honduras	5	7	93	81	0	2	0	(.)	2	10
45 Zambia	..	..	..	..	..	..	..	..	..	..
46 Egypt	4	67	84	22	9	9	(.)	(.)	3	2
47 El Salvador	0	5	94	59	3	13	(.)	3	3	20
48 Thailand	7	14	91	57	0	9	0	6	2	14
49 Philippines	10	21	86	42	1	6	0	2	3	29
50 Angola	..	..	..	..	..	..	..	..	..	..
51 Papua New Guinea	0	46	92	52	0	(.)	0	(.)	8	2
52 Morocco	38	45	54	31	1	10	1	1	6	13
53 Nicaragua	3	3	95	83	0	2	0	(.)	2	12
54 Nigeria	8	95	89	4	0	(.)	0	(.)	3	1
55 Zimbabwe	71	..	25	..	1	..	(.)	..	3	..
56 Cameroon	19	33	77	64	0	1	2	(.)	2	2
57 Cuba	2	5	93	90	1	0	(.)	0	4	5
58 Congo, People's Rep.	7	86	84	7	(.)	(.)	5	(.)	4	7
59 Guatemala	2	6	95	70	1	6	0	1	2	17
60 Peru	49	64	50	20	0	6	0	2	1	8
61 Ecuador	0	56	99	41	0	1	0	1	1	1
62 Jamaica	50	23	45	14	2	1	0	3	3	59
63 Ivory Coast	1	5	98	87	0	3	(.)	2	1	3
64 Dominican Rep.	6	3	92	73	0	(.)	0	1	2	23

	Percentage share of merchandise exports									
	Fuels, minerals, and metals		Other primary commodities		Textiles and clothing		Machinery and transport equipment		Other manufactures	
	1960[a]	1980[b]	1960[a]	1980[b]	1960[a]	1980[b]	1960[a]	1980[b]	1960[a]	1980[b]
65 Mongolia	..	..	..	..	..	..	..	..	..	..
66 Colombia	19	3	79	77	0	6	(.)	2	2	12
67 Tunisia	24	56	66	8	1	18	1	2	8	16
68 Costa Rica	0	1	95	65	0	5	0	4	5	25
69 Korea, Dem. Rep.	..	..	..	..	..	..	..	..	..	..
70 Turkey	8	8	89	65	0	16	0	3	3	8
71 Syrian Arab Rep.	0	74	81	*18*	2	4	0	*1*	17	*3*
72 Jordan	0	29	96	35	0	4	0	9	4	23
73 Paraguay	0	*(.)*	100	*88*	0	*(.)*	0	*(.)*	0	*12*
Upper middle-income	**38** *w*	**32** *w*	**46** *w*	**23** *w*	**4** *w*	**10** *w*	**2** *w*	**13** *w*	**10** *w*	**22** *w*
74 Korea, Rep. of	30	1	56	9	8	29	(.)	20	6	41
75 Iran, Islamic Rep. of	88	..	9	..	0	..	0	..	3	..
76 Iraq	97	..	3	..	0	..	0	..	0	..
77 Malaysia	20	35	74	46	(.)	2	(.)	11	6	6
78 Panama	..	24	..	67	..	3	..	(.)	..	6
79 Lebanon	..	..	..	..	..	..	..	..	..	..
80 Algeria	12	99	81	1	0	(.)	1	(.)	6	(.)
81 Brazil	8	11	89	50	0	4	(.)	17	3	18
82 Mexico	24	*39*	64	*22*	4	*3*	1	*19*	7	*17*
83 Portugal	8	7	37	21	18	27	3	13	34	32
84 Argentina	1	6	95	71	0	2	(.)	7	4	14
85 Chile	92	59	4	*21*	0	*(.)*	0	*1*	4	*19*
86 South Africa	29	*23*	42	*23*	2	*1*	4	*5*	23	*48*
87 Yugoslavia	18	9	45	18	4	9	15	28	18	36
88 Uruguay	..	1	71	61	21	16	..	4	8	18
89 Venezuela	74	98	26	(.)	0	(.)	0	(.)	(.)	2
90 Greece	9	25	81	28	1	17	1	3	8	27
91 Hong Kong	5	2	15	5	45	34	4	19	31	40
92 Israel	4	2	35	16	8	8	2	13	51	61
93 Singapore	1	28	73	18	5	4	7	26	14	24
94 Trinidad and Tobago	82	93	14	2	0	(.)	0	1	4	4
High-income oil exporters	..	**98** *w*	..	**(.)** *w*	..	**(.)** *w*	..	**1** *w*	..	**1** *w*
95 Libya	100	100	0	(.)	0	(.)	0	(.)	0	(.)
96 Saudi Arabia	95	99	5	(.)	0	(.)	0	(.)	0	1
97 Kuwait	..	89	..	1	..	1	..	3	..	6
98 United Arab Emirates	..	..	..	..	..	..	..	..	..	..
Industrial market economies	**11** *w*	**13** *w*	**23** *w*	**15** *w*	**7** *w*	**5** *w*	**29** *w*	**35** *w*	**30** *w*	**32** *w*
99 Ireland	5	3	67	39	6	8	4	19	18	31
100 Spain	21	8	57	20	7	5	2	26	13	41
101 Italy	8	7	19	8	17	11	29	33	27	41
102 New Zealand	(.)	7	97	72	0	3	(.)	5	3	13
103 United Kingdom	7	18	9	8	8	4	44	35	32	35
104 Japan	11	2	10	2	28	4	23	55	28	37
105 Austria	26	5	22	12	10	9	16	28	26	46
106 Finland	3	8	50	22	1	7	13	18	33	45
107 Australia	13	28	79	44	(.)	1	3	7	5	20
108 Canada	33	28	37	23	1	1	8	26	21	22
109 Netherlands	15	26	34	23	8	4	18	17	25	30
110 Belgium[c]	15	15	9	11	12	7	13	22	51	45
111 France	9	8	18	18	10	5	25	34	38	35
112 United States	10	9	27	23	3	2	35	40	25	26
113 Denmark	2	5	63	38	3	5	19	24	13	28
114 Germany, Fed. Rep.	9	7	4	7	4	5	44	45	39	36
115 Norway	22	59	34	9	2	1	10	12	32	19
116 Sweden	10	9	29	12	1	2	31	40	29	37
117 Switzerland	2	5	8	4	12	6	30	33	48	50
East European nonmarket economies	**18** *w*	..	**33** *w*	..	**3** *w*	..	**34** *w*	..	**21** *w*	..
118 Albania	..	..	..	..	..	..	..	..	..	..
119 Hungary	6	9	28	25	7	7	38	32	21	27
120 Romania	..	..	..	..	..	..	..	..	..	..
121 Bulgaria	3	..	75	..	12	..	6	..	4	..
122 Poland	..	20	..	9	..	6	..	36	..	29
123 USSR	24	..	28	..	1	..	21	..	26	..
124 Czechoslovakia	20	7	11	9	(.)	5	45	50	25	29
125 German Dem. Rep.	..	..	..	..	..	..	..	..	..	..

a. Figures in italics are for 1961, not 1960.   b. Figures in italics are for 1979, not 1980.   c. Includes Luxembourg.

Table 11. Structure of merchandise imports

Percentage share of merchandise imports

	Food		Fuels		Other primary commodities		Machinery and transport equipment		Other manufactures	
	1960[a]	1980[b]	1960[a]	1980[b]	1960[a]	1980[b]	1960[a]	1980[b]	1960[a]	1980[b]
Low-income economies	22 w	14 w	7 w	14 w	18 w	17 w	26 w	25 w	27 w	30 w
China and India	..	13 w	..	10 w	..	23 w	..	24 w	..	30 w
Other low-income	24 w	16 w	8 w	21 w	4 w	4 w	21 w	28 w	43 w	31 w
1 Kampuchea, Dem.	..	..	..	..	..	..	..	..	..	..
2 Bhutan	..	..	..	..	..	..	..	..	..	..
3 Lao, PDR	..	..	..	..	..	..	..	..	..	..
4 Chad	19	..	12	..	4	..	19	..	46	..
5 Bangladesh	..	25	..	11	..	8	..	24	..	32
6 Ethiopia	..	8	..	25	..	3	..	28	..	36
7 Nepal	..	4	..	18	..	2	..	32	..	44
8 Burma	14	..	4	..	9	..	17	..	56	..
9 Afghanistan	14	..	7	..	4	..	14	..	61	..
10 Mali	20	..	5	..	4	..	18	..	53	..
11 Malawi	..	8	..	15	..	2	..	34	..	41
12 Zaire	..	..	..	..	..	..	..	..	..	..
13 Uganda	6	..	8	..	8	..	25	..	53	..
14 Burundi	..	13	..	9	..	3	..	22	..	53
15 Upper Volta	21	21	4	13	1	3	24	29	50	34
16 Rwanda	..	..	..	..	..	..	..	..	..	..
17 India	21	9	6	33	28	10	30	16	15	32
18 Somalia	27	19	4	5	0	7	18	33	51	36
19 Tanzania	..	13	..	21	..	3	..	35	..	28
20 Viet Nam	..	..	..	..	..	..	..	..	..	..
21 China	..	15	..	0	..	29	..	27	..	29
22 Guinea	..	..	..	..	..	..	..	..	..	..
23 Haiti	..	..	..	..	..	..	..	..	..	..
24 Sri Lanka	39	20	7	24	5	3	15	25	34	28
25 Benin	17	..	10	..	1	..	18	..	54	..
26 Central African Rep.	15	21	9	2	2	3	26	34	48	40
27 Sierra Leone	23	..	12	..	5	..	15	..	45	..
28 Madagascar	17	9	6	15	3	4	23	34	51	38
29 Niger	24	..	5	..	4	..	18	..	49	..
30 Pakistan	22	13	10	27	2	6	27	25	39	29
31 Mozambique	..	..	..	..	..	..	..	..	..	..
32 Sudan	17	26	8	13	3	2	14	29	58	30
33 Togo	16	14	6	18	3	1	32	29	43	38
34 Ghana	19	..	5	..	4	..	26	..	46	..
Middle-income economies	15 w	11 w	9 w	19 w	13 w	7 w	28 w	31 w	35 w	32 w
Oil exporters	19 w	14 w	7 w	7 w	8 w	5 w	27 w	39 w	39 w	35 w
Oil importers	14 w	10 w	10 w	23 w	16 w	8 w	29 w	28 w	31 w	31 w
Lower middle-income	16 w	14 w	7 w	18 w	9 w	5 w	28 w	30 w	40 w	33 w
35 Kenya	12	8	11	34	8	3	27	28	42	27
36 Senegal	30	25	5	25	2	1	19	23	44	26
37 Mauritania	5	..	3	..	3	..	39	..	50	..
38 Yemen Arab Rep.	..	28	..	7	..	1	..	28	..	36
39 Yemen, PDR	..	17	..	47	..	1	..	23	..	12
40 Liberia	16	19	4	28	7	2	34	28	39	23
41 Indonesia	23	13	5	16	10	6	17	34	45	31
42 Lesotho	..	..	..	..	..	..	..	..	..	..
43 Bolivia	..	10	..	1	..	2	..	44	..	43
44 Honduras	13	10	9	16	3	2	24	30	51	42
45 Zambia	..	..	..	..	..	..	..	..	..	..
46 Egypt	23	32	11	1	16	8	25	27	25	32
47 El Salvador	17	18	6	18	6	4	26	13	45	47
48 Thailand	10	5	11	30	11	7	25	25	43	33
49 Philippines	15	8	10	28	5	5	36	24	34	35
50 Angola	..	..	..	..	..	..	..	..	..	..
51 Papua New Guinea	30	..	5	..	4	..	23	..	38	..
52 Morocco	27	20	8	24	7	10	19	21	39	25
53 Nicaragua	9	15	10	20	5	1	22	14	54	50
54 Nigeria	14	17	5	2	6	3	24	39	51	39
55 Zimbabwe	..	..	..	..	..	..	..	..	..	..
56 Cameroon	20	9	8	12	3	2	17	34	52	43
57 Cuba	..	..	..	..	..	..	..	..	..	..
58 Congo, People's Rep.	18	27	6	6	1	1	31	26	44	40
59 Guatemala	12	8	10	24	7	7	26	22	45	39
60 Peru	16	20	5	2	5	5	37	40	37	33
61 Ecuador	13	8	3	1	9	4	33	49	42	38
62 Jamaica	22	20	8	38	9	3	24	12	37	27
63 Ivory Coast	18	15	6	11	2	2	27	35	47	37
64 Dominican Rep.	..	17	..	25	..	4	..	22	..	32

	Percentage share of merchandise imports									
	Food		Fuels		Other primary commodities		Machinery and transport equipment		Other manufactures	
	1960[a]	1980[b]	1960[a]	1980[b]	1960[a]	1980[b]	1960[a]	1980[b]	1960[a]	1980[b]
65 Mongolia	..	..	..	..	..	..	..	..	..	..
66 Colombia	8	12	3	12	15	6	43	38	31	32
67 Tunisia	20	14	9	21	4	8	23	23	44	34
68 Costa Rica	13	9	6	15	6	4	26	24	49	48
69 Korea, Dem. Rep.	..	..	..	..	..	..	..	..	..	..
70 Turkey	7	4	11	48	16	5	42	18	24	25
71 Syrian Arab Rep.	24	14	8	25	5	4	15	23	48	34
72 Jordan	..	18	..	17	..	3	..	28	..	34
73 Paraguay	..	13	..	24	..	1	..	36	..	26
Upper middle-income	**15** w	**10** w	**9** w	**19** w	**15** w	**8** w	**28** w	**32** w	**33** w	**31** w
74 Korea, Rep. of	10	10	7	30	25	17	12	22	46	21
75 Iran, Islamic Rep. of	14	13	1	(.)	1	5	23	44	61	38
76 Iraq	..	..	..	..	..	..	..	..	..	..
77 Malaysia	29	12	16	15	13	6	14	39	28	28
78 Panama	15	10	10	31	1	1	22	21	52	37
79 Lebanon	..	..	..	..	..	..	14	37	54	35
80 Algeria	26	21	4	2	2	5	14	37	54	35
81 Brazil	14	10	19	43	13	6	36	19	18	22
82 Mexico	4	8	2	2	10	7	52	50	32	33
83 Portugal	15	14	10	24	28	11	26	25	21	26
84 Argentina	3	6	13	10	11	7	44	40	29	37
85 Chile	..	14	..	21	..	4	..	27	..	34
86 South Africa	6	5	7	1	9	6	37	52	41	36
87 Yugoslavia	11	8	5	24	25	12	37	28	22	28
88 Uruguay	5	8	24	29	46	7	17	30	8	26
89 Venezuela	18	15	1	2	10	5	36	43	35	35
90 Greece	11	9	8	23	16	8	44	36	21	24
91 Hong Kong	27	12	3	6	16	6	10	22	44	54
92 Israel	20	11	7	26	18	6	28	21	27	36
93 Singapore	21	9	15	29	38	7	7	29	19	26
94 Trinidad and Tobago	16	11	34	38	7	3	18	25	25	23
High-income oil exporters	..	**15** w	..	**2** w	..	**2** w	..	**38** w	..	**43** w
95 Libya	13	19	5	1	10	2	40	38	32	40
96 Saudi Arabia	..	14	..	1	..	2	..	39	..	44
97 Kuwait	..	15	..	1	..	2	..	36	..	46
98 United Arab Emirates	..	11	..	10	..	2	..	38	..	39
Industrial market economies	**22** w	**11** w	**11** w	**27** w	**24** w	**10** w	**16** w	**22** w	**27** w	**30** w
99 Ireland	18	12	12	15	11	5	21	27	38	41
100 Spain	16	13	22	39	25	11	22	18	15	19
101 Italy	20	13	14	28	31	13	13	21	22	25
102 New Zealand	8	6	8	22	16	6	29	30	39	36
103 United Kingdom	36	13	11	13	27	11	8	26	18	37
104 Japan	17	12	17	50	49	19	9	6	8	13
105 Austria	16	6	10	15	20	9	29	29	25	41
106 Finland	13	7	10	29	20	7	33	27	24	30
107 Australia	6	5	10	14	16	5	31	36	37	40
108 Canada	12	8	9	12	12	7	36	46	31	27
109 Netherlands	18	15	13	24	14	7	22	20	33	34
110 Belgium[c]	15	11	10	17	26	11	21	22	28	39
111 France	25	10	17	27	25	9	14	21	19	33
112 United States	24	8	10	33	25	7	10	25	31	27
113 Denmark	18	11	12	22	11	8	23	20	36	39
114 Germany, Fed. Rep.	26	12	8	23	28	10	10	19	28	36
115 Norway	12	8	9	17	13	8	36	29	30	38
116 Sweden	13	7	14	24	13	7	26	27	34	35
117 Switzerland	18	8	8	11	13	10	21	24	40	47
East European nonmarket economies	..	..	..	..	..	..	..	..	..	..
118 Albania	..	..	..	..	..	..	..	..	..	..
119 Hungary	8	8	12	16	28	13	28	29	24	34
120 Romania	..	..	..	..	..	..	..	..	..	..
121 Bulgaria	..	..	..	..	..	..	..	..	..	..
122 Poland	..	14	..	18	..	11	..	27	..	30
123 USSR	12	..	4	..	18	..	30	..	36	..
124 Czechoslovakia	..	10	..	19	..	15	..	36	..	20
125 German Dem. Rep.	..	..	..	..	..	..	..	..	..	..

a. Figures in italics are for 1961, not 1960.   b. Figures in italics are for 1979, not 1980.   c. Includes Luxembourg.

Table 12. Origin and destination of merchandise exports

Origin	Destination of merchandise exports (percentage of total)							
	Industrial market economies		East European nonmarket economies		High-income oil exporters		Developing economies	
	1960	1981[a]	1960	1981[a]	1960	1981[a]	1960	1981[a]
Low-income economies	51 w	50 w	21 w	5 w	1 w	4 w	27 w	41
China and India	39 w	49 w	36 w	6 w	(.) w	3 w	25 w	42w
Other low-income	66 w	52 w	3 w	5 w	2 w	7 w	29 w	36w
1 Kampuchea, Dem.	..	..	..	..	..	..	..	..
2 Bhutan	..	..	..	..	..	..	..	..
3 Lao, PDR	..	61	..	0	..	6	..	33
4 Chad	73	44	0	0	0	7	27	49
5 Bangladesh	..	34	..	8	..	1	..	57
6 Ethiopia	69	56	1	11	6	8	24	25
7 Nepal	..	50	..	0	..	(.)	..	50
8 Burma	23	25	3	1	(.)	2	74	72
9 Afghanistan	48	46	28	21	0	3	24	30
10 Mali	93	62	0	1	(.)	(.)	7	37
11 Malawi	..	83	..	0	..	0	..	17
12 Zaire	89	64	(.)	1	(.)	(.)	11	35
13 Uganda	62	78	0	(.)	0	3	38	19
14 Burundi	..	74	..	(.)	..	0	..	26
15 Upper Volta	4	39	0	(.)	0	(.)	96	61
16 Rwanda	..	61	..	0	..	(.)	..	39
17 India	66	58	7	10	2	6	25	26
18 Somalia	85	10	..	(.)	(.)	76	15	14
19 Tanzania	74	51	1	4	0	(.)	25	45
20 Viet Nam	..	40	..	9	..	(.)	..	51
21 China	14	46	61	4	(.)	2	25	48
22 Guinea	63	82	8	(.)	(.)	(.)	19	18
23 Haiti	98	97	(.)	(.)	0	(.)	2	3
24 Sri Lanka	75	42	3	4	0	6	22	48
25 Benin	90	75	2	(.)	0	(.)	8	25
26 Central African Rep.	83	77	0	(.)	0	(.)	17	23
27 Sierra Leone	99	90	0	0	0	(.)	1	10
28 Madagascar	79	75	1	1	0	(.)	20	24
29 Niger	74	64	0	(.)	0	15	26	21
30 Pakistan	56	36	4	4	2	18	38	42
31 Mozambique	29	39	(.)	0	(.)	3	71	58
32 Sudan	59	48	8	21	4	7	29	24
33 Togo	74	52	0	2	0	(.)	26	46
34 Ghana	88	77	7	10	(.)	(.)	5	13
Middle-income economies	68 w	65 w	7 w	4 w	(.) w	2 w	25 w	29w
Oil exporters	68 w	73 w	4 w	1 w	(.) w	(.)	28 w	26w
Oil importers	68 w	59 w	9 w	6 w	(.) w	4 w	23 w	31w
Lower middle-income	73 w	70 w	7 w	3 w	1 w	2 w	19 w	25w
35 Kenya	77	50	0	1	(.)	1	23	48
36 Senegal	89	40	0	1	0	(.)	11	59
37 Mauritania	89	92	0	(.)	0	(.)	11	8
38 Yemen Arab Rep.	46	48	18	3	(.)	11	36	38
39 Yemen, PDR	42	21	(.)	(.)	2	42	56	37
40 Liberia	100	92	0	2	0	1	(.)	5
41 Indonesia	54	74	11	1	(.)	(.)	42	25
42 Lesotho	..	..	..	..	..	..	..	..
43 Bolivia	88	46	0	16	0	3	12	35
44 Honduras	77	86	0	(.)	0	(.)	23	14
45 Zambia	..	71	..	1	..	(.)	..	28
46 Egypt	26	52	33	9	2	3	39	36
47 El Salvador	88	76	0	(.)	0	(.)	12	24
48 Thailand	47	53	2	5	3	5	48	37
49 Philippines	94	75	0	3	(.)	1	6	21
50 Angola	64	68	2	3	0	1	34	28
51 Papua New Guinea	..	91	..	0	..	0	..	9
52 Morocco	74	67	3	10	(.)	3	23	20
53 Nicaragua	91	69	(.)	(.)	0	(.)	9	31
54 Nigeria	95	85	1	(.)	0	(.)	4	15
55 Zimbabwe	..	..	..	..	..	..	..	..
56 Cameroon	93	93	1	(.)	(.)	(.)	6	7
57 Cuba	72	..	19	..	(.)	..	9	..
58 Congo, People's Rep.	93	81	0	(.)	0	(.)	7	19
59 Guatemala	94	51	0	1	0	2	6	47
60 Peru	84	66	(.)	4	0	(.)	16	30
61 Ecuador	91	60	1	1	0	(.)	8	39
62 Jamaica	96	81	0	5	0	(.)	4	14
63 Ivory Coast	84	70	0	5	0	(.)	16	25
64 Dominican Rep.	92	84	0	1	1	(.)	7	15

	Destination of merchandise exports (percentage of total)							
	Industrial market economies		East European nonmarket economies		High-income oil exporters		Developing economies	
Origin	1960	1981[a]	1960	1981[a]	1960	1981[a]	1960	1981[a]
65 Mongolia	..	..	..	..	..	..	..	..
66 Colombia	94	70	1	4	0	(.)	5	26
67 Tunisia	76	75	3	1	2	4	19	20
68 Costa Rica	93	62	(.)	2	(.)	(.)	7	36
69 Korea, Dem. Rep.	..	..	..	..	..	..	..	..
70 Turkey	71	47	12	7	(.)	15	17	31
71 Syrian Arab Rep.	39	60	19	18	11	7	31	15
72 Jordan	1	6	11	7	26	32	62	55
73 Paraguay	61	47	0	0	0	0	39	53
Upper middle-income	**67** w	**63** w	**6** w	**4** w	**(.)**	**3** w	**28** w	**30** w
74 Korea, Rep. of	89	67	0	(.)	0	10	11	23
75 Iran, Islamic Rep. of,	62	55	3	(.)	1	1	34	44
76 Iraq	85	47	1	(.)	(.)	(.)	14	53
77 Malaysia	58	53	7	3	0	1	35	43
78 Panama	99	72	0	(.)	0	1	1	27
79 Lebanon	21	10	8	8	32	51	39	31
80 Algeria	93	89	0	2	(.)	(.)	7	9
81 Brazil	81	54	6	7	(.)	1	13	38
82 Mexico	93	91	(.)	(.)	0	0	7	9
83 Portugal	56	77	2	2	(.)	1	42	20
84 Argentina	75	45	5	25	(.)	(.)	20	30
85 Chile	91	67	(.)	(.)	(.)	2	9	31
86 South Africa	71	80	1	(.)	(.)	0	28	20
87 Yugoslavia	48	31	31	49	1	3	20	17
88 Uruguay	82	54	7	8	0	2	11	36
89 Venezuela	62	71	0	(.)	0	(.)	38	29
90 Greece	65	56	21	8	1	13	13	23
91 Hong Kong	54	60	(.)	(.)	1	3	45	37
92 Israel	76	68	1	1	0	(.)	23	31
93 Singapore	38	41	4	1	1	7	57	51
94 Trinidad and Tobago	80	76	0	(.)	(.)	(.)	20	24
High-income oil exporters	**83** w	**64** w	**(.)** w	**(.)** w	**0** w	**8** w	**17** w	**28** w
95 Libya	67	86	7	(.)	0	(.)	26	14
96 Saudi Arabia	74	72	0	(.)	0	3	26	25
97 Kuwait	..	51	..	1	..	4	..	44
98 United Arab Emirates	91	12	0	(.)	0	45	9	43
Industrial market economies	**67** w	**65** w	**3** w	**3** w	**(.)** w	**4** w	**30** w	**28** w
99 Ireland	96	85	(.)	1	(.)	3	4	11
100 Spain	80	56	2	4	(.)	5	18	35
101 Italy	65	61	4	3	2	10	29	26
102 New Zealand	95	63	1	4	(.)	2	4	31
103 United Kingdom	57	68	3	2	2	6	38	24
104 Japan	45	46	2	3	2	7	51	44
105 Austria	69	69	13	11	(.)	3	18	17
106 Finland	69	62	19	27	(.)	1	12	10
107 Australia	75	50	3	4	1	3	21	43
108 Canada	90	84	1	3	(.)	1	9	12
109 Netherlands	78	81	1	2	1	3	20	14
110 Belgium[b]	79	83	2	2	1	2	18	13
111 France	53	66	3	4	(.)	4	44	26
112 United States	61	55	1	2	1	4	37	39
113 Denmark	83	81	4	2	(.)	2	13	15
114 Germany, Fed. Rep.	70	72	4	4	1	3	25	21
115 Norway	80	88	4	2	(.)	(.)	16	10
116 Sweden	79	76	4	4	(.)	3	17	17
117 Switzerland	72	70	3	3	1	4	24	23
East European nonmarket economies	**19**	**30** w	**59**	**53** w	**(.)**	**1** w	**22** w	**16** w
118 Albania	1	..	93	..	0	..	6	..
119 Hungary	22	27	61	53	(.)	2	17	18
120 Romania	20	35	66	37	(.)	2	14	26
121 Bulgaria	13	16	80	69	(.)	6	7	9
122 Poland	29	34	54	53	(.)	3	17	10
123 USSR	18	32	51	49	(.)	(.)	31	19
124 Czechoslovakia	16	22	67	65	(.)	3	17	10
125 German Dem. Rep.	19	24	68	65	(.)	1	13	10

a. Figures in italics are for 1980, not 1981.   b. Includes Luxembourg.

Table 13. Origin and destination of manufactured exports

Origin	Industrial market economies 1962[a]	Industrial market economies 1980[b]	East European nonmarket economies 1962[a]	East European nonmarket economies 1980[b]	High-income oil exporters 1962[a]	High-income oil exporters 1980[b]	Developing economies 1962[a]	Developing economies 1980[b]	Value of manufactured exports (millions of dollars) 1962[a]	Value of manufactured exports (millions of dollars) 1980[b]
Low-income economies	57 *w*	56 *w*	4 *w*	10 *w*	2 *w*	7 *w*	37 *w*	27 *w*		
China and India	..	..	..	..	..	..	..	..		
Other low-income	61 *w*	53 *w*	1 *w*	7 *w*	1 *w*	6 *w*	37 *w*	34 *w*		
1 Kampuchea, Dem.	30	..	1	..	(.)	..	70	..	1	..
2 Bhutan	..	..	..	..	..	..	..	..	..	..
3 Lao, PDR	35	..	0	..	0	..	65	..	(.)	..
4 Chad	19	..	0	..	6	..	75	..	1	..
5 Bangladesh	..	48	..	11	..	(.)	..	41	..	437
6 Ethiopia	47	43	2	9	1	6	50	42	2	1
7 Nepal	..	73	..	(.)	..	(.)	..	27	..	29
8 Burma	58	..	(.)	..	0	..	42	..	3	..
9 Afghanistan	96	..	1	..	0	..	3	..	9	..
10 Mali	33	..	1	..	0	..	66	..	(.)	..
11 Malawi	..	19	..	(.)	..	(.)	..	81	..	31
12 Zaire	93	..	0	..	0	..	7	..	12	..
13 Uganda	15	..	0	..	0	..	85	..	(.)	..
14 Burundi	..	40	..	(.)	..	(.)	..	60	..	1
15 Upper Volta	19	27	0	(.)	0	(.)	81	73	1	10
16 Rwanda	90	..	0	..	0	..	10	..	(.)	..
17 India	56	58	5	11	2	8	37	23	630	4,117
18 Somalia	61	48	0	1	4	2	35	49	(.)	1
19 Tanzania	93	58	0	(.)	0	(.)	7	42	16	83
20 Viet Nam	10	..	0	..	0	..	90	..	1	..
21 China	..	..	..	..	..	..	..	..	..	8,150
22 Guinea	..	..	..	..	..	..	..	..	..	..
23 Haiti	..	..	..	..	..	..	..	..	..	..
24 Sri Lanka	63	72	2	(.)	(.)	2	35	26	6	198
25 Benin	18	..	0	..	0	..	82	..	(.)	..
26 Central African Rep.	78	69	2	(.)	0	(.)	20	31	3	29
27 Sierra Leone	98	..	0	..	0	..	2	..	21	..
28 Madagascar	87	95	0	(.)	0	(.)	13	5	5	24
29 Niger	7	..	0	..	0	..	93	..	1	..
30 Pakistan	46	52	(.)	8	1	9	53	31	97	1,285
31 Mozambique	31	..	0	..	0	..	69	..	3	..
32 Sudan	37	46	1	6	3	32	59	16	(.)	15
33 Togo	44	31	0	(.)	0	(.)	56	69	1	20
34 Ghana	39	..	11	..	(.)	..	50	..	12	..
Middle-income economies	50 *w*	56 *w*	5 *w*	5 *w*	1 *w*	4 *w*	44 *w*	35 *w*		
Oil exporters	61 *w*	59 *w*	5 *w*	3 *w*	1 *w*	2 *w*	33 *w*	36 *w*		
Oil importers	48 *w*	56 *w*	5 *w*	5 *w*	1 *w*	4 *w*	46 *w*	35 *w*		
Lower middle-income	53 *w*	53 *w*	8 *w*	3 *w*	1 *w*	3 *w*	38 *w*	41 *w*		
35 Kenya	22	12	0	(.)	2	7	76	81	11	210
36 Senegal	76	30	0	(.)	0	(.)	24	70	5	72
37 Mauritania	98	..	0	..	0	..	2	..	2	..
38 Yemen Arab Rep.	..	59	..	(.)	..	7	..	34	..	11
39 Yemen, PDR	..	..	..	..	..	..	..	..	..	..
40 Liberia	94	49	(.)	(.)	0	(.)	6	51	3	20
41 Indonesia	52	33	1	(.)	1	3	46	64	2	533
42 Lesotho	..	..	..	..	..	..	..	..	..	..
43 Bolivia	82	71	0	(.)	0	(.)	18	29	4	23
44 Honduras	1	29	0	(.)	0	(.)	99	71	2	102
45 Zambia	..	..	..	..	..	..	..	..	..	..
46 Egypt	23	45	35	38	3	4	39	13	69	333
47 El Salvador	1	5	0	(.)	0	(.)	99	95	11	255
48 Thailand	51	56	(.)	(.)	(.)	5	49	39	21	1,886
49 Philippines	91	75	0	(.)	(.)	1	9	24	26	2,141
50 Angola	34	..	4	..	0	..	62	..	21	..
51 Papua New Guinea	97	83	0	2	0	(.)	3	15	4	17
52 Morocco	52	55	2	6	(.)	(.)	46	35	28	565
53 Nicaragua	55	5	0	(.)	0	(.)	45	95	2	57
54 Nigeria	91	93	(.)	1	(.)	(.)	9	6	34	137
55 Zimbabwe	44	..	0	..	0	..	56	..	31	..
56 Cameroon	25	78	0	(.)	0	(.)	75	22	4	50
57 Cuba	1	(.)	83	(.)	0	(.)	16	100	6	319
58 Congo, People's Rep.	88	90	0	(.)	0	(.)	12	10	14	39
59 Guatemala	46	6	0	(.)	0	(.)	54	94	8	359
60 Peru	53	37	0	1	0	(.)	47	62	5	553
61 Ecuador	46	15	0	(.)	0	(.)	54	85	2	57
62 Jamaica	73	74	0	8	0	1	27	17	20	611
63 Ivory Coast	61	35	0	(.)	0	(.)	39	65	2	212
64 Dominican Rep.	98	87	0	(.)	0	(.)	2	13	4	166

	Destination of manufactured exports (percentage of total)								Value of manufactured exports (millions of dollars)	
	Industrial market economies		East European nonmarket economies		High-income oil exporters		Developing economies			
Origin	1962[a]	1980[b]	1962[a]	1980[b]	1962[a]	1980[b]	1962[a]	1980[b]	1962[a]	1980[b]
65 Mongolia	. .	. .	. .	. .	. .	. .	. .	. .	. .	. .
66 Colombia	57	37	0	1	0	(.)	43	62	16	804
67 Tunisia	64	78	0	2	7	1	29	19	10	801
68 Costa Rica	78	15	0	(.)	0	(.)	22	85	9	354
69 Korea, Dem. Rep.	. .	. .	. .	. .	. .	. .	. .	. .	. .	. .
70 Turkey	73	61	17	8	(.)	5	10	26	4	782
71 Syrian Arab Rep.	17	13	7	17	1	31	75	39	9	125
72 Jordan	12	13	10	(.)	32	36	46	51	1	201
73 Paraguay	84	37	0	(.)	0	(.)	16	63	4	34
Upper middle-income	**50** w	**56** w	**4** w	**5** w	**1** w	**5** w	**45** w	**34** w		
74 Korea, Rep. of	83	64	0	(.)	0	9	17	27	10	15,722
75 Iran, Islamic Rep. of	45	. .	1	. .	3	. .	51	. .	44	. .
76 Iraq	26	. .	(.)	. .	8	. .	66	. .	2	. .
77 Malaysia	11	66	0	(.)	(.)	2	89	32	58	2,464
78 Panama	24	11	0	(.)	0	1	76	88	1	31
79 Lebanon	22	. .	4	. .	14	. .	60	. .	11	. .
80 Algeria	50	58	0	36	0	(.)	50	6	23	49
81 Brazil	60	42	3	2	0	1	37	55	39	7,770
82 Mexico	71	82	0	1	0	(.)	29	17	122	3,389
83 Portugal	56	81	(.)	1	(.)	1	44	17	205	3,322
84 Argentina	62	42	3	5	0	(.)	35	53	39	1,861
85 Chile	45	29	0	(.)	0	2	55	69	20	758
86 South Africa	54	69	(.)	(.)	(.)	(.)	46	31	317	5,166
87 Yugoslavia	31	30	30	49	1	3	38	18	344	6,570
88 Uruguay	75	47	13	2	0	(.)	12	51	7	404
89 Venezuela	94	54	0	(.)	0	(.)	6	46	158	330
90 Greece	52	56	6	5	3	13	39	26	27	2,441
91 Hong Kong	63	64	0	(.)	1	4	36	32	642	18,208
92 Israel	66	69	3	(.)	0	(.)	31	31	184	4,551
93 Singapore	4	47	0	1	2	5	94	47	328	10,452
94 Trinidad and Tobago	39	65	0	(.)	0	(.)	61	35	13	206
High-income oil exporters	**13** w	**32** w	**0** w	**(.)** w	**30** w	**21** w	**57** w	**47** w		
95 Libya	68	62	0	1	0	(.)	32	37	(.)	78
96 Saudi Arabia	64	17	0	(.)	12	14	24	69	3	705
97 Kuwait	(.)	37	0	(.)	35	24	65	39	11	2,123
98 United Arab Emirates	76	. .	0	. .	3	. .	21	. .	33	. .
Industrial market economies	**63** w	**66** w	**3** w	**3** w	**1** w	**4** w	**33** w	**27** w		
99 Ireland	76	92	0	1	(.)	1	24	6	134	4,909
100 Spain	57	57	1	2	(.)	5	42	36	205	14,967
101 Italy	65	66	5	4	2	8	28	22	3,490	65,797
102 New Zealand	90	69	0	1	0	1	10	29	23	1,174
103 United Kingdom	58	65	3	2	2	6	37	27	8,947	84,287
104 Japan	45	46	4	3	1	7	50	44	4,340	124,027
105 Austria	67	70	18	13	(.)	1	15	16	931	14,480
106 Finland	56	64	31	24	(.)	1	13	11	608	9,864
107 Australia	62	31	(.)	(.)	(.)	1	38	68	263	6,220
108 Canada	89	87	(.)	1	(.)	1	11	11	1,959	30,595
109 Netherlands	78	81	2	2	1	3	19	14	2,443	37,827
110 Belgium	83	84	2	2	1	2	14	12	3,257	47,440
111 France	63	68	4	4	(.)	3	33	25	5,317	81,654
112 United States	48	55	(.)	(.)	1	5	51	40	13,957	147,336
113 Denmark	76	82	8	2	(.)	2	16	14	627	9,252
114 Germany, Fed. Rep.	74	73	4	5	1	3	21	19	11,623	165,447
115 Norway	81	74	2	3	(.)	1	17	22	442	5,931
116 Sweden	76	77	6	3	(.)	3	18	17	1,958	24,332
117 Switzerland	74	70	3	4	1	3	22	23	2,005	26,647
East European nonmarket economies	**. .**	**. .**	**. .**	**. .**	**. .**	**. .**	**. .**	**. .**		
118 Albania	. .	. .	. .	. .	. .	. .	. .	. .	. .	. .
119 Hungary	. .	25	. .	54	. .	1	. .	20	. .	5,709
120 Romania	. .	. .	. .	. .	. .	. .	. .	. .	. .	. .
121 Bulgaria	. .	. .	. .	. .	. .	. .	. .	. .	. .	. .
122 Poland	. .	22	. .	63	. .	2	. .	13	. .	10,336
123 USSR	. .	. .	. .	. .	. .	. .	. .	. .	. .	. .
124 Czechoslovakia	. .	15	. .	69	. .	1	. .	15	. .	12,554
125 German Dem. Rep.	. .	. .	. .	. .	. .	. .	. .	. .	. .	. .

a. Figures in italics are for 1963, not 1962.   b. Figures in italics are for 1979, not 1980.

Table 14. Balance of payments and reserves

	Current account balance (millions of dollars)		Receipts of workers' remittances (millions of dollars)		Net direct private investment (millions of dollars)		Gross international reserves		
							Millions of dollars		In months of import coverage
	1970	1981[a]	1970	1981[a]	1970	1981[a]	1970	1981[a]	1981[a]
Low-income economies									4.0 *w*
China and India									5.2 *w*
Other low-income									1.9 *w*
1 Kampuchea, Dem.	..	..	..	..	..	..	..	..	..
2 Bhutan	..	..	..	..	..	..	..	..	..
3 Lao, PDR	..	..	..	..	..	..	..	..	..
4 Chad	2	..	1	..	1	..	2	12	..
5 Bangladesh	−60	−1,016	..	386	..	..	..	160	0.6
6 Ethiopia	−32	−254	..	11	4	..	72	370	5.2
7 Nepal	..	−19	..	..	..	..	94	262	6.9
8 Burma	−63	−317	..	..	..	..	98	329	3.9
9 Afghanistan	..	..	..	..	..	..	50	658	..
10 Mali	−2	−140	6	48	..	4	1	25	0.6
11 Malawi	−35	−101	10	..	9	..	29	54	1.3
12 Zaire	−64	..	2	..	42	..	189	294	..
13 Uganda	20	−161	..	2	4	3	57	17	0.3
14 Burundi	..	..	..	..	..	..	15	68	..
15 Upper Volta	9	..	18	..	(.)	..	36	75	..
16 Rwanda	7	−59	1	2	(.)	18	8	173	5.9
17 India	−394	−4,040	113	..	6	..	1,023	8,109	5.4
18 Somalia	−6	−30	..	7	5	..	21	38	1.0
19 Tanzania	−36	−533	..	11	..	..	65	19	0.2
20 Viet Nam	..	..	..	..	..	..	..	..	..
21 China	..	2,152	..	..	..	265	..	10,096	5.1
22 Guinea	..	..	..	..	..	..	..	..	..
23 Haiti	2	−146	17	123	3	18	4	31	0.6
24 Sri Lanka	−59	−441	3	230	(.)	49	43	352	1.9
25 Benin	−1	..	3	..	7	..	16	62	..
26 Central African Rep.	−12	7	(.)	(.)	1	21	1	74	2.5
27 Sierra Leone	−16	−143	..	(.)	8	8	39	16	0.5
28 Madagascar	10	..	..	..	10	..	37	..	..
29 Niger	(.)	..	..	..	1	..	19	110	..
30 Pakistan	−667	−936	..	2,056	31	107	194	1,455	2.5
31 Mozambique	..	..	..	..	..	..	..	..	..
32 Sudan	−42	−648	..	366	..	..	22	17	0.1
33 Togo	3	..	..	..	1	..	35	157	..
34 Ghana	−68	−209	..	1	68	13	58	271	2.8
Middle-income economies									3.1 *w*
Oil exporters									3.3 *w*
Oil importers									3.0 *w*
Lower middle-income									2.9 *w*
35 Kenya	−49	−736	..	10	14	61	220	263	1.2
36 Senegal	−16	..	5	..	5	..	22	20	..
37 Mauritania	−5	−148	1	4	1	22.	3	166	3.3
38 Yemen Arab Rep.	..	−659	..	926	..	40	..	964	5.0
39 Yemen, PDR	−4	−137	60	352	..	..	59	271	4.2
40 Liberia	..	−65	..	..	..	..	..	7	0.1
41 Indonesia	−310	−736	..	..	83	133	160	6,248	3.0
42 Lesotho	..	−54	265	..	..	..	..	43	1.1
43 Bolivia	4	−285	(.)	2	−76	60	46	429	3.8
44 Honduras	−64	−303	..	2	8	−4	20	107	1.0
45 Zambia	108	−649	..	(.)	−297	..	515	143	0.9
46 Egypt	−148	−2,135	29	2,181	..	746	165	1,683	1.8
47 El Salvador	9	−86	1	48	4	6	64	277	3.5
48 Thailand	−250	−2,560	..	478	43	291	912	2,721	2.7
49 Philippines	−48	−2,286	..	798	−29	403	255	2,859	3.0
50 Angola	..	..	..	..	..	..	..	..	..
51 Papua New Guinea	..	−567	..	(.)	..	86	..	478	3.4
52 Morocco	−124	−1,839	63	1,013	20	59	141	510	1.0
53 Nicaragua	−40	..	1	..	15	..	49	..	..
54 Nigeria	−368	−5,395	..	..	205	47	223	4168	2.1
55 Zimbabwe	..	−635	..	7	..	4	59	327	1.7
56 Cameroon	−30	..	(.)	..	16	..	81	90	..
57 Cuba	..	..	..	..	..	..	..	..	..
58 Congo, People's Rep.	..	−460	..	3	..	31	9	128	0.9
59 Guatemala	−8	−580	..	24	29	128	80	357	2.0
60 Peru	202	−1,512	..	(.)	−70	267	339	1,764	3.6
61 Ecuador	−113	−1,001	..	..	89	60	76	797	2.4
62 Jamaica	−153	−337	50	112	161	−12	139	85	0.5
63 Ivory Coast	−38	−1,693	6	32	31	48	119	36	0.1
64 Dominican Rep.	−102	−670	25	166	72	93	32	282	1.5

	Current account balance (millions of dollars)		Receipts of workers' remittances (millions of dollars)		Net direct private investment (millions of dollars)		Gross international reserves		
							Millions of dollars		In months of import coverage
	1970	1981[a]	1970	1981[a]	1970	1981[a]	1970	1981[a]	1981[a]
65 Mongolia	..	..	..	..	..	..	..	..	..
66 Colombia	−293	−1,943	26	124	39	209	207	6,079	10.6
67 Tunisia	−53	−450	29	357	16	294	60	610	1.8
68 Costa Rica	−74	−372	..	(.)	26	46	16	143	1.0
69 Korea, Dem. Rep.	..	..	..	..	..	..	..	..	..
70 Turkey	−44	2,175	273	2,500	58	150	440	2,783	3.3
71 Syrian Arab Rep.	−69	−511	7	581	..	..	57	622	1.3
72 Jordan	−20	−38	16	1,047	..	143	258	1,511	4.0
73 Paraguay	−16	−374	..	63	4	39	18	820	8.9
Upper middle-income									3.3 *w*
74 Korea, Rep. of	−623	−4,419	33	126	66	59	610	2,802	1.0
75 Iran, Islamic Rep. of	−507	..	..	..	25	..	217	..	..
76 Iraq	105	..	..	..	24	..	472	..	..
77 Malaysia	8	−2,911	..	5	94	1,317	667	5,024	3.9
78 Panama	−64	−627	67	13	33	45	16	120	0.3
79 Lebanon	..	..	..	..	..	..	405	5,182	..
80 Algeria	−125	249	211	406	45	315	352	5,915	5.8
81 Brazil	−837	−11,762	9	35	407	2,317	1,190	7,480	2.3
82 Mexico	−1,068	−12,933	123	216	323	2,254	756	4,971	1.4
83 Portugal	..	−2,574	..	2,896	..	156	1,565	9,345	9.4
84 Argentina	−163	−3,973	6	41	11	902	682	5,006	3.8
85 Chile	−91	−4,814	..	..	−79	376	392	3,890	4.2
86 South Africa	−1,215	−4,151	202	878	318	..	1,057	4,359	1.8
87 Yugoslavia	−372	−2,291	441	4,050	..	..	143	2,335	1.5
88 Uruguay	−45	−463	..	(.)	..	49	186	1,778	9.3
89 Venezuela	−104	3998	..	(.)	−23	160	1,047	12,719	7.5
90 Greece	−402	−2,385	339	1,177	50	520	318	2,554	2.4
91 Hong Kong	..	..	..	..	..	..	..	..	..
92 Israel	−562	−1,568	21	215	40	−414	452	3,971	3.1
93 Singapore	−572	−1,750	..	..	93	1,797	1,012	7,549	3.0
94 Trinidad and Tobago	−109	357	3	1	83	166	43	3,369	11.3
High-income oil exporters									5.7 *w*
95 Libya	645	−2,263	..	..	139	−1,079	1,596	10,425	6.7
96 Saudi Arabia	71	45,119	..	(.)	20	3,376	670	34,051	5.4
97 Kuwait	..	13,758	..	(.)	..	35	209	5,077	5.7
98 United Arab Emirates	..	..	..	..	..	..	..	3,472	..
Industrial market economies									3.8 *w*
99 Ireland	−198	−1,650	..	..	32	286	698	2,794	2.8
100 Spain	111	−4,939	469	521	179	1,440	1,851	16,611	4.9
101 Italy	902	−8,430	1,017	2,897	498	−254	5,547	46,635	5.1
102 New Zealand	−29	−1,171	..	186	22	219	258	683	1.0
103 United Kingdom	1,975	12,634	..	..	−439	−8,661	2,919	22,803	2.0
104 Japan	1,980	5,117	..	189	−260	−4,728	4,877	37,839	2.5
105 Austria	−75	−1,522	13	199	104	90	1,806	13,677	5.5
106 Finland	−239	−289	34	124	−41	−124	455	1,988	1.3
107 Australia	−837	−8,489	..	..	785	1,758	1,709	4,824	1.7
108 Canada	821	−4,413	..	..	566	−8,597	4,733	11,672	1.6
109 Netherlands	−483	3,159	116	450	−15	−1,822	3,362	26,805	3.7
110 Belgium	717	−5,231	294	1,135	140	1,343	2,947	18,539	3.6
111 France	−55	−7,254	251	1,296	248	−2,166	5,199	54,797	4.0
112 United States	2,320	4,185	..	283	−6,130	12,875	15,237	123,907	4.1
113 Denmark	−544	−1,865	..	(.)	75	−40	488	3,195	1.5
114 Germany, Fed. Rep.	850	−7,133	350	2,323	−290	−2,889	13,879	81,554	4.5
115 Norway	−242	2,301	..	24	32	493	813	6,724	3.1
116 Sweden	−265	−2,735	6	67	−104	−628	775	6,013	1.9
117 Switzerland	72	2,634	23	167	..	..	5,317	47,083	14.8
East European nonmarket economies	..	..	..	..	..	..	..	..	..
118 Albania	..	..	..	..	..	..	..	..	..
119 Hungary	..	−897	..	..	..	2	..	2,463	2.6
120 Romania	..	−832	..	..	..	..	..	1,831	1.5
121 Bulgaria	..	..	..	..	..	..	..	..	..
122 Poland	..	..	..	..	..	..	..	..	..
123 USSR	..	..	..	..	..	..	..	..	..
124 Czechoslovakia	..	..	..	..	..	..	..	..	..
125 German Dem. Rep.	..	..	..	..	..	..	..	..	..

a. Figures in italics are for 1980, not 1981.   b. See the technical notes.

Table 15. Flow of public and publicly guaranteed external capital

	Public and publicly guaranteed medium- and long-term loans (millions of dollars)					
	Gross inflow		Repayment of principal		Net inflow[a]	
	1970	1981	1970	1981	1970	1981
Low-income economies						
China and India						
Other low-income						
1 Kampuchea, Dem.	. .	. .	. .	. .	. .	. .
2 Bhutan	. .	. .	. .	. .	. .	. .
3 Lao, PDR	. .	. .	. .	. .	. .	. .
4 Chad	6	9	2	10	3	−1
5 Bangladesh	. .	513	. .	52	. .	461
6 Ethiopia	27	149	15	24	13	125
7 Nepal	1	64	2	2	−2	61
8 Burma	16	431	18	83	−2	348
9 Afghanistan	34	. .	15	. .	19	. .
10 Mali	21	116	(.)	36	21	110
11 Malawi	38	130	3	39	36	91
12 Zaire	31	260	28	90	3	170
13 Uganda	26	85	4	53	22	32
14 Burundi	1	30	(.)	3	1	27
15 Upper Volta	2	44	2	8	(.)	36
16 Rwanda	(.)	26	(.)	1	(.)	25
17 India	890	1,987	307	647	583	1,340
18 Somalia	4	175	(.)	13	4	163
19 Tanzania	50	276	10	73	40	203
20 Viet Nam	. .	. .	. .	. .	. .	. .
21 China	. .	. .	. .	. .	. .	. .
22 Guinea	90	141	10	61	80	80
23 Haiti	4	106	4	18	1	88
24 Sri Lanka	61	369	27	42	34	327
25 Benin	2	172	1	12	1	160
26 Central African Rep.	2	26	2	5	−1	21
27 Sierra Leone	8	64	10	41	−2	24
28 Madagascar	10	265	5	74	5	191
29 Niger	12	284	1	29	10	255
30 Pakistan	484	673	114	331	370	340
31 Mozambique	. .	. .	. .	. .	. .	. .
32 Sudan	60	540	22	52	39	489
33 Togo	5	38	2	21	3	17
34 Ghana	40	117	12	51	28	66
Middle-income economies						
Oil exporters						
Oil importers						
Lower middle-income						
35 Kenya	30	476	15	177	15	299
36 Senegal	15	266	5	53	10	174
37 Mauritania	4	174	3	36	1	138
38 Yemen Arab Rep. of	. .	294	. .	49	. .	245
39 Yemen, PDR	1	190	0	32	1	158
40 Liberia	7	70	12	11	−4	59
41 Indonesia	441	2,356	59	1,001	382	1,355
42 Lesotho	(.)	47	(.)	7	(.)	39
43 Bolivia	54	337	17	100	37	237
44 Honduras	29	254	3	37	26	217
45 Zambia	351	248	33	187	318	61
46 Egypt, Arab Rep. of	302	3,487	247	1,570	55	1,918
47 El Salvador	8	182	6	17	2	165
48 Thailand	51	1,461	23	226	27	1,235
49 Philippines	132	1,529	73	367	59	1,162
50 Angola	. .	. .	. .	. .	. .	. .
51 Papua New Guinea	25	138	(.)	20	25	118
52 Morocco	163	1,704	36	602	127	1,103
53 Nicaragua	44	398	17	91	28	307
54 Nigeria	62	1,164	36	361	26	803
55 Zimbabwe	0	330	5	41	−5	289
56 Cameroon	28	371	4	85	24	286
57 Cuba	. .	. .	. .	. .	. .	. .
58 Congo, People's Rep.	35	306	6	62	29	244
59 Guatemala	37	144	20	20	17	124
60 Peru	148	1,469	101	1,367	47	102
61 Ecuador	42	952	16	190	26	762
62 Jamaica	15	408	6	243	9	165
63 Ivory Coast	77	1,168	27	489	50	679
64 Dominican Rep.	38	151	7	77	31	75

	Public and publicly guaranteed medium- and long-term loans (millions of dollars)					
	Gross inflow		Repayment of principal		Net inflow[a]	
	1970	1981	1970	1981	1970	1981
65 Mongolia	. .	. .	. .	. .	. .	. .
66 Colombia	252	1,361	78	257	174	1,104
67 Tunisia	87	585	45	302	42	283
68 Costa Rica	30	603	21	80	9	523
69 Korea, Dem. Rep.	. .	. .	. .	. .	. .	. .
70 Turkey	328	1,816	128	510	200	1,306
71 Syrian Arab Rep.	59	417	30	303	30	113
72 Jordan	14	335	3	101	11	234
73 Paraguay	15	162	7	40	8	122

Upper middle-income

	1970	1981	1970	1981	1970	1981
74 Korea, Rep. of	440	6,087	198	1,820	242	4,266
75 Iran, Islamic Rep. of	940	. .	235	. .	705	. .
76 Iraq	63	. .	18	. .	46	. .
77 Malaysia	43	1,874	45	138	−1	1,736
78 Panama	67	342	24	215	44	126
79 Lebanon	12	99	2	40	9	58
80 Algeria	292	2,781	33	2,399	259	382
81 Brazil	886	8,997	255	3,619	631	5,378
82 Mexico	772	13,416	476	3,782	297	9,634
83 Portugal	18	1,622	63	606	−45	1,016
84 Argentina	487	1,845	342	1,092	146	753
85 Chile	397	1,018	163	1,175	234	−156
86 South Africa	. .		. .		. .	
87 Yugoslavia	180	1,181	168	373	12	808
88 Uruguay	38	292	47	53	−9	239
89 Venezuela	224	2,059	42	1,352	182	706
90 Greece	164	1,837	61	612	102	1,225
91 Hong Kong	0	39	(.)	155	(.)	−115
92 Israel	410	2,482	25	1,368	385	1,115
93 Singapore	58	169	6	107	52	62
94 Trinidad and Tobago	8	88	10	26	−2	62

High-income oil exporters

95 Libya
96 Saudi Arabia
97 Kuwait
98 United Arab Emirates

Industrial market economies

99 Ireland
100 Spain
101 Italy
102 New Zealand
103 United Kingdom
104 Japan
105 Austria
106 Finland
107 Australia
108 Canada
109 Netherlands
110 Belgium
111 France
112 United States
113 Denmark
114 Germany, Fed. Rep.
115 Norway
116 Sweden
117 Switzerland

East European nonmarket economies

	1970	1981	1970	1981	1970	1981
118 Albania						
119 Hungary		1,880		940		940
120 Romania						
121 Bulgaria						
122 Poland						
123 USSR						
124 Czechoslovakia						
125 German Dem. Rep.						

a. Gross inflow less repayment of principal may not equal net inflow because of rounding.

Table 16. External public debt and debt service ratios

	External public debt outstanding and disbursed				Interest payments on external public debt (millions of dollars)		Debt service as percentage of:			
	Millions of dollars		As percentage of GNP				GNP		Exports of goods and services	
	1970	1981	1970	1981	1970	1981	1970	1981	1970	1981
Low-income economies			17.5 w	18.6 w			1.1 w	1,0 w	12.0 w	8.8 w
China and India										
Other low-income			22.0 w	28.3 w			1.5 w	1.5 w	12.5 w	8.8 w
1 Kampuchea, Dem.	..	..	..	..	..	..	..	..	..	..
2 Bhutan	..	..	..	..	..	..	..	..	..	..
3 Lao, PDR	..	..	..	..	..	..	..	..	..	..
4 Chad	32	201	11.9	50.9	(.)	2	1.0	2.9	3.9	..
5 Bangladesh	..	3,850	..	31.2	..	46	..	0.8	..	6.9
6 Ethiopia	169	792	9.5	18.7	6	16	1.2	1.0	11.4	7.6
7 Nepal	3	234	0.3	9.5	(.)	3	0.3	0.2	..	1.6
8 Burma	101	1,639	4.7	28.7	3	53	0.9	2.4	15.8	22.1
9 Afghanistan	547	..	58.1	..	9	..	2.5	..	..	..
10 Mali	238	738	88.1	64.9	(.)	3	0.2	0.8	1.2	3.8
11 Malawi	122	685	39.1	42.0	3	49	1.9	5.4	7.1	24.5
12 Zaire	311	3,960	17.6	77.0	9	122	1.2	4.1	4.4	..
13 Uganda	138	540	10.5	5.2	4	2	0.6	0.5	2.6	3.9
14 Burundi	7	154	3.1	16.1	(.)	2	0.3	0.5	..	..
15 Upper Volta	21	296	6.3	23.1	(.)	6	0.6	1.1	4.0	..
16 Rwanda	2	172	0.9	13.6	(.)	2	0.2	0.2	1.3	1.5
17 India	7,940	17,975	14.9	10.8	189	378	0.9	0.6	20.9	..
18 Somalia	77	877	24.4	70.9	(.)	4	0.3	1.3	2.1	6.1
19 Tanzania	248	1,476	19.4	28.3	6	34	1.2	2.1	4.9	7.2
20 Viet Nam	..	..	..	..	..	..	..	..	..	..
21 China	..	..	..	..	..	..	..	..	..	..
22 Guinea	314	1.255	51.7	80.4	4	22	2.4	5.3	..	..
23 Haiti	40	360	10.3	22.9	(.)	7	1.0	1.6	5.8	6.6
24 Sri Lanka	317	1,585	16.1	36.6	12	49	2.0	2.1	10.3	5.7
25 Benin	41	549	16.0	55.2	(.)	10	0.7	2.2	2.2	..
26 Central African Rep.	24	213	13.7	31.5	1	1	1.7	0.9	4.8	1.5
27 Sierra Leone	59	346	14.3	31.0	2	10	2.9	4.5	9.9	24.4
28 Madagascar	93	1,258	10.8	44.6	2	47	0.8	4.3	3.5	..
29 Niger	32	605	8.7	36.7	1	34	0.6	3.8	3.8	..
30 Pakistan	3,059	8,814	30.5	29.2	76	198	1.9	1.8	23.6	9.6
31 Mozambique	..	..	..	..	..	..	..	..	..	..
32 Sudan	319	4,807	15.8	59.3	13	31	1.7	1.0	10.7	5.0
33 Togo	40	860	16.0	99.2	1	19	0.9	4.7	2.9	..
34 Ghana	489	979	22.6	4.0	12	27	1.1	0.3	5.0	9.1
Middle-income economies			13.5 w	19.6 w			1.6 w	3.4 w	9.6 w	14.4 w
Oil exporters			13.7 w	20.3 w			1.8 w	3.9 w	10.3 w	15.2 w
Oil importers			13.4 w	19.1 w			1.4 w	3.1 w	9.2 w	13.9 w
Lower middle-income			15.6 w	23.2 w			1.6 w	3.2 w	9.3 w	12.5 w
35 Kenya	313	2,228	20.3	34.4	11	116	1.7	4.5	5.3	17.1
36 Senegal	98	944	11.6	42.5	2	41	0.8	4.2	2.7	..
37 Mauritania	27	827	13.9	122.1	(.)	18	1.7	8.0	3.1	15.8
38 Yemen Arab Rep.	..	1,094	..	34.3	..	10	..	1.8	..	4.5
39 Yemen, PDR	1	640	..	73.1	0	5	..	4.3	..	2.4
40 Liberia	158	592	49.6	63.7	6	24	5.5	3.7	..	6.4
41 Indonesia	2,443	15,529	27.1	19.0	24	973	0.9	2.4	6.9	8.2
42 Lesotho	8	107	7.8	15.0	(.)	3	0.4	1.4	..	2.9
43 Bolivia	479	2,422	47.1	31.9	6	179	2.3	3.7	11.3	27.0
44 Honduras	90	1,223	12.8	47.1	3	77	0.8	4.4	2.8	12.7
45 Zambia	623	2,294	37.0	73.1	26	106	3.5	9.4	5.9	24.0
46 Egypt	1,644	13,887	23.8	43.7	38	496	4.1	6.5	28.7	22.6
47 El Salvador	88	664	8.6	19.0	4	28	0.9	1.3	3.6	3.5
48 Thailand	324	5,169	4.9	14.4	16	395	0.6	1.7	3.4	6.7
49 Philippines	633	7,388	9.0	19.3	25	507	1.4	2.3	7.4	9.9
50 Angola	..	..	..	..	..	..	..	..	..	..
51 Papua New Guinea	36	613	5.8	25.5	1	46	0.1	2.7	..	6.9
52 Morocco	711	7,879	18.0	52.4	23	631	1.5	8.2	7.7	30.1
53 Nicaragua	155	1,975	20.7	80.2	7	93	3.2	7.5	11.0	..
54 Nigeria	480	4,652	4.7	6.5	20	495	0.5	1.2	4.1	4.6
55 Zimbabwe	233	880	15.7	13.8	5	32	0.6	1.1	..	4.4
56 Cameroon	131	2,034	12.1	28.7	4	115	0.8	2.8	3.1	..
57 Cuba	..	..	..	..	..	..	..	..	..	..
58 Congo, People's Rep.	135	1,105	50.4	66.7	3	45	3.3	6.5	8.9	9.2
59 Guatemala	106	684	5.7	8.0	6	30	1.4	0.6	7.4	3.3
60 Peru	856	5,974	12.6	28.6	44	528	2.1	9.1	11.6	44.9
61 Ecuador	217	3,392	13.2	26.9	7	345	1.4	4.3	9.1	17.8
62 Jamaica	154	1,434	11.5	53.6	8	109	1.1	13.2	2.5	22.5
63 Ivory Coast	256	4,497	18.3	54.4	11	413	2.8	10.9	6.8	22.2
64 Dominican Rep.	212	1,260	14.5	17.1	4	124	0.8	2.7	4.1	10.6

	External public debt outstanding and disbursed				Interest payments on external public debt (millions of dollars)		Debt service as percentage of:			
	Millions of dollars		As percentage of GNP				GNP		Exports of goods and services	
	1970	1981	1970	1981	1970	1981	1970	1981	1970	1981
65 Mongolia	..	..	..	..	..	..	..	..	..	..
66 Colombia	1,293	5,123	18.8	14.0	44	408	1.8	1.8	11.9	13.4
67 Tunisia	541	3,171	38.2	38.0	18	204	4.5	6.1	17.5	13.9
68 Costa Rica	134	2,246	13.8	92.6	7	111	2.9	7.8	10.0	15.3
69 Korea, Dem. Rep.	..	..	..	..	..	..	..	..	..	..
70 Turkey	1,854	13,809	14.4	23.4	42	658	1.3	2.0	16.3	15.0
71 Syrian Arab Rep.	232	2,337	12.8	15.2	6	108	2.0	2.7	10.8	12.1
72 Jordan	118	1,419	..	38.7	2	81	..	5.0	3.6	5.7
73 Paraguay	112	707	19.1	12.6	4	32	1.4	1.3	11.8	9.8
Upper middle-income			12.4 w	17.8 w			1.6 w	3.5 w	10.1 w	15.4 w
74 Korea, Rep. of	1,797	19,964	20.8	32.1	70	1,777	3.1	5.8	19.4	13.1
75 Iran, Islamic Rep. of	2,193	..	20.8	..	85	..	3.0	..	12.2	..
76 Iraq	274	..	8.8	..	9	..	0.9	..	2.2	..
77 Malaysia	390	4,627	10.0	19.2	21	264	1.7	1.7	3.6	3.1
78 Panama	194	2,368	19.0	64.5	7	277	3.0	13.4	7.7	11.5
79 Lebanon	64	246	4.2	..	1	13	0.2	..	..	..
80 Algeria	937	14,392	19.3	35.2	10	1,481	0.9	9.5	3.2	24.9
81 Brazil	3,236	43,821	7.1	16.0	133	4,998	0.9	3.1	12.5	31.9
82 Mexico	3,206	42,716	9.1	18.5	216	4,700	2.0	3.7	23.6	28.2
83 Portugal	485	6,313	7.2	27.7	29	641	1.4	5.5	..	13.5
84 Argentina	1,878	10,506	8.2	8.7	121	1,058	2.0	1.3	21.5	18.2
85 Chile	2,066	4,423	25.8	14.1	78	489	3.0	5.3	18.9	27.2
86 South Africa	..	..	..	..	..	..	..	..	..	..
87 Yugoslavia	1,198	5,266	8.8	7.7	72	435	1.8	1.2	8.4	3.5
88 Uruguay	269	1,312	11.1	12.2	16	121	2.6	1.6	21.6	9.5
89 Venezuela	728	11,352	6.6	16.9	40	1,696	0.7	4.4	2.9	12.4
90 Greece	905	5,817	8.9	15.4	41	715	1.0	3.5	7.1	12.9
91 Hong Kong	2	309	0.1	1.2	0	37	(.)	0.8	..	..
92 Israel	2,274	13,868	41.3	64.3	13	707	0.7	9.6	2.7	19.1
93 Singapore	152	1,318	7.9	10.2	6	122	0.6	1.8	0.6	0.8
94 Trinidad and Tobago	101	659	12.2	9.7	6	72	1.9	1.4	4.4	6.5
High-income oil exporters										
95 Libya										
96 Saudi Arabia										
97 Kuwait										
98 United Arab Emirates										
Industrial market economies										
99 Ireland										
100 Spain										
101 Italy										
102 New Zealand										
103 United Kingdom										
104 Japan										
105 Austria										
106 Finland										
107 Australia										
108 Canada										
109 Netherlands										
110 Belgium										
111 France										
112 United States										
113 Denmark										
114 Germany, Fed. Rep.										
115 Norway										
116 Sweden										
117 Switzerland										
East European nonmarket economies										
118 Albania										
119 Hungary		6,934		31.9		672		7.4		15.6
120 Romania										
121 Bulgaria										
122 Poland										
123 USSR										
124 Czechoslovakia										
125 German Dem. Rep.										

Table 17. Terms of public borrowing

	Commitments (millions of dollars)		Average interest rate (percent)		Average maturity (years)		Average grace period (years)	
	1970	1981	1970	1981	1970	1981	1970	1981
Low-income economies	3,052 *t*	9,289 *t*	2.8 *w*	4.4 *w*	30 *w*	30 *w*	9 *w*	7 *w*
China and India	..	..	..	..	..	..	..	..
Other low-income	2,119 *t*	5,820 *t*	3.0 *w*	4.1 *w*	28 *w*	29 *w*	9 *w*	7 *w*
1 Kampuchea, Dem.	..	..	..	..	..	..	..	..
2 Bhutan	..	..	..	..	..	..	..	..
3 Lao, PDR	..	..	..	..	..	..	..	..
4 Chad	4	23	4.8	0.8	7	50	2	10
5 Bangladesh	..	937	..	2.1	..	31	..	8
6 Ethiopia	21	180	4.3	4.3	32	30	7	6
7 Nepal	17	110	2.8	1.4	27	41	6	10
8 Burma	57	257	4.3	3.8	16	25	4	7
9 Afghanistan	19	..	1.7	..	33	..	8	..
10 Mali	30	128	0.3	2.3	27	26	11	7
11 Malawi	13	158	3.8	6.6	30	30	6	7
12 Zaire	247	154	6.8	6.8	12	20	3	5
13 Uganda	12	75	3.7	5.8	28	18	7	4
14 Burundi	1	137	2.9	2.6	5	35	2	8
15 Upper Volta	9	61	2.3	3.4	37	27	8	7
16 Rwanda	9	71	0.8	1.2	50	44	11	9
17 India	933	3,469	2.4	5.0	35	33	8	7
18 Somalia	2	216	0	4.9	4	16	4	4
19 Tanzania	283	294	1.2	2.2	40	33	11	7
20 Viet Nam	..	..	..	..	..	..	..	..
21 China	..	..	..	..	..	..	..	..
22 Guinea	158	154	2.6	3.8	15	22	6	5
23 Haiti	5	109	6.7	5.3	9	26	1	5
24 Sri Lanka	79	871	3.0	5.2	27	32	5	8
25 Benin	7	92	1.8	2.6	32	38	7	8
26 Central African Rep.	7	19	2.0	3.6	36	30	8	7
27 Sierra Leone	24	66	3.5	2.7	27	28	6	6
28 Madagascar	..	193	..	2.9	..	25	..	5
29 Niger	18	218	1.2	7.1	40	17	8	5
30 Pakistan	935	872	2.8	4.2	32	29	12	7
31 Mozambique	..	..	..	..	..	..	..	..
32 Sudan	118	315	1.9	7.2	16	24	7	6
33 Togo	3	65	4.6	3.6	17	35	4	8
34 Ghana	41	44	2.4	2.4	39	45	10	8
Middle-income economies	10,504 *t*	84,198 *t*	6.1 *w*	12.5 *w*	16 *w*	12 *w*	4 *w*	4 *w*
Oil exporters	4,014 *t*	35,224 *t*	6.1 *w*	12.9 *w*	15 *w*	11 *w*	4 *w*	4 *w*
Oil importers	6,490 *t*	48,974 *t*	6.1 *w*	12.2 *w*	17 *w*	13 *w*	4 *w*	4 *w*
Lower middle-income	3,668 *t*	33,214 *t*	4.6 *w*	10.2 *w*	22 *w*	14 *w*	5 *w*	4 *w*
35 Kenya	41	375	3.0	9.5	36	22	8	5
36 Senegal	8	341	4.4	6.0	28	22	8	6
37 Mauritania	7	250	6.5	2.7	11	20	3	5
38 Yemen Arab Rep.	9	220	5.2	2.2	5	20	3	4
39 Yemen, PDR	62	86	0	2.3	21	29	11	7
40 Liberia	12	46	5.3	5.5	19	21	5	5
41 Indonesia	518	4,916	2.7	8.9	34	15	9	4
42 Lesotho	(.)	10	5.1	0.8	25	50	2	11
43 Bolivia	10	223	3.9	12.0	25	10	7	2
44 Honduras	23	249	4.1	10.7	30	19	7	4
45 Zambia	555	403	4.2	8.6	23	18	6	4
46 Egypt	246	2,381	5.6	7.5	14	13	3	3
47 El Salvador	12	128	4.7	3.7	23	24	6	7
48 Thailand	106	1,641	6.8	10.2	19	17	4	5
49 Philippines	158	2,104	7.4	11.1	11	16	2	5
50 Angola	..	..	..	..	..	..	..	..
51 Papua New Guinea	58	147	6.0	13.8	24	18	8	7
52 Morocco	182	2,546	4.6	8.4	20	10	4	4
53 Nicaragua	23	504	7.1	6.1	18	10	4	3
54 Nigeria	79	4,256	5.8	13.7	17	10	5	4
55 Zimbabwe	..	1,079	..	11.3	..	12	..	3
56 Cameroon	41	341	4.7	6.4	29	21	8	5
57 Cuba	..	..	..	..	..	..	..	..
58 Congo, People's Rep.	43	516	3.0	11.5	17	7	6	2
59 Guatemala	50	182	5.2	6.5	26	24	6	7
60 Peru	125	1,890	7.4	12.6	13	12	4	3
61 Ecuador	78	846	6.1	12.6	20	13	4	4
62 Jamaica	24	478	6.0	9.7	16	15	3	5
63 Ivory Coast	69	1,397	5.9	13.4	19	14	5	4
64 Dominican Rep.	20	171	2.5	6.0	28	24	5	5

	Commitments (millions of dollars)		Average interest rate (percent)		Average maturity (years)		Average grace period (years)	
	1970	1981	1970	1981	1970	1981	1970	1981
65 Mongolia	..	..	..	..	..	..	..	..
66 Colombia	362	1,732	5.9	12.0	21	13	5	4
67 Tunisia	141	628	3.4	8.3	27	15	6	4
68 Costa Rica	58	620	5.6	14.2	28	6	6	2
69 Korea, Dem. Rep.	..	..	..	..	..	..	..	..
70 Turkey	487	2,011	3.6	7.9	19	15	5	4
71 Syrian Arab Rep.	14	142	4.4	4.4	8	17	2	5
72 Jordan	33	11	3.9	3.1	12	16	5	5
73 Paraguay	14	346	5.6	9.9	25	16	6	4
Upper middle-income	6,836 t	50,984 t	6.9 w	14.0 w	13 w	11 w	3 w	4 w
74 Korea, Rep. of	677	5,153	6.0	12.2	19	14	5	4
75 Iran, Islamic Rep. of	1,342	..	6.2	..	12	..	3	..
76 Iraq	28		3.3	..	11	..	2	..
77 Malaysia	83	1,877	6.1	14.9	19	12	5	5
78 Panama	111	327	6.9	14.4	15	13	4	4
79 Lebanon	7	13	2.7	11.1	21	13	1	4
80 Algeria	288	2,600	6.5	9.8	10	13	2	4
81 Brazil	1,362	12,538	7.1	14.6	14	10	3	3
82 Mexico	826	13,164	8.0	15.1	12	8	3	4
83 Portugal	59	1,407	4.3	14.8	17	9	4	4
84 Argentina	488	3,638	7.4	12.2	12	14	3	5
85 Chile	343	1,214	6.9	15.0	12	11	3	4
86 South Africa	..	..	..	..	..	..	..	..
87 Yugoslavia	198	1,834	7.1	13.1	17	11	6	4
88 Uruguay	72	383	7.9	12.1	12	16	3	4
89 Venezuela	198	2,000	8.2	18.3	8	7	2	2
90 Greece	242	1,855	7.2	13.3	9	11	4	4
91 Hong Kong	..	2	..	8.1	..	12	..	4
92 Israel	439	2,778	7.3	13.6	13	19	5	5
93 Singapore	69	192	6.8	11.5	17	9	4	3
94 Trinidad and Tobago	3	10	7.5	8.8	10	8	1	(.)
High-income oil exporters								
95 Libya								
96 Saudi Arabia								
97 Kuwait								
98 United Arab Emirates								
Industrial market economies								
99 Ireland								
100 Spain								
101 Italy								
102 New Zealand								
103 United Kingdom								
104 Japan								
105 Austria								
106 Finland								
107 Australia								
108 Canada								
109 Netherlands								
110 Belgium								
111 France								
112 United States								
113 Denmark								
114 Germany, Fed. Rep.								
115 Norway								
116 Sweden								
117 Switzerland								
East European nonmarket economies								
118 Albania								
119 Hungary[a]		1,106		13.1		7		4
120 Romania								
121 Bulgaria								
122 Poland								
123 USSR								
124 Czechoslovakia								
125 German Dem. Rep.								

a. Includes only debt in convertible currencies.

Table 18. Official development assistance from OECD and OPEC members

	Amount									
	1960	1965	1970	1975	1977	1978	1979	1980	1981	1982[a]
OECD	**Millions of US dollars**									
101 Italy	77	60	147	182	198	376	273	683	666	820
102 New Zealand	..	..	14	66	53	55	68	72	68	65
103 United Kingdom	407	472	500	904	1,114	1,465	2,157	1,852	2,194	1,794
104 Japan	105	244	458	1,148	1,424	2,215	2,685	3,353	3,171	3,023
105 Austria	..	10	11	79	108	154	131	178	313	361
106 Finland	..	2	7	48	49	55	90	110	135	144
107 Australia	59	119	212	552	400	588	629	667	649	882
108 Canada	75	96	337	880	991	1,060	1,056	1,075	1,189	1,185
109 Netherlands	35	70	196	608	908	1,074	1,472	1,630	1,510	1,473
110 Belgium	101	102	120	378	371	536	643	595	575	497
111 France	823	752	971	2,093	2,267	2,705	3,449	4,162	4,177	3,991
112 United States	2,702	4,023	3,153	4,161	4,682	5,663	4,684	7,138	5,782	8,302
113 Denmark	5	13	59	205	258	388	461	481	403	415
114 Germany, Fed. Rep.	223	456	599	1,689	1,717	2,347	3,393	3,567	3,181	3,163
115 Norway	5	11	37	184	295	355	429	486	467	566
116 Sweden	7	38	117	566	779	•783	988	962	919	987
117 Switzerland	4	12	30	104	119	173	213	253	237	251
Total	4,628	6,480	6,968	13,847	15,733	19,992	22,821	27,264	25,636	27,919
OECD	**As percentage of donor GNP**									
101 Italy	.22	.10	.16	.11	.10	.14	.08	.17	.19	.24
102 New Zealand	..	..	.23	.52	.39	.34	.33	.33	.29	.28
103 United Kingdom	.56	.47	.41	.39	.45	.46	.52	.35	.44	.38
104 Japan	.24	.27	.23	.23	.21	.23	.27	.32	.28	.29
105 Austria	..	.11	.07	.21	.22	.27	.19	.23	.48	.54
106 Finland	..	.02	.06	.18	.16	.16	.22	.22	.28	.30
107 Australia	.37	.53	.59	.65	.42	.55	.53	.48	.41	.57
108 Canada	.19	.19	.41	.54	.50	.52	.48	.43	.43	.42
109 Netherlands	.31	.36	.61	.75	.86	.82	.98	1.03	1.08	1.08
110 Belgium	.88	.60	.46	.59	.46	.55	.57	.50	.59	.59
111 France	1.35	.76	.66	.62	.60	.57	.60	.64	.73	.74
112 United States	.53	.58	.32	.27	.25	.27	.20	.27	.20	.27
113 Denmark	.09	.13	.38	.58	.60	.75	.77	.74	.73	.77
114 Germany, Fed. Rep.	.31	.40	.32	.40	.33	.37	.45	.44	.47	.48
115 Norway	.11	.16	.32	.66	.83	.90	.93	.85	.82	1.01
116 Sweden	.05	.19	.38	.82	.99	.90	.97	.79	.83	1.02
117 Switzerland	.04	.09	.15	.19	.19	.20	.21	.24	.24	.25
OECD	**National currencies**									
101 Italy (billions of lire)	48	37	92	119	175	319	227	585	757	1,109
102 New Zealand (millions of dollars)	..	..	13	54	55	53	66	74	78	86
103 United Kingdom (millions of pounds)	145	169	208	409	639	764	1,018	797	1,091	1,027
104 Japan (billions of yen)	38	88	165	341	382	466	588	760	699	753
105 Austria (millions of schillings)	..	260	286	1,376	1,785	2,236	1,751	2,303	4,985	6,158
106 Finland (millions of markkaa)	..	6	29	177	197	226	351	410	583	694
107 Australia (millions of dollars)	53	106	189	422	361	514	563	586	565	870
108 Canada (millions of dollars)	73	104	353	895	1,054	1,209	1,237	1,257	1,425	1,462
109 Netherlands (millions of guilders)	132	252	709	1,538	2,229	2,324	2,953	3,241	3,768	3,933
110 Belgium (millions of francs)	5,050	5,100	6,000	13,902	13,298	16,880	18,852	17,400	21,350	22,708
111 France (millions of francs)	4,063	3,713	5,393	8,971	11,139	12,207	14,674	17,589	22,700	26,230
112 United States (millions of dollars)	2,702	4,023	3,153	4,161	4,682	5,663	4,684	7,138	5,782	8,302
113 Denmark (millions of kroner)	35	90	443	1,178	1,549	2,140	2,425	2,711	2,871	3,458
114 Germany, Fed. Rep. (millions of deutsche marks)	937	1,824	2,192	4,155	3,987	4,714	6,219	6,484	7,189	7,675
115 Norway (millions of kroner)	36	79	264	962	1,570	1,861	2,172	2,400	2,680	3,653
116 Sweden (millions of kronor)	36	197	605	2,350	3,491	3,538	4,236	4,069	4,653	6,201
117 Switzerland (millions of francs)	17	52	131	268	286	309	354	424	466	510
OECD	**Summary**									
ODA (billions of US dollars, nominal prices)	4.63	6.48	6.97	13.85	15.73	19.99	22.82	27.26	25.63	27.92
ODA as percentage of GNP	.51	.49	.34	.36	.33	.35	.35	.38	.35	.39
ODA (billions of US dollars, constant 1980 prices)	16.41	20.19	18.15	21.60	21.91	24.09	24.89	27.26	25.82	28.37
GNP (trillions of US dollars, nominal prices)	.90	1.30	2.00	3.90	4.70	5.70	6.50	7.20	7.30	7.24
ODA deflator[b]	.28	.32	.38	.64	.72	.83	.92	1.00	.99	.98

	Amount						
	1975	1976	1977	1978	1979	1980	1981[c]
OPEC	**Millions of US dollars**						
54 Nigeria	14	83	64	38	30	42	149
75 Iran, Islamic Rep. of	593	753	221	278	25	7	−150
76 Iraq	215	231	61	173	847	829	143
80 Algeria	41	54	47	44	272	65	65
89 Venezuela	31	108	56	115	109	125	67
95 Libya	259	94	113	146	105	282	105
96 Saudi Arabia	2,756	3,033	3,138	5,507	4,674	5,944	5,798
97 Kuwait	946	532	1,309	991	477	645	685
98 United Arab Emirates	1,046	1,021	1,060	891	967	906	799
Qatar	338	195	194	109	280	284	175
Total OAPEC[d]	5,601	5,160	5,922	7,861	7,622	8,955	7,770
Total OPEC	6,239	6,104	6,263	8,292	7,786	9,129	7,836
OPEC	**As percentage of donor GNP**						
54 Nigeria	.04	.19	.13	.07	.04	.05	.17
75 Iran, Islamic Rep. of	1.13	1.16	.29	.37	.03	.01	. .
76 Iraq	1.63	1.44	.33	.76	2.53	2.13	.37
80 Algeria	.27	.33	.24	.18	.89	.17	.16
89 Venezuela	.11	.34	.15	.29	.22	.21	.10
95 Libya	2.29	.63	.63	.85	.45	.92	.37
96 Saudi Arabia	7.76	6.47	5.33	8.45	6.12	5.09	4.77
97 Kuwait	7.40	3.64	8.20	5.64	1.79	2.04	1.98
98 United Arab Emirates	11.69	8.88	7.27	6.27	5.09	3.38	2.88
Qatar	15.59	7.95	7.76	3.75	6.03	4.25	2.64
Total OAPEC[d]	5.68	4.20	4.00	4.78	3.56	3.08	2.99
Total OPEC	2.92	2.32	2.03	2.46	1.88	1.74	1.46

	Net bilateral flow to low-income countries								
	1960	1965	1970	1975	1977	1978	1979	1980	1981
OECD	**As percentage of donor GNP**								
101 Italy	.03	.04	.06	.01	.02	.01	.01	.01	.02
102 New Zealand				.14	.04	.03	.02	.02	.01
103 United Kingdom	.22	.23	.15	.11	.11	.15	.16	.11	.13
104 Japan	.12	.13	.11	.08	.06	.07	.11	.11	.06
105 Austria	. .	.06	.05	.02	.01	.01	.02	.11	.02
106 Finland	. .	. .	. .	.06	.06	.04	.06	.08	.08
107 Australia	. .	.08	.09	.10	.07	.08	.09	.07	.06
108 Canada	.11	.10	.22	.24	.13	.17	.13	.11	.31
109 Netherlands	.19	.08	.24	.24	.33	.34	.30	.35	.12
110 Belgium	.27	.56	.30	.31	.24	.23	.28	.26	.21
111 France	.01	.12	.09	.10	.07	.08	.08	.09	.10
112 United States	.22	.26	.14	.08	.03	.04	.03	.03	.03
113 Denmark	. .	.02	.10	.20	.24	.21	.26	.27	.16
114 Germany, Fed. Rep.	.13	.14	.10	.12	.07	.07	.08	.07	.25
115 Norway	.02	.04	.12	.25	.30	.39	.34	.28	.09
116 Sweden	.01	.07	.12	.41	.44	.37	.40	.33	.28
117 Switzerland	. .	.02	.05	.10	.05	.08	.06	.08	.06
Total	.18	.20	.13	.11	.07	.09	.09	.09	.07

a. Preliminary estimates.   b. See the technical notes.   c. Provisional.   d. Organization of Arab Petroleum Exporting Countries.

Table 19. Population growth, past and projected, and hypothetical stationary population[a]

	Average annual growth of population (percent)			Projected population (millions)		Hypothetical size of stationary population (millions)	Assumed year of reaching reproduction rate of 1	Year of reaching stationary population
	1960–70	1970–81	1980–2000	1990	2000			
Low-income economies	**2.3** w	**1.9** w	**1.7** w	**2,624** t	**3,107** t			
China and India	**2.3** w	**1.7** w	**1.4** w	**6,937** t	**2,199** t			
Other low-income	**2.5** w	**2.6** w	**2.9** w	**687** t	**908** t			
1 Kampuchea, Dem.	2.6	..	..	..	..	..	..	..
2 Bhutan	1.8	2.0	2.3	2	2	5	2040	2155
3 Lao PDR	1.8	1.9	2.6	4	6	20	2045	2155
4 Chad	1.9	2.0	2.3	6	7	21	2045	2155
5 Bangladesh	2.5	2.6	2.9	119	156	430	2035	2145
6 Ethiopia	2.4	2.0	3.1	42	57	244	2050	2155
7 Nepal	1.9	2.6	2.6	19	24	73	2045	2155
8 Burma	2.2	2.2	2.3	42	52	114	2030	2125
9 Afghanistan	2.2	2.5	2.4	20	26	82	2045	2155
10 Mali	2.5	2.6	3.0	9	12	44	2045	2155
11 Malawi	2.8	3.0	3.4	8	12	51	2045	2155
12 Zaire	2.0	3.0	3.2	39	54	169	2035	2140
13 Uganda	3.0	2.6	3.5	18	25	93	2040	2140
14 Burundi	1.6	2.2	3.0	5	7	26	2045	2155
15 Upper Volta	2.0	2.0	2.9	8	11	34	2040	2155
16 Rwanda	2.6	3.4	3.6	7	10	44	2045	2140
17 India	2.3	2.1	2.0	836	1,001	1,838	2020	2140
18 Somalia	2.8	2.8	2.5	5	7	23	2050	2155
19 Tanzania	2.7	3.4	3.5	26	36	119	2035	2120
20 Viet Nam	3.1	2.8	2.5	70	88	164	2015	2105
21 China	2.3	1.5	1.0	1,101	1,198	1,435	2005	2040
22 Guinea	2.9	2.9	2.8	7	9	30	2040	2155
23 Haiti	1.6	1.7	2.0	6	7	15	2030	2130
24 Sri Lanka	2.4	1.7	1.9	18	21	32	2005	2090
25 Benin	2.6	2.7	3.5	5	7	25	2040	2135
26 Central African Rep.	1.9	2.3	2.3	3	4	11	2045	2155
27 Sierra Leone	2.3	2.6	2.9	5	6	20	2040	2140
28 Madagascar	2.2	2.6	3.1	12	16	54	2040	2140
29 Niger	3.4	3.3	3.3	8	11	41	2045	2155
30 Pakistan	2.8	3.0	3.0	112	148	411	2035	2150
31 Mozambique	2.1	4.2	3.4	17	24	84	2040	2155
32 Sudan	2.1	3.1	3.0	25	34	112	2040	2135
33 Togo	3.0	2.5	3.3	4	5	15	2035	2140
34 Ghana	2.3	3.0	3.9	17	24	85	2035	2135
Middle-income economies	**2.5** w	**2.4** w	**2.3** w	**1,411** t	**1,774** t			
Oil exporters	**2.6** w	**2.7** w	**2.6** w	**647** t	**833** t			
Oil importers	**2.5** w	**2.2** w	**2.1** w	**764** t	**941** t			
Lower middle-income	**2.6** w	**2.6** w	**2.5** w	**839** t	**1,074** t			
35 Kenya	3.2	4.0	4.5	26	40	157	2035	2130
36 Senegal	2.3	2.7	3.0	8	10	36	2045	2155
37 Mauritania	2.3	2.3	2.7	2	3	8	2040	2155
38 Yemen Arab Rep.	2.3	3.0	2.9	9	12	39	2040	2155
39 Yemen, PDR	2.2	2.5	3.2	3	4	12	2040	2155
40 Liberia	3.2	3.5	3.5	3	4	13	2035	2130
41 Indonesia	2.1	2.3	2.0	179	216	400	2020	2140
42 Lesotho	2.0	2.4	2.9	2	2	7	2035	2130
43 Bolivia	2.4	2.6	2.4	7	9	22	2035	2110
44 Honduras	3.1	3.4	3.1	5	7	17	2030	2090
45 Zambia	2.6	3.1	3.6	8	11	40	2035	2145
46 Egypt	2.5	2.5	2.1	53	64	117	2020	2115
47 El Salvador	2.9	2.9	2.8	6	8	16	2020	2080
48 Thailand	3.0	2.5	2.0	58	69	109	2005	2105
49 Philippines	3.0	2.7	2.3	62	76	137	2015	2105
50 Angola	2.1	2.5	2.8	10	13	46	2045	2155
51 Papua New Guinea	2.2	2.1	2.0	4	5	10	2035	2125
52 Morocco	2.6	3.1	3.5	29	40	113	2030	2120
53 Nicaragua	2.6	3.9	2.9	4	5	12	2030	2105
54 Nigeria	2.5	2.5	3.5	119	169	623	2040	2140
55 Zimbabwe	3.4	3.2	4.4	11	16	71	2035	2130
56 Cameroon	1.8	2.2	2.8	11	15	43	2035	2135
57 Cuba	2.0	1.1	1.2	11	12	16	2000	2075
58 Congo, People's Rep.	2.4	2.9	3.5	2	3	9	2030	2120
59 Guatemala	3.0	3.1	2.6	10	12	25	2025	2120
60 Peru	2.9	2.6	2.3	21	26	50	2020	2110
61 Ecuador	3.0	3.4	2.8	11	14	32	2025	2115
62 Jamaica	1.4	1.5	2.1	3	3	5	2005	2065
63 Ivory Coast	3.8	5.0	3.1	11	15	52	2040	2140
64 Dominican Rep.	2.9	3.0	2.5	7	9	16	2015	2095

184

	Average annual growth of population (percent)			Projected population (millions)		Hypothetical size of stationary population (millions)	Assumed year of reaching reproduction rate of 1	Year of reaching stationary population
	1960–70	1970–81	1980–2000	1990	2000			
65 Mongolia	3.0	2.9	2.4	2	3	5	2020	2110
66 Colombia	3.0	1.9	2.0	32	38	62	2010	2110
67 Tunisia	2.0	2.3	2.4	8	10	20	2020	2110
68 Costa Rica	3.4	2.8	2.1	3	3	5	2005	2065
69 Korea, Dem. Rep.	2.9	2.6	2.3	23	28	49	2015	2105
70 Turkey	2.5	2.3	2.1	56	68	119	2015	2110
71 Syrian Arab Rep.	3.2	3.7	4.0	14	19	48	2020	2105
72 Jordan	3.1	3.5	3.7	5	7	18	2025	2110
73 Paraguay	2.6	2.6	2.3	4	5	8	2020	2105
Upper middle-income	2.5 w	2.2 w	2.1 w	572 t	700 t			
74 Korea, Rep. of	2.6	1.7	1.6	45	52	74	2005	2095
75 Iran, Islamic Rep. of	3.0	3.1	3.2	54	72	174	2025	2115
76 Iraq	3.2	3.4	3.5	19	26	73	2030	2120
77 Malaysia	2.9	2.5	2.1	17	21	35	2010	2100
78 Panama	2.9	2.3	2.1	2	3	5	2010	2090
79 Lebanon	2.9	0.6	2.0	3	4	7	2010	2095
80 Algeria	2.4	3.3	3.6	27	38	111	2030	2120
81 Brazil	2.8	2.1	2.1	147	177	299	2015	2110
82 Mexico	3.3	3.1	2.6	91	115	215	2015	2105
83 Portugal	0.3	0.8	0.9	11	11	14	2000	2070
84 Argentina	1.4	1.6	1.0	31	34	45	2010	2080
85 Chile	2.1	1.7	1.5	13	15	22	2010	2070
86 South Africa	2.4	2.8	3.1	39	52	123	2025	2120
87 Yugoslavia	1.0	0.9	0.7	24	26	30	2005	2070
88 Uruguay	1.0	0.4	0.9	3	4	5	2010	2075
89 Venezuela	3.4	3.4	2.3	19	24	41	2010	2095
90 Greece	0.6	0.9	0.4	10	10	12	2000	2065
91 Hong Kong	2.6	2.4	1.2	6	6	8	2000	2060
92 Israel	3.5	2.6	1.5	5	5	8	2010	2085
93 Singapore	2.4	1.5	1.2	3	3	4	2000	2035
94 Trinidad and Tobago	2.1	1.4	1.5	1	2	2	2000	2065
High-income oil exporters	4.3 w	4.9 w	3.4 w	20 t	28 t			
95 Libya	3.9	4.1	3.7	4	6	19	2030	2120
96 Saudi Arabia	3.5	4.5	3.4	12	18	59	2035	2125
97 Kuwait	9.9	6.3	2.6	2	2	5	2015	2085
98 United Arab Emirates	9.3	16.6	2.0	1	2	3	2020	2110
Industrial market economies	1.1 w	0.7 w	0.7 w	754 t	792 t			
99 Ireland	0.4	1.3	0.9	4	4	6	2000	2070
100 Spain	1.0	1.1	0.7	41	43	53	2000	2080
101 Italy	0.7	0.4	0.4	58	60	65	2000	2065
102 New Zealand	1.7	1.5	1.0	4	4	5	2000	2070
103 United Kingdom	0.6	0.1	0.2	57	59	61	2000	2025
104 Japan	1.0	1.1	0.6	124	131	137	2000	2030
105 Austria	0.5	0.1	0.2	8	8	8	2000	2025
106 Finland	0.4	0.4	0.4	5	5	5	2000	2020
107 Australia	2.0	1.4	0.7	16	17	20	2000	2055
108 Canada	1.8	1.2	0.8	26	28	32	2000	2030
109 Netherlands	1.3	0.8	0.6	15	16	17	2000	2025
110 Belgium	0.6	0.2	0.2	10	10	10	2000	2020
111 France	1.1	0.5	0.5	56	59	65	2000	2050
112 United States	1.3	1.0	0.6	245	259	289	2000	2040
113 Denmark	0.8	0.3	0.3	5	5	6	2000	2020
114 Germany, Fed. Rep.	0.9	0.0	0.1	62	63	63	2000	2000
115 Norway	0.8	0.5	0.3	4	4	5	2000	2030
116 Sweden	0.7	0.3	0.1	8	9	9	2000	2000
117 Switzerland	1.5	0.1	0.3	7	7	7	2000	2025
East European nonmarket economies	1.1 w	0.8 w	0.7 w	411 t	437 t			
118 Albania	2.8	2.5	1.9	3	4	6	2005	2060
119 Hungary	0.3	0.4	0.2	11	11	12	2000	2040
120 Romania	0.9	0.9	0.7	24	25	31	2000	2085
121 Bulgaria	0.8	0.5	0.4	9	10	11	2000	2080
122 Poland	1.0	0.9	0.7	39	41	49	2000	2080
123 USSR	1.2	0.9	0.8	291	312	373	2000	2090
124 Czechoslovakia	0.5	0.7	0.5	16	17	20	2000	2085
125 German Dem. Rep.	−0.1	−0.2	0.2	17	17	18	2000	2015
Total[b]				5,220	6,138			

a. For the assumptions used in the projections, see the technical notes.   b. Excludes countries with populations of less than one million.

Table 20. Demographic and fertility-related indicators[a]

	Crude birth rate per thousand population		Crude death rate per thousand population		Percentage change in:		Total fertility rate 1981[a]	Percentage of married women using contraceptives[a]	
					Crude birth rate 1960–81[a]	Crude death rate 1960–81[a]			
	1960	1981[a]	1960	1981[a]				1970	1981
Low-income economies	42 w	31 w	23 w	12 w	−28.9 w	−50.1 w	4.3 w	..	..
China and India	41 w	27 w	23 w	10 w	−35.0 w	−55.5 w	3.7 w	..	..
Other low-income	48 w	44 w	24 w	17 w	−9.3 w	−32.7 w	6.2 w	..	..
1 Kampuchea, Dem.	45	..	19	..	..	..	..	..	..
2 Bhutan	43	40	26	19	−7.1	−25.0	5.7	..	..
3 Lao, PDR	44	43	23	21	−2.5	−8.8	6.4	..	..
4 Chad	45	43	29	22	−5.5	−24.5	5.5	..	..
5 Bangladesh	54	47	28	18	−12.2	−37.5	6.4	..	12
6 Ethiopia	51	48	28	24	−5.5	−14.7	6.5	..	..
7 Nepal	44	44	26	20	0.1	−25.3	6.4	1	4
8 Burma	43	37	21	13	−13.7	−37.2	5.2	..	..
9 Afghanistan	50	47	31	26	−6.6	−16.2	6.9	..	1
10 Mali	50	49	27	21	−2.7	−19.9	6.5	..	..
11 Malawi	56	56	27	23	0.1	−15.9	7.8	..	..
12 Zaire	48	46	24	16	−3.7	−32.8	6.3	..	..
13 Uganda	50	50	23	18	−0.1	−20.1	7.0	..	..
14 Burundi	47	46	27	20	−1.2	−23.9	6.5	..	..
15 Upper Volta	49	48	27	22	−1.5	−19.5	6.5	..	..
16 Rwanda	53	54	27	20	1.5	−26.5	8.3	..	..
17 India	44	35	22	13	−18.8	−38.8	4.8	12	23
18 Somalia	48	48	29	25	0.1	−12.4	6.5	..	..
19 Tanzania	47	47	22	15	0.8	−32.3	6.5	..	..
20 Viet Nam	47	35	21	8	−23.9	−60.7	5.1	..	..
21 China	39	21	24	8	−46.3	−67.1	2.9	..	74
22 Guinea	47	47	30	22	1.3	−25.9	6.3	..	..
23 Haiti	39	33	19	13	−14.1	−32.6	4.7	..	5
24 Sri Lanka	36	27	9	6	−24.3	−34.8	3.5	8	41
25 Benin	51	49	27	17	−3.1	−36.2	6.5	..	..
26 Central African Rep.	43	43	28	22	1.5	−22.6	5.5	..	..
27 Sierra Leone	47	46	27	18	−2.3	−33.0	6.1	..	..
28 Madagascar	47	47	27	18	−0.1	−32.9	6.5	..	..
29 Niger	52	51	27	21	−0.8	−22.7	7.0	..	..
30 Pakistan	51	46	24	16	−11.2	−34.9	6.4	..	6
31 Mozambique	..	..	..	..	..	..	6.5	..	..
32 Sudan	47	47	25	18	0.2	−25.1	6.7	..	..
33 Togo	51	49	23	18	−2.6	−20.1	6.5	..	..
34 Ghana	50	49	20	13	−1.7	−34.2	7.0	2	4
Middle-income economies	43 w	35 w	17 w	11 w	−20.2 w	−38.5 w	4.8 w	..	..
Oil exporters	47 w	40 w	20 w	12 w	−16.2 w	−40.6 w	5.4 w	..	..
Oil importers	41 w	32 w	15 w	9 w	−23.6 w	−38.6 w	4.3 w	..	..
Lower middle-income	47 w	38 w	20 w	12 w	−18.9 w	−41.7 w	5.2 w	..	..
35 Kenya	55	55	24	13	0.1	−45.5	8.0	1	..
36 Senegal	48	48	26	21	0.1	−20.7	6.5	..	..
37 Mauritania	51	44	27	20	−14.0	−25.2	6.0	..	..
38 Yemen Arab Rep.	50	48	29	23	−2.5	−21.1	6.8	..	..
39 Yemen, PDR	50	48	29	20	−4.9	−31.7	7.0	..	..
40 Liberia	50	50	21	14	−0.8	−30.9	6.9	..	..
41 Indonesia	46	35	22	13	−24.4	−41.8	4.4	..	36
42 Lesotho	42	42	23	15	(.)	−36.3	5.8	..	..
43 Bolivia	46	42	22	16	−9.4	−29.0	6.0	..	..
44 Honduras	51	44	19	11	−13.0	−42.3	6.6	..	9
45 Zambia	51	49	24	16	−2.4	−34.4	6.9	..	..
46 Egypt	44	36	19	12	−17.9	−38.0	4.8	9	17
47 El Salvador	49	40	16	8	−18.4	−50.3	5.6	..	20
48 Thailand	44	30	15	8	−32.1	−48.8	3.9	8	59
49 Philippines	47	34	15	7	−27.4	−50.1	4.6	2	48
50 Angola	50	49	31	23	−1.5	−26.9	6.5	..	..
51 Papua New Guinea	44	36	23	15	−18.3	−36.0	5.2	..	..
52 Morocco	52	46	23	13	−10.6	−46.4	6.9	1	5
53 Nicaragua	51	44	19	11	−12.6	−39.9	6.1	..	..
54 Nigeria	52	50	25	17	−4.5	−34.2	6.9	..	..
55 Zimbabwe	55	54	17	13	−1.8	−23.0	8.0	..	14
56 Cameroon	43	43	27	17	−0.8	−37.2	5.8	..	..
57 Cuba	32	18	9	6	−43.3	−29.4	2.2	..	..
58 Congo, People's Rep.	40	43	18	10	6.2	−44.0	6.0	..	..
59 Guatemala	48	39	18	10	−19.0	−44.0	5.3	7	18
60 Peru	46	36	18	11	−20.2	−39.5	5.1	..	..
61 Ecuador	47	40	17	9	−14.9	−44.4	5.9	..	6
62 Jamaica	39	29	9	6	−26.7	−32.6	3.8	..	..
63 Ivory Coast	49	46	27	18	−6.0	−33.7	6.8	..	..
64 Dominican Rep.	50	36	16	8	−28.9	−49.6	4.6	..	31

186

	Crude birth rate per thousand population		Crude death rate per thousand population		Percentage change in:		Total fertility rate	Percentage of married women using contra-ceptives[a]	
					Crude birth rate	Crude death rate			
	1960	1981[a]	1960	1981[a]	1960–81[a]	1960–81[a]	1981[a]	1970	1981
65 Mongolia	41	34	15	7	−16.3	−50.6	4.9	..	..
66 Colombia	46	29	16	8	−32.2	−51.1	3.7	34	46
67 Tunisia	49	34	21	9	−30.1	−56.7	5.1	10	21
68 Costa Rica	47	30	10	4	−36.5	−56.4	3.5	..	65
69 Korea, Dem. Rep.	42	31	13	6	−26.2	−50.4	4.2	..	..
70 Turkey	43	33	16	9	−23.0	−41.4	4.6	3	38
71 Syrian Arab Rep.	47	47	18	8	1.0	−56.4	7.4	..	..
72 Jordan	47	46	20	9	−1.9	−55.0	7.3	..	..
73 Paraguay	43	32	13	7	−26.5	−42.9	4.3	..	16
Upper middle-income	39 w	31 w	13 w	9 w	−22.1 w	−34.0 w	4.2 w	..	..
74 Korea, Rep. of	43	24	13	7	−43.7	−48.5	3.0	32	55
75 Iran, Islamic Rep. of	46	43	17	11	−6.1	−36.7	6.0	3	23
76 Iraq	49	47	20	12	−4.8	−38.9	7.0	..	23
77 Malaysia	45	31	16	7	−31.0	−53.9	4.0	7	42
78 Panama	41	30	10	5	−26.2	−46.4	3.8	..	54
79 Lebanon	43	30	14	8	−30.8	−43.5	4.0	..	..
80 Algeria	50	45	23	13	−4.5	−41.7	7.3	..	..
81 Brazil	43	30	13	8	−28.6	−36.7	4.0	..	..
82 Mexico	45	36	12	7	−20.6	−42.8	5.0	..	38
83 Portugal	24	16	11	10	−32.6	−8.3	2.3	..	..
84 Argentina	24	20	9	9	−13.6	0.6	2.8	..	..
85 Chile	37	25	12	7	−31.6	−39.5	3.0	..	..
86 South Africa	39	39	15	9	0.1	−39.7	5.1	..	..
87 Yugoslavia	24	17	10	9	−28.9	−9.1	2.2	59	..
88 Uruguay	22	20	10	10	−9.0	−0.5	2.8	..	..
89 Venezuela	46	35	11	6	−24.4	−51.1	4.4	..	..
90 Greece	19	15	7	9	−18.5	24.7	2.3	..	..
91 Hong Kong	35	19	8	5	−45.0	−33.9	2.2	50	80
92 Israel	27	25	6	7	−5.8	13.1	3.3	..	..
93 Singapore	38	18	8	5	−53.0	−35.0	1.7	45	71
94 Trinidad and Tobago	38	29	8	8	−23.0	−10.1	2.5	44	..
High-income oil exporters	49 w	44 w	21 w	12 w	−9.0 w	−43.2 w	7.1 w	..	..
95 Libya	49	47	19	12	−4.0	−38.5	7.4	..	..
96 Saudi Arabia	49	45	23	13	−6.9	−40.0	7.3	..	..
97 Kuwait	44	38	10	4	−13.4	−59.3	5.9	..	..
98 United Arab Emirates	46	30	19	7	−34.9	−61.6	6.8	..	..
Industrial market economies	20 w	14 w	10 w	9 w	−31.1 w	−7.7 w	1.8 w	..	..
99 Ireland	21	21	12	9	−1.9	−18.3	3.2	..	..
100 Spain	22	14	9	8	−35.0	−13.6	2.5	..	..
101 Italy	18	11	10	10	−39.8	−1.0	1.9	..	..
102 New Zealand	27	16	9	8	−38.5	−9.1	2.1	..	..
103 United Kingdom	18	13	12	12	−25.1	2.6	1.7	..	..
104 Japan	17	13	8	6	−24.9	−19.7	1.7	56	61
105 Austria	18	13	13	12	−30.2	−3.1	1.6	..	..
106 Finland	19	13	9	9	−28.6	1.1	1.6	77	..
107 Australia	22	16	9	7	−29.5	−15.1	1.9	66	..
108 Canada	27	16	8	7	−41.9	−7.7	1.9	..	..
109 Netherlands	21	13	8	8	−39.9	5.2	1.6	59	75
110 Belgium	17	13	12	11	−25.4	−9.7	1.7	76	87
111 France	18	15	11	10	−16.8	−9.6	1.9	64	79
112 United States	24	16	10	9	−32.6	−8.4	1.8	65	68
113 Denmark	17	10	10	11	−37.3	15.8	1.6	67	..
114 Germany, Fed. Rep.	18	10	12	12	−42.3	0.9	1.4	..	..
115 Norway	17	13	9	10	−26.0	8.8	1.8	..	..
116 Sweden	14	11	10	11	−17.5	11.0	1.7	..	..
117 Switzerland	18	12	10	9	−34.1	−4.1	1.5	..	..
East European nonmarket economies	23 w	18 w	8 w	11 w	−21.2 w	37.5 w	2.3 w	..	..
118 Albania	43	29	10	6	−33.6	−41.2	3.8	..	..
119 Hungary	15	13	10	14	−9.5	32.4	1.9	6	28
120 Romania	19	18	9	10	−5.8	19.5	2.5	..	..
121 Bulgaria	18	14	8	11	−20.8	37.0	2.1	..	..
122 Poland	23	19	8	9	−16.4	21.1	2.2	57	..
123 USSR	25	19	7	10	−24.9	45.1	2.4	..	..
124 Czechoslovakia	16	16	9	12	−2.5	27.2	2.4	66	..
125 German Dem. Rep.	17	14	14	14	−16.5	2.2	1.4	..	..

a. Figures in italics are for years or periods other than those specified. See the technical notes.

Table 21. Labor force

	Percentage of population of working age (15–64 years)		Percentage of labor force in:						Average annual growth of labor force (percent)		
			Agriculture		Industry		Services				
	1960	1981	1960	1980	1960	1980	1960	1980	1960–70	1970–81	1980–2000
Low-income economies	55 w	59 w	77 w	70 w	9 w	15 w	14 w	15 w	1.7 w	1.9 w	2.0 w
China and India	56 w	60 w	74 w	69 w	11 w	17 w	15 w	14 w	1.7 w	1.9 w	1.8 w
Other low-income	54 w	54 w	82 w	73 w	7 w	11 w	11 w	16 w	1.8 w	2.3 w	3.0 w
1 Kampuchea, Dem.	53	..	82	..	4	..	14	..	2.0	..	..
2 Bhutan	56	55	95	93	2	2	3	5	1.6	1.8	2.4
3 Lao, PDR	56	51	83	75	4	6	13	19	1.0	0.7	2.7
4 Chad	57	54	95	85	2	7	3	8	1.5	1.8	2.5
5 Bangladesh	53	55	87	74	3	11	10	15	2.1	2.9	3.0
6 Ethiopia	53	52	88	80	5	7	7	13	2.0	1.6	3.0
7 Nepal	57	55	95	93	2	2	3	5	1.3	2.3	2.7
8 Burma	59	55	..	67	..	10	..	23	1.1	1.4	2.2
9 Afghanistan	55	52	85	79	6	8	9	13	1.9	2.0	2.6
10 Mali	54	51	94	73	3	12	3	16	2.1	2.0	3.0
11 Malawi	52	50	92	86	3	5	5	9	2.4	2.5	3.2
12 Zaire	53	52	83	75	9	13	8	12	1.4	2.3	3.1
13 Uganda	54	52	89	83	4	6	7	11	2.6	2.1	3.6
14 Burundi	55	53	90	84	3	5	7	11	1.2	1.5	2.8
15 Upper Volta	54	52	92	82	5	13	3 .	5	1.6	1.5	2.8
16 Rwanda	53	52	95	91	1	2	4	7	2.2	3.2	3.4
17 India	54	57	74	69	11	13	15	18	1.7	1.9	2.2
18 Somalia	54	54	88	82	4	8	8	10	2.1	3.0	2.0
19 Tanzania	54	51	89	83	4	6	7	11	2.1	2.7	3.4
20 Viet Nam	..	54	..	71	..	10	..	19	..	..	2.7
21 China	56	62	..	69	..	19	..	12	1.7	1.8	1.6
22 Guinea	55	53	88	82	6	11	6	7	2.5	2.2	2.6
23 Haiti	55	53	80	74	6	7	14	19	0.6	1.3	2.1
24 Sri Lanka	54	60	56	54	14	14	30	32	2.1	2.0	2.2
25 Benin	53	51	54	46	9	16	37	38	2.1	2.1	2.9
26 Central African Rep.	58	55	94	88	2	4	4	8	1.4	1.7	2.1
27 Sierra Leone	55	53	78	65	12	19	10	16	1.5	1.9	2.8
28 Madagascar	55	53	93	87	2	4	5	9	1.7	2.1	3.0
29 Niger	53	51	95	91	1	3	4	6	3.0	3.0	3.4
30 Pakistan	52	51	61	57	18	20	21	23	1.9	2.7	3.3
31 Mozambique	56	53	81	66	8	18	11	16	1.8	3.3	3.1
32 Sudan	53	53	86	72	6	10	8	18	2.0	2.7	3.1
33 Togo	53	51	80	67	8	15	12	18	2.5	1.7	3.1
34 Ghana	53	51	64	53	14	20	22	27	1.6	2.3	3.9
Middle-income economies	54 w	55 w	62 w	45 w	15 w	21 w	23 w	34 w	2.1 w	2.3 w	2.7 w
Oil exporters	54 w	54 w	66 w	47 w	13 w	21 w	22 w	32 w	2.0 w	2.6 w	2.9 w
Oil importers	55 w	57 w	60 w	44 w	16 w	21 w	24 w	35 w	2.1 w	2.1 w	2.5 w
Lower middle-income	54 w	55 w	71 w	55 w	11 w	17 w	18 w	28 w	1.9 w	2.5 w	2.8 w
35 Kenya	50	47	86	78	5	10	9	12	2.7	3.2	4.2
36 Senegal	54	52	84	77	5	10	11	13	1.7	2.0	2.6
37 Mauritania	53	51	91	69	3	8	6	23	1.9	2.0	2.5
38 Yemen Arab Rep.	54	52	83	75	7	11	10	14	1.6	1.8	3.4
39 Yemen, PDR	52	52	70	45	15	15	15	40	1.7	1.8	3.6
40 Liberia	52	51	80	70	10	14	10	16	2.4	3.1	3.5
41 Indonesia	56	57	75	55	8	15	17	30	1.7	2.5	2.0
42 Lesotho	57	55	93	87	2	4	5	9	1.6	1.9	2.8
43 Bolivia	55	53	61	50	18	24	21	26	1.7	2.3	2.9
44 Honduras	52	50	70	63	11	15	19	23	2.5	3.1	3.5
45 Zambia	53	50	79	67	7	11	14	22	2.1	2.3	3.2
46 Egypt	55	57	58	50	12	30	30	20	2.2	2.5	2.4
47 El Salvador	52	52	62	50	17	22	21	27	2.6	2.8	3.5
48 Thailand	53	56	84	76	4	9	12	15	2.1	2.8	2.3
49 Philippines	52	53	61	46	15	17	24	37	2.1	2.5	2.9
50 Angola	55	53	69	59	12	16	19	25	1.6	2.0	2.9
51 Papua New Guinea	57	55	89	82	4	8	7	10	1.7	1.7	1.7
52 Morocco	53	51	62	52	14	21	24	27	1.5	3.1	4.2
53 Nicaragua	50	50	62	43	16	20	22	37	2.3	3.8	3.9
54 Nigeria	52	50	71	54	10	19	19	27	1.8	1.7	3.5
55 Zimbabwe	52	50	69	60	11	15	20	25	2.7	2.5	4.5
56 Cameroon	57	54	87	83	5	7	8	10	1.3	1.5	2.8
57 Cuba	61	61	39	23	22	31	39	46	0.8	1.7	1.9
58 Congo, People's Rep.	56	52	52	34	17	26	31	40	1.8	2.1	3.7
59 Guatemala	51	54	67	55	14	21	19	25	2.8	3.2	2.9
60 Peru	52	54	52	39	20	18	28	43	2.1	2.9	3.0
61 Ecuador	52	52	57	52	19	17	23	31	2.9	3.3	3.5
62 Jamaica	54	54	39	21	25	25	36	53	0.4	2.2	3.3
63 Ivory Coast	54	53	89	79	2	4	9	17	3.6	4.3	2.9
64 Dominican Rep.	49	53	67	49	12	18	21	33	2.2	3.6	3.3

	Percentage of population of working age (15–64 years)		Percentage of labor force in:						Average annual growth of labor force (percent)		
			Agriculture		Industry		Services				
	1960	1981	1960	1980	1960	1980	1960	1980	1960–70	1970–81	1980–2000
65 Mongolia	54	54	70	55	13	22	17	23	2.1	2.4	3.1
66 Colombia	50	60	51	26	19	21	29	53	3.0	3.3	2.5
67 Tunisia	52	56	56	35	18	32	26	33	0.7	3.0	3.2
68 Costa Rica	50	59	51	29	19	23	30	48	3.5	3.9	2.8
69 Korea, Dem. Rep.	53	56	62	49	23	33	15	18	2.4	2.9	2.9
70 Turkey	55	57	79	54	11	13	11	34	1.4	2.0	2.5
71 Syrian Arab Rep.	52	49	54	33	19	31	27	36	2.1	3.4	4.7
72 Jordan	52	51	44	20	26	20	30	60	2.8	3.1	4.3
73 Paraguay	51	53	56	44	19	20	25	36	2.3	2.9	3.0
Upper middle-income	55 w	57 w	49 w	30 w	20 w	28 w	31 w	42 w	2.3 w	2.0 w	2.6 w
74 Korea, Rep. of	54	62	66	34	9	29	25	37	3.1	2.6	2.2
75 Iran, Islamic Rep. of	51	52	54	39	23	34	23	27	2.7	2.8	3.9
76 Iraq	51	51	53	42	18	26	29	32	2.9	2.9	4.0
77 Malaysia	51	56	63	50	12	16	25	34	2.8	2.9	3.1
78 Panama	52	56	51	27	14	18	35	55	3.4	2.4	2.6
79 Lebanon	53	56	38	11	23	27	39	62	2.1	1.0	2.8
80 Algeria	52	49	67	25	12	25	21	50	0.5	3.6	4.7
81 Brazil	54	55	52	30	15	24	33	46	2.7	1.0	3.0
82 Mexico	51	52	55	36	20	26	25	39	2.8	3.2	3.5
83 Portugal	63	63	44	28	29	35	27	37	0.4	0.6	0.9
84 Argentina	64	63	20	13	36	28	44	59	1.3	1.4	1.1
85 Chile	57	62	31	19	20	19	50	61	1.4	2.0	2.2
86 South Africa	55	55	32	30	30	29	38	41	3.0	2.9	3.2
87 Yugoslavia	63	67	63	29	18	35	19	36	0.6	0.6	0.7
88 Uruguay	64	63	21	11	30	32	50	57	0.8	0.2	1.1
89 Venezuela	51	55	35	18	22	27	43	55	2.8	4.0	3.1
90 Greece	65	64	56	37	20	28	24	35	0.0	0.8	0.5
91 Hong Kong	56	66	8	3	52	57	40	40	3.3	3.7	1.2
92 Israel	59	58	14	7	35	36	51	57	3.6	2.5	2.0
93 Singapore	55	66	8	2	23	39	69	59	2.8	2.7	1.3
94 Trinidad and Tobago	53	63	22	10	34	39	44	51	2.5	2.6	2.1
High-income oil exporters	54 w	52 w	62 w	46 w	13 w	19 w	25 w	35 w	3.7 w	4.3 w	3.5 w
95 Libya	53	51	53	19	17	28	30	53	3.6	3.7	3.9
96 Saudi Arabia	54	52	71	61	10	14	19	25	3.3	4.4	3.5
97 Kuwait	63	52	1	2	34	34	65	64	7.0	4.5	2.8
98 United Arab Emirates	. .	53	. .	. .	. .	. .	. .	. .	. .	. .	. .
Industrial market economies	63 w	66 w	18 w	6 w	38 w	38 w	44 w	56 w	1.2 w	1.2 w	0.7 w
99 Ireland	58	59	36	18	25	37	39	44	0.0	1.1	1.5
100 Spain	64	63	42	14	31	40	27	45	0.2	1.1	0.9
101 Italy	66	65	31	11	40	45	30	44	−0.1	0.6	0.4
102 New Zealand	58	64	15	9	37	35	49	56	2.2	2.1	1.2
103 United Kingdom	65	64	4	2	48	42	48	56	0.6	0.4	0.3
104 Japan	64	68	33	12	30	39	37	49	1.9	1.3	0.8
105 Austria	66	65	24	9	46	37	30	55	−0.7	0.9	0.5
106 Finland	62	68	36	11	31	35	33	54	0.4	0.9	0.5
107 Australia	61	65	11	6	40	33	49	62	2.6	1.8	1.0
108 Canada	59	67	13	5	34	29	52	66	2.5	2.0	1.0
109 Netherlands	61	67	11	6	42	45	47	49	1.6	1.4	0.7
110 Belgium	65	66	8	3	48	41	44	56	0.3	0.7	0.3
111 France	62	64	22	8	39	39	39	53	0.7	1.1	0.7
112 United States	60	66	7	2	36	32	57	66	1.8	1.9	0.9
113 Denmark	64	65	18	7	37	35	45	58	1.1	0.6	0.5
114 Germany, Fed. Rep.	68	67	14	4	48	46	38	50	0.2	0.8	0.1
115 Norway	63	63	20	7	37	37	44	57	0.5	0.7	0.7
116 Sweden	66	64	14	5	45	34	41	61	1.0	0.3	0.4
117 Switzerland	66	67	11	5	50	46	38	49	2.0	0.3	0.3
East European nonmarket economies	63 w	66 w	42 w	18 w	30 w	44 w	28 w	39 w	0.8 w	1.1 w	0.6 w
118 Albania	54	58	71	61	18	25	11	14	2.3	2.8	2.4
119 Hungary	66	65	37	21	35	43	28	36	0.5	0.3	0.1
120 Romania	64	64	67	29	15	36	18	35	0.9	0.6	0.7
121 Bulgaria	66	66	56	37	25	39	19	24	0.7	0.3	0.2
122 Poland	61	66	48	31	29	39	23	30	1.7	1.4	0.8
123 USSR	63	66	42	14	29	45	29	41	0.7	1.2	0.6
124 Czechoslovakia	64	64	26	11	46	48	28	41	0.8	0.7	0.7
125 German Dem. Rep.	65	64	18	10	48	50	34	40	−0.2	0.5	0.3

Table 22. Urbanization

| | Urban population | | | | Percentage of urban population | | | | Number of cities of over 500,000 persons | |
| | As percentage of total population | | Average annual growth rate (percent) | | In largest city | | In cities of over 500,000 persons | | | |
	1960	1981[a]	1960–70	1970–81[a]	1960	1980	1960	1980	1960	1980
Low-income economies	17 w	21 w	4.2 w	4.4 w	10 w	16 w	31 w	55 w	55 t	145 t
China and India	18 w	22 w	3.3 w	3.7 w	7 w	. .	33 w	59 w	49 t	114 t
Other low-income	12 w	20 w	5.4 w	5.3 w	25 w	28 w	19 w	40 w	6 t	31 t
1 Kampuchea, Dem.	11	. .	3.5	. .	. .	. .	. .	. .	. .	. .
2 Bhutan	2	4	4.0	4.4	0	0	0	0	0	0
3 Lao, PDR	8	14	3.7	5.2	69	48	0	0	0	0
4 Chad	7	19	6.7	6.5	. .	39	0	0	0	0
5 Bangladesh	5	12	6.3	6.5	20	30	20	51	1	3
6 Ethiopia	6	14	6.5	5.5	30	37	0	37	0	1
7 Nepal	3	6	6.3	5.0	41	27	0	0	0	0
8 Burma	19	28	3.9	3.9	23	23	23	23	1	2
9 Afghanistan	8	16	5.4	5.8	33	17	0	17	0	1
10 Mali	11	19	5.4	4.6	32	24	0	0	0	0
11 Malawi	4	10	6.6	7.0	. .	19	0	0	0	0
12 Zaire	16	36	5.2	7.5	14	28	14	38	1	2
13 Uganda	5	9	7.1	3.4	38	52	0	52	0	1
14 Burundi	2	2	1.6	2.7	. .	. .	0	0	0	0
15 Upper Volta	5	11	5.7	6.0	. .	41	0	0	0	0
16 Rwanda	2	4	5.4	6.4	. .	0	0	0	0	0
17 India	18	24	3.3	3.7	7	6	26	39	11	36
18 Somalia	17	31	5.7	5.4	. .	34	0	0	0	0
19 Tanzania	5	12	6.3	8.6	34	50	0	50	0	1
20 Viet Nam	15	19	5.3	3.3	32	21	32	50	1	4
21 China	18	21	. .	. .	6	. .	42	73	38	78
22 Guinea	10	20	6.2	6.0	37	80	0	80	0	1
23 Haiti	16	28	4.0	4.7	42	56	0	56	0	1
24 Sri Lanka	18	27	4.3	3.6	28	16	0	16	0	1
25 Benin	10	15	5.4	4.1	. .	63	0	63	0	1
26 Central African Rep.	23	29	. .	. .	40	36	0	0	0	0
27 Sierra Leone	13	22	5.5	4.4	37	47	0	0	0	0
28 Madagascar	11	19	5.0	5.2	44	36	0	36	0	1
29 Niger	6	13	7.0	7.2	. .	31	0	0	0	0
30 Pakistan	22	29	4.0	4.3	20	21	33	51	2	7
31 Mozambique	4	9	6.5	8.2	75	83	0	83	0	1
32 Sudan	10	26	6.7	7.1	30	31	0	31	0	1
33 Togo	10	21	5.9	6.6	. .	60	0	0	0	0
34 Ghana	23	37	4.6	5.0	25	35	0	48	0	2
Middle-income	33 w	45 w	4.3 w	4.1 w	28 w	29 w	35 w	48 w	54 t	128 t
Oil exporters	27 w	39 w	4.3 w	4.3 w	27 w	30 w	32 w	48 w	15 t	42 t
Oil importers	37 w	51 w	4.4 w	4.0 w	28 w	28 w	36 w	48 w	39 t	86 t
Lower middle-income	24 w	33 w	4.4 w	4.3 w	27 w	32 w	28 w	47 w	22 t	60 t
35 Kenya	7	15	6.4	7.3	40	57	0	57	0	1
36 Senegal	23	34	4.9	3.7	53	65	0	65	0	1
37 Mauritania	3	24	15.5	8.1	. .	39	0	0	0	0
38 Yemen Arab Rep.	3	11	8.0	8.2	. .	25	0	0	0	0
39 Yemen, PDR	28	37	3.5	3.8	61	49	0	0	0	0
40 Liberia	20	34	5.6	5.7	. .	. .	0	0	0	0
41 Indonesia	15	21	3.6	4.0	20	23	34	50	3	9
42 Lesotho	2	12	7.5	16.1	. .	. .	0	0	0	0
43 Bolivia	24	45	3.9	6.9	47	44	0	44	0	1
44 Honduras	23	36	5.4	5.5	31	33	0	0	0	0
45 Zambia	23	44	5.2	6.5	. .	35	0	35	0	1
46 Egypt	38	44	3.6	2.9	38	39	53	53	2	2
47 El Salvador	38	41	3.2	3.4	26	22	0	0	0	0
48 Thailand	13	15	3.5	3.4	65	69	65	69	1	1
49 Philippines	30	37	3.8	3.7	27	30	27	34	1	2
50 Angola	10	22	5.7	5.8	44	64	0	64	0	1
51 Papua New Guinea	3	19	15.2	8.2	. .	25	0	0	0	0
52 Morocco	29	41	4.2	4.6	16	26	16	50	1	4
53 Nicaragua	41	54	4.0	5.0	41	47	0	47	0	1
54 Nigeria	13	21	4.7	4.8	13	17	22	58	2	9
55 Zimbabwe	13	24	6.3	6.3	40	50	0	50	0	1
56 Cameroon	14	36	5.6	7.4	26	21	0	21	0	1
57 Cuba	55	66	2.9	1.9	32	38	38	32	1	1
58 Congo, People's Rep.	30	46	5.0	4.4	77	56	0	0	0	0
59 Guatemala	33	39	3.8	3.9	41	36	41	36	1	1
60 Peru	46	66	5.3	3.5	38	39	38	44	1	2
61 Ecuador	34	45	4.4	4.6	31	29	0	51	0	2
62 Jamaica	34	42	2.4	2.5	77	66	0	66	0	1
63 Ivory Coast	19	41	7.3	8.3	27	34	0	34	0	1
64 Dominican Rep.	30	52	5.6	5.3	50	54	0	54	0	1

190

	Urban population				Percentage of urban population				Number of cities of over 500,000 persons	
	As percentage of total population		Average annual growth rate (percent)		In largest city		In cities of over 500,000 persons			
	1960	1981[a]	1960–70	1970–81[a]	1960	1980	1960	1980	1960	1980
65 Mongolia	36	51	5.2	4.0	53	52	0	0	0	0
66 Colombia	48	64	5.2	2.6	17	26	28	51	3	4
67 Tunisia	36	53	3.8	4.0	40	30	40	30	1	1
68 Costa Rica	37	44	4.2	3.6	67	64	0	64	0	1
69 Korea, Dem. Rep.	40	60	5.1	4.3	15	12	15	19	1	2
70 Turkey	30	47	5.1	4.1	18	24	32	42	3	4
71 Syrian Arab Rep.	37	49	4.8	4.6	35	33	35	55	1	2
72 Jordan	43	57	4.5	4.7	31	37	0	37	0	1
73 Paraguay	36	40	2.9	3.3	44	44	0	44	0	1
Upper middle-income	45 w	63 w	4.2 w	3.8 w	28 w	29 w	38 w	51 w	32 t	68 t
74 Korea, Rep. of	28	56	6.4	4.6	35	41	61	77	3	7
75 Iran, Islamic Rep. of	34	51	4.9	5.0	26	28	26	47	1	6
76 Iraq	43	72	6.2	5.3	35	55	35	70	1	3
77 Malaysia	25	30	3.5	3.3	19	27	0	27	0	1
78 Panama	41	55	4.4	3.6	61	66	0	66	0	1
79 Lebanon	44	77	6.2	2.8	64	79	64	79	1	1
80 Algeria	30	44	3.5	5.6	27	12	27	12	1	1
81 Brazil	46	68	4.7	3.9	14	15	35	52	6	14
82 Mexico	51	67	4.7	4.2	28	32	36	48	3	7
83 Portugal	23	31	1.8	2.4	47	44	47	44	1	1
84 Argentina	74	83	2.0	2.0	46	45	54	60	3	5
85 Chile	68	81	3.1	2.4	38	44	38	44	1	1
86 South Africa	47	50	2.6	3.1	16	13	44	53	4	7
87 Yugoslavia	28	43	3.2	2.9	11	10	11	23	1	3
88 Uruguay	80	84	1.3	0.6	56	52	56	52	1	1
89 Venezuela	67	84	4.7	4.2	26	26	26	44	1	4
90 Greece	43	63	2.6	2.5	51	57	51	70	1	2
91 Hong Kong	89	90	2.6	2.5	100	100	100	100	1	1
92 Israel	77	89	4.3	3.1	46	35	46	35	1	1
93 Singapore	100	100	2.4	1.5	100	100	100	100	1	1
94 Trinidad and Tobago	22	22	1.8	1.4	. .	. .	0	0	0	0
High-income oil exporters	30 w	68 w	8.5 w	8.2 w	29 w	28 w	0 w	34 w	0 t	3 t
95 Libya	23	54	8.0	8.1	57	64	0	64	0	1
96 Saudi Arabia	30	68	8.4	7.4	15	18	0	33	0	2
97 Kuwait	72	89	10.0	7.5	75	30	0	0	0	0
98 United Arab Emirates	40	73	12.7	16.6	. .	. .	. .	. .	. .	. .
Industrial market economies	68 w	78 w	1.9 w	1.4 w	18 w	18 w	48 w	55 w	104 t	152 t
99 Ireland	46	58	1.6	2.5	51	48	51	48	1	1
100 Spain	57	75	2.6	2.2	13	17	37	44	5	6
101 Italy	59	70	1.5	1.1	13	17	46	52	7	9
102 New Zealand	76	85	2.4	1.9	25	30	0	30	0	1
103 United Kingdom	86	91	0.9	0.3	24	20	61	55	15	17
104 Japan	62	79	2.4	2.0	18	22	35	42	5	9
105 Austria	50	55	0.9	0.6	51	39	51	39	1	1
106 Finland	38	63	3.2	2.4	28	27	0	27	0	1
107 Australia	81	89	2.5	2.0	26	24	62	68	4	5
108 Canada	69	76	2.7	1.2	14	18	31	62	2	9
109 Netherlands	80	76	1.0	0.6	9	9	27	24	3	3
110 Belgium	66	73	1.2	0.4	17	14	28	24	2	2
111 France	62	78	2.4	1.4	25	23	34	34	4	6
112 United States	70	77	1.8	1.5	13	12	61	77	40	65
113 Denmark	74	85	1.6	0.8	40	32	40	32	1	1
114 Germany, Fed. Rep.	77	85	1.4	0.5	20	18	48	45	11	11
115 Norway	32	53	3.5	2.7	50	32	50	32	1	1
116 Sweden	73	88	1.8	1.0	15	15	15	35	1	3
117 Switzerland	51	59	2.2	1.0	19	22	19	22	1	1
East European nonmarket economies	48 w	62 w	2.6 w	1.8 w	9 w	7 w	23 w	32 w	35 t	64 t
118 Albania	31	37	3.8	3.4	27	25	0	0	0	0
119 Hungary	40	54	2.1	1.4	45	37	45	37	1	1
120 Romania	32	50	3.4	2.8	22	17	22	17	1	1
121 Bulgaria	39	65	3.8	2.4	23	18	23	18	1	1
122 Poland	48	57	1.8	1.7	17	15	41	47	5	8
123 USSR	49	63	2.7	1.8	6	4	21	33	25	50
124 Czechoslovakia	47	64	2.1	1.9	17	12	17	12	1	1
125 German Dem. Rep.	72	77	0.1	0.2	9	9	14	17	2	3

a. Figures in italics are for years or periods other than those specified.

Table 23. Indicators related to life expectancy

	Life expectancy at birth (years)		Infant mortality rate (aged 0–1)		Child death rate (aged 1–4)	
	1960	1981	1960	1981[a]	1960	1981[a]
Low-income economies	41 w	58 w	165 w	99 w	27 w	14 w
China and India	41 w	61 w	165 w	92 w	26 w	11 w
Other low-income	41 w	50 w	163 w	124 w	30 w	21 w
1 Kampuchea, Dem.	46	..	146	..	22	..
2 Bhutan	38	45	195	148	33	22
3 Lao, PDR	40	43	155	126	24	18
4 Chad	35	43	195	146	46	32
5 Bangladesh	37	48	159	135	25	20
6 Ethiopia	..	46	175	145	40	31
7 Nepal	38	45	195	148	33	22
8 Burma	44	54	158	98	25	12
9 Afghanistan	33	37	233	205	41	35
10 Mali	37	45	195	152	46	33
11 Malawi	37	44	207	169	49	38
12 Zaire	40	50	150	110	33	21
13 Uganda	41	48	139	96	29	17
14 Burundi	37	45	150	120	33	24
15 Upper Volta	37	44	252	208	63	50
16 Rwanda	37	46	147	137	32	29
17 India	43	52	165	121	26	17
18 Somalia	35	39	175	145	40	31
19 Tanzania	42	52	152	101	33	19
20 Viet Nam	43	63	157	97	25	12
21 China	41	67	165	71	26	7
22 Guinea	..	43	208	163	50	36
23 Haiti	44	54	182	112	47	17
24 Sri Lanka	62	69	71	43	7	3
25 Benin	37	50	206	152	49	33
26 Central African Rep.	35	43	195	146	46	32
27 Sierra Leone	37	47	234	205	57	49
28 Madagascar	37	48	109	69	21	11
29 Niger	37	45	191	143	45	31
30 Pakistan	43	50	162	123	25	17
31 Mozambique	..	..	160	113	36	22
32 Sudan	40	47	168	122	40	21
33 Togo	42	48	182	107	42	20
34 Ghana	45	54	143	101	31	19
Middle-income economies	50 w	60 w	127 w	81 w	22 w	11 w
Oil exporters	45 w	57 w	145 w	97 w	27 w	14 w
Oil importers	54 w	63 w	113 w	69 w	18 w	8 w
Lower middle-income	46 w	57 w	145 w	95 w	27 w	14 w
35 Kenya	41	56	138	85	29	15
36 Senegal	37	44	182	145	42	31
37 Mauritania	37	44	185	141	43	30
38 Yemen Arab Rep.	36	43	212	190	60	50
39 Yemen, PDR	36	46	209	143	59	29
40 Liberia	44	54	194	152	46	33
41 Indonesia	41	54	150	105	23	14
42 Lesotho	42	52	144	113	31	22
43 Bolivia	43	51	167	129	40	23
44 Honduras	46	59	145	86	30	9
45 Zambia	40	51	151	104	33	20
46 Egypt	46	57	128	110	34	16
47 El Salvador	51	63	136	75	26	7
48 Thailand	52	63	103	53	13	4
49 Philippines	53	63	106	53	14	4
50 Angola	33	42	208	152	50	33
51 Papua New Guinea	41	51	165	102	26	13
52 Morocco	47	57	161	104	37	15
53 Nicaragua	47	57	144	88	30	10
54 Nigeria	39	49	183	133	42	28
55 Zimbabwe	49	55	118	72	23	11
56 Cameroon	37	50	162	106	36	20
57 Cuba	63	73	66	19	5	1
58 Congo, People's Rep.	48	60	171	127	39	26
59 Guatemala	47	59	92	66	10	5
60 Peru	47	58	163	85	38	9
61 Ecuador	51	62	140	80	28	8
62 Jamaica	64	71	52	16	3	(.)
63 Ivory Coast	37	47	173	125	39	25
64 Dominican Rep.	51	62	119	66	20	5

	Life expectancy at birth (years)		Infant mortality rate (aged 0–1)		Child death rate (aged 1–4)	
	1960	1981	1960	1981[a]	1960	1981[a]
65 Mongolia	52	64	109	53	14	4
66 Colombia	53	63	103	55	14	4
67 Tunisia	48	61	159	88	36	9
68 Costa Rica	62	73	83	27	8	1
69 Korea, Dem. Rep.	54	66	78	33	9	2
70 Turkey	51	62	190	119	50	20
71 Syrian Arab Rep.	50	65	132	60	25	4
72 Jordan	47	62	136	67	26	5
73 Paraguay	56	65	86	46	9	2
Upper middle-income	**57** *w*	**65** *w*	**103** *w*	**62** *w*	**15** *w*	**6** *w*
74 Korea, Rep. of	54	66	78	33	9	2
75 Iran, Islamic Rep. of	50	58	163	105	26	14
76 Iraq	46	57	139	76	28	7
77 Malaysia	53	65	72	30	7	2
78 Panama	62	71	68	21	5	1
79 Lebanon	58	66	68	40	5	2
80 Algeria	47	56	165	114	39	18
81 Brazil	55	64	118	75	19	7
82 Mexico	57	66	91	54	10	4
83 Portugal	63	72	82	*26*	9	*1*
84 Argentina	65	71	61	44	4	2
85 Chile	57	68	114	42	18	2
86 South Africa	53	63	135	94	28	17
87 Yugoslavia	63	71	92	31	11	2
88 Uruguay	68	71	50	39	3	2
89 Venezuela	57	68	85	40	9	2
90 Greece	69	74	40	18	3	1
91 Hong Kong	67	75	37	10	2	(.)
92 Israel	69	73	31	15	2	1
93 Singapore	64	72	36	12	2	(.)
94 Trinidad and Tobago	64	72	54	*31*	4	1
High-income oil exporters	**44** *w*	**57** *w*	**173** *w*	**96** *w*	**43** *w*	**13** *w*
95 Libya	47	57	158	97	36	*12*
96 Saudi Arabia	43	55	185	111	48	17
97 Kuwait	60	70	89	33	10	1
98 United Arab Emirates	47	63	135	52	26	3
Industrial market economies	**70** *w*	**75** *w*	**30** *w*	**11** *w*	**2** *w*	**(.)** *w*
99 Ireland	70	73	29	11	2	(.)
100 Spain	68	74	50	10	4	(.)
101 Italy	69	74	44	14	3	1
102 New Zealand	72	74	23	12	1	(.)
103 United Kingdom	71	74	23	*12*	1	(.)
104 Japan	68	77	30	7	2	(.)
105 Austria	69	73	38	13	3	1
106 Finland	68	75	21	8	1	(.)
107 Australia	71	74	20	10	1	(.)
108 Canada	71	75	27	10	2	(.)
109 Netherlands	73	76	18	8	1	(.)
110 Belgium	70	73	31	12	2	(.)
111 France	70	76	27	10	2	(.)
112 United States	70	75	26	12	1	(.)
113 Denmark	72	75	22	8	1	(.)
114 Germany, Fed. Rep.	70	73	34	*13*	2	1
115 Norway	73	76	19	8	1	(.)
116 Sweden	73	77	17	7	1	(.)
117 Switzerland	71	76	21	9	1	(.)
East European nonmarket economies	**68** *w*	**72** *w*	**38** *w*	**25** *w*	**3** *w*	**1** *w*
118 Albania	62	70	83	. .	9	. .
119 Hungary	68	71	48	21	2	1
120 Romania	65	71	77	29	8	2
121 Bulgaria	69	73	45	20	3	1
122 Poland	67	73	56	21	5	1
123 USSR	68	72	33	. .	2	. .
124 Czechoslovakia	70	72	24	17	1	1
125 German Dem. Rep.	69	73	39	12	3	(.)

a. Figures in italics are for years other than that specified.

Table 24. Health-related indicators

| | Population per: | | | | Daily per capita calorie supply | |
| | Physician[a] | | Nursing person[a] | | Total | As percentage of requirement |
	1960	1980	1960	1980	1980	1980
Low-income economies	12,222 w	5,785 w	7,217 w	4,668 w	2,218 w	97 w
China and India	6,977 w	2,626 w	6,727 w	3,322 w	2,270 w	99 w
Other low-income	37,737 w	15,846 w	9,707 w	8,953 w	2,050 w	92 w
1 Kampuchea, Dem.	35,440	..	4,010	..	2,053	88
2 Bhutan	..	..			..	90
3 Lao, PDR	54,140	20,060	4,980	3,040	1,829	97
4 Chad	72,190	47,530	5,780	3,850	1,768	74
5 Bangladesh	..	10,940	..	24,450	1,960	84
6 Ethiopia	100,470	58,490	14,920	5,440	1,735	76
7 Nepal	73,800	30,060	..	33,420	1,977	86
8 Burma	15,560	4,660	8,520	4,750	2,174	113
9 Afghanistan	28,700	16,730	19,590	25,990	1,775	73
10 Mali	64,130	22,130	4,710	2,380	1,871	85
11 Malawi	35,250	40,950	12,940	3,830	2,095	94
12 Zaire	79,620	14,780	3,510	1,920	2,180	94
13 Uganda	15,050	26,810	10,030	4,180	1,760	83
14 Burundi	96,570	45,020	4,530	6,180	2,114	96
15 Upper Volta	81,650	48,510	4,090	4,950	1,791	95
16 Rwanda	143,290	31,510	11,620	9,840	2,364	88
17 India	4,850	3,640	10,980	5,380	1,880	87
18 Somalia	36,570	14,290	4,810	2,330	1,952	100
19 Tanzania	18,220	17,560	11,890	2,980	2,051	83
20 Viet Nam	..	4,190	..	2,930	1,977	90
21 China	8,330	1,920	4,020	1,890	2,539	107
22 Guinea	26,900	16,630	3,260	2,490	2,071	77
23 Haiti	9,230	8,200	4,020	2,490	1,620	96
24 Sri Lanka	4,490	7,170	4,170	1,340	2,238	102
25 Benin	23,030	17,050	2,700	1,670	2,292	103
26 Central African Rep.	49,610	27,050	3,280	1,760	2,198	94
27 Sierra Leone	20,420	18,280	2,960	2,130	2,053	89
28 Madagascar	8,900	10,170	3,110	3,660	2,466	109
29 Niger	82,170	38,790	8,460	4,650	2,327	92
30 Pakistan	5,400	3,480	16,960	5,820	2,184	106
31 Mozambique	20,390	39,110	4,720	5,600	2,170	70
32 Sudan	33,420	8,800	3,030	1,410	2,447	101
33 Togo	47,060	18,100	5,340	1,430	2,101	95
34 Ghana	21,600	7,630	5,430	780	1,964	88
Middle-income economies	17,011 w	5,332 w	3,889 w	1,769 w	2,579 w	110 w
Oil exporters	29,989 w	6,706 w	4,118 w	1,979 w	2,498 w	106 w
Oil importers	6,681 w	4,174 w	3,685 w	1,580 w	2,644 w	113 w
Lower middle-income	27,807 w	7,751 w	4,925 w	2,261 w	2,476 w	106 w
35 Kenya	10,690	10,500	2,270	550	2,078	88
36 Senegal	24,990	13,800	2,840	1,400	2,406	100
37 Mauritania	40,420	14,350	5,430	2,080	1,941	97
38 Yemen Arab Rep.	130,090	11,670	..	4,580	2,712	76
39 Yemen, PDR	13,290	7,390	..	850	2,122	84
40 Liberia	12,600	9,610	1,410	1,420	2,390	114
41 Indonesia	46,780	11,530	4,510	2,300	2,315	110
42 Lesotho	23,490	18,640	6,540	4,330	2,444	107
43 Bolivia	3,830	1,850	..	3,070	2,084	87
44 Honduras	12,620	3,120	..	700	2,171	96
45 Zambia	9,540	7,670	9,920	1,730	2,051	93
46 Egypt	2,550	970	1,930	1,500	2,972	117
47 El Salvador	5,260	3,040	..	870	2,031	99
48 Thailand	7,950	7,180	4,860	2,420	2,308	104
49 Philippines	6,940	7,970	..	6,000	2,275	116
50 Angola	14,910	..	6,650	..	2,232	83
51 Papua New Guinea	28,840	13,590	2,450	960	2,164	90
52 Morocco	9,410	11,200	..	1,830	2,628	110
53 Nicaragua	2,690	1,800	1,250	550	2,135	99
54 Nigeria	73,710	12,550	4,040	3,010	2,595	91
55 Zimbabwe	4,790	6,580	1,000	1,190	1,793	86
56 Cameroon	48,110	13,670	3,280	1,910	2,439	105
57 Cuba	1,060	700	950	360	2,723	122
58 Congo, People's Rep.	16,100	5,510	1,300	790	2,277	94
59 Guatemala	4,420	8,600	9,040	1,620	2,045	93
60 Peru	1,910	1,390	2,210	690	2,057	99
61 Ecuador	2,670	1,620	2,360	..	2,181	88
62 Jamaica	2,590	2,830	420	630	2,624	119
63 Ivory Coast	29,190	21,040	2,920	1,590	2,746	112
64 Dominican Rep.	8,220	4,020	..	2,150	1,980	105

194

| | Population per: | | | | Daily per capita calorie supply | |
| | Physician[a] | | Nursing person[a] | | Total | As percentage of requirement |
	1960	1980	1960	1980	1980	1980
65 Mongolia	1,070	450	300	240	2,681	111
66 Colombia	2,640	1,920	4,220	1,220	2,529	108
67 Tunisia	10,030	3,690	. .	890	2,789	116
68 Costa Rica	2,700	1,470	710	450	2,766	116
69 Korea, Dem. Rep.	. .	440	. .	. .	3,073	126
70 Turkey	2,800	1,630	16,310	1,130	2,965	122
71 Syrian Arab Rep.	4,630	2,310	6,660	1,440	2,909	117
72 Jordan	5,800	1,890	1,930	1,310	2,355	96
73 Paraguay	1,810	1,710	1,380	1,100	2,741	134
Upper middle-income	**2,606** w	**1,689** w	**2,678** w	**1,010** w	**2,724** w	**115** w
74 Korea, Rep. of	3,540	1,690	3,250	380	2,957	128
75 Iran, Islamic Rep. of	4,060	2,320	8,090	2,520	2,018	81
76 Iraq	5,270	1,790	3,030	2,140	2,677	111
77 Malaysia	7,020	7,910	1,790	940	2,625	121
78 Panama	2,730	980	3,460	420	2,163	103
79 Lebanon	1,210	530	2,080	720	2,476	100
80 Algeria	5,530	2,650	. .	740	2,433	101
81 Brazil	2,670	1,700	2,810	820	2,447	109
82 Mexico	1,830	1,260	3,650	1,420	2,791	121
83 Portugal	1,250	540	1,420	650	3,101	129
84 Argentina	740	530	750	. .	3,494	125
85 Chile	1,780	1,920	640	450	2,790	114
86 South Africa	2,180	. .	480	. .	2,778	118
87 Yugoslavia	1,620	680	630	280	3,565	140
88 Uruguay	960	540	800	190	2,896	110
89 Venezuela	1,510	950	2,840	370	2,525	112
90 Greece	800	420	800	600	3,685	147
91 Hong Kong	3,060	1,220	2,880	790	2,898	128
92 Israel	400	370	360	130	3,020	118
93 Singapore	2,360	1,150	650	320	3,158	134
94 Trinidad and Tobago	2,370	1,490	760	410	2,744	113
High-income oil exporters	**13,285** w	**1,295** w	**4,496** w	**841** w	**3,036** w	**127** w
95 Libya	6,580	730	1,320	400	3,459	147
96 Saudi Arabia	16,370	1,640	5,850	1,150	2,895	120
97 Kuwait	1210	590	270	180	. .	. .
98 United Arab Emirates	. .	900	. .	340	. .	. .
Industrial market economies	**816** w	**554** w	**474** w	**183** w	**3,433** w	**134** w
99 Ireland	950	760	190	120	3,718	148
100 Spain	850	460	1,290	330	3,361	135
101 Italy	640	340	1,330	330	3,662	150
102 New Zealand	850	670	. .	130	3,685	126
103 United Kingdom	940	650	210	140	3,306	132
104 Japan	930	780	310	240	2,912	124
105 Austria	550	400	440	230	3,579	135
106 Finland	1,570	530	170	100	3,196	118
107 Australia	750	560	. .	120	3,159	117
108 Canada	910	550	290	90	3,369	127
109 Netherlands	900	540	. .	130	3,514	131
110 Belgium	780	400	450	120	3,916	160
111 France	930	580	530	120	3,391	134
112 United States	750	520	340	150	3,658	139
113 Denmark	810	480	220	210	3,566	133
114 Germany, Fed. Rep.	670	450	370	170	3,561	133
115 Norway	900	520	330	90	3,315	124
116 Sweden	1,050	490	100	60	3,202	119
117 Switzerland	740	410	350	160	3,551	133
East European nonmarket economies	**683** w	**356** w	**358** w	**212** w	**3,412** w	**133** w
118 Albania	3,620	960	530	310	2,664	110
119 Hungary	720	400	330	150	3,534	134
120 Romania	790	680	420	270	3,337	126
121 Bulgaria	710	410	550	190	3,646	146
122 Poland	1,070	570	460	240	3,521	134
123 USSR	560	280	340	210	3,372	132
124 Czechoslovakia	620	360	230	130	3,477	141
125 German Dem. Rep.	1,180	520	. .	. .	3,780	144

a. Figures in italics are for years other than those specified. See the technical notes.

Table 25. Education[a]

	Primary Total 1960	1980	Primary Male 1960	1980	Primary Female 1960	1980	Secondary 1960	1980	Higher education 1960	1979	Adult literacy 1960	1980
Low-income economies	80 w	93 w	68 w	105 w	34 w	80 w	18 w	29 w	2 w	4 w	34 w	52 w
China and India	90 w	100 w	80 w	111 w	40 w	86 w	21 w	32 w	..	4 w	37 w	56 w
Other low-income	37 w	70 w	50 w	83 w	24 w	55 w	6 w	19 w	1 w	2 w	23 w	40 w
1 Kampuchea, Dem.	64	..	82	..	46	..	3	..	(.)	..	31	..
2 Bhutan	3	11	..	15	..	7	3	1	..	(.)	..	..
3 Lao, PDR	25	96	34	104	16	88	1	17	(.)	(.)	28	44
4 Chad	17	35	29	51	4	19	..	3	..	(.)	6	15
5 Bangladesh	47	62	66	76	26	47	8	15	1	3	22	26
6 Ethiopia	7	43	11	56	3	30	..	11	(.)	1	..	15
7 Nepal	10	91	19	126	1	53	6	21	1	3	9	19
8 Burma	56	84	61	87	52	81	10	20	1	4	60	66
9 Afghanistan	9	30	15	49	2	10	1	10	(.)	2	8	20
10 Mali	10	27	14	35	6	20	1	28	..	1	2	10
11 Malawi	..	62	..	73	..	51	1	4	..	(.)	..	25
12 Zaire	60	90	88	104	32	75	3	23	(.)	1	31	55
13 Uganda	49	50	65	58	32	42	3	5	(.)	1	25	52
14 Burundi	18	29	27	35	9	23	1	3	(.)	1	14	25
15 Upper Volta	8	19	12	24	5	14	1	3	..	(.)	2	5
16 Rwanda	49	70	68	74	30	67	2	2	..	(.)	16	50
17 India	61	76	80	90	40	61	20	28	3	9	28	36
18 Somalia	9	41	13	53	5	29	1	6	(.)	1	2	60
19 Tanzania	25	104	33	110	18	98	2	4	..	(.)	10	79
20 Viet Nam	..	116	..	124	..	109	..	48	..	3	..	87
21 China	109	117	..	126	..	106	21	34	..	1	43	69
22 Guinea	30	33	44	44	16	22	2	16	..	5	7	20
23 Haiti	46	64	50	69	42	59	4	12	(.)	1	15	23
24 Sri Lanka	95	100	100	103	90	97	27	51	1	3	75	85
25 Benin	27	62	38	84	15	39	2	16	..	1	5	28
26 Central African Rep.	32	70	53	92	12	49	1	10	..	1	7	33
27 Sierra Leone	23	39	30	45	15	30	2	12	(.)	1	7	15
28 Madagascar	52	100	58	..	45	..	4	12	(.)	3	..	50
29 Niger	5	23	7	29	3	17	..	4	..	(.)	1	10
30 Pakistan	30	57	46	81	13	30	11	15	1	2	15	24
31 Mozambique	48	93	60	107	36	79	2	6	..	(.)	8	33
32 Sudan	25	51	35	60	14	43	3	16	(.)	2	13	32
33 Togo	44	116	63	144	24	89	2	33	..	2	10	18
34 Ghana	38	69	52	77	25	60	5	36	(.)	1	27	..
Middle-income economies	75 w	100 w	84 w	106 w	67 w	95 w	14 w	39 w	3 w	11 w	48 w	65 w
Oil exporters	63 w	101 w	75 w	109 w	52 w	93 w	9 w	34 w	2 w	10 w	36 w	58 w
Oil importers	85 w	100 w	91 w	104 w	80 w	97 w	18 w	44 w	4 w	13 w	58 w	72 w
Lower middle-income	66 w	98 w	78 w	105 w	56 w	91 w	10 w	33 w	3 w	10 w	39 w	59 w
35 Kenya	47	108	64	114	30	101	2	18	(.)	1	20	47
36 Senegal	27	44	36	53	17	35	3	10	1	3	6	10
37 Mauritania	8	33	13	43	3	23	..	10	..	(.)	5	17
38 Yemen Arab Rep.	8	47	14	82	..	12	..	5	..	1	3	21
39 Yemen, PDR	13	72	20	93	5	51	5	28	..	2	..	40
40 Liberia	31	66	45	82	18	50	2	20	(.)	2	9	25
41 Indonesia	71	98	86	104	58	91	6	28	1	..	39	62
42 Lesotho	83	104	63	84	102	123	3	17	(.)	2	..	52
43 Bolivia	64	84	78	90	50	78	12	36	4	..	39	63
44 Honduras	67	89	68	92	67	85	8	21	1	8	45	60
45 Zambia	42	95	51	101	34	89	2	17	..	2	29	44
46 Egypt	66	76	80	89	52	63	16	52	5	15	26	44
47 El Salvador	80	74	82	74	77	74	13	23	1	8	49	62
48 Thailand	83	96	88	..	79	..	13	29	2	13	68	86
49 Philippines	95	110	98	111	93	108	26	63	13	25	72	75
50 Angola	21	..	28	..	13	..	2	..	(.)	(.)	..	..
51 Papua New Guinea	32	62	59	70	7	54	1	12	..	..	29	32
52 Morocco	47	76	67	95	27	58	5	24	1	4	14	28
53 Nicaragua	66	100	65	97	66	103	7	43	1	9	..	90
54 Nigeria	36	98	46	..	27	..	4	16	(.)	2	15	34
55 Zimbabwe	96	115	107	118	86	113	6	13	(.)	(.)	39	69
56 Cameroon	65	104	87	113	43	94	2	18	..	1	19	..
57 Cuba	109	112	109	116	109	109	14	71	3	20	..	95
58 Congo, People's Rep.	78	156	103	163	53	148	4	69	1	5	16	..
59 Guatemala	45	69	50	74	39	63	7	16	2	9	32	..
60 Peru	83	112	95	116	71	108	15	56	4	16	61	80
61 Ecuador	83	107	87	109	79	105	12	40	3	35	68	81
62 Jamaica	92	99	92	98	93	100	45	57	2	..	82	90
63 Ivory Coast	46	76	68	92	24	60	2	17	(.)	2	5	35
64 Dominican Rep.	98	106	99	105	98	107	7	32	1	10	65	67

196

		Number enrolled in primary school as percentage of age group						Number enrolled in secondary school as percentage of age group		Number enrolled in higher education as percentage of population aged 20–24		Adult literacy rate (percent)	
		Total		Male		Female							
		1960	1980	1960	1980	1960	1980	1960	1980	1960	1979	1960	1980
65	Mongolia	79	105	79	107	78	102	51	89	8	9	95	..
66	Colombia	77	128	77	127	77	130	12	46	2	11	63	81
67	Tunisia	66	103	88	118	43	88	12	27	1	5	16	62
68	Costa Rica	96	108	97	109	95	106	21	48	5	26	..	90
69	Korea, Dem. Rep.	..	116	..	118	..	114	..	..	..	..	..	..
70	Turkey	75	101	90	110	58	93	14	37	3	6	38	60
71	Syrian Arab Rep.	65	100	89	112	39	87	16	46	4	15	30	58
72	Jordan	77	108	94	..	59	..	25	79	1	27	32	70
73	Paraguay	98	102	105	106	90	98	11	26	2	7	75	84
Upper middle-income		**88** *w*	**104** *w*	**93** *w*	**108** *w*	**83** *w*	**101** *w*	**20** *w*	**48** *w*	**4** *w*	**13** *w*	**61** *w*	**76** *w*
74	Korea, Rep. of	94	107	99	108	89	105	27	85	5	14	71	93
75	Iran, Islamic Rep. of	41	101	56	121	27	80	12	44	1	5	16	50
76	Iraq	65	116	94	122	36	110	19	57	2	9	18	
77	Malaysia	96	92	108	94	83	91	19	53	1	3	53	60
78	Panama	96	113	98	115	94	111	29	65	5	23	73	85
79	Lebanon	102	118	105	..	99	..	19	58	6	35	..	..
80	Algeria	46	95	55	108	37	81	8	33	(.)	5	10	35
81	Brazil	95	93	97	93	93	93	11	32	2	12	61	76
82	Mexico	80	120	82	123	77	116	11	37	3	15	65	83
83	Portugal	..	118	..	120	..	116	..	55	4	11	63	78
84	Argentina	98	116	98	116	99	116	23	56	11	23	91	93
85	Chile	109	117	111	118	107	116	24	55	4	12	84	..
86	South Africa	89	..	94	..	85	..	15	..	3	..	57	..
87	Yugoslavia	111	99	113	100	108	98	58	83	9	23	77	85
88	Uruguay	111	105	111	107	111	104	37	60	8	16	..	94
89	Venezuela	100	104	100	104	100	104	21	39	4	21	63	82
90	Greece	102	103	104	104	101	103	37	81	4	17	80	..
91	Hong Kong	87	109	93	111	79	107	20	62	4	10	70	90
92	Israel	98	96	99	95	97	97	48	71	10	26	84	..
93	Singapore	111	107	121	108	101	105	32	55	6	8	..	83
94	Trinidad and Tobago	88	94	89	93	87	95	24	56	1	..	93	95
High-income oil exporters		**29** *w*	**83** *w*	**44** *w*	**93** *w*	**12** *w*	**74** *w*	**5** *w*	**44** *w*	**1** *w*	**7** *w*	**9** *w*	**32** *w*
95	Libya	59	123	92	128	24	119	9	67	1	6	22	..
96	Saudi Arabia	12	64	22	77	2	51	2	30	(.)	7	3	25
97	Kuwait	117	96	131	98	102	93	37	75	..	12	47	60
98	United Arab Emirates	..	116	..	117	..	115	..	52	(.)	3	..	56
Industrial market economies		**114** *w*	**102** *w*	**107** *w*	**103** *w*	**112** *w*	**103** *w*	**64** *w*	**89** *w*	**16** *w*	**36** *w*	**96** *w*	**99** *w*
99	Ireland	110	102	107	101	112	102	35	93	9	19	97	98
100	Spain	110	109	106	109	116	110	23	87	4	22	87	..
101	Italy	111	102	112	102	109	101	34	73	7	27	91	98
102	New Zealand	108	105	110	105	106	104	73	81	13	25	..	99
103	United Kingdom	92	104	92	104	92	105	66	82	9	20	..	99
104	Japan	103	101	103	101	102	101	74	91	10	30	98	99
105	Austria	105	98	106	99	104	98	50	74	8	23	99	99
106	Finland	97	83	100	83	95	83	74	90	7	21	99	100
107	Australia	103	110	103	110	103	110	51	86	13	26	..	100
108	Canada	107	100	108	100	105	100	46	89	16	36	..	99
109	Netherlands	105	101	105	100	104	102	58	94	13	30	..	99
110	Belgium	109	101	111	101	108	101	69	89	9	24	..	99
111	France	144	112	98	112	143	111	46	85	10	25	..	99
112	United States	118	98	..	..	..	..	86	97	32	55	98	99
113	Denmark	103	98	103	97	103	98	65	87	10	29	..	99
114	Germany, Fed. Rep.	133	..	132	..	134	..	53	..	6	26	..	99
115	Norway	100	100	100	99	100	100	57	94	7	25	..	99
116	Sweden	96	97	95	97	96	97	55	86	9	37	..	99
117	Switzerland	118	86	118	86	118	87	26	55	7	17	..	99
East European nonmarket economies		**101** *w*	**104** *w*	**101** *w*	**97** *w*	**101** *w*	**97** *w*	**45** *w*	**92** *w*	**11** *w*	**20** *w*	**97** *w*	**99** *w*
118	Albania	94	108	102	111	86	105	20	63	5	6	..	..
119	Hungary	101	97	103	97	100	97	23	40	7	13	97	99
120	Romania	98	101	101	101	95	101	24	75	5	11	89	98
121	Bulgaria	93	97	94	97	92	96	55	86	11	17	91	..
122	Poland	109	100	110	100	107	99	50	77	9	18	95	98
123	USSR	100	106	100	..	100	..	49	101	11	21	99	100
124	Czechoslovakia	93	91	93	91	93	92	25	44	11	16	95	..
125	German Dem. Rep.	112	96	111	95	113	97	39	88	16	30	..	..

a. Figures in italics are for years other than those specified. See the technical notes.

Table 26. Defense and social expenditure

	Defense expenditure as percentage of				Central government expenditure per capita (1975 dollars)					
	GNP		Central government expenditure		Defense		Education		Health	
	1972[a]	1980[b]	1972[a]	1980[b]	1972[a]	1980[b]	1972[a]	1980[b]	1972[a]	1980[b]
Low-income economies	3.6 w	3.5 w	19.5 w	16.9 w	5 w	7 w	3 w	6 w	1 w	1 w
China and India	..	4.0 w	..	16.7 w	..	8 w	..	6 w	..	(.) w
Other low-income	3.6 w	2.5 w	19.5 w	18.9 w	5 w	7 w	3 w	3 w	1 w	1 w
1 Kampuchea, Dem.	..	..	..	..	..	..	..	..	..	..
2 Bhutan	..	..	..	..	..	..	..	..	..	..
3 Lao, PDR	..	..	..	..	..	..	..	..	..	..
4 Chad	4.5	..	24.6	..	..	..	3	..	1	..
5 Bangladesh	0.5	..	5.1	..	(.)	..	1	..	(.)	..
6 Ethiopia	2.0	..	14.3	..	2	..	2	..	1	..
7 Nepal	0.6	0.9	7.1	6.6	1	1	1	2	(.)	1
8 Burma	6.3	3.5	31.6	24.2	7	5	3	2	1	1
9 Afghanistan	..	..	..	..	..	..	..	..	..	..
10 Mali	..	2.9	..	17.4	..	3	..	5	..	1
11 Malawi	0.6	3.7	3.2	12.8	1	5	4	4	1	2
12 Zaire	..	..	..	..	..	..	..	..	..	..
13 Uganda	5.1	0.4	23.2	13.7	16	1	10	2	4	(.)
14 Burundi	2.0	..	10.3	..	2	..	6	..	1	..
15 Upper Volta	1.3	2.5	11.5	16.9	1	4	3	4	1	1
16 Rwanda	3.0	1.6	25.6	12.4	4	2	3	3	1	1
17 India	..	2.8	..	19.4	..	4	..	(.)	..	(.)
18 Somalia	6.2	..	23.3	..	7	..	2	..	2	..
19 Tanzania	2.3	9.0	11.9	24.5	4	16	5	8	2	4
20 Viet Nam	..	..	..	..	..	..	..	..	..	..
21 China	..	4.6	..	15.9	..	10	..	10	..	..
22 Guinea	..	..	..	..	..	..	..	..	..	..
23 Haiti	..	..	..	..	..	..	..	..	..	..
24 Sri Lanka	1.3	..	4.1	..	4	..	12	..	6	..
25 Benin	..	..	..	..	..	..	..	..	..	..
26 Central African Rep.	..	..	..	..	..	..	..	..	..	..
27 Sierra Leone	..	0.9	..	3.2	..	2	..	6	..	2
28 Madagascar	0.8	..	3.6	..	2	..	5	..	2	..
29 Niger	..	1.0	..	3.8	..	2	..	8	..	2
30 Pakistan	6.6	5.0	39.9	30.6	10	10	(.)	1	(.)	(.)
31 Mozambique	..	..	..	..	..	..	..	..	..	..
32 Sudan	3.5	2.6	23.0	13.2	8	7	3	5	2	1
33 Togo	..	2.5	..	7.0	..	7	..	13	..	6
34 Ghana	1.6	0.5	8.0	3.8	8	2	20	11	6	3
Middle-income economies	3.1 w	3.0 w	13.9 w	14.2 w	26 w	28 w	20 w	27 w	8 w	10 w
Oil exporters	3.0 w	2.1 w	17.5 w	10.8 w	33 w	23 w	25 w	32 w	8 w	9 w
Oil importers	3.1 w	3.4 w	12.5 w	16.8 w	23 w	32 w	17 w	22 w	9 w	11 w
Lower middle-income	3.2 w	3.8 w	12.7 w	15.6 w	15 w	18 w	15 w	16 w	4 w	5 w
35 Kenya	1.3	4.4	6.0	16.4	3	11	11	13	4	5
36 Senegal	..	..	..	..	..	..	..	..	..	..
37 Mauritania	..	12.6	..	29.4	..	36	..	13	..	3
38 Yemen Arab Rep.	..	10.6	..	33.2	..	21	..	8	..	3
39 Yemen, PDR	..	..	..	..	..	..	..	..	..	..
40 Liberia	..	1.7	..	5.8	..	6	..	13	..	6
41 Indonesia	..	3.4	..	13.5	..	10	..	6	..	2
42 Lesotho	..	..	..	..	..	..	..	..	..	..
43 Bolivia	1.5	2.0	16.1	16.6	7	10	13	19	4	5
44 Honduras	1.9	2.4	12.4	11.4	7	9	13	15	6	7
45 Zambia	..	..	..	..	..	..	33	17	13	9
46 Egypt	..	3.0	..	7.4	..	14	..	19	..	6
47 El Salvador	0.8	1.6	6.6	8.6	4	7	11	15	6	7
48 Thailand	3.5	3.8	19.5	20.6	11	17	11	16	2	4
49 Philippines	1.5	1.8	10.1	14.6	5	7	7	7	1	2
50 Angola	..	..	..	..	..	..	..	..	..	..
51 Papua New Guinea	..	1.6	..	4.5	..	7	..	27	..	14
52 Morocco	2.8	6.1	12.3	17.9	13	36	21	35	5	7
53 Nicaragua	1.9	3.4	12.3	11.0	12	16	16	17	4	21
54 Nigeria	5.2	..	40.2	..	20	..	2	..	2	..
55 Zimbabwe	..	..	..	..	..	..	..	..	..	..
56 Cameroon	..	1.5	..	9.1	..	7	..	9	..	4
57 Cuba	..	..	..	..	..	..	..	..	..	..
58 Congo, People's Rep.	..	..	..	..	..	..	..	..	..	..
59 Guatemala	1.1	1.3	11.0	9.9	3	8	5	11	2	9
60 Peru	2.5	2.5	14.8	12.5	23	23	35	20	10	8
61 Ecuador	2.0	1.9	16.9	12.5	11	14	20	37	3	8
62 Jamaica	..	..	..	..	..	..	..	..	..	..
63 Ivory Coast	..	1.3	..	3.9	..	8	..	33	..	8
64 Dominican Rep.	1.5	1.9	8.5	10.3	11	15	18	20	15	13

	Defense expenditure as percentage of				Central government expenditure per capita (1975 dollars)					
	GNP		Central government expenditure		Defense		Education		Health	
	1972[a]	1980[b]	1972[a]	1980[b]	1972[a]	1980[b]	1972[a]	1980[b]	1972[a]	1980[b]
65 Mongolia	. .	. .	. .	. .	. .	. .	. .	. .	. .	. .
66 Colombia	. .	. .	. .	. .	. .	. .	. .	. .	. .	. .
67 Tunisia	1.1	3.9	4.8	12.0	7	36	46	50	11	21
68 Costa Rica	0.5	0.7	2.6	2.6	5	7	48	71	6	15
69 Korea, Dem.Rep.	. .	. .	. .	. .	. .	. .	. .	. .	. .	. .
70 Turkey	3.4	3.8	15.4	15.3	27	36	32	34	6	9
71 Syrian Arab Rep.	10.9	17.3	37.2	47.7	64	144	19	15	2	3
72 Jordan	. .	13.1	. .	25.5	. .	74	. .	28	. .	12
73 Paraguay	1.8	1.0	13.8	11.7	9	9	8	10	2	3
Upper middle-income	**3.1** w	**2.6** w	**14.3** w	**13.6** w	**36** w	**42** w	**25** w	**42** w	**15** w	**17** w
74 Korea, Rep. of	4.9	6.6	25.8	34.3	22	49	14	25	1	2
75 Iran, Islamic Rep. of	7.4	. .	24.1	15.0	104	78	45	77	16	23
76 Iraq	. .	. .	. .	. .	. .	. .	. .	. .	. .	. .
77 Malaysia	5.1	4.0	18.5	16.6	33	38	42	50	12	15
78 Panama	. .	. .	. .	. .	. .	. .	. .	60	. .	58
79 Lebanon	. .	. .	. .	. .	. .	. .	. .	. .	. .	. .
80 Algeria	. .	. .	. .	. .	. .	. .	. .	. .	. .	. .
81 Brazil	1.4	0.7	8.3	4.3	13	10	11	15	10	20
82 Mexico	0.6	0.4	4.9	2.3	8	7	27	55	8	7
83 Portugal	. .	. .	. .	. .	. .	. .	. .	. .	. .	. .
84 Argentina	1.0	2.3	9.0	11.8	18	36	19	27	7	5
85 Chile	2.4	. .	6,1	. .	4	. .	9	. .	5	. .
86 South Africa	. .	. .	. .	. .	. .	. .	. .	. .	. .	. .
87 Yugoslavia	4.1	4.5	20.5	48.6	54	81	. .	. .	66	. .
88 Uruguay	1.4	2.6	5.6	11.6	16	41	28	31	5	17
89 Venezuela	2.1	1.2	9.7	5.9	41	28	73	95	27	41
90 Greece	7.8	. .	14.6	. .	90	. .	54	. .	44	. .
91 Hong Kong	. .	. .	. .	. .	. .	. .	. .	. .	. .	. .
92 Israel	17.6	31.2	39.8	24.9	620	1,103	141	261	55	98
93 Singapore	6.0	5.5	35.3	24.9	126	192	56	112	28	53
94 Trinidad and Tobago	. .	0.8	. .	2.5	. .	23	. .	107	. .	58
High-income oil exporters	. .	. .	. .	. .	. .	. .	. .	. .	. .	. .
95 Libya	. .	. .	. .	. .	. .	. .	. .	. .	. .	. .
96 Saudi Arabia	. .	. .	. .	. .	. .	. .	. .	. .	. .	. .
97 Kuwait	2.7	2.9	8.4	12.2	314	366	559	276	206	154
98 United Arab Emirates	. .	6.2	24.5	47.5	. .	1,119	. .	296	. .	200
Industrial market economies	**5.0** w	**3.6** w	**21.3** w	**12.2** w	**281** w	**254** w	**77** w	**111** w	**141** w	**240** w
99 Ireland	. .	. .	. .	. .	. .	. .	. .	. .	. .	. .
100 Spain	1.3	1.3	6.5	5.2	34	41	43	64	5	7
101 Italy	2.0	1.6	6.3	3.4	70	66	178	164	150	246
102 New Zealand	1.7	1.9	5.8	5.1	70	83	203	237	180	248
103 United Kingdom	5.5	4.6	16.7	14.5	217	246	34	45	158	217
104 Japan	. .	. .	. .	. .	. .	. .	. .	. .	. .	. .
105 Austria	1.0	1.2	3.0	3.1	47	71	160	229	156	302
106 Finland	1.5	1.7	6.1	5.6	80	107	203	280	140	199
107 Australia	2.8	2.3	14.5	9.4	188	170	55	152	108	182
108 Canada	. .	1.8	. .	7.7	. .	136	. .	68	. .	118
109 Netherlands	. .	3.1	. .	5.5	. .	208	. .	495	. .	447
110 Belgium	2.6	2.8	6.6	5.4	157	206	364	551	34	63
111 France	. .	2.8	. .	7.3	. .	208	. .	258	. .	431
112 United States	6.3	4.9	32.2	21.2	453	392	45	49	120	193
113 Denmark	2.3	. .	7.0	. .	169	. .	377	. .	231	. .
114 Germany, Fed. Rep.	3.0	2.7	12.4	9.6	200	225	24	22	281	463
115 Norway	3.4	. .	9.4	. .	201	. .	206	. .	255	. .
116 Sweden	3.6	3.2	12.2	7.5	283	288	335	460	81	87
117 Switzerland	2.0	2.0	15.1	10.2	184	189	51	62	122	215
East European nonmarket economies	. .	. .	. .	. .	. .	. .	. .	. .	. .	. .
118 Albania	. .	. .	. .	. .	. .	. .	. .	. .	. .	. .
119 Hungary	. .	. .	. .	. .	. .	. .	. .	. .	. .	. .
120 Romania	. .	2.0	6.2	3.7	. .	. .	. .	. .	. .	. .
121 Bulgaria	. .	. .	. .	. .	. .	. .	. .	. .	. .	. .
122 Poland	. .	. .	. .	. .	. .	. .	. .	. .	. .	. .
123 USSR	. .	. .	. .	. .	. .	. .	. .	. .	. .	. .
124 Czechoslovakia	. .	. .	. .	. .	. .	. .	. .	. .	. .	. .
125 German Dem. Rep.	. .	. .	. .	. .	. .	. .	. .	. .	. .	. .

a. Figures in italics are for 1973, not 1972   b. Figures in italics are for 1979, not 1980.

Table 27. Income distribution

	Year	Percentage share of household income, by percentile groups of households[a]					
		Lowest 20 percent	Second quintile	Third quintile	Fourth quintile	Highest 20 percent	Highest 10 percent
Low-income economies							
China and India							
Other low-income							
1 Kampuchea, Dem.		. .	. .	. .	. .	. .	. .
2 Bhutan		. .	. .	. .	. .	. .	. .
3 Lao, PDR		. .	. .	. .	. .	. .	. .
4 Chad		. .	. .	. .	. .	. .	. .
5 Bangladesh	1973–74	6.9	11.3	16.1	23.5	42.2	27.4
6 Ethiopia		. .	. .	. .	. .	. .	. .
7 Nepal	1976–77	4.6	8.0	11.7	16.5	59.2	46.5
8 Burma		. .	. .	. .	. .	. .	. .
9 Afghanistan		. .	. .	. .	. .	. .	. .
10 Mali		. .	. .	. .	. .	. .	. .
11 Malawi	1967–68	10.4	11.1	13.1	14.8	50.6	40.1
12 Zaire		. .	. .	. .	. .	. .	. .
13 Uganda		. .	. .	. .	. .	. .	. .
14 Burundi		. .	. .	. .	. .	. .	. .
15 Upper Volta		. .	. .	. .	. .	. .	. .
16 Rwanda		. .	. .	. .	. .	. .	. .
17 India	1975–76	7.0	9.2	13.9	20.5	49.4	33.6
18 Somalia		. .	. .	. .	. .	. .	. .
19 Tanzania	1969	5.8	10.2	13.9	19.7	50.4	35.6
20 Viet Nam		. .	. .	. .	. .	. .	. .
21 China		. .	. .	. .	. .	. .	. .
22 Guinea		. .	. .	. .	. .	. .	. .
23 Haiti		. .	. .	. .	. .	. .	. .
24 Sri Lanka	1969–70	7.5	11.7	15.7	21.7	43.4	28.2
25 Benin		. .	. .	. .	. .	. .	. .
26 Central African Rep.		. .	. .	. .	. .	. .	. .
27 Sierra Leone	1967–69	5.6	9.5	12.8	19.6	52.5	37.8
28 Madagascar		. .	. .	. .	. .	. .	. .
29 Niger		. .	. .	. .	. .	. .	. .
30 Pakistan		. .	. .	. .	. .	. .	. .
31 Mozambique		. .	. .	. .	. .	. .	. .
32 Sudan	1967–68	4.0	8.9	16.6	20.7	49.8	34.6
33 Togo		. .	. .	. .	. .	. .	. .
34 Ghana		. .	. .	. .	. .	. .	. .
Middle-income economies							
Oil exporters							
Oil importers							
Lower middle-income							
35 Kenya	1974	2.6	6.3	11.5	19.2	60.4	45.8
36 Senegal		. .	. .	. .	. .	. .	. .
37 Mauritania		. .	. .	. .	. .	. .	. .
38 Yemen Arab Rep.		. .	. .	. .	. .	. .	. .
39 Yemen, PDR		. .	. .	. .	. .	. .	. .
40 Liberia		. .	. .	. .	. .	. .	. .
41 Indonesia	1976	6.6	7.8	12.6	23.6	49.4	34.0
42 Lesotho		. .	. .	. .	. .	. .	. .
43 Bolivia		. .	. .	. .	. .	. .	. .
44 Honduras		. .	. .	. .	. .	. .	. .
45 Zambia		. .	. .	. .	. .	. .	. .
46 Egypt		. .	. .	. .	. .	. .	. .
47 El Salvador		. .	. .	. .	. .	. .	. .
48 Thailand	1975–76	5.6	9.6	13.9	21.1	49.8	34.1
49 Philippines	1970–71	5.2	9.0	12.8	19.0	54.0	38.5
50 Angola		. .	. .	. .	. .	. .	. .
51 Papua New Guinea		. .	. .	. .	. .	. .	. .
52 Morocco		. .	. .	. .	. .	. .	. .
53 Nicaragua		. .	. .	. .	. .	. .	. .
54 Nigeria		. .	. .	. .	. .	. .	. .
55 Zimbabwe		. .	. .	. .	. .	. .	. .
56 Cameroon		. .	. .	. .	. .	. .	. .
57 Cuba		. .	. .	. .	. .	. .	. .
58 Congo, People's Rep.		. .	. .	. .	. .	. .	. .
59 Guatemala		. .	. .	. .	. .	. .	. .
60 Peru	1972	1.9	5.1	11.0	21.0	61.0	42.9
61 Ecuador		. .	. .	. .	. .	. .	. .
62 Jamaica		. .	. .	. .	. .	. .	. .
63 Ivory Coast		. .	. .	. .	. .	. .	. .
64 Dominican Rep.		. .	. .	. .	. .	. .	. .

		Percentage share of household income, by percentile groups of households[a]					
	Year	Lowest 20 percent	Second quintile	Third quintile	Fourth quintile	Highest 20 percent	Highest 10 percent
65 Mongolia		. .	. .	. .	. .	. .	. .
66 Colombia		. .	. .	. .	. .	. .	. .
67 Tunisia		. .	. .	. .	. .	. .	. .
68 Costa Rica	1971	3.3	8.7	13.3	19.9	54.8	39.5
69 Korea. Dem. Rep.		. .	. .	. .	. .	. .	. .
70 Turkey	1973	3.5	8.0	12.5	19.5	56.5	40.7
71 Syrian Arab Rep.		. .	. .	. .	. .	. .	. .
72 Jordan		. .	. .	. .	. .	. .	. .
73 Paraguay		. .	. .	. .	. .	. .	. .

Upper middle-income

74 Korea. Rep. of	1976	5.7	11.2	15.4	22.4	45.3	27.5
75 Iran. Islamic Rep. of		. .	. .	. .	. .	. .	. .
76 Iraq		. .	. .	. .	. .	. .	. .
77 Malaysia	1973	3.5	7.7	12.4	20.3	56.1	39.8
78 Panama	1970	2.0	5.2	11.0	20.0	61.8	44.2
79 Lebanon		. .	. .	. .	. .	. .	. .
80 Algeria		. .	. .	. .	. .	. .	. .
81 Brazil	1972	2.0	5.0	9.4	17.0	66.6	50.6
82 Mexico	1977	2.9	7.0	12.0	20.4	57.7	40.6
83 Portugal		. .	. .	. .	. .	. .	. .
84 Argentina	1970	4.4	9.7	14.1	21.5	50.3	35.2
85 Chile	1968	4.4	9.0	13.8	21.4	51.4	34.8
86 South Africa		. .	. .	. .	. .	. .	. .
87 Yugoslavia	1978	6.6	12.1	18.7	23.9	38.7	22.9
88 Uruguay		. .	. .	. .	. .	. .	. .
89 Venezuela	1970	3.0	7.3	12.9	22.8	54.0	35.7
90 Greece		. .	. .	. .	. .	. .	. .
91 Hong Kong	1980	5.4	10.8	15.2	21.6	47.0	31.3
92 Israel		. .	. .	. .	. .	. .	. .
93 Singapore		. .	. .	. .	. .	. .	. .
94 Trinidad and Tobago	1975–76	4.2	9.1	13.9	22.8	50.0	31.8

High-income oil exporters

95 Libya		. .	. .	. .	. .	. .	. .
96 Saudi Arabia		. .	. .	. .	. .	. .	. .
97 Kuwait		. .	. .	. .	. .	. .	. .
98 United Arab Emirates		. .	. .	. .	. .	. .	. .

Industrial market economies

99 Ireland		. .	. .	. .	. .	. .	. .
100 Spain	1974	6.0	11.8	16.9	23.1	42.2	26.7
101 Italy	1977	6.2	11.3	15.9	22.7	43.9	28.1
102 New Zealand		. .	. .	. .	. .	. .	. .
103 United Kingdom	1979	7.3	12.4	17.7	23.4	39.2	23.8
104 Japan	1969	7.9	13.1	16.8	21.2	41.0	27.2
105 Austria		. .	. .	. .	. .	. .	. .
106 Finland	1977	6.8	12.8	18.7	24.9	36.8	21.2
107 Australia	1966–67	6.6	13.5	17.8	23.4	38.8	23.7
108 Canada	1977	3.8	10.7	17.9	25.6	42.0	26.9
109 Netherlands	1977	8.1	13.7	17.9	23.3	37.0	22.1
110 Belgium		. .	. .	. .	. .	. .	. .
111 France	1975	5.3	11.1	16.0	21.8	45.8	30.5
112 United States	1972	4.5	10.7	17.3	24.7	42.8	26.6
113 Denmark	1976	7.4	12.6	18.3	24.2	37.5	22.4
114 Germany. Fed. Rep.	1974	6.9	11.0	15.4	21.9	44.8	28.8
115 Norway	1970	6.3	12.9	18.8	24.7	37.3	22.2
116 Sweden	1979	7.2	12.8	17.4	25.4	37.2	21.2
117 Switzerland		. .	. .	. .	. .	. .	. .

East European nonmarket economies

118 Albania		. .	. .	. .	. .	. .	. .
119 Hungary		. .	. .	. .	. .	. .	. .
120 Romania		. .	. .	. .	. .	. .	. .
121 Bulgaria		. .	. .	. .	. .	. .	. .
122 Poland		. .	. .	. .	. .	. .	. .
123 USSR		. .	. .	. .	. .	. .	. .
124 Czechoslovakia		. .	. .	. .	. .	. .	. .
125 German Dem. Rep.		. .	. .	. .	. .	. .	. .

a. These estimates should be treated with caution. See the technical notes.

Technical notes

This edition of the World Development Indicators provides economic indicators for periods of years and social indicators for selected years in a form suitable for comparing economies and groups of economies. Although the statistics and measures have been carefully selected to provide a comprehensive picture of development, readers are urged to exercise care in interpreting them. This is particularly true of comparing indicators across economies, because statistical methods, coverage, practices, and definitions differ widely. The statistical systems in many developing economies still are weak, and this affects the availability and reliability of the data, the more so for countries that are not members of the World Bank.

All growth rates shown are in real terms and, unless otherwise noted, have been computed by using the least-squares method. The least-squares growth rate, r, is calculated by regressing the annual values of the variable in the relevant period using the logarithmic form: Log $X_t = a + bt + e_t$, where X_t is the variable, a is the intercept, b is the slope coefficient, t is time, and e_t is the error term. Then r is equal to [antilog b] $-$ 1, the least-squares estimate of the growth rate.

Table 1. Basic indicators

The estimates of *population* for mid-1981 are primarily based on data from the UN Population Division. In many cases the data take into account the results of recent population censuses. The data on *area* are from the FAO *Production Yearbook 1980*.

Gross national product (GNP) measures the total domestic and foreign output claimed by residents. It comprises gross domestic product (see the note for Table 2) and factor incomes (such as investment income and workers' remittances) accruing to residents from abroad, less the income earned in the domestic economy accruing to persons abroad. It is calculated without making deductions for depreciation.

The *GNP per capita* figures were calculated according to the *World Bank Atlas* method, under which the conversion of GNP proceeds in the fol-

lowing manner. The first step is to convert the GNP series in constant market prices and national currency units to one measured in constant average 1979–81 prices. This is done by multiplying the original constant price series by the weighted-average domestic GNP deflator for the base period (that is, by the ratio of total GNP in current prices to total GNP in constant prices for the 1979–81 period). The second step is to convert the series measured in constant average 1979–81 prices in national currency to one in US dollars by dividing that series by the weighted-average exchange rate for the base period. The weighted-average exchange rate is the ratio of the sum of GNP in current prices to the sum of the GNP divided by the annual average exchange rate in national currency per US dollar for 1979, 1980, and 1981. The third step is to convert the series measured in constant average 1979–81 US dollars to one measured in current US dollars by multiplying that series by the implicit US GNP deflator for 1979–81. This procedure was followed for most economies.

The *GNP per capita* figures were obtained by dividing GNP at market prices in US dollars by the population in mid-1981. The use of the three-year base period is intended to smooth the impact of fluctuations in prices and exchange rates. Because the base period is changed every year, the per capita estimates presented in the various editions of the World Development Indicators are not comparable.

Because of problems associated with the availability of data and the determination of exchange rates, information on GNP per capita is shown only for East European nonmarket economies that are members of the World Bank. The World Bank has a research project under way to estimate GNP per capita for nonmarket economies that are not members. But until a broadly acceptable method is prepared, figures will not be shown for the GNP per capita of such economies.

For Romania the GNP per capita figure has been derived, following the World Bank Atlas method, by using adjusted official Romanian national accounts data and converting them into US dollars at the effective exchange rate for foreign trade transactions in convertible currencies. For Hungary the GNP per capita figure has been derived by applying the Atlas method to official GNP estimates with the official commercial exchange rate. Several factors may influence the level and comparability of these estimates with those of other countries. The World Bank is also aware of other estimates that have been made for Hungary: these estimates have been derived by using methods that attempt to account for taxes, subsidies, wage and price distortions, and other possible distortions introduced through the exchange rate; they cover a range of different results.

The use of official exchange rates to convert national currency figures to US dollars does not accurately measure the relative purchasing power of currencies. In particular, differences between developing and industrial economies in their real income, measured by their GNP per capita in US dollars, are likely to be exaggerated. The reason is that exchange rates are based on prices of internationally traded goods and services and may bear little relation to the prices of goods and services that do not enter international trade but that make up the bulk of the national product of most developing economies.

The inadequacy of the exchange rate has been demonstrated by the UN International Comparison Project, which has developed reliable measures of real GNP on an internationally comparable scale (see Irving Kravis and others, *A System of International Comparisons of Gross Product and Purchasing Power* [Baltimore: Johns Hopkins University Press, 1975]; Kravis and others, *International Comparisons of Real Product and Purchasing Power* [1978]; and Kravis and others, *World Product and Income: International Comparisons of Real GDP* [1982]). This project has already covered 34 countries and will ultimately cover about 75. The World Bank, the United Nations, and several other international and regional agencies are engaged in data gathering and research on appropriate ways of extending purchasing power comparisons to all the countries of the world. Until such coverage is comprehensive, however, exchange rates remain the only available means of converting GNP from national currencies to US dollars for purposes of comparison.

The table on this page gives examples of the differences between gross domestic product per capita as conventionally computed and as computed using the ICP method.

The *average annual inflation rate* is the implicit gross domestic product (GDP) deflator, which is calculated by dividing, for each year of the period, the value of GDP in current market prices by the

Gross domestic product per capita computed conventionally and computed by using the ICP method, selected countries, 1975

| Country | Index of GDP per capita (United States = 100) | | GDP per capita at purchasing-power-parity exchange rate as percentage of that at official rate |
	US dollars converted at official exchange rate	International dollars converted at purchasing-power-parity exchange rate[a]	
Africa			
Kenya	3.4	6.6	195
Malawi	1.9	4.9	255
Zambia	6.9	10.3	149
Asia			
India	2.0	6.6	322
Iran, Islamic Rep. of	22.1	37.7	171
Japan	62.3	68.4	110
Korea, Rep. of	8.1	20.7	254
Malaysia	10.9	21.5	198
Pakistan	2.6	8.2	312
Philippines	5.2	13.2	251
Sri Lanka	2.6	9.3	365
Syrian Arab Rep.	10.0	25.0	250
Thailand	5.0	13.0	261
Europe			
Austria	69.8	69.6	100
Belgium	87.8	77.7	88
Denmark	104.5	82.4	79
France	89.6	81.9	91
Germany, Fed. Rep.	94.7	83.0	88
Hungary	29.6	49.6	168
Ireland	37.2	42.5	114
Italy	47.9	53.8	112
Luxembourg	90.2	82.0	91
Netherlands	84.5	75.2	89
Poland	36.0	50.1	139
Romania	24.3	33.3	137
Spain	41.0	55.9	136
United Kingdom	57.6	63.9	111
Yugoslavia	23.2	36.1	156
Latin America and Caribbean			
Brazil	16.0	25.2	158
Colombia	7.9	22.4	283
Jamaica	19.6	24.0	123
Mexico	20.4	34.7	170
Uruguay	18.2	39.6	217

a. An international dollar has the same purchasing power over total GDP as a US dollar.
Source: Kravis and others, "World Product and Income: International Comparisons of Real Gross Product (Baltimore: Johns Hopkins University Press, 1982).

value of GDP in constant market prices, both in national currency. This measure of inflation has limitations, especially for the oil-producing countries in the light of sharp increases in oil prices. It is used as an indicator of inflation because it is the most broadly based deflator, showing annual price movements for all goods and services produced in an economy.

The *adult literacy rate* is the percentage of persons aged 15 and over who can read and write. These rates are based primarily on information from the UN Educational, Scientific, and Cultural Organization (UNESCO), supplemented by World Bank data. Because such data are normally gathered in large-scale demographic surveys and censuses, they often are not available for the most recent year. For some countries the estimates are for years other than, but generally not more than two years distant from, those specified. Thus the series are not comparable for all countries.

Life expectancy at birth indicates the number of

years newborn children would live if subject to the mortality risks prevailing for the cross-section of population at the time of their birth. Data are from the UN Population Division, supplemented by World Bank estimates.

The table on this page shows basic indicators for 34 countries that have a population of less than a million and are members of the United Nations, the World Bank, or both. For most of these countries, comprehensive data are not available.

The weighted averages in Table 1 are weighted by population.

Basic indicators for UN/World Bank members with a population of less than 1 million

UN/World Bank member	Population (millions) Mid-1981	Area (thousands of square kilo-meters)	GNP per capita		Average annual rate of inflation[a] (percent)		Adult literacy rate (percent) 1980[d]	Life ex-pectancy at birth (years) 1981[d]
			Dollars 1981	Average annual growth (percent) 1960–80[b]	1960–70	1970–81[c]		
Equatorial Guinea	0.3	28	180	..	3.7	..	..	48
Guinea-Bissau	0.8	36	190	..	..	7.2	28	37
Maldives	0.2	(.)	..	1.4	1.0	14.0	82	47
Comoros	0.4	2	320	0.7	3.4	11.8	..	48
Cape Verde	0.3	4	340	..	..	11.2	..	61
Vanuatu	0.1	15	350	0.4	..	..	..	..
Gambia, The	0.6	11	370	2.5	2.2	10.7	15	42
Sao Tome and Principe	0.1	1	370	0.0	..	8.8	..	..
Djibouti	0.4	22	480	..	..	12.6	10	45
St. Vincent and the Grenadines	0.1	(.)	630	0.3	4.0	14.0	..	..
Western Samoa	0.2	3	..	..	..	..	..	68
Solomon Islands	0.2	28	640	1.3	3.0	6.8	..	..
Guyana	0.8	215	720	1.8	2.4	9.9	..	70
Dominica	0.1	1	750	−1.0	3.8	16.9	..	..
Swaziland	0.6	17	760	5.5	2.2	11.5	65	54
Grenada	0.1	(.)	850	1.7	3.4	14.1	..	69
St. Lucia	0.1	1	970	3.4	3.6	11.5	..	..
Botswana	0.9	600	1,010	7.9	2.4	11.6	35	57
Belize	0.1	23	1,080	3.0	3.4	8.7	..	..
Mauritius	0.9	2	1,270	2.1	2.2	15.0	85	65
Antigua and Barbuda	0.1	(.)	1,550	−0.2	3.1	11.7	..	..
Seychelles	0.1	(.)	1,800	2.9	..	..	..	66
Fiji	0.6	18	2,000	3.3	2.5	12.5	75	72
Suriname	0.4	163	3,030	5.1	2.7	9.1	65	69
Barbados	0.3	(.)	3,500	4.9	2.3	13.9	99	71
Malta	0.4	(.)	3,600	8.1	1.5	4.6	..	72
Bahamas	0.2	14	3,620	−0.2	3.4	6.9	93	69
Cyprus	0.6	9	3,740	6.3	1.3	5.9	89	73
Gabon	0.7	268	3,810	4.9	5.4	19.5	..	48
Oman	0.9	300	5,920	8.3	2.4	27.2	..	49
Bahrain	0.4	1	8,960	..	..	..	..	67
Iceland	0.2	103	12,860	3.3	12.2	36.8	..	77
Luxembourg	0.4	3	15,910	4.1	3.7	6.9	100	74
Qatar	0.2	11	27,720	2.6	2.6	..	..	58

a. See the technical notes for Table 1. b. Because data for the early 1960s are not available, figures in italics are for periods other than that specified. c. Figures in italics are for 1970–80, not 1970–81. d. Figures in italics are for years other than that specified. See the technical notes.

Tables 2 and 3. Growth and structure of production

Most of the definitions used are those of the UN *System of National Accounts.*

Gross domestic product (GDP) measures the total final output of goods and services produced by an economy—that is, by residents and nonresidents, regardless of the allocation to domestic and foreign claims. It is calculated without making deductions for depreciation. For most countries, GDP by industrial origin is measured at factor cost, but for some countries without complete national accounts series at factor cost, market price series were used. GDP at factor cost is equal to GDP at market prices, less indirect taxes net of subsidies. The figures for GDP are dollar values converted from domestic currency by using the average annual exchange rate for the year in question: that is, they were not calculated by using the *World Bank Atlas* method described in the note for Table 1. Because of these differences in concept and in method of conversion, the figures in these tables are not comparable with the GNP-based numbers in Table 1. The GDP figures nevertheless show the relative size of different economies.

As in Table 1, data are shown only for East European nonmarket economies that are members of the World Bank.

The *agricultural sector* comprises agriculture, forestry, hunting, and fishing. The *industrial sector* comprises mining, *manufacturing*, construction, and electricity, water, and gas. All other branches of economic activity are categorized as *services.*

National accounts series in domestic currency units were used to compute the indicators in these tables. The growth rates in Table 2 were calculated from constant price series; the shares of GDP in Table 3, from current price series.

The average growth rates for the summary measures in Table 2 are weighted by country GDP in 1970 dollars. The average sectoral shares in Table 3 are weighted by GDP in current dollars for the years in question.

Tables 4 and 5. Growth of consumption and investment; Structure of demand

GDP is defined in the note for Table 2.

Public consumption (or general government consumption) includes all current expenditure for purchases of goods and services by all levels of government. Capital expenditure on national defense and security is regarded as consumption expenditure.

Private consumption is the market value of all goods and services purchased or received as income in kind by households and nonprofit institutions. It includes imputed rent for owner-occupied dwellings.

Gross domestic investment consists of the outlays for additions to the fixed assets of the economy, plus changes in the net value of inventories.

Gross domestic saving shows the amount of gross domestic investment financed from domestic output. Comprising public and private saving, it is gross domestic investment plus the net exports of goods and nonfactor services.

Exports of goods and nonfactor services represent the value of all goods and nonfactor services sold to the rest of the world; they include merchandise, freight, insurance, travel, and other nonfactor services. The value of factor services, such as investment income and workers' remittances from abroad, is excluded.

The *resource balance* is the difference between exports and imports of goods and nonfactor services.

National accounts series in domestic currency units were used to compute the indicators in these tables. The growth rates in Table 4 were calculated from constant price series; the shares of GDP in Table 5, from current price series.

The summary measures in Table 5 are weighted by GDP in current dollars for the years in question.

Table 6. Agriculture and food

The figures for *value added in agriculture* are from the World Bank's national accounts series in national currencies, converted to 1975 dollars.

Cereal imports and *food aid in cereals* are measured in grain equivalents and defined as comprising all cereals under the Revised Standard International Trade Classification (SITC) Groups 041–046. The figures have discrepancies attributable to the use of crop-year and calendar-year data and donor-country and recipient-country data.

Fertilizer consumption is measured in relation to arable land, defined as comprising arable land and land under permanent crops, including land under temporary crops (double-cropped areas are counted once), temporary meadows for mowing or pastures, land under market or kitchen gardens, and land temporarily fallow or lying idle.

The figures on food and fertilizer are from the Food and Agriculture Organization (FAO): from computer tapes for *Production Yearbook 1981, Trade Yearbook 1981,* and *Fertilizer Yearbook 1981;* and from *Food Aid Bulletin,* October 1980 and January 1983. In some instances data are for 1974 because they provide the earliest available information.

The *index of food production per capita* shows the average annual quantity of food produced per capita in 1979–81 in relation to that in 1969–71. The estimates were derived from those of the FAO, which are calculated by dividing indices of the quantity of food production by indices of total population. For this index, food is defined as comprising cereals, starchy roots, sugar cane, sugar beet, pulses, edible oils, nuts, fruits, vegetables, livestock, and livestock products. Quantities of food production are measured net of animal feed, seeds for use in agriculture, and food lost in processing and distribution.

Table 7. Industry

The percentage *distribution of value added* among manufacturing industries was calculated from data obtained from the UN Industrial Development Organization (UNIDO), with the base values expressed in 1975 dollars.

The classification of manufacturing industries is in accord with the UN International Standard Industrial Classification of All Economic Activities (ISIC). *Food and agriculture* comprise ISIC Major Groups 311, 313, and 314; *textiles and clothing* 321–24; *machinery and transport equipment* 382–84; and *chemicals* 351 and 352. *Other manufacturing* comprises ISIC Major Division 3, less all of the above.

The figures for *value added in manufacturing* are from the World Bank's national accounts series in national currencies, converted to 1975 dollars.

Table 8. Commercial energy

The data on energy generally are from UN sources. They refer to commercial forms of primary energy: petroleum and natural gas liquids, natural gas, solid fuels (coal, lignite, and so on), and primary electricity (nuclear, geothermal, and hydroelectric power)—all converted into coal equivalents. Figures on liquid fuel consumption include petroleum derivatives that have been consumed in nonenergy uses. For converting primary electricity into coal equivalents, a notional thermal efficiency of 34 percent has been assumed. The use of firewood and other traditional fuels, though substantial in some developing countries, is not taken into ac-

count because reliable and comprehensive data are not available.

The summary measures of growth rates of *energy production* are weighted by volumes of production in 1974; those of growth rates of *energy consumption,* by volumes of consumption in 1974; those of *energy consumption per capita,* by population in 1974.

Energy imports refer to the dollar value of energy imports—SITC (Revised) Section 3—and are expressed as a percentage of earnings from merchandise exports. The summary measures are weighted by merchandise exports in current dollars.

Because data on energy imports do not permit a distinction between petroleum imports for fuel and for use in the petrochemicals industry, these percentages may be overestimates of the dependence on imported energy.

Table 9. Growth of merchandise trade

The statistics on merchandise trade are from UN publications and the UN trade data system, supplemented by statistics from the UN Conference on Trade and Development (UNCTAD), the International Monetary Fund (IMF), and in a few cases World Bank country documentation.

Merchandise exports and imports cover, with some exceptions, all international changes in ownership of goods passing across customs borders. Exports are valued f.o.b. (free on board), imports c.i.f. (cost, insurance, and freight), unless otherwise specified in the foregoing sources. These values are in dollars at prevailing exchange rates. Note that they do not include trade in services and are thus different from the trade figures in Part I of this year's *World Development Report.*

The *growth rates of merchandise exports and imports* are in real terms and are calculated from quantum (volume) indices of exports and imports. For most developing economies these indices are from the UNCTAD *Handbook of International Trade and Development Statistics* and supplementary data that show revisions and updates. For industrial economies the indices are from the UN *Yearbook of International Trade Statistics* and UN *Monthly Bulletin of Statistics.* The summary measures are median values. Note again that these values do not include trade in services and are thus different from the trade figures in Part I of this year's *World Development Report.*

The *terms of trade,* or the net barter terms of trade, are calculated as the ratio of a country's index of export unit values to that of import unit values. The terms-of-trade index numbers shown for 1978 and 1981, with 1975 = 100, thus indicate changes in export prices in relation to import prices. Note in this year's edition that data are given for 1978 rather than 1960. The unit value indices are from the same sources cited above for the growth rates of exports and imports.

Tables 10 and 11. Structure of merchandise trade

The shares in these tables are derived from trade values in current dollars reported in UN trade tapes and the UN *Yearbook of International Trade Statistics*, supplemented by other regular statistical publications of the UN and the IMF.

Merchandise exports and imports are defined in the note for Table 9.

In the categorization of exports in Table 10, *fuels, minerals, and metals* are the commodities in SITC (Revised) Section 3, Divisions 27 and 28, and the nonferrous metals of Division 68. *Other primary commodities* comprise SITC Sections 0, 1, 2, and 4 (food and live animals, beverages and tobacco, inedible crude materials, oils, fats, and waxes) less Divisions 27 and 28 (minerals, crude fertilizers, and metalliferous ores). *Textiles and clothing* represent SITC Divisions 65 and 84 (textiles, yarns, fabrics, and clothing). *Machinery and transport equipment* are the commodities in SITC Section 7. *Other manufactures*, calculated as the residual from the total value of manufactured exports, represent SITC Sections 5 to 9 less Section 7 and Divisions 65, 68, and 84.

In the categorization of imports in Table 11, *food* commodities are those in SITC (Revised) Sections 0, 1, and 4 and in Division 22 (food and live animals, beverages and tobacco, and oils and fats). *Fuels* are the commodities in SITC Section 3 (mineral fuels, lubricants, and related materials). *Other primary commodities* comprise SITC Section 2 (crude materials excluding fuels), less Division 22 plus Division 68 (nonferrous metals). *Machinery and transport equipment* are the commodities in SITC Section 7. *Other manufactures*, calculated as the residual from the total value of manufactured imports, represent SITC Sections 5 to 9 less Section 7 and Division 68.

The summary measures in Table 10 are weighted by merchandise exports in current dollars; those in Table 11, by merchandise imports in current dollars.

Table 12. Origin and destination of merchandise exports

Merchandise exports are defined in the note for Table 9. Trade shares in this table are based on statistics on the value of trade in current dollars from the UN and the IMF except those for nonmember East European nonmarket economies, which are based on data from the Secretariat of the Council for Mutual Economic Aid (COMECON). Unallocated exports are distributed among the economy groups in proportion to their respective shares of allocable trade. *Industrial market economies* also include Gibraltar, Iceland, and Luxembourg; *high-income oil exporters* also include Qatar. The summary measures are weighted by merchandise exports in current dollars.

Table 13. Origin and destination of manufactured exports

The data in this table are from the United Nations and are among those used to compute special Table B in the UN *Yearbook of International Trade Statistics*. *Manufactured goods* are the commodities in SITC (Revised) Sections 5 through 9 (chemicals and related products, manufactured articles, and machinery and transport equipment) excluding Division 68 (nonferrous metals).

The economy groups are the same as those in Table 12. The summary measures are weighted by manufactured exports in current dollars.

Table 14. Balance of payments and reserves

The *current account balance* is the difference between (i) exports of goods and services plus inflows of unrequited official and private transfers and (ii) imports of goods and services plus unrequited transfers to the rest of the world. The current account estimates are from IMF data files.

Net direct private investment is the net amount invested or reinvested by nonresidents in enterprises in which they or other nonresidents exercise significant managerial control. Including equity capital, reinvested earnings, and other capital, these net figures also take into account the value of direct investment abroad by residents of the reporting country. IMF data files were used in compiling these estimates.

Workers' remittances cover remittances of income by migrants who are employed or expected to be employed for more than a year in their new economy, where they are considered residents.

Gross international reserves comprise holdings of gold, special drawing rights (SDRs), the reserve position of IMF members in the Fund, and holdings of foreign exchange under the control of monetary authorities. The gold component of these reserves is valued throughout at year-end London prices: that is, $37.37 an ounce in 1970 and $397.50 an ounce in 1981. The data on holdings of international reserves are from IMF data files. The reserve levels for 1970 and 1981 refer to the end of the year indicated and are in current dollars at prevailing exchange rates. The reserve holdings at the end of 1981 are also expressed in the number of months of imports of goods and services they could pay for, with imports at the average level for 1980 or 1981. The summary measures are weighted by imports of goods and services in current dollars.

Table 15. Flow of public and publicly guaranteed external capital

The data on debt in this and successive tables are from the World Bank Debt Reporting System. That system is concerned solely with developing economies and does not collect data on external debt for other groups of borrowers. Nor are comprehensive comparable data available from other sources.

Data on the *gross inflow* and *repayment of principal* (amortization) are for public and publicly guaranteed medium- and long-term loans. The *net inflow* is the gross inflow less the repayment of principal.

Public loans are an obligation of a public debtor, including the national government, its agencies, and autonomous public bodies. Publicly guaranteed loans are external obligations of private debtors that are guaranteed for repayment by a public entity.

The data in this table and in successive tables on debt do not cover unguaranteed private debt because comprehensive data are not available; for some borrowers such debt is substantial. The debt contracted for purchases of military equipment is also excluded because it usually is not reported.

Table 16. External public debt and debt service ratios

External public debt outstanding and disbursed represents the amount of public and publicly guaranteed loans that has been disbursed, net of repayments of principal and write-offs at year-end. In estimating external public debt as a percentage of GNP, GNP was converted from national currencies to dollars at the average official exchange rate for the year in question. The summary measures are weighted by GNP in current dollars.

Interest payments are those on the disbursed and outstanding public and publicly guaranteed debt in foreign currencies, goods, or services; they include commitment charges on undisbursed debt if information on those charges was available.

Debt service is the sum of interest payments and repayments of principal on external public and publicly guaranteed debt. The ratio of debt service to exports of goods and services is one of several rules of thumb commonly used to assess the ability to service debt. The average ratios of debt service to GNP for the economy groups are weighted by GNP in current dollars. The average ratios of debt service to exports of goods and services are weighted by exports of goods and services in current dollars.

Table 17. Terms of public borrowing

Commitments refer to the public and publicly guaranteed loans for which contracts were signed in the year specified.

Interest rates, *maturities*, and *grace periods* are averages weighted by the amounts of loans. Interest is the major charge levied on a loan and is usually computed on the amount of principal drawn and outstanding. The maturity of a loan is the interval between the agreement date, when a loan agreement is signed or bonds are issued, and the date of final repayment of principal. The grace period is the interval between the agreement date and the date of the first principal repayment.

The summary measures in this table are weighted by the amounts of loans.

Table 18. Official development assistance from OECD and OPEC members

Official development assistance (ODA) consists of net disbursements of loans and grants made at concessional financial terms by official agencies of the members of the Development Assistance Committee (DAC) of the Organisation for Economic Co-operation and Development (OECD) and members of the Organization of Petroleum Exporting Countries (OPEC) with the objective of promoting economic development and welfare. It includes the value of technical cooperation and assistance. All data shown were supplied by the OECD.

Amounts shown are net disbursements to developing countries and multilateral institutions. The disbursements to multilateral institutions are now reported for all DAC members on the basis of the date of issue of notes; some DAC members previously reported on the basis of the date of encashment. *Net bilateral flows to low-income countries* exclude unallocated bilateral flows and all disbursements to multilateral institutions.

The nominal values shown in the summary for ODA from OECD countries were converted into 1980 prices using the dollar GNP deflator. This deflator is based on price increases in OECD countries (excluding Greece, Portugal, and Turkey) measured in dollars. It takes into account the parity changes between the dollar and national currencies. For example, when the dollar depreciates, price increases measured in national currencies have to be adjusted upward by the amount of the depreciation to obtain price increases in dollars.

The table, in addition to showing totals for OPEC, shows totals for the Organization of Arab Petroleum Exporting Countries (OAPEC). The donor members of OAPEC are Algeria, Iraq, Kuwait, Libya, Qatar, Saudi Arabia, and United Arab Emirates. ODA data for OPEC and OAPEC were also obtained from the OECD.

Table 19. Population growth, past and projected, and hypothetical stationary population

The *growth rates of population* are period averages calculated from midyear populations. The summary measures are weighted by population in 1970.

The *projections of population* for 1990 and 2000, and to the year in which it will eventually become stationary, were made for each economy separately. Starting with information on total population by age and sex, fertility rates, and mortality rates in the base year 1980, these parameters were projected at five-year intervals on the basis of generalized assumptions until the population became stationary. The base-year estimates are from updated computer printouts of UN, *World Population Prospects as Assessed in 1980*, from the most recent issue of UN, *Population and Vital Statistics Report*,

and from the World Bank, the Population Council, the US Bureau of the Census, and recent national censuses.

The *net reproduction rate* (NRR) indicates the number of daughters that a newborn girl will bear during her lifetime, assuming fixed age-specific fertility rates and a fixed set of mortality rates.

The NRR thus measures the extent to which a cohort of newborn girls will reproduce themselves under given schedules of fertility and mortality. An NRR of 1 indicates that fertility is at replacement level: at this rate childbearing women, on the average, bear only enough daughters to replace themselves in the population. A population continues to grow after replacement-level fertility has been reached because its past higher birth rates will have produced an age distribution with a relatively high proportion of women in, or still to enter, the reproductive ages. The time taken for a country's population to become stationary after reaching replacement-level fertility thus depends on its age structure and previous fertility patterns.

A *stationary population* is one in which age- and sex-specific mortality rates have not changed over a long period, while age-specific fertility rates have simultaneously remained at replacement level (NRR = 1). In such a population, the birth rate is constant and equal to the death rate, the age structure also is constant, and the growth rate is zero.

To make the projections, assumptions about future mortality rates were made in terms of female life expectancy at birth (that is, the number of years a newborn girl would live if subject to the mortality risks prevailing for the cross-section of population at the time of her birth). Economies were first divided according to whether their primary-school enrollment ratio for females was above or below 70 percent. In each group a set of annual increments in female life expectancy was assumed, depending on the female life expectancy in 1975–80. For a given life expectancy at birth, the annual increments during the projection period are larger in economies having a higher primary-school enrollment ratio in 1975–80 and a life expectancy of up to 62.5 years. At higher life expectancies, the increments are the same.

To project the fertility rates, the first step was to estimate the year in which fertility would reach replacement level. These estimates are speculative and are based on information on trends in crude birth rates (defined in the note for Table 20), total fertility rates (also defined in the note for Table 20), female life expectancy at birth, and the performance of family planning programs. For most economies it was assumed that the total fertility rate would decline between 1980 and the year of reaching a net reproduction rate of 1, after which fertility would remain at replacement level. For sub-Saharan Africa, total fertility rates were assumed to remain constant until 1990–95 and then to decline until replacement level was reached. For a few other countries in Asia and the Middle East, those rates were also assumed to remain constant for some years before beginning to decline. In several industrial economies, fertility is already below replacement level. Because a population will not remain stationary if its net reproduction rate is other than 1, it was necessary to assume that fertility rates in these economies would regain replacement levels in order to make estimates of the stationary population for them. For the sake of consistency with the other estimates, the total fertility rates in the industrial economies were assumed to increase to replacement level by 2000 and then to remain constant.

For all the projections, it was assumed that international migration would have no effect.

The estimates of the hypothetical size of the stationary population, the assumed year of reaching replacement-level fertility, and the year of reaching a stationary population are speculative. *They should not be regarded as predictions.* They are included to provide a summary indication of the long-run implications of recent fertility and mortality trends on the basis of highly stylized assumptions. They differ from the corresponding figures in last year's edition because of the assumption of a higher life expectancy at birth: 82.5 years compared with 77.5. A fuller description of the methods and assumptions used to calculate the estimates is available from the Population, Health, and Nutrition Department of the World Bank.

Table 20. Demographic and fertility-related indicators

The *crude birth and death rates* indicate the number of live births and deaths per thousand population in a year. They are from the same sources mentioned in the note for Table 19. Percentage changes are computed from unrounded data.

The *total fertility rate* represents the number of children that would be born per woman, if she were to live to the end of her childbearing years and bear children at each age in accord with prevailing age-specific fertility rates. The rates given

are from the same sources mentioned in the note for Table 19.

The *percentage of married women using contraceptives* refers only to married women of childbearing age (15–44 years). These data are mainly derived from Dorothy Nortman and Ellen Hofstatter, *Population and Family Planning Programs: A Factbook* (New York: Population Council, various issues); Dorothy Nortman, "Changing Contraceptive Patterns: A Global Perspective," *Population Bulletin*, vol. 32, no. 3 (Washington, D.C.: Population Reference Bureau, August 1977); Office of Population, *Family Planning Service Statistics, Annual Report 1976* (Washington, D.C.: US Agency for International Development); and publications of the World Fertility Survey. The data refer to a variety of years, generally not more than two years distant from those specified.

All summary measures are weighted by population.

Table 21. Labor force

The *population of working age* refers to the population aged 15–64. The estimates are based on the population estimates of the World Bank for 1981 and previous years. The summary measures are weighted by population.

The *labor force* comprises economically active persons age 10 years and over, including the armed forces and the unemployed, but excluding housewives, students, and other economically inactive groups. *Agriculture, industry, and services* are defined in the same manner as in Table 2. The estimates of the sectoral distribution of the labor force are from International Labour Office (ILO), *Labour Force Estimates and Projections, 1950–2000,* and from the World Bank. The summary measures are weighted by labor force.

The *labor force growth rates* were derived from the Bank's population projections and ILO data on age-specific activity rates, from the source cited above. The summary measures for 1960–70 and 1970–81 are weighted by labor force in 1970; those for 1980–2000, by estimates of labor force in 1980.

The application of ILO activity rates to the Bank's latest population estimates may be inappropriate for some economies in which there have been important changes in unemployment and underemployment, in international and internal migration, or in both. The labor force projections for 1980–2000 should thus be treated with caution.

Table 22. Urbanization

The data on *urban population as a percentage of total population* are from the UN (*Patterns of Urban and Rural Population Growth*, Population Studies, no. 68, 1980), supplemented by data from the World Bank and from various issues of the UN *Demographic Yearbook*.

The *growth rates of urban population* were calculated from the World Bank's population estimates; the estimates of urban population shares were calculated from the sources cited above.

Data on urban agglomeration are also from the United Nations.

Because the estimates in this table are based on different national definitions of what is "urban," cross-country comparisons should be interpreted with caution.

The summary measures for urban population as a percentage of total population are weighted by population; the other summary measures in this table are weighted by urban population.

Table 23. Indicators related to life expectancy

Life expectancy at birth is defined in the note for Table 1.

The *infant mortality rate* is the number of infants who die before reaching one year of age, per thousand live births in a given year. The data are from a variety of sources—including different issues of the UN *Demographic Yearbook* and UN, "Infant Mortality: World Estimates and Projections, 1950–2025," *Population Bulletin of the United Nations*, no. 14 (1982)—and from the World Bank.

The *child death rate* is the number of deaths of children aged 1–4 per thousand children in the same age group in a given year. Estimates were based on the data on infant mortality and on the relation between the infant mortality rate and the child death rate implicit in the appropriate Coale-Demeny Model life tables; see Ansley J. Coale and Paul Demeny, *Regional Model Life Tables and Stable Populations* (Princeton, N.J.: Princeton University Press, 1966). The summary measures in this table are weighted by population.

Table 24. Health-related indicators

The estimates of *population per physician and nursing person* were derived from World Health Organization (WHO) data, some of which have been revised to reflect new information. They also take into account revised estimates of population. Nursing persons include graduate, practical, assistant, and auxiliary nurses; the inclusion of auxiliary nurses enables a better estimation of the availability of nursing care. Because definitions of nursing personnel vary—and because the data shown are for a variety of years, generally not more than two years distant from those specified—the data for these two indicators are not strictly comparable. The *daily calorie supply per capita* was calculated by dividing the calorie equivalent of the food supplies in an economy by the population. Food supplies comprise domestic production, imports less exports, and changes in stocks; they exclude animal feed, seeds for use in agriculture, and food lost in processing and distribution. The *daily calorie requirement per capita* refers to the calories needed to sustain a person at normal levels of activity and health, taking into account age and sex distributions, average body weights, and environmental temperatures. Both sets of estimates are from the Food and Agriculture Organization.

The summary measures in this table are weighted by population.

Table 25. Education

The data in this table refer to a variety of years, generally not more than two years distant from those specified, and are mostly from UNESCO.

The data on *number enrolled in primary school* refer to estimates of total, male, and female enrollment of students of all ages in primary school; they are expressed as percentages of the total, male, or female populations of primary-school age to give gross primary enrollment ratios. Although primary-school age is generally considered to be 6–11 years, the differences in country practices in the ages and duration of schooling are reflected in the ratios given. For countries with universal primary education, the gross enrollment ratios may exceed 100 percent because some pupils are below or above the official primary-school age.

The data on *number enrolled in secondary school* were calculated in the same manner, with secondary-school age generally considered to be 12–17 years.

The data on *number enrolled in higher education* are from UNESCO.

The *adult literacy rate* is defined in the note for Table 1.

The summary measures in this table are weighted by population.

Table 26. Defense and social expenditure

Data on the central government transactions are from the IMF *Government Finance Statistics Yearbook*, IMF data files, and World Bank country documentation. These transactions include current and capital (development) expenditure. The inadequate statistical coverage of state, provincial, and local governments and the nonavailability of data for these lower levels of government has dictated the use only of central government data. This may seriously understate or distort the statistical portrayal of the allocation of resources for various purposes, especially in large countries where lower levels of government have considerable autonomy and are responsible for many social services.

Central government expenditure comprises the expenditure by all government offices, departments, establishments, and other bodies that are agencies or instruments of the central authority of a country. It does not necessarily comprise all public expenditure.

Defense expenditure comprises all expenditure, whether by defense or other departments, for the maintenance of military forces, including the purchase of military supplies and equipment, construction, recruiting, and training. Also falling under this category is expenditure for strengthening the public services to meet wartime emergencies, for training civil defense personnel, and for foreign military aid and contributions to military organizations and alliances.

Education expenditure comprises public expenditure for the provision, management, inspection, and support of preprimary, primary, and secondary schools; of universities and colleges; and of vocational, technical, and other training institutions by central governments. Also included is expenditure on the general administration and regulation of the education system; on research into its objectives, organization, administration, and methods; and on such subsidiary services as transport, school meals, and medical and dental services in schools.

Health expenditure covers public expenditure on hospitals, medical and dental centers, and clinics with a major medical component; on national health and medical insurance schemes; and on family planning and preventive care. Also included is expenditure on the general administration and regulation of relevant government departments, hospitals and clinics, health and sanitation, and national health and medical insurance schemes.

It must be emphasized that the data presented, especially those for education and health, are not comparable for a number of reasons. In many economies private health and education services are substantial; in others public services represent the major component of total expenditures but may be financed by lower levels of government. Great caution should therefore be exercised in using the data for cross-economy comparisons.

The summary measures for defense expenditure as a percentage of GNP are weighted by GNP in current dollars; those for defense expenditure as a percentage of central government expenditure, by central government expenditure in current dollars. The other summary measures in this table are weighted by population.

Table 27. Income distribution

The data in this table refer to the distribution of total disposable household income accruing to percentile groups of households ranked by total household income. The distributions cover rural and urban areas and refer to different years between 1966 and 1981.

The estimates for developing economies in Asia and Africa are from the results of a joint project of the World Bank and the International Labour Office (ILO). Those for Turkey, Hong Kong, Malaysia, and the Republic of Korea are from data gathered by the World Bank from national sources but not adjusted. The estimates for Sri Lanka are from the results of a joint project of the World Bank and the Economic and Social Commission for Asia and the Pacific. The estimates for Latin American countries other than Mexico come from the results of two joint projects of the World Bank, one with the ILO, the other with the Economic Commission for Latin America. Those for Mexico are the results from the 1977 Household Budget Survey.

Data for industrial market economies other than the Netherlands are from Malcolm Sawyer, *Income Distribution in OECD Countries* (OECD Occasional Studies, July 1976); the joint project of the ILO and the World Bank; and the UN Statistical Office, *A Survey of National Sources of Income Distribution Statistics* (Statistical Papers, Series M, no. 72, 1981). Data for the Netherlands are from that country's statistical office.

Because the collection of data on income distribution has not been systematically organized and integrated with the official statistical system in many countries, estimates were typically derived from surveys designed for other purposes, most often consumer expenditure surveys, which also collect some information on income. These surveys use a variety of income concepts and sample designs. Furthermore, the coverage of many of these surveys is too limited to provide reliable nationwide estimates of income distribution. Thus, although the estimates shown are considered the best available, they do not avoid all these problems and should be interpreted with extreme caution.

The scope of the indicator is similarly limited. Because households vary in size, a distribution in which households are ranked according to per capita household income, not according to their total household income, is superior for many purposes. The distinction is important because households with low per capita incomes frequently are large households, whose total income may be relatively high. Information on the distribution of per capita household income exists, however, for only a few countries. The World Bank Living Standards Measurement Study is developing procedures and applications that can assist countries in improving their collection and analysis of data on income distribution.

Bibliography of data sources

National accounts and economic indicators	*A System of National Accounts.* New York: UN Department of International Economic and Social Affairs, Statistical Office, 1968. *Statistical Yearbook.* New York: UN Department of International Economic and Social Affairs, Statistical Office, various issues. *World Bank Atlas, 1983.* Washington, D.C.: World Bank, 1983. World Bank data files. FAO and UNIDO data files. National sources.
Energy	*World Energy Supplies.* UN Statistical Papers, Series J, various numbers. New York: UN Department of International Economic and Social Affairs, various years. World Bank data files.
Trade	*Direction of Trade.* Washington, D.C.: International Monetary Fund (IMF), various issues. *International Financial Statistics.* Washington, D.C.: IMF, various issues. *Handbook of International Trade and Development Statistics.* New York: UN Conference on Trade and Development, various issues. *Monthly Bulletin of Statistics.* New York: UN Department of International Economic and Social Affairs, Statistical Office, various issues. *Yearbook of International Trade Statistics.* New York: Department of International Economic and Social Affairs, Statistical Office, various issues. United Nations trade tapes.
Balance of payments, capital flows and debt	*Balance of Payments Manual.* 4th ed. Washington, D.C.: IMF, 1977. International Monetary Fund balance-of-payments data files. *Development Co-operation.* Paris: OECD, various annual issues. World Bank Debt Reporting System.
Population	*World Population Prospects as Assessed in 1980.* New York: UN Department of International Economic and Social Affairs, Population Division, 1979. United Nations population tapes. *World Population: 1977.* Washington, D.C.: US Bureau of the Census, International Statistical Programs Center, 1978. *World Bank Atlas, 1983.* Washington, D.C.: World Bank, 1983. World Bank data files.
Labor force	*Labour Force Estimates and Projections, 1950–2000.* 2nd ed. Geneva: International Labour Office, 1977. International Labour Office tapes. World Bank data files.
Social indicators	*Demographic Yearbook.* New York: UN Department of International Economic and Social Affairs, Statistical Office, various issues. *Statistical Yearbook.* New York: UN Department of International Economic and Social Affairs, Statistical Office, various issues. *Statistical Yearbook.* Paris: UNESCO, various issues. *World Health Statistics Annual.* Geneva: WHO, various issues. *World Health Statistics Report.* Special Issue on Water and Sanitation, vol. 29, no. 10. Geneva: WHO, 1976. *Government Finance Statistics Yearbook, Vol. IV, 1980.* Washington, D.C.: IMF, 1980. World Bank data files.